Also by Frances FitzGerald
FIRE IN THE LAKE
AMERICA REVISED

Frances FitzGerald

✠ Cities on a Hill

A JOURNEY THROUGH CONTEMPORARY AMERICAN CULTURES

A TOUCHSTONE BOOK
Published by Simon & Schuster, Inc.
NEW YORK   LONDON   TORONTO   SYDNEY   TOKYO

FIRST TOUCHSTONE EDITION, 1987

PUBLISHED BY SIMON & SCHUSTER, INC.
SIMON & SCHUSTER BUILDING
ROCKEFELLER CENTER
1230 AVENUE OF THE AMERICAS
NEW YORK, NY 10020

TOUCHSTONE AND COLOPHON IS A REGISTERED TRADEMARK
OF SIMON & SCHUSTER, INC.

DESIGNED BY KAROLINA HARRIS

MANUFACTURED IN THE UNITED STATES OF AMERICA

10 9 8 7 6 5 4 3 2 1
10 9 8 7 6 5 4 3 2 1 PBK.

LIBRARY OF CONGRESS CATALOGING IN PUBLICATION DATA
FITZGERALD, FRANCES, DATE.
CITIES ON A HILL.

1. COMMUNITY ORGANIZATION—UNITED STATES—CASE
STUDIES. 2. RELIGIOUS COMMUNITIES—UNITED STATES—
CASE STUDIES. 3. RETIREMENT COMMUNITIES—UNITED STATES—
CASE STUDIES. 4. HOMOSEXUALS—UNITED STATES—CASE
STUDIES. 5. UNITED STATES—SOCIAL CONDITIONS—1960-1980
—CASE STUDIES. 6. LIFESTYLE—CASE STUDIES. I. TITLE.
HN59.F57 1986 307'.0973 86-13499
ISBN: 0-671-55209-0
ISBN: 0-671-64561-7 PBK.

MOST OF THIS BOOK APPEARED ORIGINALLY IN *THE NEW YORKER*.

✣ Acknowledgments

Three people gave me invaluable help with the research on this book. Elizabeth Taylor worked with me on the Sun City study, gathering research materials and going with me to Florida to do interviews. Her enthusiasm sustained me, and I learned to rely on her sensitivity and good judgment. A better colleague would be hard to find. For the research on Rajneeshpuram I am much indebted to Professor Erhard Dortmund of Western Oregon State College, who for three years kept me abreast of the news by sending me what now amounts to a trunkful of clippings from the Oregon press. For his selfless efforts and his friendship I am most grateful. I had much help on the Castro piece, but my thanks go principally to Ken Maley, who, over the years, gave me every kind of assistance from introductions to research materials to his own good counsel.

Professor Susan Harding of the University of Michigan at Ann Arbor was kind enough to tell me about her own exploration of Reverend Falwell's community in 1984–85. But her contribution to this book goes far beyond that. Reading much of the book (though not the original Liberty Baptist chapter) in manuscript, she offered me not only excellent criticism but new ideas and new ways to look at the large questions of community, religion, and culture in the United States. Our discussions and her bibliographic suggestions informed the concluding chapter a great deal. All writers should have such an interlocutor.

Several other people were kind enough to read parts of the book in manuscript and to offer helpful criticism and advice. In particular my thanks go to Professor Thomas Bender and Professor Richard Sennett of New York University, Professor William Taylor of the State University of New York, and Professor Ronald Steel of the University of Southern California. The New York Institute for the Humanities at New York University provided a collegial forum for the discussion of many of the ideas in this book. Needless to say, none of its fellows, nor anyone here mentioned, should bear any responsibility for any error of commission or omission in the book.

Much of the book appeared initially in *The New Yorker*, and, as always, I owe an enormous debt of thanks to William Shawn. Without his support this book would probably not exist. He and others at *The New Yorker* made important contributions. John Bennet and Patrick Crow improved the manuscript; Martin Baron, Hal Espin, Sara Lippincott, Richard Sacks and Robert Walsh performed the heroic feats of fact-checking.

My thanks go also to my friend and editor at Simon and Schuster, Alice Mayhew, who has always understood this book as well or better than I have. Last but far from least, they go to my champion, Robert Lescher, who has often saved me from my own worst instincts and the moral equivalent of on-rushing trains.

✛ Contents

✠ Introduction

THIS book began with a story I heard about the mayor of San Francisco making an appearance at a drag ball and a chance visit I paid to Jerry Falwell's church a year later. It began with a sensation—in both cases the same—of strangeness inside the familiar: a kind of shock of non-recognition.

In the first instance I was teaching a class in journalism at the University of California, Berkeley, when a student brought me an account of the gala coronation ball held for the Emperor and Empress of San Francisco at which Mayor George Moscone made a brief political appearance. I had seen no mention of the event in the city newspapers. To local journalists the mayor's appearance at it was apparently no more newsworthy than his appearance at a Garibaldi or a Hibernian dinner. It was, after all, the third year he had attended the annual Beaux Arts Costume Ball.

That was the early spring of 1978, the time when, as it happened, the gay community in San Francisco had reached its greatest extent and the height of its powers. Over the past six years tens of thousands of young gay men had moved into the city, settling a neighborhood they called "the Castro" and creating an entire world for themselves. In the Castro the bars were gay, but so also were the clothing stores, the stock brokerages, and the real-estate agencies. There were gay theater companies, a gay marching band, gay policemen and gay lawbreakers, gay churches, gay foundations, and gay holidays. There was a gay yellow pages for residents and, for tourists, a gay visitors' guide. The previous November the Castro had elected an openly gay man, Harvey Milk, to the city Board of Supervisors, and under Milk's leadership the gay community was becoming a force to be reckoned with in city politics. Enthusiasm ran high, and as gay immigration kept increasing, Harvey Milk, among others, thought gay people might dominate the city in five or ten years.

The Castro was the first gay neighborhood in the country, and as such it was something quite new under the sun. But the Castro was also a movement; it was a part of the national movement for gay liberation, but Castro activists thought of it as the cutting edge. Gay liberation was a civil rights struggle, but it was much more than that. Now that the feminist movement had passed its radical phase, gay activists saw themselves as the avant-garde of the sexual revolution and the revolutionary change in sex and gender roles. Specifically, their goal was to overturn one of the oldest and strongest taboos in the culture, but beyond that it was to challenge all the conventions surrounding the "traditional" nuclear family. The Castro—or what they called their "liberated zone"—was a kind of laboratory for exper-imentation with alternate ways to live. It was also a carnival where social conventions were turned upside down just for the pleasure of seeing what they looked like the wrong way up. At the Castro Street Fair, on Halloween or on any of the other gay holidays, men would turn up as Betty Grable look-alikes, as Hell's Angels toughs, as nuns on roller skates, and as men in Brooks Brothers shirts and tasseled loafers. This was play; it was at the same time a meditation on the arbitrary nature of gender roles and costumes; it was also real life for men who had found themselves in the excluded middle of the terms male/female.

The Castro and its carnival were perfectly open. The gay activists I met encouraged me to visit the drag balls and leather bars even though they themselves knew little about these costumed worlds. Openness was for them the supreme virtue: after so much conceal-ment and subterfuge, nothing should be hidden, nothing repressed. "Coming out" as a homosexual was the essence of gay liberation; it was a personal and a political statement at the same time. What was odd, then, was how few other San Franciscans knew anything about the Castro or the growing gay minority in their midst. They learned about it after George Moscone and Harvey Milk were murdered. But they did not know about it then. Once, leaving a party on Telegraph Hill, where fifty young men were talking about the coming cultural revolution, I walked a few blocks to a restaurant, where young mar-rieds at a nearby table were expressing surprise at the very existence of gay bars in the city.

I had heard of Jerry Falwell while writing a short magazine piece on the Castro; Falwell, along with the actress Anita Bryant, had led the campaign against a gay rights ordinance in Dade County, Florida, in

1978. All the same, it was something of an accident that I visited his church in February 1979. I had been invited to lecture at a small liberal arts college in Lynchburg, Virginia, and Falwell's Liberty Baptist Church was a block away from the edge of the campus. The Reverend Jerry Falwell had not yet launched the Moral Majority, but he and his church were the talk of the college, and a young professor and his wife took me to a Wednesday-evening service. Walking into the church I remembered the television commercials I had watched as a child in the fifties: commercials that showed a family at breakfast in a sunlit kitchen, the two towheaded children clamoring for Sugar Pops or Tastee Treats, their mother lovingly explaining how she kept the wash so clean, and their father kissing her, then waving at a neighbor as he went off to work. As a New York City child, I had never met people such as this: I knew no one who lived this suburban family idyll with sparkling linoleum and perfect teeth. At the same time I was quite convinced that this was the way most Americans lived. I supposed that these were the real Americans—as opposed to myself, my friends, and everyone I saw on the city streets. The people in Falwell's church looked so much like those television-commercial Americans it was as if the images had walked off the screen twenty-five years later. Only now it was they who looked exotic. Certainly the Lynchburg college students in their blue jeans and down jackets regarded them as such.

That evening, or perhaps the following Sunday, Falwell asked for donations for the "I Love America" rallies he was holding on the steps of state capitols around the country; in return he was offering American flag lapel pins and the thought that every contribution helped the cause of bringing America back to morality again. He also spoke of a recent trip to New York City during which he had braved dark streets full of muggers and thieves and talked with one of the princes of industry in his skyscraper office—the prince confessing to loneliness in his world of wealth, luxury, and power. This, I discovered later, was the way Billy Graham had been describing his trips to foreign parts for at least twenty years. But at the time the story amazed me, for in a few sentences Falwell had managed to turn my hometown into Baghdad.

Eight months later Jerry Falwell was seated on daises at the right hand of the presidential nominee, Ronald Reagan, and was appearing regularly on TV talk shows. Conservative evangelicals had become the political phenomenon of the eighties, and Falwell, now the head of the Moral Majority, was the most articulate spokesman for the religious Right. But it was still Falwell's church that interested me. As a New Yorker I had never been to a fundamentalist church before, and Falwell's Thomas Road Church not only preached a different gospel from the Episcopal Church I had grown up in but it seemed to belong to a different category of institution. A "separatist" church, it provided its members with a way of living in American society (or, what its pastors called "the world") without being a part of it: it educated their children, gave them an entire social life, and occupied most of their nonworking hours. Its pastors taught people how to conduct their family lives and instructed them not just in theology but in a comprehensive worldview. They involved them in an entire culture quite different from the one just outside. Falwell's church was the wellspring of his politics; indeed, the politics of the New Right was, in great degree, merely the overflow of this particular brand of fundamentalism from the churches into the public domain. This was so chronologically as well as ontologically, for in the seventies, well before the launching of the Moral Majority, the fundamentalist churches had experienced a large-scale revival. It was this revival that had to be explained.

For some time it had been quite generally assumed that Western society was moving slowly and inexorably in the direction of secularization. The movement had seemed quite as evident within the churches as outside of them, given the ground that most of them had ceded to science. What, then, was the meaning of the fact that the churches preaching the literal truth of the Bible, the immanence of Christ and the approach of Armageddon were making widespread conversions in the United States? Fundamentalism was sweeping the Islamic world as well, but in Iran, Pakistan, and Lebanon, fundamentalism could be explained—if not explained away—as a reaction to violent social and economic change. In the Middle East it was clearly the religion of the poor and the dispossessed—the religion of those who had suffered from the culturally disruptive process their Westernized elites called "modernization." A hundred years ago, when the industrial revolution swept this country, the withdrawal of Appalachian coal miners and dirt farmers into speculation about Armageddon and the Second Coming could be understood as a similar phenomenon. But the new fundamentalist revival seemed to be quite different. The people flocking into the churches affiliated with the Moral Majority were, generally speaking, not poor by American standards and apparently not at all alienated from the economic system. The preachers, at least, defended capitalism as they defended motherhood, and while they denounced secular education as the work of the devil, they taught children the importance of success in economic terms. Fundamentalists rejected Darwinian biology, but they found practical, and theologically permissible, applications for science in refrigerators, television sets, and missile technology. They came from a tradition of separation and world rejection, but now they wanted the political power to bring the whole society into conformity with their religious vision. Falwell's brand of fundamentalism was clearly something new. More than a way of life, it was a social experiment and a dynamic political movement. Like gay liberation, it raised some profound questions.

One of these questions, certainly, was the accuracy of the general picture most Americans had of their society. In an age of mass communications, in an age when instantaneous electronic floods of information washed back and forth across the country, the very gatekeepers of the information sluices—journalists, pollsters, and politicians—were in 1980 surprised by the very existence of an "evangelical vote" and, in the main, shocked to hear what the fundamentalist Christians were proposing. That most journalists (myself included) knew nothing about fundamentalist theology even though Falwell and many others had been preaching it for a decade on national television suggested a blind spot. It suggested a gap in our education and a gap that had developed relatively recently. H. L. Mencken, after all, never underestimated the number of fundamentalists in the country.

In the fifties our textbooks, like our television commercials, pictured the United States as a more or less homogeneous society: a nation of happy families, white and middle class, or, on the other hand, a nation of individuals with a common understanding of good citizenship and common virtues such as optimism, pragmatism, love of compromise, and belief in progress. In the sixties this picture changed. It was shattered in one way by the bitter conflict over the Vietnam War and all the other angry confrontations of the period: Americans, it seemed, were not always tolerant and pragmatic; the United States was not always a consensus society. It was shattered in another way by the black civil rights movement and all the succeeding movements that brought racial minorities, European ethnic groups, and women into focus for the first time. In the textbooks of the late sixties and seventies, the United States was not a "melting pot," as it had been until then in their pages, it was a "stew" or "salad" of different groups: it was "multiracial, multicultural and pluralistic." What the textbooks did not suggest was that some of the most profound cultural differences in the country lay between white, middle-class American men—and on the other hand, women.

These textbook accounts were, of course, crude and sketchy, but they were, among other things, crude and sketchy descriptions of the concerns of American scholars in each period. In the fifties American historians—the best of them—had given their attentions to the unique character of American intellectual life and the development of American political institutions. Henry Steele Commager, Daniel Boorstin, and Richard Hofstadter wrote books with titles such as *The American Mind*, *The National Experience*, and *The American Political Tradition*. In the sixties and seventies, however, social history superseded political and intellectual history as a discipline. Arguing that consensus, or synthetic political, history was merely a study of dominant groups, the new social historians looked to the subordinate groups—in particular to blacks, women, workers, the newer immigrants, and American Indians. In writing about those generally left out of the composite picture of the society, they focused on conflict rather than on consensus, on the persistence of local tradition rather than on assimilation. The social scientists of the period did the same. Anthropologists, when they worked inside the United States, worked on Indian tribes, Appalachian villages, or the most traditional of ethnic neighborhoods. In 1965 the sociologists Daniel Patrick Moynihan and Nathan Glazer published an enormously influential work, *Beyond the Melting Pot*, on the persistence of ethnic traditions in the blue-collar neighborhoods of New York City. The white middle class of David Riesman's *The Lonely Crowd* and John Kenneth Galbraith's *The Affluent Society* was set aside as a subject for the next twenty years.

Looking back, however, it's apparent that in the sixties and seventies, white middle-class society changed more decisively than it had in many decades—perhaps even since the turn of the century. In San Francisco and in Lynchburg, Virginia, some of these changes were visible in the landscape. Standing on top of the Castro hills in 1980, you could, for example, see the new office towers of downtown San Francisco—and what remained of some of the old ethnic neighborhoods. Until 1965 San Francisco was much as it had been since the turn of the century: a manufacturing city, a port, and a collection of ethnic villages—Irish, Italian, and German as well as Asian, Hispanic, and black. But in the sixties much of the shipping and manufacturing moved out—to be replaced, eventually, by financial and service industries. With the flight of manufacturing the European ethnic communities scattered into the suburbs and beyond. Their members had conceivably "melted" into the white middle class (there to join the sons and daughters these communities had been sending out into it for decades). But to look at the city and its suburbs was to imagine that the mechanism at work was not a melting pot but a centrifuge that spun them around and distributed them out again across the landscape according to new principles: families with incomes of, say, thirty to sixty thousand dollars a year went to one suburb; families with incomes of, say, sixty to a hundred thousand dollars went to another; and young, single people were flung, en masse, into the recently evacuated downtown neighborhoods.

Many of the young people came from blue-collar backgrounds, and from ethnic neighborhoods in other cities, but Moynihan and Glazer would not have called them Irish- or Italian-Americans, and they did not think of themselves as such. Approximately 50 percent of them were college educated, but even those who were not lacked blue-collar traditions. A computer programmer or an executive secretary might make less money than a foreman in an automobile plant, but he or she was not a hyphenated American. Possibly by no coincidence a hundred new flowers bloomed around the Bay Area in the sixties and seventies: not only the Beats and the flower-child culture of Haight-Ashbury, but the New Left, a dozen new, or imported, religions, est, and the cult of serious jogging.

Similarly in Lynchburg you could—from the height of a new twenty-story building—see the remnants of the old economy in the boarded-up stores and warehouses on the main street. Until the late fifties, Lynchburg was almost as it had been since the Civil War: a market and mill town and the center of the local agricultural economy. But then highways had replaced the railroad, and corporations from the North and from Europe had turned it into a modern manufacturing town. In the fifties there had been a gentry of landowners and merchants, a poor white population of small farmers, workers, and tradesmen, and an even poorer black population. Now there were corporate executives and a large middle class that included some blacks. Lynchburg, in other words, had become a part of the New South: a South of sleek, landscaped manufacturing plants and men in polyester suits riding local commuter airlines. In a time of transition Jerry Falwell's church outdrew all the other churches in town.

The changes in Lynchburg and in San Francisco merely pointed to the large economic and demographic shifts which took place across the country during the sixties and seventies: the decline of heavy industry and the flight of manufacturing from the old northern cities; the migration of population and industry to the Sun Belt; the economic development of the South that, a hundred years after the Civil War, brought the region to some rough economic parity with the rest of the country; and the development of what economists called "the postindustrial economy." The period of the sixties and seventies was one of enormous prosperity for the country. It was not one of economic growth comparable to that of the fifties, but the dividends were now paying off. In those two decades the federal and the state governments subsidized a vast expansion of educational facilities to accommodate the huge generational cohort born just after World War II. The result was that members of the "baby-boom generation" had far more education than their parents—or, at any rate, had many more years in school. Eighty-three percent of them completed high school and 25 percent of them—as opposed to 6 percent of their parents' generation—completed college.

In the same two decades a major transformation took place in the structure of the American family. With the advent of the Pill a sexual revolution passed over the country. (According to one authoritative study, the percentage of eighteen-year-old girls who admitted to premarital sex went from 29 percent in 1971 to 42 percent in 1976.) Domestic arrangements changed radically. In the first place, the women of the baby-boom generation went to work outside the home as a matter of course, whether or not they were married. Whereas in 1960 70 percent of all married women were full-time homemakers, only 25 percent of the baby-boom generation women did not have work outside the home in 1980. Between 1960 and 1980 the birth rate declined from 3.7 births per woman to 1.8 births per woman; in the same period the divorce rate climbed from twenty-six to fifty divorces per hundred marriages. The number of families headed by women increased significantly, as did the number of people living alone and the number of "nonfamily households." If the American family was alive and well, as some researchers claimed, then it was a family quite different from the one Jerry Falwell presented as the norm. In 1980 only 8 percent of all American families fit the model of a working husband-father and a full-time wife-mother with dependent children living at home.

The sixties and seventies were also decades of political, social, and cultural upheaval, beginning with the black civil rights movement and ending with the political crusade of the new fundamentalists. The events of "the sixties" are, of course, very well known, but they are still very little understood—the discussion about causality, interrelation, and consequence having just begun. One of the striking things about the period—in contrast to that of the New Deal—was that most of the major protest movements had a social or cultural dimension to them: they came from outside the normal political channels and they were never wholly absorbed by the usual business of politics and government. This was obviously true of the black civil rights movement and the American Indian movement even though these had clear economic and political grievances and programs. But it was even more true of the movements that came from the white middle class. Some of these (feminism, for example) developed political and economic programs as they went along, but many of them (the various counterculture movements) did not, as they had nothing to do with politics in the usual sense of that word. Even the New Left was not exclusively "political" in that it had some concerns that no government could possibly address: it aimed, after all, to end racism and otherwise morally reform the white middle class. During the sixties and early seventies all of these movements put together seemed to be on the verge of effecting a major cultural transformation in the country, changing the whole society radically and at once. By the eighties, however, it was clear that something less than a revolution had occurred. Some of the sixties enthusiasms had, it now seemed, been a function of youthful rebellion and nothing more. A number of endeavors—as feminism—had changed the society, but not all of it, or not all of it evenly. A reaction had set in and was gaining ground. One consequence was that while modernization of the technical sort (television, capital flows, and so on) had broken down white ethnic and regional folk cultures, it had not homogenized the country in the way that was expected of it. Indeed by the eighties white American society seemed rather less homogeneous than it had been before.

After writing on the Falwell church and on the gay community in San Francisco, I began to look for other communities—or cultural enclaves—that had taken shape during the sixties and seventies to explore. Studying relatively small groups seemed to me one way to look at some of the changes that had taken place in those decades. There were other ways, of course: taking soundings in Middletown was certainly one of them, but these new cultural enclaves had the virtue of distillation and explicitness (a virtue indeed for a single journalist). They had a prismatic quality. The majority would never belong to them, but they served to show what was happening in a much more diffuse fashion in the society around them. Falwell's church, for example, not only illuminated the new fundamentalist movement but it cast some light on the conservative evangelical movement as a whole. Likewise, the gay community in the Castro reflected the much more general revolution in sex and gender roles. A great deal, of course, could be learned from studying the larger social movements —gay liberation, for example, or the New Right as a whole—but these communities were more than collections of people bound together by a set of beliefs and programs. They were more like single organisms or personalities: they had manners and morals as well as beliefs, aesthetic sensibilities as well as political goals. As anthropologists would put it, they had kinship systems, customs, and rituals. What was more, they were changing, and not just as all things change, but as a consequence of their purposefulness. As they were carrying on social experiments, so they were themselves exploring the American scene and themselves, asking the essential questions of who we, as Americans, are, and how we ought to live.

As I thought about new forms of community, it occurred to me that in many ways the most radical of them were the retirement communities. These communities were not, of course, ideological or programmatic; many of them had been conceived and built by commercial developers. But they were radical in the sense that never before in history had older people taken themselves off to live in isolation from the younger generations. Like the gay community in the Castro, they were something new under the sun. The migrations of retired people had begun in the thirties, but retirement communities built exclusively for people over a certain age dated only from the sixties. Florida, the first state where retired people had settled in large numbers, now had a great variety of them—the planned housing developments ranging in form from single high-rise buildings to trailer parks to tract housing built around recreational facilities. After visiting a number of them and talking to representatives from others at a senior citizens' congress in Tallahassee, I fastened upon Sun City Center, an unincorporated town of 8,500 people set off by itself in the countryside south of Tampa. It was not demographically representative—none of the retirement communities were—but its inhabitants came from all over the country, and while most of them were Protestants, there were some Catholics and some Jews. More important to me was the fact that most Sun Citians were well enough off so that settling in the town—and staying there—was a matter of choice rather than one of necessity. Even more important, it was a true community—a social unit; founded in 1960, it had, like any small town, evolved its own institutions and customs. Then, too, Sun Citians were involved in a social experiment.

In his *Centuries of Childhood*, the French historian Philippe Ariès described how the conception of "childhood" evolved over three centuries: how children, once treated as small adults, came to have their own distinctive forms of work and play, their own dress, their own literature, and their own customs. In much the same way Sun Citians were now evolving a distinct culture at the other end of the age spectrum. Belonging to the first generation to reach old age en masse, in good health, and with the resources to live independently of their children, they were people for whom society had as yet no set of expectations and no vision. They were people who had to invent, and along with others of their generation, they were creating a conception of how their stage in life should be led. They were, I thought, pioneers on the frontier of age.

As a contrast to Sun City, but also in the interests of representing

an important change in sensibilities, I then thought to look for a quintessential New Age community of the sort that had flourished during
the sixties. New Age values were by now very familiar. If you thought
of them as amounting to a monistic vision of the world without traditional (bourgeois) oppositions between man and nature, work and
leisure, men and women, the natural and the supernatural, and so
on, then they were also very widespread. They were almost an orthodoxy in some parts of the country, and they were held in some part
by such various groups as solar heating advocates, craftsmen, dows-
ers, midwives, herbalists, astrologers, Zen Buddhists, and consumers
of natural food. In one form or another the monistic vision had inspired the nuclear freeze movement, the environmental movement,
the feminist movement, and the hospice movement. But for all of the
influence of this vision, a pure, unadulterated New Age community
proved very difficult to find in the eighties. After spending a weekend
in southern Vermont, I became quite discouraged about ever finding
one. In the early seventies there had been five large interconnected
communes on the southern border of Vermont engaged variously in
New Left politics, subsistence farming, community Shakespeare, gay
and feminist consciousness-raising, and cooking with, or smoking,
fresh herbs. Farm work, however, turned out not to be play for the
intellectuals involved; none of the communes made enough money,
and there were political fallings-out. By 1980 three of them had disappeared entirely, and two of them had been transformed into communal vacation houses for their former members, now editors,
writers, and professors in Boston and New York. In compensation,
however, the communes had changed the countryside. The very
same local Vermonters who in the seventies had wanted to run them
out of town were now voting for the nuclear freeze at town meetings,
selling natural foods, inviting Marxist scholars to join their Fourth of
July parades, and, in the case of one farm family, growing bumper
crops of marijuana instead of corn. The editors of *New Age* magazine
told me that these developments were fairly standard throughout the
country: the idealistic rural communes had disbanded—after influ-
encing their neighbors in some degree. The only large communes that
survived, they said, were religious in nature.

I was lecturing at a college in western Oregon in 1983 when I heard
about the Rajneeshee. There had been a number of articles about
them in the local papers, and "the red people," as they were called,
were the talk of the campus. One professor I met had gone with a
tour group to visit them, but as Rancho Rajneesh was far away in the
eastern part of the state and fifty miles from a town of any size, he,
like most other visitors, had spent only a few hours with them. What

he had discovered was that the Rajneeshee were highly educated people—doctors, lawyers, accountants, and the like—with a great deal of money. They had gone to the back of beyond to build a Utopia for themselves; they had brought in bulldozers and prefabs, and already they were making the desert bloom. The idea of doctors, lawyers, and accountants building a Utopia interested me, so a few months later I went out to Rancho Rajneesh.

The Rajneeshee were, as it turned out, building a New Age commune—organic farming, recycled wastes, and all—and while they said they had no belief system as such, their practices included Zen meditations, encounter groups, tarot card reading, Tantric sex, disco dancing, past life revelations, and primal screaming. They seemed in fact to be trying to roll all the California youth religions up into one. They had found their guru, Bhagwan Shree Rajneesh, in India and, two years before, had brought him to the United States along with a silver, bulletproof stretch Rolls-Royce limousine. They dressed entirely in shades of red and had Hindi names, such as Swami Prem Siddha, but as characters they seemed quite familiar. Some were doctors and lawyers, but many were psychotherapists and social workers: the aura of the Human Potential Movement surrounded Rancho Rajneesh. While some university people in the state thought their experiment idealistic and exciting, their immediate neighbors in central Oregon thought them sinister—if not the devil's work. A year earlier they had taken over Antelope, a tiny town near the ranch inhabited by retired people from around the state. As Falwell's congregation seemed to be moving into the world, so the Rajneeshee, from the other end of the spectrum, seemed to be moving away from it to create a separatist community with hard-and-fast borders. But, like Falwell's people, they were involved in an epic social drama that included not just themselves but everyone within their reach: in the Rajneeshee case, the whole state of Oregon.

Four different social experiments, then, and four very different new communities. Looked at in one way, they formed a kind of parallelogram: two religious movements and two social groups; two sixties communities and two groups with conservative views. And there were connections between them. The strongest connection was, of course, between the gay liberationists and the fundamentalists, who, almost literally, haunted each others' dreams. The Rajneeshee were similarly linked to the fundamentalists in central Oregon; also their group included a few gay men from San Francisco, and in the end their connection was AIDS. They also, as it happened, had a year-long fight with a group of retired people in Antelope. This last was, however, sheer coincidence, and in truth there was no real congruence between any of the groups. When fundamentalists and Rajnee-shee shouted at each other across an Oregon highway, or when fundamentalists and gay activists faced each other across a ballot box in Dade County, Florida, they were not matched adversaries. In fact they did not really see each other, so different were their experiences of the world. Essentially they stood not in the relationship of opposition so much as in that of exemplary difference, as the Dobu, the Zuni, and the Kwakiutl. Each community worked out its own destiny quite independently of the others. In many ways they might have lived in different countries.

And yet to step back a certain distance from all of them—to step back across the Atlantic—was to see that the four groups had some rather important things in common. To imagine, say, Parisians creating a gay colony or a town for grandparents was to make the point in a negative way. From a European perspective all four groups appeared quintessentially American. In the first place, the people who joined such groups had the extraordinary notion that they could start all over again from scratch. Uncomfortable with, or simply careless of, their own personal histories and their family traditions, they thought they could shuck them off and make new lives, new families, even new societies. They aimed to reinvent themselves. From a European perspective this was an absurd enterprise. Man could change the political system by reform or revolution; he could change the social system by changing the means of production. But he—or she—could not erase history or pull himself up by his own bootstraps. Yet Americans characteristically continued to try.

That individuals could start over again, and if necessary reinvent themselves, was one of the great legends of American life. It was the stuff of self-improvement manuals, generation after generation, and the attempt was a major theme in American literature. But the American attempt to start over again in groups or en masse was not a theme so well explored. The myth of the rugged individual dominated popular literature. And when in novels or histories the group appeared around the individual, that group was by and large a stable cultural entity: the Puritans, the southern plantocracy, the Quakers of Pennsylvania—or in this century ethnic blue-collar communities and the WASP Establishment. These groups certainly existed and endured for long periods of time. But it also happened with some fair frequency that groups of Americans just stopped doing what they were doing, took themselves off, and started something quite new. In certain periods of history—as the 1840s—Americans began a great variety and profusion of new enterprises: Utopian communities, new religions, and reform movements—enterprises indeed as different in nature as

Sun City and Rajneeshpuram. In these periods, visionaries would appear—Joseph Smith, Susan B. Anthony, William Lloyd Garrison, Mary Baker Eddy—all kinds of them, and in a country known for its pragmatism and the rule of the marketplace, these visionaries would find mass followings. The country, of course, was founded by visionaries. "We must consider that we shall be a City Upon a Hill, the eyes of all people are upon us," John Winthrop told his Puritan company crossing the Atlantic to found the Massachusetts Bay Colony. The remarkable thing was that four centuries later Americans were still self-consciously building cities on a hill.

The Castro

It was one of those days in San Francisco when the weather is so perfect there seems to be no weather. The sun shone out of a cerulean sky lighting the streets to a shadowless intensity. It was a Sunday morning, and the streets were almost empty, so our pickup truck sped uninterrupted up and down the hills, giving those of us in the back a Ferris wheel view of the city. In Pacific Heights the roses were blooming, the hollies were in berry, and enormous clumps of daisies billowed out from under palm trees. On Russian Hill the Victorian houses with their ice-cream-colored facades seemed to reflect this bewilderment of seasons. At the bottom of the hill the sky-scrapers of the financial district wheeled through our horizon, and the truck careened through the deserted canyons of the financial district heading for the waterfront.

"Don't worry," said Armistead. "We're on gay time, so the parade won't have started yet."

He was right, of course. Rounding a corner, we came upon a line of stationary floats. The balloons were flying—the lavender, pink, and silver bouquets crowding the sky—and the bands were just warming up. People in costumes milled about amid a crowd of young men and women in blue jeans. The Gay Freedom Day Parade had not yet begun.

Our truck nosed itself into the parade lineup behind a group of marchers with signs reading LUTHERANS CONCERNED FOR GAY PEOPLE and a hay wagon advertising a gay rodeo in Reno, Nevada. Our truck had no sign on it, but it carried in addition to myself and another journalist, two people well known to the gay community of the city: the writer and humorist Armistead Maupin and the professional football player Dave Kopay. In the front seat were Ken Maley and a couple of other friends of Armistead's.

In a few minutes our part of the parade began to move forward; a country-and-western band struck up somewhere behind us, and a number of men dressed as cowboys and clowns took their places in and around the hay wagon. A clown in whiteface with baggy overalls came and walked alongside our truck. I asked about the rodeo, and he said matter-of-factly, "This is only our second year, so we don't expect any bulldogging, but we've got a lot of calf ropers, some bronc riders, and some really wonderful Dale Evans imitations. You've *got* to come."

The clown paused, distracted by the sight of a huge person in velvet robes with ermine trim and red velvet hat to match hurrying along the sidewalk. "Just *who* does she think *she* is?" he asked rhetorically. The "Boris Gudunov" personage was followed by what seemed to be a frowsy middle-aged woman with an enormous bosom. The woman was wearing a kerchief and a cheap cloth coat, and she was having some trouble with her high heels—so the red-robed person kept having to go back to right her and pull her along. "Well, it's certainly not the Empress," the clown said. "Far too tacky."

The clown drifted off, and I turned to watch a man in a Batman cape and a sequined jockstrap roller-skating by. He had the torso of a dancer, and he moved with liquid, dreamlike movements, crossing and recrossing the street. He glided through the Lutheran contingent and then swept through another group of clergymen carrying large placards of Christ on the cross. At the intersection he looped around a yellow taxicab filled with young women in T-shirts. The young women were leaning out of the windows cheering and bouncing about a sign that read LESBIAN TAXI DRIVERS OF SAN FRANCISCO. One of them, a slim young woman with long blond hair, I recognized as the taxi driver who had brought me in from the airport a few weeks before.

Eventually our pickup truck turned onto Market Street, the main thoroughfare of the city, and we had suddenly a view of the whole first half of the parade—its floats and lines of marchers filling the street in front of us—on its way to City Hall. The sun was now harsh as a kleig light overhead; it burnished the streets and set the windows of the skyscrapers on fire. Nearby an elderly Chinese man with a dog walked along the sidewalk close to the buildings, his head bowed, his eyes averted from the marchers. A block away a woman in a baggy coat and kerchief scuttled into a doorway—just in time to avoid the sight of the transvestite copy of herself hulking down the avenue. Otherwise the sidewalks and the streets leading off into the down-town were deserted—as empty as if a neutron bomb had hit, cleaning away the weekday mass of humanity and leaving the skyscrapers perfectly intact for a new civilization to move in. At this point there were no spectators; there was no one to watch this horde in its out-landish costumes march into the city.

That summer—it was 1978—estimates of the gay population of San Francisco ranged from 75,000 to 150,000. If the off-cited figure of 100,000 were correct, this meant that in this city of less than 700,000 people, approximately one out of every five adults and one out of every three or four voters was gay. A great proportion of these people —half of them or more—had moved into the city within the past eight years. And most of these new immigrants were young, white, and male. There were now some 90 gay bars in the city and perhaps 150 gay organizations including church groups, social services, and busi-ness associations. There were 9 gay newspapers, 2 foundations, and 3 Democratic clubs. While the gay men and women had settled all over the city, they had created an almost exclusive area of gay settle-ment in the Eureka Valley, in a neighborhood known as the Castro. The previous year the Castro had elected a city supervisor, Harvey Milk, who ran as a gay candidate—against 16 opponents including another gay man. Now, quite visibly, this area of settlement was spreading in all directions: up into the hills above the Castro, down into the Mission District, and across into the lower Haight Street neighborhood. While New York and Los Angeles probably had more gay residents, the proportions were nowhere as high as they were in San Francisco. Possibly the sheer concentration of gay people in San Francisco had no parallel in history.

At that time most San Franciscans still contrived to ignore the growing gay population in their midst. The local press reported on gay
events and on the growth of the Castro, but most San Franciscans I
talked to seemed not to have noticed these pieces—or they had forgotten them. Small wonder, perhaps, for the articles were not sensational in any sense. The local reporters seemed to have gotten quite
used to the gay community without ever giving it its due. They now
took certain things for granted. Earlier that year a young journalist
from out of town had gone with the mayor and other city officials to
the annual Beaux Arts Costume Ball. The event had shaken him, but
the local newspapers had reported it as they would a mayoral visit to
a Knights of Columbus dinner. It was, after all, the third year the
mayor had gone to a drag ball in the civic auditorium.

The program in my press kit showed that there were 138 contingents in the parade, and that with a few exceptions, such as Straights
for Gay Rights and the San Francisco Commission on the Status of
Women, all of them represented gay organizations of one sort or
another. With the program it was possible to sort these organizations
into certain categories: political organizations, human rights groups,
professional associations, social-service organizations, ethnic minority
groups, religious organizations, college groups, out-of-town contingents, such as the Napa Gay People's Coalition, fraternal organizations, such as those for transsexuals and bisexuals for gay rights,
sports groups, and commercial enterprises. Perhaps for variety's
sake, however, the organizers had chosen to mix up the categories to
some degree, so that the actual order of the parade might have come
from the pages of Claude Lévi-Strauss.

By the time our truck turned onto Market Street, I was in fact too
late to see the head of the parade: the Gay American Indian contingent followed by Disabled Gay People and Friends, followed by a
ninety-piece marching band and the gay political leaders of the city.
But leaving my truck to walk along the sidelines where a crowd was
now gathering, I was able to make my way up to number forty-one:
the Gay Latino Alliance, or GALA, a group of young men dancing
down the street to mariachi music. Just behind them was a group
representing the gay Jewish synagogue, a rather serious group of
people, the men with yarmulkes on carrying a banner with the Star of
David. This contingent was closely followed by a Marilyn Monroe
look-alike on stilts batting six-inch-long eyelashes and swaying to the
music of the disco float just behind her. Farther back there were people in country work clothes with a sign for the Order of Displaced
Okies. The Local Lesbian Association Kazoo Marching Band led a
number of women's groups, including the San Francisco Women's

Center, UC Berkeley Women's Studies, and Dykes on Bikes. This latter group could be easily located, as every time they came to an intersection, the six or seven petite women in tight jeans, men's undershirts, and boots would rev up their motorcycles, bringing loud applause from the crowd. Farther back, behind the Gay Pagans, the Free Beach Activists, the Zimbabwe Medical Drive, and the Alice B. Toklas Democratic Club, came the float that many had been waiting for: the sequined, spangled, and tulle-wrapped chariot of the Council of Grand Dukes and Duchesses of San Francisco. Somewhere in this neighborhood there was a truly unfortunate juxtaposition. The Women Against Violence in Pornography and the Media had taken their proper places in line, but then somehow, perhaps as a result of some confusion in the Society of Janus, elements of the sadomasochistic liberation front had moved in just behind them. The pallid-looking men in uniforms were not dragging chains—the parade organizers had counseled against it—but they were carrying a sign of questionable grammar that read BLACK AND BLUE IS BEAUTIFUL.

At that time—the very height of gay liberation—many Americans believed that the homosexual population of the United States had greatly increased in the past ten or twenty years. And they were willing to explain it. Some said the country was going soft: there was no discipline anymore, and no morality. Others, including a number of gay men, said that the country was finding its ecological balance and creating natural limits to population growth. There was, however, no evidence for the premise—never mind for the theories built upon it. What demographic studies there were showed that male homosexuals had remained a fairly stable percentage of the population since 1948 when the first Kinsey study came out. What had happened since then, but particularly in the past decade, was that homosexuals had assumed much greater visibility. Gay liberation was, more than anything else, a move into consciousness. The movement "created" some homosexuals in that it permitted some people to discover their homosexual feelings and to express them. But its main effect was to bring large numbers of homosexuals out of the closet—and into the consciousness of others. Its secondary effect was to create a great wave of migration into the tolerant cities of the country. All the gay immigrants I talked to said that they had always known they were attracted to the same sex; their decision was not to become a homosexual but to live openly as one and in a gay community. "I lived in Rochester," a young political consultant told me. "I was white, male, and middle class, and I had gone to Harvard. I thought I could do anything I wanted, so I resented having to conceal something as basic as sex. I resented being condemned to repress or ignore my homosexuality and to live in turmoil for the rest of my life. The solution was to move here."

The parade was moving slowly, but the farther we went up Market Street, the more spectators there were. First there was a line of people and then a crowd filling the sidewalks and spilling out into the streets behind. Many of the spectators were young men, and though we had no sign on our truck, it now happened frequently that one of them would call out, "Hey, it's Armistead!" or, "Look, it's Dave Kopay!"

Kopay, tall, broad-shouldered, and lantern-jawed, was not hard to recognize: he looked like a movie version of a football player. A veteran running back, he had played pro ball for eight years with the 49ers, the Lions, the Redskins, the Saints, and the Green Bay Packers. He retired in 1975 and three years later, convinced that rumors of his homosexuality had denied him a coaching job, he decided to come out to a newspaper reporter doing a story on homosexuality in professional sports. The reporter had talked to a number of gay athletes, but only Kopay permitted his name to be used. His gesture created a scandal in the sports world, for while everyone knew there were homosexuals in professional sports, no one wanted the evidence of it. But Kopay became something of a hero among gay men.

Armistead Maupin might have been more difficult to recognize, as he was wearing a lavender-and-yellow hockey jersey with a matching cap pulled down over his bright blue eyes. But in San Francisco he was just as well known as Kopay. A journalist and fiction writer, he was the author of *Tales of the City*, a humorous serial on San Francisco life that had appeared in the *San Francisco Chronicle*. The terrain he mapped in his *Tales* was the world of young single people, gay and straight, who came to San Francisco to change their lives. It was a world he knew well. Maupin, as it happened, came from an aristocratic and ultraconservative North Carolina family. On graduating from the University of North Carolina at Chapel Hill, he had joined the Navy, gone through officers' school, and served a tour of duty in Vietnam. He had then spent another summer in Vietnam as a volunteer building refugee housing with some fellow officers. On his return, President Richard Nixon invited him to the White House and honored him as the very model of patriotic young Republicanism. A year later Maupin left for San Francisco.

Because of his writing but also because of his enormous southern charm, Armistead had become the Gay Personality of San Francisco. The year before he had been master of ceremonies at the gay parade, and he had opened the annual game between the San Francisco Sheriff's Department and the Gay Softball League by throwing out an orange. Once, to demonstrate that nothing is sacred, including *amour-propre*, he turned up in a white rabbit suit to sell jockstraps for a gay charity. The epigraph for his book was a quotation from Oscar Wilde: "It's an odd thing, but anyone who disappears is said to be seen in San Francisco."

Most of the spectators crowding the sidewalks appeared to be in their twenties or thirties. Dressed California-style in natural fibers and hiking or jogging shoes, both the men and women looked lean, tan, and athletic. Many of the men, now shirtless in the sun, had admirably muscled chests. "Just think," Armistead said, looking out at a row of them sunbathing on a wall, "of all the fortunes spent in bodybuilding equipment." There were some older people, including a group of four women with butch haircuts and lined faces and a couple of men with identical beards and canes, but not very many. And apart from a few glum-looking tourist families, there were hardly any mixed couples or children. To the expert observers on my truck, most of the spectators appeared to be gay.

The majority of San Franciscans could still ignore the growing gay population in their midst in part because the city—in spite of the endless views of self afforded by its hills—was still decentralized, its residential neighborhoods a series of ethnic villages: black, Hispanic, Irish, Italian, and Chinese. Like all the other minorities, the gays had their own neighborhoods and places of entertainment which other San Franciscans circumnavigated as they went from work to home. But then, too, unlike the rest, gay people had no distinguishing marks, no permanent badges of color, class, or accent. Going to work in the downtown, gay people, black or white, men or women, were invisible to others for as long as they wanted to be. Politically speaking, they acted like a highly organized ethnic group—indeed this year (1978) they had persuaded the city government to give the gay parade the same sum it gave ethnic parades for the purpose of encouraging tourism. Yet this minority, being defined by desire alone, materialized only once a year, in June, on Gay Freedom Day.

From time to time during the slow march up Market Street it came to me to see the gay parade as the unfurling of a municipal dream sequence—the clowns, the drag queens, and the men in their leather suits being the fantastic imagery of the city's collective unconscious. Sigmund Freud, after all, had believed that man was born bisexual and that every human being had homosexual desires in some degree. From this perspective it seemed unreasonable that the parade should not include everyone in San Francisco. On the other hand, Freud believed that each individual's inner world was quite unique—individual desires having different qualities or textures, different degrees of intensity and modes of expression. And from this perspective it seemed unreasonable that all these thousands of people should pick up a banner labeled GAY and march with it to City Hall. What made the experience more bewildering still was that to watch the contingents pass by was to watch a confusion of categories something like that of Borges's Chinese list: Dykes on Bikes, California Human Rights Advocates, Sutro Baths, Lesbian Mothers, the Imperial Silver Fox Court. Looking at the costumes—the leather and the tulle—I wondered which were new and which had been worn for decades, even centuries, in the undergrounds of Paris or London. Which were the permanent archetypes of desires, and which merely fashions or the jokes of the young? My friends on the truck would answer with the counterculture koan that everyone—all of us—were in drag. And yet some of these costumes and dream images had settlement patterns in the city. There were in fact four gay centers in San Francisco, each geographically distinct, each containing what appeared to be distinct subcultures or culture parts.

The oldest gay center in the city lay in the Tenderloin—that triangle of sleazy bars and cheap hotels bordered by the business district, the theater district, and Market Street. The Tenderloin, like its counterparts in other cities, was far from exclusively gay. The home of winos and bums, it was the transit station for sailors and other impecunious travelers, and it harbored most of the prostitution, both gay and straight, for the entire city. In the late afternoon female prostitutes, male hustlers, and transvestite whores could be seen performing a complicated street corner ballet as they tried at once to evade the police and sort out their initially undifferentiated customers. In the fifties the district had harbored most of the gay bars in the city—but now only hustler and drag queen bars were left. The Kokpit, owned by a queen called Sweet Lips, had been in operation for about a decade. Now lined with trophies and photographs of countless drag balls, it had become a kind of Toots Shor's of drag San Francisco. A few blocks away there was a bar of a professional and much more highly specialized nature, where six- to seven-foot-tall black transvestites hustled white men in business suits, who were, necessarily, shorter.

Chronologically speaking, Polk Street, or Polk Gulch, was the second gay center of the city. It was the decorators' district, and in the sixties a number of gay bars had moved into the blocks lined with antique shops and furniture stores. Since then it had been the major site of the Halloween festivities. On that one night a year the police stood by, leaving the street to a carnival of witches, clowns, nuns on roller skates, and Jackie Kennedy look-alikes or Patty Hearst look-alikes with toy machine guns. Polk Street was a mixed neighborhood —both gay and straight people lived there, and its restaurants catered to both crowds. Its gay bars were thus not conspicuous except at night when groups of young hustlers stood out on the sidewalks around them. A number of them still catered to the stylish and the well-to-do. They had low lights, expensive furniture, and music by the old favorites: Marlene Dietrich, Noel Coward, and Judy Garland. Even to outsiders their patrons would be recognizable, for Polk Street was still the land of good taste and attitude: the silk scarf so perfectly knotted, the sentimentality, the witty little jab.

A newer gay center lay around Folsom Street in the old warehouse district south of Market. At night Folsom Street was the complement to Polk Street—the raw, as it were, to the cooked—for it was lined with leather bars: the Stud, the Brig, the Ramrod, the Black and Blue. Late at night groups of men in blue jeans, motorcycle jackets, and boots would circle around ranks of Triumphs and Harley-Davidsons, eyeing each other warily. The bars had sawdust on the floors, and men drank beer standing up, shoulder to shoulder, in a din of heavy metal and hard rock. In the Black and Blue some of them wore studded wristbands, studded neckbands, and caps with Nazi insignia; above the bar a huge motorcycle was suspended in a wash of psychedelic lights. On Wednesday nights the Arena bar had a slave auction: men would be stripped almost naked, chained up by men in black masks with whips, prodded, and sold off to the highest bidder. Such was the theater of Folsom Street. The men in leather came from Polk Street and other quiet neighborhoods, the money went to charity, and the "slave" put on a business suit and went to work the next day.

Folsom Street was a night town—the Valley of the Kings, it was called, as opposed to the Valley of the Queens in the Tenderloin and the Valley of the Dolls on Polk Street. But in addition to the leather bars, a variety of gay restaurants, discotheques, bathhouses, and sex clubs had moved into its abandoned warehouses and manufacturing lofts. It was an entertainment place, and few people lived there.

The Castro, by contrast, was a neighborhood. Though first settled by gays—homesteaded, as it were—in the early seventies, it was now the fulcrum of gay life in the city. At first glance it was much like other neighborhoods: a four-block main street with a drugstore, corner groceries, a liquor store, dry cleaners, and a revival movie house whose facade had seen better days. Here and there upscale money was visibly at work: a café advertised Dungeness crab, a store sold expensive glass and tableware, and there were two banks. But there was nothing swish about the Castro. The main street ran off into quiet streets of two- and three-story white-shingle houses; the main haberdashery, The All-American Boy, sold clothes that would have suited a conservative Ivy Leaguer. In fact the neighborhood was like other neighborhoods except that on Saturdays and Sundays you could walk for blocks and see only young men dressed as it were for a hiking expedition. Also the bookstore was a gay bookstore, the health club a gay health club; and behind the shingles hung out on the street there was a gay real-estate brokerage, a gay lawyer's office, and the office of a gay psychiatrist. The bars were, with one exception, gay bars, and one of them, the Twin Peaks bar near Market Street, was, so Armistead told me, the first gay bar in the country to have picture windows on the street.

Armistead and his friends liked to take visitors to the Castro and point out landmarks such as the Twin Peaks. But in fact the only remarkable-looking thing on the street was the crowd of young men. Even at lunchtime on a weekday there would be dozens of good-looking young men crowding the café tables, hanging out at the bars, leaning against doorways, or walking down the streets with their arms around each other. The sexual tension was palpable. "I'd never live here," Armistead said. "Far too intense. You can't go to the laundromat at ten A.M. without the right pair of jeans on." The Castro was the place where most of the young gay men came. Fifty to a hundred thousand came as tourists each summer, and of these, thousands decided to settle, leaving Topeka and Omaha for good. New York and Los Angeles had their Polk Streets and Folsom Districts, but the Castro was unique: it was the first settlement built by gay liberation.

The denizens of the Castro were overwhelmingly male, but occasionally in a crowd of men on the street you would see two or three young women dressed in jeans or jumpsuits. Some gay women lived in the Castro—they considered it safe—and close by there were a few small lesbian settlements in the Haight, the Duboce Triangle and the Mission District. But you could not find these settlements unless you knew where to look, so inconspicuous were they. On one quiet street there was a comfortable neighborhood bar with a jukebox and a pool table; on the walls were framed photographs of the softball team its regulars organized each summer. This was Maud's Study, and the bartender plus all of the customers were women. But there were only five or six lesbian bars in the entire city. There were many more women's organizations, theater groups, social-service organizations, and so on—but there was no female equivalent of the Castro. In Berkeley and north Oakland across the Bay, young political women had taken over some of the big, slightly run-down, shingle houses and started a newspaper, a crafts cooperative, a recording company, and various other enterprises. And there were a number of lesbian farm communes up the coast in northern California. But nowhere did gay women congregate the way gay men did. In the city—feeling themselves vulnerable—they took on protective colorings and melted into the landscape. No one ever knew how many of them there were in San Francisco, as no research money was ever allotted to finding that out. They appeared in large numbers only on Gay Freedom Day.

The front of the parade had long ago reached its terminus at City Hall when our truck pulled into the Civic Center Plaza. A rotunda building like the U.S. Capitol, the San Francisco City Hall looked large and imposing, fronted, as it was, by tree-lined malls and a reflecting pool. At the same time, recently cleaned and bright white against a bright blue sky, it looked like an enormous wedding cake of the sort displayed in old-fashioned Italian bakeries. As we arrived, a tall, handsome woman standing on the dais before its steps was chanting something like a prayer. She was saying:

"In the memory of the recorded nine million women, many of whom were lesbians, who were executed on charges of witchcraft, we invoke the name of the Great Goddess.

"In memory of the uncounted number of gay men who were thrown into the fire as faggots to light the pyres of their sisters, we invoke the name of the Great Goddess, the Mother of all living things."

The speaker, I discovered later, called herself Bayta Podos. She was a secretary and an instructor in women's studies at San Francisco State University. She was also the priestess of a feminist religion that she herself had conceived out of her research into matriarchal or matrilineal societies. She practiced magic and invented rituals to be used on ceremonial occasions. Recently she had closed a feminist conference on violence against women by producing a large wooden sword and instructing the women to meditate upon it, filling it with all their fears and all the anger they felt against the patriarchate. Then she broke the sword in two.

"We invoke you, Great One," she continued. "You whose names have been sung from time beyond time: You who are Inanni, Isis, Ishtar, Anath, Ashtoreth, Amaterasu, Neith, Selket, Turquoise Woman, White Shell Woman, Cihuacotl, Tonantzin, Demeter, Artemis, Earthquake Mother, Kail . . ."

Next to the dais Harvey Milk was standing with a lei of purple orchids around his neck and a bunch of daisies in one hand, giving interviews to a small group of radio and television correspondents. He had already made his speech—a strong one, I was told—denouncing the so-called Briggs Initiative, a proposition on the California ballot which, if passed, would drive all openly gay teachers and all discussion of gay rights out of the public schools. He was now calling for a national gay march on Washington for the following year. Nearby, beside the dais, a woman in a gypsy costume was swinging her child around through the air; a man in a tuxedo with makeup on and long red fingernails strolled past her humming to himself.

In front of the dais a large crowd had assembled—a very large crowd. Indeed, it seemed to me when I looked at it from the top of City Hall steps that I must be looking at all the twenty- to thirty-year-olds in northern California. The young people in front were following the proceedings on the dais enthusiastically. Some were waving banners; others were standing with linked arms, chanting and cheering. Behind them groups of people were lying on the grass, their heads pillowed on backpacks, talking and rolling joints while other groups of young people drifted around them. From the front the crowd looked like an early antiwar demonstration; from the back it looked like the Woodstock nation. Both seemed to be crowds of the sixties returned, only now, both of them were gay.

The next day, June 26, 1978, the *San Francisco Chronicle* reported that 240,000 people turned out for the annual Gay Freedom Day Parade. It quoted the police estimate rather than the chamber of commerce estimate of 300,000 made later in the day or the figure of 375,000 quoted by the *Los Angeles Times*. Even the second figure would make the turnout one of the largest in San Francisco's history and would equal nearly half of the adult population of the city. The local press tended to avoid figures leading to such arithmetic. It did not like to advertise that San Francisco had become the gay capital of the country, if not of the world.

Just why so many gay people came to San Francisco was a question few nongay San Franciscans asked themselves in the summer of 1978. But after the death of Harvey Milk in November, local journalists would be called upon to explain the Castro every time events focused national attention on San Francisco. The explanation they evolved had to do with the Gold Rush. In an article for *The New York Times Magazine* just before the Democratic Convention of 1984, the reporter and novelist Lacey Fosburgh told the story in a fairly typical fashion, thus: Founded during the Gold Rush, San Francisco was a shanty-town built by miners; it was a city of young men, and it thrived on the sale of liquor, its dance halls, and its gambling. Eventually women came and fortunes were made in trade and manufacturing, but the city retained its Gold Rush flavor. Tolerant of unconventional behav-

ior, tolerant of diversity, it became an outpost "for everything that
was strange and different" and "a mecca for people who wanted to
change their lives, break with the past." First came the Beats drinking
espresso; then in the sixties came the hippies winding flowers in their
hair; in the seventies the gays appeared walking hand in hand down
the street. San Francisco was surely one of the "most tolerant, most
diverse and most democratic" of American cities, and as such it had a
"driving pertinence" for the country as a whole.

This boosterish history had a good deal of truth to it, but, of course,
there were countercurrents and contrary facts. San Francisco was, for
example, not always so tolerant vis-à-vis its Chinese and Japanese
residents, and from time to time it exhibited a rather strong strain of
middle-class morality. The city, it was true, grew up as a wide-open
miners' town, and long after the Gold Rush was over it continued to
attract a raffish crowd of fortune seekers and adventurers—not for
tradition's sake, but because it became a port city, the largest on the
West Coast and the main jumping-off place for the American outback.
During the Spanish-American War and then again during World War
II, it was a center for American naval operations in the Pacific. Like
most port cities, it had a big, raunchy waterfront which expanded
mightily during wartime. But it was also, by the end of the nineteenth
century, a manufacturing city with a solid citizenry of blue-collar
workers and prosperous, civic-minded entrepreneurs. In peacetime
its citizenry would wage strenuous and often successful campaigns
against vice and sin on the waterfront. Its preachers mounted a successful effort after 1906 by claiming the earthquake was divine intervention against the new "Sodom and Gommorah"; the city
government cracked down in the twenties and thirties and then again
in the fifties and early sixties. During this last period the police championed bourgeois morality to the extent of closing all the gay bars and
confiscating copies of Allen Ginsberg's *Howl* from the City Lights
Bookstore. But then, as had happened so often in the past, a new
wave of invaders came to disrupt the order so carefully restored.
There was, in other words, a cyclical motion to San Francisco's tolerance for "unconventional behavior."

What was certainly true about the booster version of San Francisco
history was that among the immigrants to San Francisco, and to California in general, were a great many people who were looking for
personal freedom and who wanted to break with the past. Such was
Henry Hay, the founder of the Mattachine Society, the first homosexual rights organization in the United States. Very little was known
about Hay until the late seventies, when the gay historian, John
D'Emilio, interviewed him, for Hay and his first two associates,

Chuck Rowland and Bob Hull, had Communist party backgrounds. Well-educated and highly cultivated men—Hull was a classical musician—all three of them were immigrants to California. They had worked as organizers in Communist party cultural committees and affiliates in the forties. Hay, who had been married, met Rowland and Hull in Los Angeles in 1950 and asked them to join him in creating an organization whose aim would be to raise the consciousness of homosexuals and take political action on behalf of what he defined as an "oppressed cultural minority." Hay and his colleagues founded a society along lines familiar to them: its membership was secret and its structure cell-like and hierarchical. The need for secrecy seemed evident to them, for the House Un-American Activities Committee and other agencies operating in California had already begun a hunt for Communists—and for homosexuals with security clearances. In 1955 Hay was called up before HUAC for his Communist associations, but perhaps because of the security system he had instituted, HUAC never discovered his connection with the Mattachine Society. The committee members thus missed the chance to demonstrate its thesis that Communists and homosexuals were almost the same thing. Hay, however, had quit the party because of its hostility to homosexuals and was now engaged in the most all-American of endeavors: a civil rights struggle and the pursuit of happiness.

The Mattachine Society was enormously successful in California; so popular were Hay's consciousness-raising sessions that it grew to several hundred members in the first few years. The new members, however, insisted that it have a democratic structure, and as secrecy could no longer be assured, Hay, Hull, and Rowland had to resign their positions, fearing that their former associations might become a liability to it. The leadership then passed into the hands of people who were defensively anti-Communist, and who did their best to erase all memory of the founders. The headquarters moved from Los Angeles to San Francisco, and in 1955 two other San Franciscans, Del Martin and Phyllis Lyon, founded what became a sister organization called the Daughters of Bilitis.

These two "homophile" organizations, as they were known, did not, of course, create the homosexual population in San Francisco; rather the reverse was true. According to gay historians, the city had homosexual baths and meeting places as far back as the 1890s. (According to legend, the gay fashion for wearing colored bandannas to signify sexual preferences came from the Gold Rush—from the miners' practice of using bandannas to indicate "female" partners in their all-male square dances.) Though gay history remains anecdotal until the fifties, it is clear that the homosexual population increased after

World War II, when homosexual soldiers and sailors, demobilized in the city, took a look at the waterfront and decided not to return to Kansas City and Duluth. In any case there were some thirty homosexual bars in the city in 1961 when a new police crackdown occurred.

The proximate cause of this crackdown was a charge made by a mayoral candidate that the incumbent mayor had allowed "sex deviates" to establish their national headquarters in the city. The candidate was, of course, referring to the members of the Mattachine Society and Daughters of Bilitis. There was a good deal of irony in this, for at the time two groups of more conservative and respectable people could hardly have been found. During the witch-hunts of the fifties the Mattachine Society had rejected Hay's aggressive program of "consciousness-raising" and direct political action; indeed it had rejected it so totally that most of its members never knew it had existed at all. The emphasis in both societies was now on improving the "image" of homosexuals through educational programs and through appeals to clergymen, psychologists, and sex researchers. So anxious were their members to demonstrate their respectability that they would have nothing whatever to do with the people who went to the bars. As a result, their memberships were extremely small and remained so into the sixties.

For most of the sixties and into the seventies San Francisco was not always a tolerant city as far as homosexuals were concerned. Police harassment was often ferocious: most of the bars were closed (some temporarily, some permanently) and hundreds of men were picked up each year—often simply for dancing together or holding hands. In 1961, Jose Sarrio, a talented drag entertainer at the Black Cat bar ran for supervisor in protest against this harassment. He won six thousand votes, but the Black Cat was closed for good. In 1965 the police even raided a New Year's dance held by a group of local clergymen to raise money for their newly formed Council on Religion and the Homosexual. Under the circumstances the homophile organizations made little headway, and the center of gravity in the Mattachine Society moved to New York. The year before a new organization, the Society for Individual Rights, known as SIR, was created to provide a meeting ground for gay men that was safer than the much-besieged bars. SIR differed from the homophile groups in that it addressed the needs of gay men—rather than what the larger community thought about homosexuality. Though mainly a social organization, it had committees to deal with legal and political issues and to offer social services. And as a result of entering the world of the bars, it attracted a great many more members than the Mattachine Society, some twelve hundred at its peak. But it was not until the early seventies that gay organizations gained the strength to challenge city policies. And by that time two almost seismic changes had taken place. One of them was an economic transformation of the city. The other was gay liberation.

Our truck was idling at an intersection during the parade when Larry Glover appeared out of the crowd and came up to say hello. He was wearing only shorts and hiking boots; with a backpack slung over his tanned shoulders, he looked like an advertisement for a wilderness trip or natural foods. I had met Larry on my first trip through gay night town. It was Saturday—Sunday morning, actually—and the Black and Blue bar was packed so tight that it had taken me and a journalist-friend fifteen minutes to work our way across the room. The crowd was not of the yielding variety. There were no other women, and all the men were dressed in heavy leather, Hell's Angels' style: leather boots, studded leather belts, motorcycle jackets. They were big men, many of them, with a lot of muscle and shoulder, and they had tough-guy, watch-it-buster expressions. My colleague, though gay, had never been to a bar like this before, and he, too, was feeling distinctly out of place. All of a sudden he disappeared into the crowd and a moment later came back, smiling, with one of the more imposing figures there—a tall man with chest muscles bulging out from beneath an undershirt. "Old friend of mine," he shouted at me over the din. "College together . . . Ann Arbor. . . SDS."

I thought I had heard wrong. But no. Larry left the bar with us and volunteering to act as our guide, took us around to several other Folsom Street bars and after-hours clubs. A few days later I went to see him in his apartment. It was a plain apartment, but the living room had a lot of hanging plants and a Victorian sofa covered with ancient, hairless teddy bears. Larry was, as it turned out, a gentle soul; he had a job he didn't like much and was studying to be an actor. Over white wine he told me about his days at the University of Michigan. He had gone to Ann Arbor in the late sixties, and though he came from a conservative, blue-collar family, he had joined the antiwar movement and become a member of Students for a Democratic Society. He heard about the gay liberation movement soon after it began in 1969, and, feeling that it was closer to his own concerns than the peace movement, had started a chapter in Ann Arbor. From then on he devoted himself entirely to it, organizing educational programs and gay dances; once, because he was an actor, he had lectured a seminar on sexism dressed in a woman's jumper. The period was, he said, an exhilarating one for him. But it was also a sad time because his lover, who was running for Congress on a peace ticket, decided he was too radical and left him. Then his best friend, a lesbian, became a separatist and would not speak to him again.

Larry was somber that day, and he seemed a little lonely. But on the street in the midst of the parade he looked much happier. "I'm in a good space," he said. "I'm jogging now as well as doing weights. Then we've got two plays in rehearsal, and I'm really getting into Brecht." He smiled and waved as our truck pulled away.

The 1978 Gay Freedom Day Parade marked the ninth anniversary of gay liberation. The event heralding its birth was a riot on Christopher Street in Greenwich Village, New York. On June 27, 1969, the New York City police raided the Stonewall Inn, a bar that catered to effeminate young street people and drag queens among others. Instead of acquiescing, the customers and onlookers fought back with beer bottles and paving stones. The scene was iconic, and as the rioting continued for a second night, there appeared graffiti on the walls and sidewalks announcing the birth of a revolutionary new movement. Extraordinarily, a movement came into being that summer and was an immediate success. In the first year it spread like wildfire across the campuses—from Columbia to Berkeley and Ann Arbor to colleges across the nation.

As John D'Emilio had shown in his history of the movement, gay liberation owed something to the older homophile organizations. But the gay liberationists were largely college and university students, a generation younger than most of the members of the Mattachine Society, and most of them were involved with the other radical movements of the sixties rather than with the homophile groups. For them gay liberation was simply a logical extension of the New Left, the counterculture, black power, and the feminist movement. Whereas the homophile groups retained a moderate, reformist character long past the time when other social movements had passed into a radical phase, the gay liberationists adopted militant, confrontational tactics. The rhetoric of oppression, consciousness, and revolution came naturally to them, as did a sense of an impending apocalyptic change. They were not out to persuade and educate, they were out to shock the society into a sudden "change of consciousness." Abandoning the old networks, they used the platforms provided by the other radical sixties movements. Gay rights contingents carried banners at antiwar demonstrations; lesbian groups ran workshops at feminist conferences; gay speakers addressed New Left and black power rallies, and gay students did guerrilla theater on the campuses. Whereas the older groups had counseled self-acceptance, the gay liberationists called upon homosexuals to make an open avowal of their sexual identity. "Coming out" symbolized the shedding of self-hatred, but it was also a political act directed toward the society as a whole. In San Francisco, Leo Laurence, a thirty-six-year-old radio journalist, returned from the 1968 Democratic Convention "radicalized" to write for the *Berkeley Barb* and *Vector,* the publication of the Society for Individual Rights. He wrote of the "homosexual revolution" and called upon homosexuals to "come out from behind a double life." He and his lover posed for a seminaked photograph in the *Barb,* and he lambasted homophile activists as "timid," "bigoted," and a "bunch of middle-class, uptight, bitchy old queens." This was gay liberation speaking.

The movement caught on the way the homophile movement never had. The students, of course, had less to lose than their elders, and when called upon to do so, they came out and went out into the streets to demonstrate. In just a few years the movement did "change the consciousness" of young gay men and women across the country: not just in the colleges but in the high schools, not just in the cities but in the small towns—and among those who otherwise had no interest in radical politics. This change in turn set off a wave of migrations. In the seventies thousands upon thousands of young gay men and women left their small towns and went to the cities. They went to New York and Los Angeles as well as San Francisco; they also went to Chicago, Boston, Washington, D.C., Atlanta, New Orleans, and Houston. Roughly speaking, they went from the interior of the country to the cosmopolitan cities of the coasts. There were no reliable statistics, but the movement was clearly national, and in many cities on a scale to be of some significance to city planners and politicians.

In the early seventies San Francisco seemed a logical place for movement activists to settle; not only was there a large and fairly open homosexual community there, but it was the place where gay liberation had its longest and probably its strongest roots. In the fifties the poets Allen Ginsberg, Lawrence Ferlinghetti, Kenneth Rexroth, and others had created a small literary community in the North Beach and launched a bohemian protest against literary conventions and also against the social and political conformity of the period. A number of them, including Ginsberg, but also Robert Duncan and Jack Spicer, were homosexuals and proclaimed it, often raucously, joyously. They, unlike the homophile groups of the period, were not purveyors of good taste: indeed, they thought good taste the enemy. Ginsberg's first major epic *Howl* created a scandal on many counts, but one of them was its celebration of homosexual sex, and it was on that count that the San Francisco police confiscated copies of it from Ferlinghetti's bookstore. The "Beats," as the North Beach writers came to be known, captured the attentions of the press, and before long, North Beach was inundated by young drifters, hipsters, and dropouts, enchanted with the notion of rebellion, or simply escape, from social and parental authority. Later, a number of the writers who had given the North Beach its bohemian cachet moved to quieter quarters in the Haight-Ashbury, where, predictably, the young people followed them.

The young who moved into the Haight in the sixties belonged to the front ranks of a generation so large it seemed to have no parents and no memory. In the Haight the taste was for drugs rather than drink, metaphysics rather than poetry, and instead of despair with the condition of the world, there was the arrogant optimism of the young. But the Haight was in some sense a fulfillment of the North Beach prophecy, for the hippies were pacifists in an age of war, critics of consumerism in an age of plenty, and the enemies of all convention. They believed love had the power to sweep away all repressive social institutions: love or an altered state of consciousness. Articulation was not their forte, and reasonably enough, since their whole endeavor was to disarticulate the society and the intellectual frames they had grown up in. Their long hair and loose clothes blurred the shape of the family and the sexual exclusivity that went with it. If people over thirty were not to be trusted, people under thirty were to be trusted implicitly: they were brothers and sisters, and everyone had a right to do his or her own thing. If they were gay, that was their thing, and it had to be respected.

As the Haight was the successor to North Beach, so the Castro was the direct descendant of the Haight. It grew out of its side, geographically speaking, for its main street, the Castro, was only a few blocks away from the Haight settlement. When the first wave of gay settlers arrived there in 1972, what they found was a decaying Irish neighborhood with two gay bars catering to hippies from the Haight. And the new settlers fit right in. One of them, Harvey Milk, had been looking for a place to drop out. He had worked for years as a financial analyst in New York, but then the sixties hit him, and at the age of forty-three he had long hair and friends in the avant-garde theater. The Castro with its cheap housing and good weather suited him, and he bought a camera store with his lover. Milk, as it happened, was not a man in flight. He had lived most of his life quite openly as a gay man. Most of the others who moved there in the first wave, however, were looking for the shelter of bohemia in order to become gay. Indeed, they equated gay and hip. Frank Robinson, for example, a science fiction writer, had been an editor of *Playboy* magazine in Chicago and deep in the closet until he picked up a sign at a gay rights demonstration one day. Harry Britt, a Methodist minister from Texas, had been deeply involved in the civil rights movement—and married. He quit the church in 1968, and got a divorce; three years later he moved to San Francisco, went into the Human Potential movement and finally realized he was a homosexual. He took a job as a mailman in the Castro and began to think out his life anew.

The counterculture helped to bring the younger men of the post-Stonewall generation to San Francisco. But for them there were other attractions as well. There was cheap housing in nice parts of the city; there were also jobs available, and as most of the younger men were not dropouts—far from it—this was important to them. In addition the city was now well known for its tolerance of "unconventional behavior" and "diverse life-styles." In fact all of these things were quite new, and all were related to the fundamental transformation of the city's economy that occurred during the sixties—a transformation that in turn changed the population of the city and its politics.

In 1960 San Francisco was a commercial and industrial city with a wide variety of manufacturing enterprises. Its population was heavily blue collar, and though racially and ethnically diverse, the city was not truly integrated. It was low-lying and decentralized: a city of neighborhoods, each with its own main street, its own shops and restaurants. It was a city of villages—Irish, Italian, black, Hispanic, and Chinese. And much as most San Franciscans resented being told it, the city was quite provincial. Its WASP Establishment was more than a little stuffy, and its police and politicians, being largely Irish or Italian Catholics, had no respect whatsoever for "diverse life-styles." During the sixties, however, the economic base of the city eroded. Manufacturing declined as factories moved out to cheaper quarters across the Bay; the port lost shipping to Oakland. New York City went through the same kind of decline in the same period, but as San Francisco was a much smaller city—it was like Manhattan with its Brooklyn and Queens in separate cities across the Bay—so the decline was sharper and more thoroughgoing in its effects. The flight of manufacturing emptied the factories and warehouses south of Market Street; the flight of blue-collar workers in its wake emptied the ethnic neighborhoods, among them Haight-Ashbury and the Castro. It emptied the Irish and Italian neighborhoods, and it thinned the black population in the Fillmore District and the Hispanic population in the Mission District. Great tracts of the Fillmore District were razed to the ground and never rebuilt, but the other neighborhoods offered good cheap housing—though no jobs. This was ideal for the tribes of sixties children who came to live on the fringes of the economy.

In the sixties the city fathers sought to compensate for the losses by building up the already strong financial sector, attracting corporate headquarters and making San Francisco a major tourist and convention center. In the late sixties, Mayor Joseph Alioto cleared the path for real-estate developers. Hotels and office buildings now sprouted like so many giant beanstalks out of the downtown; corporate executives arrived, tourists arrived, and the city soon had a demand for white-collar office workers, professional people, and service industry personnel. What it needed were young people with college educations—and as these were the most mobile people in the population, they came very quickly.

Mayor Alioto, an Italian Catholic, was a big-city Democrat of the old school. He ruled the city with an iron hand, and in part through the old networks: the ward bosses, the unions, and the construction firms. He changed the city and at the same time swept away the very base of his own power. As the manufacturing left, so did his supporters. By the mid-seventies only one of the city's eleven voting districts had a majority of conservative, blue-collar Democrats. And, ironically, those for whom he had remade the city detested him and his politics. By the early seventies the city was electing liberals to its Board of Supervisors, the state legislature, and the U.S. Congress—liberals who believed that government should be more open, more democratic, more open to racial minorities, and more tolerant of "diverse life-styles." Even before the new wave of gay immigration began, a number of these liberals were attending candidates' nights organized by the homophile groups. Dianne Feinstein went in 1969, when as a thirty-five-year-old housewife from the affluent Pacific Heights district she took more votes than any other candidate in her first run for the Board of Supervisors. The same year Willie Brown, the flamboyant state assemblyman, who later became speaker of the California State Assembly, made his first attempt to repeal state statutes proscribing various forms of consensual sex. (In 1975 he and George Moscone, then majority leader of the State Senate, engineered passage of the legislation.) In 1971 Richard Hongisto, a civil rights and antiwar activist, was elected sheriff of San Francisco County; on taking office he gave a great deal of attention to improving relations between the gay population and the police. It was under the stewardship of these liberals that San Francisco politics gained its now well-deserved reputation for tolerance.

How many gay immigrants came to San Francisco during the seventies it was difficult to say exactly, at the time, for they came in a flood of other young immigrants, most of them white, most of them single, themselves shaken loose from their hometowns by the nation-wide shift from an industrial to a "postindustrial" economy. The 1980 census showed that, while the population of the city had declined by 5 percent since 1970, the number of people between twenty-five and thirty-four showed a net increase of more than 25 percent. A great many of the gay immigrants moved into the Castro and the neighbor-hoods around it. Beginning in 1973 the price of residential property began to climb sharply; the boom was citywide, but nowhere as great as it was in the Castro. A federal survey of a small neighborhood near the Castro showed that business transactions increased by 700 percent in the decade 1968–78. In 1977 Harvey Milk estimated through pre-cinct counts that twenty-five to thirty thousand gay people had moved into the Castro. That year the annual Castro Street Fair at-tracted seventy thousand gay tourists and immigrants—most of them men.

It was Armistead Maupin who first introduced me to what he and his friends called alternately "the ghetto" and "the liberated zone." Literally this was the Castro, but figuratively speaking it was the world of gay immigrants in their twenties and thirties throughout the city. At the time Armistead did not live in the Castro. He had an apartment in a small wooden house on Telegraph Hill overlooking the Filbert Steps. A number of his friends, including Ken Maley, Dan-iel Detorie, and Steve Beery, lived within shouting distance; their houses and apartments, backed up to the precipitous hillside, had clear views across San Francisco Bay. It was like the pueblo of some cliff-dwelling tribe. How many lived there I never really knew, for the friends seemed so much alike. Blond, pleasant, collegiate-looking, they wore khakis and Brooks Brothers shirts and went about in groups, often with other young men of the same general description. In the course of a year there would be substitutes—a Greg for a Bob, a Steve for another Steve—and, as they introduced themselves Cali-fornia-style by their first names alone, the substitutions could be eas-ily missed. They were full of high spirits. On weekends they would often hang out at someone's apartment for hours, smoking a little dope and talking, talking. Then they would suddenly bust off down the hill to some adventure, laughing at some private joke. Their group was much like a college fraternity—the one they had never belonged to. At the bottom of the Filbert Steps a garden bench had a plaque on it that read: "I HAVE A FEELING WE'RE NOT IN KANSAS ANYMORE." The plaque with the *Wizard of Oz* inscription had been put up by Armistead for Ken, who came from Kansas, and from a fundamentalist family to boot.

Through Armistead, but also through Ken, who was working as a publicist for gay organizations, I met a number of young men then active in the cause of gay liberation. At a party that Ken and Daniel had at their house after the gay parade, I met, among others, Randy Shilts, then a correspondent for the local public television station, KQED, and the only openly gay journalist working for the major news organizations in town; Peter Adair, a documentary filmmaker, whose latest film, *Word Is Out,* explored the lives of twenty-six gay men and women from several generations; Toby Marotta, a Harvard-trained social scientist who was doing a study of gay hustlers for a policy research institute and writing a history of gay liberation in New York; and Jim Rivaldo, a political consultant who with his partner Dick Pabich had worked on the Harvey Milk campaigns. Through them I in turn met a number of other gay activists. Both personally and politically it was an exhilarating time for these men. They were too young to have suffered in any overt way for their homosexuality, but, having recognized that they were homosexual in school or in college, they had looked forward to a life of suffering. They had, as Toby Marotta wrote, equated homosexuality with "a world of eccentric bachelors and effeminate characters, of unsavory public sex scenes and dingy bars and steam baths"—a shadowy world of indirection and conflict, guilt and tragedy. They had been very isolated even in college. "I used to think that all gay people were hairdressers," Rivaldo said. "It took coming here to find that there were gay lawyers, gay businessmen—a lot of people like myself." For these young men coming out was a profound experience. It was, Ken Maley said, something like the evangelical experience of being "born again": it lifted a huge burden and gave them a fresh start. Just the possibility of leading a normal life was heady, but on the top of it was the fact that, historically, they were an avant-garde. "We're the first generation to live openly as homosexuals," Randy Shilts said. "We have no role models. We have to find new ways to live."

In San Francisco these young men had not only changed their lives but they had found a community, a cause, and an intellectual endeavor all in one. The homophile leaders had been engaged in a civil rights struggle, but gay liberation had widened the task, for it, like feminism, offered a new perspective on the whole culture. The taboo against homosexuality went, after all, to the heart of it; to deny the taboo was therefore to throw into question the traditional family structure, traditional gender roles, and sexual mores. Homosexuals had always been marginal to the culture—anomalies within it; thus, liberated homosexuals—that is, gay men and women—had, as they saw it, a privileged position from which to observe it. In changing their own lives they would provide a model for other gay men and women in the generations to come; in breaking sex and gender taboos they would change the whole society. Gay liberation was, of course, a national movement, and its theorists lived largely in New York, but what was a matter of theory elsewhere seemed a matter of imminent realization here. The Castro was, after all, the first gay settlement, the first true "gay community," and as such it was a laboratory for the movement. It served as a refuge for gay men, and a place where they could remake their lives; now it was to become a model for the new society—"a gay Israel," as someone once put it.

In fact by the summer of 1978 the new society of the Castro had already taken shape; indeed from the perspective of some years later (after Milk was dead and the AIDS crisis had begun) that summer marked a high point in its development. Given the homogeneity of its inhabitants, it had quite quickly and spontaneously evolved a new kind of politics, a new style of dress and behavior, new forms of couple relationships, and new sexual mores. It had an ideology rather different from that of gay groups on the East Coast, and it had, as the sociologists put it, institutional completeness. It was something new under the sun.

The politics of the Castro were, essentially, the politics of Harvey Milk—the hip politics that the forty-three-year-old convert to bohemia devised in the front room of his camera store. They were difficult to define without reference to the man himself. Randy Shilts, who later wrote Milk's biography, traced Milk's decision to run for city supervisor a few months after he settled in the Castro to three incidents: first, the contretemps Milk had with a city official over a hundred-dollar deposit against sales tax; second, to his discovery that the local public school could not afford to buy enough slide projectors—a teacher had to borrow one from him; and third, to his indignation at former Attorney General John Mitchell's performance at the Senate Watergate hearings. This was typical Milk politics. The man had no politics when he decided to run for office—certainly no received political opinions. He had once professed right-wing Republicanism, but recently he had turned into an antiwar demonstrator. Abstractions didn't interest him; his own immediate experience did. Energetic, sociable, gusty of temperament, he had a great capacity for sympathy and an even greater one for outrage. In many ways he was the perfect representative for the Castro—a community coming out of the counterculture and trying out something new.

Up until then Milk had drifted—though respectably enough. Born in Woodmere, Long Island, to a middle-class Jewish family, he had attended teachers' college in upstate New York, then gone into the Navy and quickly became an officer. He had spent three years in the Pacific working, when he got the chance, as a deep-sea diver. He later claimed to have been dishonorably discharged, as many homosexuals were, but this was not true: he simply left the Navy after four years, restive under the discipline. He returned to Long Island and taught high-school history and math for a few years; then he left and went to Dallas with a lover for no better reason than to get out of the cold weather. He soon moved back to New York. He took a job as an actuarial statistician for an insurance company, then one as a researcher for a Wall Street investment firm. Both jobs bored him eventually—as did running a camera store in the Castro. He seemed to be a hippie who had taken a long time to find that out. He was in fact a born politician, and at the age of forty-three he had finally found his vocation.

Otherwise his first campaign for supervisor made no sense at all. In the first place, the Castro was still a working-class neighborhood in 1973; largely Irish, it was known to its inhabitants as the parish of the Most Holy Redeemer Church. In the second place, Milk had no money, no staff, and no roots in San Francisco. And he presented himself quite openly as gay. This did not help him on any score, since the gay community in San Francisco already had well-entrenched political leaders—people who stood up to be counted during the sixties and who had recently taken the cause of gay rights a giant step forward. In the mid-sixties the homophile leaders had of necessity remained largely anonymous to the outside world; by the end of the decade, however, a number of well-educated professional people were working openly for the cause: Del Martin and Phyllis Lyon became well known in the city. Jim Foster, a sales representative and founder of SIR, took over the political committee at SIR and made it an effective organization. With him at SIR was Larry Littlejohn, a public health worker, among a number of others. In addition there was David Goodstein, a financier from New York, and Rick Stokes, a Texas-born lawyer. Many of these people had been victimized because of their homosexuality. Foster had received a dishonorable discharge from the Army, Goodstein had been fired as vice president of a bank, and Stokes had been institutionalized and submitted to electrical shock treatment. (He had later studied law in order to fight for gay rights.) In 1971 Foster turned his political committee into a Democratic club—the Alice B. Toklas Democratic Club—and put it to work for George McGovern, the presidential candidate that year with the strongest stand on gay rights. At the Democratic Convention, Foster, at the invitation of the California McGovern Committee, made a major speech on gay rights. His speech marked a turning point for the movement nationally: now a mainstream political party had recognized a spokesman for a minority with legitimate grievances and claims to equality before the law.

In 1972, therefore, Foster, Stokes, and their colleagues had the best of credentials to represent "the gay vote." They had stood up when it was dangerous to do so and had won major battles. In alliance with the liberal Democratic politicians in the city—Feinstein, Brown, Moscone, and Congressman Phillip Burton—they had changed city politics. Electorally they had proved that they did not need the local New Left organization, the Bay Area Gay Liberation Front (BAGL had few members in San Francisco proper, and these seemed preoccupied with ideological hairsplitting). And now, as far as they could see, they did not need an aging hippie just arrived in town with a disheveled camera store in the Castro. Yet, running for supervisor in citywide elections in 1973, Milk came tenth in a field of thirty-two candidates and proved to be the top vote-getter in the heavily gay precincts around Polk Street and the Castro. In 1975 he ran again for supervisor and finished seventh behind the six incumbents who were running that year. In 1976 he ran for the State Assembly and was defeated by a liberal, Art Agnos, who was backed not only by all the important liberal politicians in the city but the gay leaders as well. In 1977, after a referendum that changed the electoral laws so that candidates for supervisor ran in their own districts and not citywide, Milk ran for supervisor from the Castro and won.

Harvey Milk loved campaigning—that was the real secret of his success. For months out of every year, according to Shilts, he would let his business drift into further disarray in order to get up at five in the morning and shake hands at bus stops, in order to visit people in the neighborhood, in order to speak at every meeting that he was invited to. He organized a Castro Village business association and an annual street fair; he persuaded gay bars across the city to boycott Coors beer in aid of a Teamster campaign. He became a figure in the neighborhood—and eventually one who could get things done. At the same time he had a flair for the dramatic and knew how to attract press attention. Outspoken, he attacked Foster and Stokes as the Uncle Toms of the gay movement, and when Moscone was elected mayor, lambasted Moscone's "machine." His early supporters included a Eureka Valley housewife; the head of the Teamsters local; Jose Sarrio, the famous drag queen entertainer; and a young lesbian, Anne Kronenberg, who wore black leather jackets and rode a motorcycle. Defeated once, Milk cut his hair—a sign of the times—and took to wearing three-piece suits he picked up second-hand. As an outsider running against liberals, he became at once a fiscal conservative and a populist: he was for "the little people" in the neighborhoods against the downtown interests and the landlords; he was for mass transit, better schools, better city services for the elderly; to pay for that, he would end waste in government and tax the corporations and commuters from Marin County. Along the way, his support came from the Teamsters, the Firefighters' Union, the Building and Construction Trades Council, and small businessmen; but in the end his main supporters were the thousands upon thousands of young gay men settling in the Castro.

In many respects, these young men did not differ very much from the older generation of gay immigrants constituting Foster and Stokes's constituency. Most of them were white, most came from middle-class families, and the majority had college degrees. Those who went to work for Milk were liberal Democrats rather than New Leftists, and in the end their dispute with Foster and Stokes was largely a fight over turf—a struggle of the newcomers to make a place for themselves in city politics. On the other hand, the newcomers were virtually all in their twenties or early thirties. As members of the baby-boom generation, they were used to collective self-assertion and used to getting their way. They had grown up with gay liberation, and they were still young enough to take risks. Furthermore, the very concentration of them in the Castro constituted a kind of critical mass. On June 7, 1977, the night the born-again singer Anita Bryant proclaimed victory in her campaign to repeal a gay rights ordinance in Dade County, Florida, three thousand people gathered on Castro Street to shout their protests. The police, fearing a riot, called upon Harvey Milk for help, and to provide a release for the anger, Milk led the crowd on a five-mile march through the city. At midnight he rallied the marchers in Union Square and, taking up a bullhorn, told them, "This is the power of the gay community. Anita's going to create a national gay force." Ten days later when Vice President Walter Mondale came to Golden Gate Park to address an open-air rally on the subject of human rights, Milk and a number of his supporters picketed the rally and heckled Mondale for not speaking about gay rights. This was how the Castro expressed itself: not by alliances and persuasion but by demonstrations and nonnegotiable demands.

Harvey Milk's victory in the 1977 election was a victory for the Castro and a proof of its new political power. At the same time it signified a much more general triumph for gay liberation in the city. The homophile organizations had long been forgotten, and SIR collapsed shortly thereafter for lack of a role to play. Foster and Stokes —whatever Milk said of them—had long ago accepted the basic tenets of gay lib, and with the help of the liberals they had already made such changes in the city that Milk had a relatively short agenda of gay rights items to take to City Hall. Then, too, emboldened by the Castro, important businessmen and lawyers were coming out of the closet to join the cause. Between them, both older and younger immigrants were introducing the concepts of gay liberation into fields far more resistant to change than city politics.

In the early seventies John Schmidt, an insurance broker, left the big company he had been working for to start his own firm. In his former employ he had learned that most insurance companies penalized single people and gay couples by the structure of their premiums. His new firm equalized the premium structure and attracted a good deal of business in the gay community. A few years later he founded a savings and loan association on the similar premise that loan officers in banks often discriminated—consciously or unconsciously—against gay and single people. Founded in the depths of the S and L depression of 1980 on $2 million scraped together from sixteen hundred shareholders, the Atlas Savings & Loan Association was making an annual profit of a million dollars three years later.

During the seventies a great many other gay businessmen and women followed much the same model, starting travel agencies, hotels, financial services, and so on, specially tailored to a gay clientele. Gay professionals, too, developed specialized gay practices. Lawyers, for example, became expert not only in discrimination cases but in cases involving child custody and inheritance. Some gay doctors specialized in the diseases common to the gay population, while others came out far enough to assure their gay patients that they found their way of life quite normal and natural. The same went for gay psychotherapists. In 1978 Don Clark, a clinical psychologist, told me that when he came to San Francisco in 1970, he knew only a couple of openly gay therapists—and they lacked credentials. Now, eight years later, he knew almost fifty; he had worked with a number of them in rethinking all the questions involved in treating gay patients. In Clark's view, gay therapists were almost always better qualified than others to treat gay patients because "they knew about gay life-styles and could love and celebrate homosexual desires."

In San Francisco a number of liberal Protestant clergymen, headed by Rev. Cecil Williams of the Glide Memorial Methodist Church, had been active in the gay civil rights struggle of the sixties. They had

developed gay fellowships in their own churches, which now welcomed the gay immigrants in. Other churches, however, were not so
accommodating, and as the same was true all over the country, many
gay people had simply lost their faith—or lost interest in organized
religion. Others had led double lives. Now, however, in the spirit of
gay liberation a number of these undertook to create churches where
they could worship as gay men and women. Bernard Pechter, for
example, a playwright and a stock broker, had founded a gay synagogue. When I asked him about it, he told me that he had gone
regularly to a Conservative synagogue until the mid-sixties. At that
point it had occurred to him that however accepting of homosexuals
the rabbi seemed to be, the synagogue was family-oriented—and thus
it excluded him. He could not go back. Some years later, however, a
friend told him about a gay synagogue in New York and after visiting
it he became, as he put it, "a born-again Jew." He formed a congregation in San Francisco; it had no rabbi—a learned layman had written the liturgy and the congregants took turns performing the services
—but the group now had 250 members, most of whom, Pechter said,
had come back to Judaism only because of it.

The gay Catholics in San Francisco had done much the same thing.
Because the Catholic Church still viewed homosexual sex—along
with all forms of extramarital sex—as a sin, gay Catholics had
founded a separate congregation; they, however, had found a priest
to perform the services—though outside church sanctuaries. Protestants, too, now had an entirely gay church: the Metropolitan Community Church, a member of the nondenominational association
founded by Reverend Troy Perry in Los Angeles. The pastors would
perform gay marriages and were rather more accepting of the far-out
fringes of the gay community than most other Protestant clergymen.
In 1978 the church in San Francisco, for example, took donations from
drag balls held for charity and had a bike club described on its posters
as "outreach to the Western leather community." Gay women as well
as men went to these separatist churches, but a number of radical
feminists were in the process of developing a whole religion of their
own. Having abandoned the Judeo-Christian tradition as essentially
and unalterably patriarchal, they researched other traditions and discovered a host of female spirits and deities. Bayta Podos, the woman
who had spoken at the gay parade, had done some of this work at
San Francisco State, and was helping to reconstruct witchcraft and
other—similarly misunderstood—female rites. "I don't take the position of a spiritual leader," she said when I went to see her, "but I
guess I am one in that I had a lot to do with bringing this information
out at women's studies' programs."

To a great degree gay men—and to a lesser degree gay women—were building themselves a world apart from the rest of the city. Gay men, after all, could spend days, or an entire week, going to their offices, to the cleaner, the bank, and the health club, dining in restaurants, attending political meetings, and going to church without coming into contact with anyone who was not gay. Some, such as Bob Ross, publisher of a local gay newspaper, said that they actually did just that on occasion. Others normally lived all but their working lives within gay society. While the density of gay institutions gave them a good deal of power and influence in the city, it also, paradoxically, had the effect of separating them from it. The gay community thus evolved according to its own logic and became more and more articulated and distinct. It now had not only its own political leaders but its own habits and customs and its own holidays: Gay Freedom Day, Halloween, and the Castro Street Fair. As for the Castro, it was a great hive where everyone knew everything that happened that day. To an outsider it seemed self-preoccupied and claustrophobic. Gay activists might argue among themselves, but they presented a united front to the outside world. In the Castro gay men even presented a uniform appearance.

Looking back, Randy Shilts felt that 1978 was the year when the Castro clone style reached an almost Platonic perfection. In the early seventies, the look had been unisex hippie: the green fatigues and the pea jackets snatched from military surplus stores and added, willy-nilly, to items found on the racks at the Salvation Army. Now "the Castroids," as they sometimes called themselves, were dressing with the care of Edwardian dandies—only the look was cowboy or bush pilot: tight blue jeans, preferably Levi's with button flies, plaid shirts, leather vests or bomber jackets, and boots. Accessories included reflecting sunglasses and keys dangling from leather belts; in the hot weather there were muscle T-shirts. The counterculture style had been loose and flowing, concealing of gender differences; the new look was male to the point of what the psychologist C. A. Tripp called "gender-eccentricity." Short hair was now the style—very short hair cut far above the ears; mustaches were clipped, and there wasn't a beard or a ponytail to be seen anywhere. And the new gear was cut to show off bulging deltoids, slim hips, and rippling stomachs. The muscles seemed to belong to the uniform—as did the attitude. Men would swagger slightly walking down the street and watch each other from under lowered lids, a slightly hostile air about them. Bellied up to a bar, they would look around them with a studied casualness and with one foot on the rail, communicate with their neighbor in grunts. The look, Shilts wrote, was supermacho. "It was as if this new generation of gays were out to deliver one big 'fuck you' to society. Tell 'em they're femmy queers who need wrist splints and lisp lessons and they'll end up looking like a bunch of cowboys, loggers, and MPs. Whaddya think of that?"

Shilts, Maupin, Adair, and their friends had—personally—no interest in the clone style. I knew Armistead worked out only because he once gave a party for *le tout* San Francisco in the Market Street health club and floated gardenias in the Jacuzzis. Randy dressed conservatively and Peter, tall and bearded, wore baggy trousers and oversize checked coats from the time they were hip to the time they were New Wave. They saw the Castro style as a caricature; all the same they saw it as an important step forward. "The culture proceeds by contradictions," Shilts told me. "These days the style is straight but sensitive, gay but macho. There's some compensation involved. Gay men used to be expected to play women, so now they're playing superstud." What it meant in particular, he felt, was that the Judy Garland style was really dead: there would be no more hostile mimicry of women, no more bitchiness, no exaggerated sense of vulnerability, and no self-destructiveness. "Younger people can't relate to that kind of thing anymore," he said. "Life is so much easier for us now. It's the juggernaut effect of openness." Gone, too, so my friends said, was gay mimicry of heterosexual marriages with the "male" and "female" role-playing it had involved. "In the Castro there are all kinds of experiments going on with communal arrangements and open relationships," Adair said. "You have a roommate, or perhaps several of them. Or you have a lover but not an exclusive one. How you live together is a matter of negotiation." It was in the domain of relationships, my friends felt, that gay men were leading the way for the rest of the society; there, and in the area of sexual freedom.

By 1978 the Castro had become the most active cruising strip in the city—and perhaps in the country. Even in the daytime there were hundreds of young men out cruising in the bars, the bookshops, the restaurants, and the stores—even in the vast supermarket some distance down Market Street. At night the bars were jammed—there were lines out on the sidewalks—and cars had trouble getting through the crowds of men. The scene was mind-boggling to newcomers: the openness of it and the sheer turnover. It was crazy, one gay activist told me, speaking of his first visit to the Castro. "I belonged to the Yippies at home, and I'd been through a Smash Monogamy period, but, you know, we were still very sexually oppressed. I came out here with my lover, and we couldn't believe it. . . . Everyone seemed to be living out their fantasies from day to day. We had dates at breakfast, lunch, and dinner. It was like opening up a treasure chest and rummaging through it in some hysterical way." The gay activists had had a political vision, but few of them had imagined what a sexually liberated society might be like; few, certainly, had imagined the sexual carnival of the Castro in the late seventies, for it was something new. In 1978 two Kinsey Institute researchers, Alan P. Bell and Martin S. Weinberg, published the results of a survey they had done of gay men and women in the San Francisco area. Even in 1970, when they did their interviews, nearly 40 percent of the white males they had interviewed (about a third of the black males) said that they had had over five hundred sexual partners in the course of their careers; 28 percent said that they had had over a thousand.

The extent of the sexual free-for-all in the Castro surprised gay women as much as anyone else. A decade before, gay liberationists had generally supposed that gay men and gay women had a great deal in common: the society, after all, assigned them to the same category. But as gay liberation revealed to them—and as their social worlds developed—they provided little more than a study in contrasts. According to the Kinsey Institute researchers, for example, over half of the gay white females they interviewed said they had ten sexual partners or fewer in the course of their careers. The gay women they talked to rarely cruised and rarely had casual sex outside a relationship; they tended to be monogamous, serially. According to the gay therapists I spoke with, the problem for gay men often lay in developing intimate relationships; the problem for gay women was often the reverse in that their relationships were generally so close and so emotionally intense that even the unhappiest of couples had difficulty separating. If gay male society seemed in many ways impersonal and atomistic, lesbian society seemed to be private and intimate to the point of claustrophobia. While gay men flocked to bars and bathhouses, gay women nested at home or gathered together in small groups. The female cochair of the 1978 Gay Parade told me that after the parade the women organizers would go to a retreat in the countryside. "It's a lovely place," she said. "It has Jacuzzis and steam baths. When we go there, we usually ditch our clothes and do a lot of chanting. It's very sensual, but there's not much sex." While gay men built businesses, gay women built communes—both literally and figuratively speaking. That is, while gay male organizations tended to be rationalized and, in the case of businesses, hierarchical, women's organizations were structured for cooperation and the melding of individuals into the collective enterprise. The most businesslike of lesbian organizations would build in encounter-group techniques as a management strategy: the emotions, they understood, had always to be considered. Liberated gay women, in other words, turned out to be archetypically women, and gay men in the Castro archetypically men—as if somehow their genders had been squared by isolation from the other sex.

In a sense the oddest thing about gay liberation in general and the Castro in particular was that neither gay men nor gay women had any agreed-upon explanation for homosexuality. The gay men I knew said that they had known they were homosexuals so early on in their lives that they felt it must be a matter of chemistry or biology. They felt this intuitively, but, lacking evidence to prove it, they did not insist upon it. Perhaps it was nurture rather than nature, they said, but, if so, the psychologists had no very convincing explanation. Look, they said, until 1973 the American Psychiatric Association listed homosexuality as a mental illness. In that year its board members voted to take it off the list—but as a result of political pressure from gay activists and from the gay caucus within the association. This was an advance, they felt, but the procedure was hardly scientific.

What gay activists generally believed was that, whatever the genesis of homosexuality, there was always—for reasons unknown—a fixed proportion of homosexuals in the population: 10 percent was their estimate. The figure derived from the Kinsey reports of 1948 and 1953. In those surveys Kinsey researchers had found that 4 percent of American men were exclusively homosexual, and 10 percent almost exclusively so. (A later survey showed that one to three percent of single American women were homosexual.) Changing attitudes about sex would, the activists thought, have changed these figures somewhat: but a figure of 10 percent would be roughly correct. Beyond that they were resolute agnostics—indifferent or actually hostile to any further attempts at explanation.

As it happened, Wardell Pomeroy, one of the original members of the Kinsey research team, was now running an institute for the study of human sexuality in San Francisco. Pomeroy told me that he thought the 1948 figures were still approximately correct but that he did not see them as permanent—as an attribute of nature. Pomeroy believed, with Freud, that man was innately bisexual. After all, he said, anthropologists have found that in many societies—including that of ancient Greece—homosexuality was ubiquitous. "The real question," he said, "is not why anyone is homosexual but why everyone is not." His own theory was that, if cultural constraints were set aside, sexual behavior in the United States would be quite different.

Perhaps a half of the population would continue to be exclusively heterosexual and 4 percent would be exclusively homosexual, but the rest would be bisexual in one degree or another. As it was, he said, the culture pushed most people into the exclusively heterosexual end of the spectrum by labeling homosexual desires as sick or sinful. Therefore, in his view, the major thrust of the gay movement was correct, as homosexuals who were willing to stand up and be counted as such had a liberating effect on the whole society.

Pomeroy's theoretical spectrum was a counterculture idea in that it assumed—if only for purposes of argument—that cultural constraints could be put aside. While anthropologists would have rejected it categorically (on his own grounds that cultures conditioned sexual expressions), it served to point up the dilemmas involved in gay liberation and in the particular society of the Castro. Gay liberationists were, of course, reacting to a culture that understood homosexuals as a distinct category of people and endowed them with all kinds of attributes from effeminacy to mental illness. But though they rejected the attributes, they accepted the category: that is, they viewed homosexuals as a distinct group of people who had to unite and fight their oppression. In the view of many European gay intellectuals, this was a mistake. The philosopher and historian Michel Foucault cautioned the gay movement in the United States against accepting the terms of its enemies (and not just its enemies but everyone's). The real task, as he saw it, was to subvert all such distinctions, since the isolation of any sexual category could only lead to further oppression or at best to further marginalization of the group.

By 1978 many gay liberationists in New York had discussed the Foucault argument and rejected it on the grounds that it was politically infeasible: gay men and gay women had to unite to break the taboo—there was no other possible strategy. In San Francisco the argument was not discussed (few knew it existed) and yet the dilemma was nowhere more apparent than in the Castro: by uniting they were hardening the category. In the Castro, a gay society was coming into being, and along with it a "gay identity," which, though still superficial, tended to divide gay men from others. In 1978 that society was still defining itself. It was pulling further and further away from its origins in the counterculture. It was doing so in part for reasons that had little to do with homosexuality and a great deal to do with the fact that its inhabitants were well-educated young white men. It had become a male preserve—and a society that more or less ignored gay women; it was now becoming a class preserve as well. For most young gay activists in the Castro, this was the tension, and this was the real issue.

By 1978 Harvey Milk had succeeded in representing the Castro and all that it stood for in the city. But ironically the Castro was no longer the place he had represented in his campaigns. By 1978 it was not a poor neighborhood anymore. The Irish working-class families had largely gone, but so, too, had the hippies. On Castro Street there was now an expensive home furnishings shop, a wine-and-quiche café, a card and gift shop, and two upscale men's clothing stores; boutiques were moving in. The neighboring streets looked equally prosperous, for gay men had bought up the old houses, stripped them of their aluminum sidings, painted them, and renovated their interiors. The price of real estate continued to climb, and by 1976 the old houses were fetching five times their earlier value. In 1977 the rent on Milk's camera store tripled. Milk denounced the landlord, and all of land-lordism, but to no avail, as the rents up and down the street were now doubling every six months. He moved his store to a cubbyhole on Market Street, and the space he vacated was quickly occupied by a boutique selling Waterford crystal.

The Castro was not a poor neighborhood anymore, and in some sense it was not even a neighborhood. Milk had railed against the city policy of spending to make San Francisco a tourist center, but now the Castro had become a "mecca" (as journalists kept putting it) for gay tourists. The air shuttle between Los Angeles and San Francisco was now known on weekends as "the gay express," for every Friday night it was filled with gay Angelenos coming to town for the week-end. New Yorkers, Chicagoans, and others would spend their vaca-tions in San Francisco, staying at gay hotels, going to gay restaurants, and shopping at gay stores. In the summertime on the streets of the Castro you could hear the accents of New York and Houston but also of London, Paris, and Sydney. Then, too, as many who came as tourists returned to settle, the Castro was becoming the hub of a vast redevelopment project. Gay men—and some gay women—were moving into Noe Valley and the Mission District; they were moving into the Haight-Fillmore District and settling the back slopes of Pacific Heights, painting and refurbishing as they went. In some of the poor-est neighborhoods in the city, Victorian facades blossomed with dec-orator paint.

Harvey Milk, the populist, spoke of gay people as an oppressed minority and promised to make common cause with the racial minor-ity groups in the city and with the poor. But the gay immigrants were now putting this alliance into question. They might be refugees from oppression, but they were also, by and large, young white men who had arrived in town at the very moment to begin careers. In practice they were taking professional and managerial jobs, or they were staffing the numerous new service industries, or they were starting businesses of their own. In many ways they were proving a boon to the city. By pioneering the dilapidated neighborhoods, they were helping to reverse the white and middle-class flight to the suburbs, thus increasing the tax base both directly and indirectly. As they had no children, they made no demands on the schools—and they had more discretionary income than the average family man or woman to spend on entertainment as well as housing. In practice, they were supporting the opera, the ballet, and other cultural institutions of the city. But in settling the poor neighborhoods, they were pushing up real-estate prices and pushing out black and Hispanic families.

This was not, of course, their aim. Jim Rivaldo was one of the early settlers of the Haight-Fillmore, and when he arrived there in 1972, the main street was a combat zone of alcoholics, drug dealers, and thugs. He set up a neighborhood association to make the area livable for black and white residents. The association under his leadership brought in the police, demanded efficient city services, and began to reverse the process of decay and dereliction in the area. Many black residents applauded his efforts, but as one resident black social worker pointed out, the alcoholics and drug dealers were the people who were keeping the rents down. The safer the streets were, the more attractive they would become to white settlers and real-estate developers, and the more black families would be pushed out—including the poorest families with nowhere else to go. The logic was inescapable. Rivaldo understood it—he was defensive on that score. What he wanted—as Harvey Milk had some years before in the Castro—was to maintain an integrated neighborhood. But he could not ensure it any better than Milk had, and for many other gay settlers it was simply not a priority. And while Milk worried about gentrification, he predicted with some relish that along with the Asian immigrants they would control the city in a matter of years. It was, as Shilts wrote, a time of gay manifest destiny.

The new Castro, and all that it represented, had set off a debate within the gay community—a debate whose terms were quintessentially Californian. One side of that debate was represented by David Goodstein, the financier and now the publisher of The Advocate, the best-selling gay publication in the country. Published out of plush offices in San Mateo, The Advocate combined political and cultural journalism with photos of beautiful seminaked men and ads for gay baths, skin flicks, and hustlers. It was a kind of Playboy for the gay community, and Goodstein, short, plump, and forty-five, had Hugh

Hefner views—except that he was considerably to the right of Hefner on economic issues. "I'm a libertarian," he said when I went to see him. "I believe freedom is indivisible: political and economic freedom are the same thing. I think that people have the right to laetrile if they want it. I'm for the decriminalization of marijuana and prostitution. And I'm pro- abortion." Goodstein was also very much in favor of the new Castro. "Our cities are in very bad trouble as the groups moving into them are generally without skills, education, or affluence. The gay immigrants have these things, and they have a real interest in the cities." Of course, he said, people were upset by the rise in rents, so gay landlords had to be tactful and careful to establish communication within their communities.

It was on the grounds of individual freedom that Goodstein defended the sexually explicit, if not pornographic, advertisements in the second section of *The Advocate*. "Sexuality is a private matter," he said. "You should be able to regulate street signs but not censor books. Every expert I've talked to believes that pornography is good for sex. We support all forms of human sexuality that are freely consensual, not medically harmful, and not offensive to bystanders—so that rules out sex in public, anything to do with children, and extreme forms of S and M. There's nothing wrong with ads for male prostitutes, though. For people who use prostitutes it's much better to find them in a magazine than to have to look for them on the streets."

Goodstein was a friend of Werner Erhard's, and this year he was putting together a national organization to conduct *est*-type seminars for homosexuals called "The Advocate Experience." On this subject Goodstein, a man known to his staff as a hardheaded businessman and political broker, talked like a religious visionary. "I believe the Human Potential Movement is more important for humanity than anything that has ever happened. *Est* is just one aspect of it. What we're all aiming for is transformation." He seemed quite surprised to be asked transformation into what. "Oh," he replied, "transformation means the all-rightness of people. Health, happiness, love, and full expression."

On the other side of the debate were young gay activists from the left wing of the movement. Bill Hartman and others from Bay Area Gay Liberation put the case most vehemently. They believed in the Castro as a liberated zone—a place of refuge for gay men. At the same time they deplored what was happening to it. Gay men, they said, were becoming "fodder for Wall Street West"; they were being "scapegoated" for driving out ethnic minorities when what was really happening was that the real-estate speculators and other forces for gentrification were seeing to it that only young white professionals or paraprofessionals could settle in San Francisco. A number of gay bars, they said, now discriminated against blacks, women, and effeminate gay men. The new Castro was the sign and symbol of this tendency. And *The Advocate*, which ran only photos of beautiful white men, was encouraging "ageism, sexism, and beauty snobbery."

The interest of this analysis was that it went far beyond the conventional Marxist analysis of political and economic factors and into the domains of psychology and aesthetics. The left-wingers were, in other words, joining Goodstein from the other side of the political spectrum to insist on the importance of social and psychological criteria. What they were saying, Goodstein to the contrary, was that *The Advocate* made a lot of people feel bad. Just how far they could take this radical egalitarianism remained to be seen, but Bill Hartman told me that friends of his were now suing a popular gay bathhouse on the grounds that it discriminated against both older and more effeminate men. It was, he said, "a class action suit on behalf of sissies."

Armistead Maupin, Randy Shilts, and Ken Maley did not fully sympathize with either side of this debate. The three of them had gone through The Advocate Experience by invitation from Goodstein and had come out profoundly unmoved. Goodstein had arrived to take up his role as Facilitator and dramatically unveiled a blackboard with the word toilet on it; in their view things had gone—aesthetically speaking—downhill from there. The Facilitator had in the end asked them to contribute to various organizations, including a political action fund, that he himself had set up, and as they saw it he was trying to transform himself into Chief and them into Indians. They were having none of it. On the other hand, they tended to take a more philosophical view of the new Castro than did Hartman et al. Gay irony, after all, dictated that everyone, including the pin-striped banker and the long-haired truck driver, was in drag. Still, they believed that this Nautilus-machine look was only a stage in gay development and that Castro denizens would eventually grow up and come to look like normal human beings without any distinctive style to speak of. When discussing the subject in dead earnest, they said that the Castro was a stage in gay development—and that in the end "the ghetto" would no longer be necessary to gay men.

Right now, however, the Castro burgeoned. And rather than returning to normal, whatever that might be, gay styles were proliferating, becoming more various. That is, while the Castro presented a fairly uniform look to outsiders, its denizens could point out a huge number of species and subspecies, each as distinct as warblers. There was the clone style proper: short hair, clipped mustache, blue jeans, and bomber jacket. There was the preppie-athletic look: Lacoste or rugby shirts and well-shined loafers. There was the cowboy look, the logger look, the bodybuilder look, and so on. Randy Shilts—observer that he was—used to speak of the Folsom District leather bars as something alien to the Castro. But in fact black leather had already made its debut on the street. What was surprising was not that these varieties of dress existed but rather that the wearers did not seem to mix any more than did warbler species. If the limp wrist had been a sign of fraternity between one homosexual man and another, the number of signs had multiplied so as to require the interpretive assistance of a Jacques Derrida. Some of the items of apparel—the hot hankies, the keys—were encoded for sexual preference. Other signs, however, belonged to the realm of aesthetics rather than to that of the sex manual. And these were so precisely and exquisitely articulated as to confound those who fought the grosser forms of discrimination, as "ageism" and "sexism." They were a type of "beauty snobbery" all right, but what was a Bill Hartman to do about them?

One evening John Abney, one of the dozen or so openly gay sheriffs in San Francisco, took me to a cocktail party given by two TV journalists in a luxurious bachelor apartment in the Castro hills. There were about fifty men at the party and three women. The men came from various professions—there were businessmen, journalists, waiters, musicians, and city employees—but with one or two exceptions they looked remarkably alike. They were between twenty-five and thirty-five years old, between five feet nine inches, and six feet two inches, and athletic-looking but not overly so (the bodybuilding equipment had been in moderate use); they were all clean-shaven and dressed in well-cut golf shop sports clothes. They might have been members of the same fraternity at some private college in the South —except that it would have been hard to find a fraternity where *every* man wore a shirt with a crocodile on the front.

"It's my kind of party," John said, smiling happily. "Clean-cut types. No mustaches."

"Come on, John," I protested. "No mustaches?"

"No mustaches."

John came from a military family, and he had the bearing of a marine captain. He was getting along well in the sheriff's department and liked his job. In college at the University of New Mexico he had been engaged to a nice, clean-cut girl from Albuquerque; then the spirit of gay liberation had hit and he moved to San Francisco.

"Really no mustaches?"

"No mustaches."

These minute forms of discrimination testified, of course, to the sheer numbers of young men in the Castro and the extraordinarily high volume of sexual activity. Figuratively speaking, it was as if a small general store with staple items had been replaced by a vast supermarket where anyone could find virtually anything at any hour of the day. New choices were available, and so new distinctions had to be made. Bars became more specialized, and so did sex clubs. Gay entrepreneurs were now creating the sexual equivalent of supermarkets, specialty markets, and boutiques. Some of these—high-volume, quick turnover—were the equivalent of fast-food shops. In the South of Market Club, for example, a dark warehouse filled with plywood cubicles, customers could take a cubicle and have sex through holes in the partitions without even the delay occasioned by eye contact. The entrance fee was only three dollars. There were eight of these "glory hole" establishments in the city now and nine bathhouses. In the distant past the baths had been squalid places where men deep in the closet had secret, guilty liaisons; now they were well-appointed clubs—some with Jacuzzis and video screens—where young men went for fun and a change of scene. They had private rooms, lounges, public rooms for orgies, and specialty rooms. At least one of them had a room full of S and M machinery—racks, pulleys, and the like.

In addition to the increase in volume of sexual activity, there was also an increase in experimentation with new techniques. Bell and Weinberg did not explore this subject, but in fact there was a vogue for various extremist practices, some of which, like fist-fucking, were medically harmful. Sado-masochism, once confined to a tiny minority and considered perverse, was now rising to the surface of acceptability. "Why get hung up with higher prices when all you want is a place to hang your handcuffs?" one Folsom District hotel brochure asked jauntily. Gay boosters—when they did not deny it existed—would explain that S and M was only theater, involving fantasies, not bodily harm. Theater was certainly the idea behind it, but, perhaps because of the number of amateurs involved, violence did occur. In 1981 the San Francisco coroner, Dr. Boyd Stephens, warned that he was seeing an "alarming increase in injuries and death from S and M sex."

Most San Franciscans did not really know what went on in the Castro and Folsom districts at night: they avoided the two areas, and they avoided knowing about it if they could. But the sexual exuberance tended to spill over into the other areas of the city. Those who lived near the Castro or Buena Vista Park in the Haight sometimes could not help but see gay men having sex with each other in public and in broad daylight. Such sights were not unknown in other parts of the city, particularly on gay holidays such as Halloween or Gay Freedom Day. And with the growing fad for S and M garb, men with spiked collars on their necks and Nazi insignia on their caps would appear on the downtown streets. Dianne Feinstein, in her third term as president of the Board of Supervisors, spoke to this issue in an interview published in the *Bay Area Reporter*, a gay newspaper distributed in the bars. "I know of no city in the United States where gay people live and work and create as constructively as they do in San Francisco," she said, but "What I see happening in San Francisco—in the bar scene, in the street scene, in the S and M scene—is an imposition of lifestyle on those who do not wish to participate in that lifestyle . . . I've tried to talk to various leaders in the gay community to say that the community needs to set some standards. I was not able to get a commitment. I am very concerned that unless some standards are set . . . many people will want to see a crackdown." Feinstein said much the same thing on one other occasion that year.

The Castro reacted to such expressions of concern with ridicule or outrage. How dare she say such a thing! Feinstein was a prude—that was Ken Maley's view; her "interest in the gay leather scene bordered on an obsession"—that was Randy Shilts's. "What if she told blacks their behavior was offensive?" someone asked indignantly at a gay political club meeting. To report that the sight of gay men in Nazi caps or gay men having sex in public *did* offend other San Franciscans —that Feinstein was not making it up—was to call forth a storm of objections from many gay activists. The very same people would argue (a) that it did not happen, (b) that those who proclaimed themselves offended were closet cases or voyeurs, and (c) that those people better just get used to it. The fact that an outsider had asked the gay community to "set some standards" was seen as a challenge to the movement as a whole and a threat to the civil rights of all gay men. The editorial in the issue of *BAR* in which the Feinstein interview appeared said: "What Feinstein cannot or will not face is that the Gay movement is much more than a civil rights affair. . . . It is a revolution. To digest that the Gay movement has to do with the reevaluation of sexuality . . . is more than she can handle. Her solution is tolerance —not to be confused with acceptance. To Feinstein a gay presence is possible, gay dominance a disaster." This was indeed a time of gay manifest destiny.

That the whole bar and sex culture of the Castro might be harmful to gay men themselves was not at the time given any serious consideration in the gay community. And yet it clearly was unhealthy in many respects. "In the seventies you used to go into someone's refrigerator and see no food, only dope," one gay activist told me years later. The bar scene involved a great deal of alcohol and various sorts of drugs, including amyl nitrate, which was stressful to the heart.

Alcoholism was prevalent—as were a good many sexually transmitted diseases. Syphilis and gonorrhea were epidemic in the Castro. According to Bell and Weinberg, two-thirds of the thousand gay men they interviewed had had VD at least once, and according to public health authorities, homosexuals accounted for 50 to 55 percent of all VD cases across the country. In 1978 the San Francisco Health Department announced that in the past three years there had been a dramatic increase in hepatitis and intestinal infections among males in their twenties and thirties. In 1979 there were 744 cases of hepatitis and 220 cases of amebic dysentary in the city; a year later health officials found that 60 to 70 percent of gay men in San Francisco had the virus for hepatitis B. Some gay leaders, including some of the bar owners, worried about the casualties from alcoholism—to the extent at least of raising money for treatment centers and outdoor activities. No one worried about the sexually transmitted diseases because they were curable. "Clap was a big joke," Shilts told me years later. "Going to the city clinic was part of the routine. There would be all this camaraderie, and people would tell each other how many times they'd been there."

The idea that the sexual free-for-all might be aesthetically unpleasing, emotionally unrewarding, or morally troubling in its disregard for the individual was generally rejected by the Castro generation. Older men, however, expressed concern. Zohn Artman, then the chief of public relations for the rock impresario Bill Graham and a respected figure in the city, said of the bars and the baths, "They're meat palaces. Grade A, Grade B, Choice, USDA approved. I worry a lot about the young right now. They think they are free, but they are getting locked in behind their genitalia. So much of life seems concentrated there. It worries me that they don't have more of a sense of self."

Dianne Feinstein had warned of a political backlash against gay men in San Francisco. There was no evidence of this now, but another kind of backlash had already taken shape outside the city. In the mid-seventies conservative churches across the country experienced a revival, and fundamentalist preachers drew huge new audiences on radio and television. Now preachers such as Jerry Falwell and political strategists such as Richard Viguerie translated fundamentalists' concerns into politics, reviving the right wing of the Republican party. The New Right, as it was called, made the Panama Canal Treaty its first major foreign-policy issue, and gay rights its first major domestic issue. In fundamentalist doctrine homosexuality was simply a choice —a sexual preference, as it were—except that it was a sinful choice in the same general category as adultery or rape. For fundamentalists the very notion of gay rights was an abomination—and at the same time made no sense at all. (Falwell and others, however, adopted the general parlance and spoke of "homosexuals," thereby implying that homosexuality was not a choice, but the logical problem was generally overlooked.) In 1977, the year Anita Bryant won her campaign against a gay rights ordinance in Dade County, Florida, similar ordinances were defeated by voters in St. Paul, Minnesota, Wichita, Kansas, and Eugene, Oregon. In Oklahoma and Arkansas, legislators passed laws banning homosexuals from teaching in the public schools and in Arkansas denied them credentials as pediatricians and social workers. On the strength of these victories State Senator John Briggs of California in 1978 gathered enough signatures from fundamentalist constituencies around the state to put a proposition on the November ballot mandating the dismissal of any schoolteacher who advocated or encouraged homosexuality. The wording of the proposition, known as the Briggs Initiative, was vague enough to threaten the job of any teacher who so much as discussed gay rights in class. That spring Briggs put out a series of pamphlets associating all homosexuals with child molesters and pornographers. The "moral decay in this country" was, he said, "a greater danger than Communism."

Since the spring a number of gay organizations in San Francisco and Los Angeles had been preparing a riposte to the Briggs Initiative and the fundamentalist crusade in general. Harvey Milk had organized a voter registration drive through his own political organization, the San Francisco Gay Democratic Club. In the Castro, leaflets had been distributed, demonstrations held, and committees formed. Countering the Briggs Initiative was the major political theme of the Gay Freedom Day Parade. In the gay community there was a good deal of consternation about the backlash: many thought the Briggs Initiative would pass and that would be only the beginning. Leaflets and placards announced that Anita Bryant—alternately, Falwell or Briggs—wanted to put all gay people in concentration camps. In his speech at the Gay Parade, Harvey Milk said:

> I want to recruit you for the fight to preserve your democracy from the John Briggs and the Anita Bryants who are trying to constitutionalize bigotry. We are not going to allow this to happen. We are not going to sit back in silence as 300,000 of our gay brothers and sisters did in Nazi Germany. We are not going to allow our rights to be taken away and then march with bowed heads into the gas chamber.

Just as among fundamentalists, there was among gay activists a general propensity to seek out signs of impending doom and to imagine the worst. Milk had this vision, but at the same time he was delighted with the opportunity the initiative presented. Judging that the proposition would not pass, he saw it as a means to raise the issue of gay rights in places it had not been raised before. Briggs, a very recent born-again Christian with ambitions for the governorship, for his part virtually acknowledged that the issue was an attention-getting device for himself. When Milk challenged him to a series of debates in towns and cities across the state, he accepted with alacrity, and the two went on the road together, joking with each other in airports and lambasting each other in front of audiences. At one point Briggs brought up the Bell and Weinberg statistic on the percentage of gay men with over five hundred sexual partners. "I wish," Milk replied, laughing.

Milk could afford to laugh, for in five years of campaigning he had become a powerful speaker—articulate, witty, and capable of pulling out the full range of rhetorical stops. On the podium Briggs was no contest for him, and in November Milk's political judgment turned out to be correct. The teachers' association viewed the Briggs Initiative as threatening to teachers and to the cause of civil liberties in general, and campaigned vigorously against it. The liberal politicians in the state came out against it, but so, too, did former Governor Ronald Reagan, who at the beginning of his term had vowed not to pass any gay rights legislation. President Jimmy Carter came out against it, as did ex-President Gerald Ford. On Election Day Californians voted 2 to 1 against the proposition.

The defeat of the Briggs Initiative was a personal triumph for Milk. In San Francisco the campaign against it had brought a number of wealthy conservatives out of the closet and focused the attention of the Castro on politics. The attention went to Milk. In addition the campaign brought him statewide and even national coverage. In a movement that had no well-known leaders Milk began to stand out as the most effective spokesman for gay rights. Politician that he was, Milk understood this very well. In his speech at the parade he had called for a national gay march on Washington for the following year; his assistance would clearly be required in mounting such an effort, and he was looking forward to it. Then, too, he was thinking (as most city supervisors do) of running for mayor one day. The idea was not wholly unreasonable.

In the ten months since his inauguration Milk had proved a popular and effective member of the Board of Supervisors. His colleagues, who had seen him as a single-issue candidate, found him hardworking and concerned with all issues from the city transport system to social services for the elderly. He worked for his own district like a good ward boss, seeing that more streetlights were put in, that the streets were cleaned regularly, and that the local branch of the public library had adequate funds. At board meetings he was sometimes abrasive—gleefully so—and his talent for attracting the spotlight was hardly collegial, but he was an engaging man with a talent for disarming. He made friends. And on a board that often split 6 to 5, he voted consistently with the liberal minority in support of the mayor, George Moscone. Milk's own bill forbidding discrimination against gays in housing and employment, however, passed by a majority of 10 to 1. When I went to see him that summer, he spoke enthusiastically about new projects, including the revamping of the Civil Service Commission and a pooper-scooper bill he himself had introduced. He said that the direction of the board was changing: the Old Guard was losing ground, the liberals and minority representatives gaining power. Self-confident, outspoken, he seemed very much at home in City Hall.

On November 27, 1978, just three weeks after the election and the defeat of the Briggs Initiative, Harvey Milk and George Moscone were shot and killed. They were shot down in their City Hall offices by Dan White, a former member of the Board of Supervisors. Dianne Feinstein was one of the first to see Milk's body; later she announced the news to the press in a horror-stricken voice in a milling crowd of people at the head of the stairs in City Hall. It was just eight days after the news of the mass suicide at Jonestown reached the city where Jones had been a prominent minister. San Francisco lay in shock. That night forty thousand people walked from the Castro to City Hall, carrying candles, singing, and weeping.

Some months later, in May 1979, Dan White was tried for murder. He was charged with two counts of first-degree murder (murder committed with premeditation, deliberation, and malice) and it was generally assumed that the state prosecutor would make the case for deliberation on circumstantial evidence. The question was why White shot his two colleagues; the answer was not obvious. Now thirty-two years old, White had been elected to his first term on the Board of Supervisors in district elections the year before. A former policeman, he represented District Eight, the last of the conservative blue-collar districts in the city—and the only one with precincts voting for the Briggs Initiative. His campaign photographs showed a good-looking young man with sideburns, well-groomed and dressed in a three-piece suit. White had served only eight months on the board. He had resigned in early November, explaining that his supervisor's salary of $9600 a year was not enough to support him, his wife, and their new baby. The mayor accepted his resignation. Four days later, however, White asked for his job back, giving no clear reason for his change of mind. Moscone was inclined to reappoint White, but Milk persuaded him not to, arguing that he now had the opportunity to change the majority on the board and get his programs through. Milk then told the press what he told the mayor.

White heard of the mayor's decision from a radio journalist the evening before it was to be announced. He stayed up all night long, and the next morning he took out his loaded .38 Smith-Wesson police revolver, put ten extra dumdum bullets in a handkerchief, and put the handkerchief in his pocket. His aide picked him up and drove him to City Hall. After she dropped him off, he went into City Hall through a window below the ground floor, thus avoiding the metal detector at the door. He walked into the mayor's office, asked the secretary to announce him, and talked with her until the mayor ushered him in. Shortly after Moscone told White of his decision, White pulled out his revolver, and shot him once in the arm and once in the body. As Moscone slumped to the floor, White walked over to him and, bending over, shot him twice in the head at very close range. He then reloaded and ran to Harvey Milk's office. Finding Milk there, he asked if he could see him in his own empty office across the hall. Ushering Milk into the office ahead of him, he closed the door and, after some words, shot Milk five times, three times in the body, twice in the head. He then ran out of City Hall, called his wife from a pay phone, and asked her to meet him at St. Mary's. When his wife arrived, he went with her to the Northern police station, where he had once worked, gave himself up, and confessed to the killings.

The trial lasted three weeks, and at the end of it the jurors returned a verdict of voluntary manslaughter. San Franciscans were shocked. District Attorney Joe Freitas said he did not think justice had been done; the judge in the case, who gave White the maximum sentence for third-degree murder—seven years and eight months—said he thought the punishment "inappropriate." Dianne Feinstein, now mayor, called a press conference when she heard the verdict. She had been in her City Hall office when the killings occurred; she had heard the shooting and had been the first to rush to Milk. She had looked at her colleague on the floor in a pool of blood, and felt for his pulse. She had no doubt, she said, what the verdict should have been. "As far as I'm concerned these were two murders," she said.

How the jury had reached its verdict was not entirely clear. The defense counsel, Douglas Schmidt, had pleaded temporary insanity for his client (or "diminished capacity" as California law had it) and he had made a good case, given the shreds of evidence he had to go on. He constructed a picture of Dan White that looked like this: White was a good person from a fine background. A native of San Francisco, he went to school in the city and was a noted high-school athlete. He served in the Army in Vietnam and thereafter joined the San Francisco police force. "A brief hiatus developed" (so said Schmidt) and he rejoined the police force and later transferred to the fire department. As a fireman he was decorated for saving a woman and a child from a burning building. He was an idealistic young man who believed strongly in traditional American values; he was "supremely frustrated with crime and the politics of the city and saw the city deteriorating as a place for the average and decent people to live." He was moral—almost rigidly moral—but he was a fair man and "perhaps too fair for politics in San Francisco." He had sought to befriend Harvey Milk, though the man represented a different lifestyle and different values from his own. He had worked hard over issues, only to find that the politicians had no interest in their merits. What no one knew until after "those tragedies" occurred was that White had a history of mental illness. That summer he had been depressed and under great strain in his job.

To fill in this picture Schmidt introduced a battery of psychiatrists to testify to White's depression. According to one of them, White, when depressed, would consume inordinate quantities of junk food: Cokes, Twinkies, double-scoop chocolate ice-cream cones, and the like. Junk food, according to the psychiatrist, produced extreme variations in blood sugar levels and was known to exacerbate antisocial behavior. (The proof he offered was the mention of a study done that showed that criminal junk-food addicts were better behaved on prison diets than they had been before.) Schmidt's insistence on White's junk food habit became known as "the Twinkie Defense." Significant help for the defense came from a tape recording of the confession White had given to homicide inspector Frank Falzon; on it White tearfully described the great stress he was under and how he had heard a roaring in his ears after Moscone told him that he would not reappoint him to the board. White, the defense counsel concluded, had had a lapse of sanity caused by his history of mental illness, his high consumption of junk food, and the strain resulting from his entanglement with a lot of devious politicians. It had to be that, he said, because "Good people, fine people with fine backgrounds, simply don't kill people in cold blood."

On the face of it the problem with this story was that White had no clinical history of manic-depression; he was depressed at the time—

that was all the defense psychiatrists knew. Then, too, if he had had a lapse of sanity, he had never, on returning to sanity, expressed any remorse in public for what he had done. His confession was full of self-pity. It was a story about all the pressures he had been under, how he had worked hard and tried to be honest, and how Milk and Moscone had deceived and mocked him. (He said that in the end Milk had "smirked" at him as if to say "too bad.") He had given this confession to a homicide inspector whom he had worked with and whom he had known since grammar school. Falzon, as was clear on the tape, had not pressed him about his intention in going to City Hall but allowed him to narrate his own version of events—in which stress played such a big role.

To the journalists following the trial it seemed that at least some of the responsibility for this "miscarriage of justice" lay with the jury. The defense counsel had eliminated all prospective jurors who belonged to racial minorities or who acknowledged that they supported gay rights. The prosecution did not question Schmidt's choices, and, as a result, the jury was largely made up of white working-class people, most of them Catholic. A number of them lived in or around White's old district, and one was a retired security guard: thus they were precisely Dan White's peers. Long after the trial, however, a few of the jurors came forward to say that they had agonized over the decision: they had deliberated for thirty-six hours. They had dismissed premeditation early on, but some had voted for second degree murder; eventually, however, they had come to the conclusion that, given the trial record, they had no choice but voluntary manslaughter. In their view the responsibility for the verdict lay squarely with the prosecution.

Whether or not the jurors were justified in taking this view, the fact was that the state prosecutor, Thomas F. Norman, had made a very poor case. He took only three days to make it, and he relied heavily on a bare presentation of facts. In addition he made a number of blunders. First, he apparently did not anticipate that the jurors would react sympathetically to White's tearful confession. Second, rather than to rake Falzon over the coals for failing to interrogate his friend aggressively, he allowed him to testify to White's good character and to his impression that White was "a broken individual" after the killings—and not at all the man he had known. In cross-examining the psychiatrists called in by the defense counsel, he had failed to make them differentiate between signs of "diminished capacity" and the agitation any normal person might feel before shooting two men in cold blood. Finally, and most importantly, he failed to address the question of motive adequately. He had to prove malice, and he merely pointed to the fact that Moscone and Milk had blocked White's reappointment to the board. To the jury this did not seem an adequate reason for any wholly sane man to shoot down two of his colleagues.

But what was the motive—if there was a motive? What could it have been? The question haunted San Francisco journalists. After the trial a number of them came up with a good deal more information about Dan White and the political circumstances surrounding the killings than had ever been presented to the jury—though without satisfactorily resolving the question. From what they found out, however, it was possible to construct a rather different picture of Dan White than the one presented by Schmidt; what they found out, too, was that there were people in the city, and more particularly in the police department, who were not at all sorry to see Harvey Milk and George Moscone dead.

During his campaign for supervisor Dan White had been a spokesman for conservative social values—for the importance of the family and the neighborhood. Interviewed on television, he had sounded concerned, civic-minded, and moderate, but some of his constituents had noticed signs of a mean streak in him. According to them, he packed other candidates' meetings with gangs of young hecklers; at one joint meeting four hecklers had showed up with White buttons on—and with Nazi insignia. White had refused all requests to ask them to leave. One of his campaign leaflets read, "I am not going to be forced out of San Francisco by splinter groups of radicals, deviates and incorrigibles."

When he joined the Board of Supervisors in January, the board members—who knew nothing of these incidents—found him a nice young man, though a bit naive. Dianne Feinstein undertook to educate him in the ways of city government, and Harvey Milk, who saw him as a potential ally on neighborhood issues, made an effort to cultivate him. As the defense attorney suggested, the two had a cordial relationship for some time. White had voted for Milk's gay rights bill in committee after making a long statement about how as a paratrooper in Vietnam he had found "a lot of things that I had read about —that had been attributed to certain people—blacks, Chinese, gays, whites—just didn't hold up under fire—literally under fire," and how he had learned "the sooner we leave discrimination in any form behind, the better off we'll be." As time went on, however, it became clear the two would never be allies. White drifted to the pro-big-business side of the board that was cool to neighborhood preservationists: he voted for bills favored by the real-estate developers —one of whom got him the lease on a baked potato stand on one of the piers renovated for the tourist trade. Also, he became the voice of the conservative Police Officers' Association, championing every single request it made. Milk lost his initial interest in him; but so, too, in another way did the more conservative members of the board. After working with him for a while Feinstein found him neither very bright nor very reliable: he hated to lose and would erupt into a fury of temper if he could not make his point. After John Molinari, a board member who had befriended him, voted with all the other members of the board against a trivial request from the police department that he was pushing, he would not speak to Molinari for days. For a time White seemed to have inhaled a whiff of political ambition. When asked whether he might run for mayor, he answered diplomatically, "Not yet." To his colleagues, however, it became clear that he was not cut out to be a politician. He seemed unable to compromise and unable to "disagree without being disagreeable," as the Irish political credo went. Mel Wax, the mayor's imperturbable aide, felt there was an extraordinary tension in him. Playing softball in the city league, he would, Wax said, play "as though this were the World Series," while the other players swapped stories and drank beer in the sun.

During the spring a feud broke out between Dan White and Harvey Milk. From the beginning White had attached great importance to the defeat of a bill that would put a psychiatric outpatient clinic for teen-agers in his district. Milk initially suggested to White he would vote against the bill, but then after examining the needs of the patients, he changed his mind and voted for the bill. After the bill passed, White refused to speak to Milk or any of his aides. He cast the only vote against the gay rights bill when it came to the floor and opposed every request Milk made on behalf of the gay community. The feud became public—but neither the defense counsel nor the prosecutor gave it any weight at the trial. In early November, Milk told his friends and aides that he thought White "a closet case" and "dangerous"; he did not explain why he thought so, but he repeated the remark several times.

A few days after the November election White went to the mayor and tendered his resignation from the board. He spoke of financial pressures, and these were real enough. The salary of a supervisor was not enough to support a family, and he, unlike most of his colleagues, had no outside source of income. The baked potato stand had only added to his worries as his wife had to leave her baby to go out and tend it—and still it looked as if it might fail. Molinari, who sympa-thized with him, thought he had made the right decision and thought he looked relieved and happy because of it—as though a great weight had been lifted from him. But then four days later White, after meet-ing with the leaders of the Police Officers' Association and representatives from the Board of Realtors, asked for his job back. He gave no clear explanation for his change of mind.

Harvey Milk, who had cheered when White resigned, now set out to try and block his reappointment. Hearing that the mayor was inclined to reappoint him, he went to Moscone and pointed out that White's vote had been crucial to the defeat of a number of the mayor's projects. He also pointed out that if Moscone reappointed the only antigay spokesman on the board, he, Moscone, stood to lose every gay vote in the city in the next election. Milk was not kidding, and he gave the mayor to understand that. "You won't get elected dogcatcher," he said.

At the trial both the defense and the prosecution had generally avoided the whole subject of city politics, but, as White had the swing vote on the board, there were real political issues at stake on his reappointment. There were also real political tensions in the city. Harvey Milk took the question of White's reappointment seriously, but so too did the Police Officers' Association. The old-line police had a number of problems with the mayor. In the first place, they disliked the police chief Moscone had appointed the year before. Charles R. Gain was an outsider—he had not come up through SFPD ranks—and he was not one whose values they respected. According to Frank Falzon, the trouble had begun when on his arrival Gain had removed the American flag from his office and replaced it with plants. The gesture in their view symbolized the man. The disaffection grew when Gain had the police cars painted powder blue and when he backed the mayor on minority hiring. For some months Moscone had been pushing the board to settle a discrimination suit brought by the few black officers in the department—a settlement that would have required the police to take affirmative action to hire and promote members of racial minorities. The Police Officers' Association had come out against it, and thus far the board had blocked it 6 to 5. What was more, Moscone and Gain were now promising to hire openly gay policemen, and Moscone had said he would put an acknowledged homosexual on the police commission. It had only been less than ten years since the police had been asked to raid gay bars and lock up gay men as perverts—and this was too much for them. The year before there had been loose talk in the department about killing the police chief. Now there was loose talk about getting rid of the mayor.

Investigating the police connection during the trial, Warren Hinckle of the *Chronicle* found an undersheriff who had witnessed White's arraignment and his first evening in jail. White, he said, had not shown any signs of "diminished capacity"—nor had he seemed at all sorry for what he had done. And why should he? The police were

laughing and joking with him and giving him friendly pats on the
ass. The undersheriff worried about this. It wasn't—he said—that he
suspected a police conspiracy in the killings; he simply thought that
the prosecution should have made the well-known police hostility to
the mayor a part of the case.

Later, journalists reexamining the case investigated the possibility
that there might have been a police conspiracy. They found no evidence for one—though they did find considerable animosity toward
the former mayor among conservative policemen. (Police were wearing FREE DAN WHITE T-shirts shortly after the assassination.) From a
factual standpoint the better hypothesis seemed to be that White had
acted independently for the purposes of making himself a hero in
their eyes. But this was problematic in another way. White had been
of great service to the Police Officers' Association on the board—the
proof being that the officers wanted him back on it again. If he wanted
their approbation, then why had he resigned? Then, too, if he had
killed Moscone and Milk simply because he knew—or thought he
knew—that the police wanted them out of the way, then his act
would not have been that of a totally sane man. Yet the journalists
refused to believe that White was insane—even temporarily. The killings had been too deliberate. White, after all, had sat up all night after
he heard of the mayor's decision; then he had acted methodically. His
former aide had testified that he seemed agitated that morning, but
the mayor's secretary had noticed nothing unusual about him. He
had killed the two men like an executioner; then he had called his
wife, gone to the police station where he had worked, and confessed
—not to murder but to voluntary manslaughter. He had seemed quite
himself in the police lockup. When he went to the state prison to
serve his term, psychiatrists had examined him and decided against
prescribing therapy: he had "no apparent signs" of mental disorder,
they said. He served his term without incident and was out on parole
in January 1984.

But there was a workable hypothesis. There was a story the prosecutor might have told about Dan White had he wished to construct a
plausible motive for murder. The story went like this: Dan White had
resigned from the Board of Supervisors for purely personal reasons.
He had financial problems and he worried that his wife and child
were suffering because of him. At the same time the job did not suit
him: he was too tense, too controlled, and too controlling a man to
get along in the rough-and-tumble world of politics. Because of this
he had fallen into a depression—a depression that had been alleviated
by his decision to resign. But he had also quit because he was a
quitter. In a television interview after the trial Frank Falzon said that

White had finally left the police department for good because he had objected to the treatment of a prisoner in handcuffs and could not get his way. "He had a tendency to run occasionally, from situations," Falzon had said on the stand. White did not lack physical courage—that was not the point; rather he lacked the psychological flexibility to deal with the everyday politics of any organization. He quit the police department twice, then he served in the fire department and left it to run for office, then he had quit the board.

Being politically naive, White did not realize the political consequences of his private decision until the realtors and the police came to him. What kind of pressure was put on him remains unknown, but the pressure was certainly great enough to make him put himself in the humiliating position of asking the mayor to give him his job back after only four days—and with no real explanation for his change of heart. The developers meant nothing to him—that was politics. But the police—well, they were his buddies: he hung around with them even while on the board. And if you are a policeman or a fireman, and if you have been a trooper in Vietnam, you know your honor and your life depend on not letting your buddies down. White (as someone may have reminded him) had let his buddies down—had let them down by quitting, the way he always did.

For a time White thought he could get his job back. "I've got a real surprise for the gay community," he told a reporter from a gay newspaper a day or so after he heard that Harvey Milk opposed his reappointment. He hoped, but then he learned that the mayor had decided otherwise. That evening after the reporter called him, the realization hit him: he had sold out his buddies for his family life and a baked potato stand. He wrestled with his guilt all night long, then in the morning he made his plan. He executed it, and afterward his conscience was clear: he had done the right thing; he had sacrificed himself for his buddies.

Of course no one knew, or could know, what went through Dan White's mind the day he shot George Moscone and Harvey Milk. But a plausible scenario was what a prosecutor needed to establish premeditation and to convict him. For a prosecutor, however, the difficulty was that to construct a plausible motive for White was necessarily to bring city politics into the courtroom. Such a prosecutor would have had to bring witnesses to testify to the conflict between the mayor and the old-line policemen. He would have had to talk about the police opposition to the anti-discrimination suit brought by the black officers, and about the hostility many of them felt toward their own police chief. Further, he would have had to expose the repugnance the police felt for what went on every night in the Castro and the Folsom districts. He would have had to reveal the vein of anger against the gay community that lay below the surface of city politics and public discourse—the anger that Dianne Feinstein had warned the gay community about. He would have had to show that San Francisco was not the perfectly tolerant city that it seemed to be. But the prosecutor did not do this, and instead the conflict broke out into the open.

The voluntary manslaughter verdicts were announced on May 21. That night an angry crowd gathered in the Castro shouting, "Dan White was a cop" and "Avenge Harvey Milk." Cleve Jones, one of Milk's young lieutenants, took up a bullhorn and led the crowd out of the Castro down Market Street, as Milk had once done, with the aim of averting a riot. By the time the crowd reached Civic Center Plaza at dusk there were over five thousand marchers, most of them young men, chanting, "Kill Dan White! Kill Dan White! We want justice." The crowd continued to grow and the anger mounted. A rock crashed through the central doors of City Hall; the crowd roared its approval and rushed forward. Milk's close friends and supporters, including Harry Britt and Jim Rivaldo, ran to the top of the stairs and, linking arms, stood across the door while rocks and chunks of asphalt shattered the windows around them. A detachment of riot policemen pushed through the crowd and shoved aside those nearest the door; after beating some of them up, the police took their places across the door.

At eight-thirty Dianne Feinstein arrived, and not long afterward rocks came through her office windows and Carol Ruth Silver, Milk's closest ally on the Board of Supervisors, was laid out with an ugly cut on her mouth. The riot then began in earnest. The police tried to move forward, and young men pushed them back using torn-out parking meters for spears and garbage-can lids for shields. A group of young men moved down the line of empty police cars parked on the north side of the plaza and set one after another of them on fire; there were explosions from the gas tanks and a low moaning of sirens as the electrical wires melted. Police reinforcements had entered City Hall from the other side, and now platoons of them stood under the rotunda tapping their nightsticks. The police chief, Charles Gain, fearing bloodshed, refused to let them move out to join the detachment outside the door.

Finally, three hours after the first stone hit the door, Gain ordered the police to move out. The crowd had dispersed somewhat, but the police still had to battle their way across the plaza and then chase the looters who had broken into the nearby stores. It was midnight before

the riot was over and the plaza quiet again. Feinstein praised the
police for the restraint they had shown.

But then a procession of police cars moved up Market Street and
into the Castro, where the bars were full to overflowing with excited
young men. The police poured out of their cars in full riot gear, went
into battle formation, and marched down Castro Street. Beer bottles
flew. When Warren Hinckle protested that the action would start
another riot, the police captain replied, "We lost the battle at City
Hall. We're not going to lose here." A few blocks down the street two
dozen officers, their shields torn off to avoid identification, burst into
the Elephant Walk bar swinging their nightsticks and shouting ob-
scenities. People tried to get away from them and get out of the bar,
but the crowd was too thick; the police beat up everyone around
them, randomly, savagely. A dozen other policemen outside began
beating up men on the street. Chief Gain had by now reached the
corner of Market and Castro; informed of the rampage going on some
blocks away, he ordered his men out of the Castro just in time to stop
a battle—whose lines were already forming on the street.

The next day officials of the Police Officers' Association denounced
Gain for not ordering a police drive through Civic Center Plaza earlier
in the evening and for withdrawing the police from Castro Street.
Gain replied that his orders had stopped a great deal of bloodshed.
As it was, there had been no fatalities, but sixty-one policemen had
been hospitalized along with about a hundred gay men.

Strangely enough, the gay riot and the police rampage had no consequence. For the gay community the riot was a kind of catharsis—
even for those who did not participate in it and even for those who
did not approve. Other San Franciscans were shocked by it, but then
there had been so many shocks in the past few months. To many San
Franciscans gay anger at the trial verdict was perfectly understandable; the riot could not therefore be condoned, but no more could
police brutality in the Castro. Fortunately, perhaps, there was some
symmetry between the two events. Dianne Feinstein urged no prosecution, and in the weeks that followed, made a sustained and master-
ful effort to diffuse the tensions. She reassured everyone and talked
endlessly, soothingly, never making a point. The city that had gone
through the assassinations of its mayor and a supervisor, the Jonestown suicides, and the rioting, seemed grateful for the sheer prosi-
ness of her response. Civic peace returned.

The Castro continued to mourn Harvey Milk. His friends and supporters celebrated his birthday and memorialized the day of his assassination that year and the next and the next. A library and an arts center were named after him, and so was the plaza at the corner of Castro and Market streets. Aspiring gay politicians and community leaders quoted him often and talked of carrying on his legacy. Years later, after the talk had finally died, filmmakers and playwrights recreated the drama of his life and death. In 1984 a film called *The Times of Harvey Milk* was shown in movie theaters around the country and won the Oscar for that year's documentary film feature. Based on interviews with Milk's friends and associates, the film painted a glowing portrait of the man—his warmth, charm, and bohemian insouciance unmarred by any blemish. That same year a docudrama about Milk's assassination and the trial of Dan White was shown on national television, and in 1986 a play about the miscarriage of justice in the trial ran on Broadway—even while the last act of the drama took place in life. In January 1985 Dan White returned to San Francisco, where he lived for ten months as an outcast, unable to find a job, moving around and hiding his whereabouts from all but his family and a few friends. In October he committed suicide in the garage of his family's house by funneling carbon monoxide into the family car.

The Castro mourned Harvey Milk, and yet it could not seem to make him into a living legend—that is, into a legend that would nourish and sustain it. The Castro saw him as a martyr but understood his martyrdom as an end rather than a beginning. He had died, and with him a great deal of the Castro's optimism, idealism, and ambition seemed to die as well. The Castro could find no one to take his place in its affections, and possibly it wanted no one.

Shortly after his election to the Board of Supervisors, Milk tape-recorded a political will and testament to be played "only in the event of my death by assassination." Milk believed that, as a gay activist, he presented a likely target for "a person who is insecure, terrified, afraid, or very disturbed themselves." In his will he named four people that the mayor might consider appointing in his place. He did not, he said, want "the Jim Fosters, the Rick Stokes"; he wanted people who had been close to "the movement": Frank Robinson, Bob Ross, Harry Britt, or Anne Kronenberg. Some time after his death Feinstein, in consultation with his supporters, appointed Harry Britt. The former minister and civil rights activist had the political and the intellectual credentials to succeed Milk. He was a thoughtful man with a good deal of charm, and the following year he was elected to the Board of Supervisors in citywide balloting. Britt, however, lacked Milk's extraordinary political energy and his sheer chutzpah. As a result, the gay political community returned to its usual state of factionalism. There were now three gay Democratic clubs: Foster's Alice B. Toklas Club, the club Milk had founded, now called the Harvey Milk Gay Democratic Club, and a smaller group called the Stonewall Gay Democratic Club. The three held slightly different positions on the ideological spectrum and often supported different candidates. In the 1984 Democratic primaries, for example, the Toklas club backed Walter Mondale, the Milk club supported Gary Hart, and Stonewall came out for Jesse Jackson. More important, perhaps, the three had rather different styles of leadership. But the differences between them were neither very deep nor very bitter, and when gay interests were at stake, there was a "gay vote" in the city. This vote, however, did not represent a movement so much as it represented an interest group that had become "realistic" and even a bit cynical. The mayoral election of 1979 made that abundantly clear.

The 1979 mayoral race focused on three candidates: Dianne Feinstein, Quentin Kopp, a conservative member of the Board of Supervisors, and David Scott, a gay real estate investor and former member of the Board of Permit Appeals and a political unknown. Scott ran well behind Feinstein and Kopp, but he won 18,500 votes, or 10 percent of the total: enough votes, as it turned out, to deprive Feinstein of a clear majority and to force a runoff election. In a press conference before the runoff, Scott announced he would withhold his endorsement until the eve of the election and then come out for the candidate who best satisfied his demands. What he asked was that the candidates appoint a gay police commissioner, give the gay community a hand in the selection of a police chief when Gain retired, and retract certain statements he found offensive. In an interview with the *Ladies' Home Journal* the acting mayor had said, "The right of an individual to live as he or she chooses can become offensive. The gay community is going to have to face this. It's fine for us to live here respecting each other's life-styles, but this doesn't mean imposing them on others." Quentin Kopp had objected to Board of Supervisors' decision to honor Del Martin and Phyllis Lyon for their twenty-five years together. "Tolerance, yes," he said, "glorification, no." These were the remarks that had to be taken back.

Scott's ploy was brilliant. Almost certainly he could not personally deliver the 18,500 votes he had won to either candidate, but he had made demands that all gay organizations supported, and the candidates knew that. In the weeks before the runoff, Kopp and Feinstein made separate visits to Scott's house, and in the viewfinders of the television cameras stationed outside his door, they looked very much like supplicants. Then they went together to a meeting at the Harvey Milk Gay Democratic Club and retracted their offending remarks.

"Maybe my choice of words was wrong," Quentin Kopp said. Feinstein went further: "If I said things that offended the community, I apologize. I can't always be inside your head. I ask you to accept me for not always being what one would want." Feinstein, unlike Kopp, had promised to appoint a gay police commissioner and to make other commission appointments relative to gay numbers. David Scott endorsed her candidacy eight days before the election; after that, he took her to gay leather bars and campaigned vigorously with her. She won the election handily, taking 80 percent of the gay vote.

To the producers of a CBS documentary on San Francisco, "Gay Power, Gay Politics," the concessions Feinstein had made to Scott seemed to signify the capitulation of city politicians before a militant gay movement determined to impose its "life-style" on the city. Feinstein, however, had not capitulated, and she was amazed that anyone could see her campaign in this light. Once elected, she fulfilled her promises to the letter—to the letter. She appointed a gay police commissioner, for example, but her choice was a woman—Jo Daly—a Foster supporter, a former president of the Toklas club, and a conservative on the so-called life-style issues. And just before the election the mayor asked for Charles Gain's resignation. When gay politicians complained, she said sweetly that the police couldn't have a leader they wouldn't follow. In his stead she appointed Cornelius Murphy, an Irish Catholic who had made his way up through the ranks and who had the support of the department. One of Murphy's first acts, however, was to attend a fund-raising drive to recruit gay men and women for the police force. In 1980 the city in a special election voted to return to citywide elections for the Board of Supervisors. Now that the mayor had an electoral system in which the neighborhoods could not prevail over the downtown and rule the city as a whole, she could proceed to steer the city back to a more conservative, probusiness course. Though a liberal Democrat, she would not be out of step in the eighties.

In the second week of July in 1984 fourteen thousand reporters made their way to the Democratic Convention in San Francisco. Some of them were actually going to sit in the new Moscone Convention Center and listen to speeches; the rest were going into the streets, for mayhem was predicted. In previous weeks there had been a spate of press stories about "the unconventional city" with its bohemian subcultures and weirdo life-styles. As the flower children had long since gone, what they referred to, for the most part, was the gay community. San Francisco journalists did the best they could to defend the city from its "negative stereotype" with articles about the "driving pertinence" of its tolerance and its diversity for the country as a whole. But they, too, were battening down the hatches. The week before the convention, Jerry Falwell was to bring a road show of New Right personalities to discuss "family issues" and to denounce what he called San Francisco's "Wild Kingdom." His Family Forum seemed to be a probe designed to draw a group of transvestite nuns on roller skates, the Sisters of Perpetual Indulgence, within the range of the nightly network news cameras. In fact the Sisters had announced plans for a puke-in and an exorcism of Falwell. More important, a gay rights march was planned for the convention itself, and it was generally supposed that a horde of witches, warlocks, drag queens, leather men, and so on would descend on the convention center and embarrass the Democrats.

In the event, however, the speeches inside the convention center and the nomination of Geraldine Ferraro as the vice-presidential candidate were rather more spectacular than the goings-on outside in the streets. Guerrilla theater groups did turn up at the Family Forum to perform their tribal rites, but there were probably more police than demonstrators in attendance. And Falwell, who sent his youngest son out into the Castro to report on the "Wild Kingdom," came back with disappointingly few details for the *Moral Majority Report.* The gay march from the Castro to the convention center was orderly and not at all colorful. There were contingents of gay union members and nuclear freeze supporters; there were groups of gay parents and gay businessmen in three-piece suits; there were Democratic clubs, human rights coalitions, and medical groups, including a contingent of men with AIDS. In the lead were the sixty-five gay elected officials, gay delegates, and gay alternates to the convention. The march, one of the delegates told the press, was not a protest but a show of support for the Democratic party. Gay men and women have become "a part of the problem-solving family of the Democratic party," said City Supervisor Harry Britt.

Of course the parade organizers and gay Democrats had put a good deal of effort into seeing that the march turned out as it did. But an era was nonetheless over, and the march was a sign of the times. The gay rights movement continued, but gay liberation, the last wave emanating from the seismic disturbances of the sixties, had worn itself out by 1984. What it left in San Francisco was a small gay city—a city of perhaps 100,000 men and women with political organizations, newspapers, professional associations, businesses, churches, cultural institutions, and recreational facilities. A survey done by a market research corporation on gay men in San Francisco that year revealed a good deal about that city, or rather about the male part of it. From a survey sample of 529 gay or bisexual men researchers found that 78 percent had arrived since 1969, and most of them were living as openly gay men. About half of them lived in the Castro proper and its adjacent neighborhoods; about 80 percent lived in three major gay enclaves. The city was still young—half of the men were in their thirties—and it was prospering. Over half of the men were working in managerial or professional positions—or they had businesses of their own. Forty-three percent of them were making $25,000 a year or more (as opposed to 28 percent of San Franciscans generally), and 39 percent of those living in the Castro proper were making $30,000 or more. The vast majority of them lived in one- or two-person households, and just over half of them had a "primary relationship" with another man. But the city was not growing: immigration had dropped off considerably in the past few years, and thus possibly the population was the same or not much greater than it had been in 1978. It was also aging. A generation of gay men had come to San Francisco, and the next generation was not replacing it (only 18 percent were in their twenties). The gay community was thus becoming a minority in the sense that it had not been one while on the increase. And it was accepting its status as such. It was still powerful politically, but the old militance had gone. Even for those who lived there, the Castro was no longer the shining ideal. If anywhere, West Hollywood, where homosexuals won the majority of seats on the city council in 1984, now held claim to the title of the gay Camelot.

The looks of the Castro proper had changed quite noticeably since 1978. The main street, which six years ago had been in lively transition betwen hip and chic, now had an uneven and unlived-in look to it. Boutiques selling trendy clothes and expensive home furnishings had crowded out a number of the neighborhood stores; a building and an alleyway had been turned into a boutique mall. The gay bars were still there, but one had become a video discotheque and several of the others had acquired the tired, seedy air of those North Beach bars too long at the center of the tourist routes. Restaurants on the street now advertised pretentious "Continental" food on huge, engraved menus. A chain bookstore had replaced the gay political bookshop, and a new brick-and-plate-glass office building now occupied a whole block on the corner of Market Street. There were noticeably more women in the street—several of the boutiques sold women's clothes—and while the men still wore tight blue jeans and T-shirts, the Castro styles had grown vague and confused. The one shop selling gay leather gear looked musty by contrast to the shops selling three-hundred-dollar suede jackets. In the Folsom District, straight restaurants and discos were crowding the gay bars out.

On the bulletin board at the corner of Castro and Market were fliers from the Alice B. Toklas and the Harvey Milk Gay Democratic clubs. Half of the officers of both clubs were now women—and the same seemed to be true of most of the gay, now "gay and lesbian," social-service groups. Asking around for the veterans of the Harvey Milk campaigns and the Castro marches, I found that some of them had moved away, left the scene, while others had moved into the political mainstream. Cleve Jones was now working for Art Agnos, the state assemblyman who had won his seat for the first time by defeating Harvey Milk. Jim Rivaldo and Dick Pabich each had successful political consulting businesses and were at work for liberal candidates around the state. Bill Kraus worked for Congresswoman Sala Burton. Anne Kronenberg spent several years working in city government, no longer riding a motorcycle to work. Randy Shilts, who had written a biography of Harvey Milk, *The Mayor of Castro Street*, was now a reporter on the *San Francisco Chronicle*. Calling my friends, I found Peter Adair working on a film about antinuclear-war protesters, Ken Maley working on earthquake preparedness measures, and Armistead Maupin finishing another book in the *Tales of the City* series and horribly depressed. Another friend of his had come down with AIDS.

AIDS—the Acquired Immune Deficiency Syndrome—had hit the Castro hard. As of July 30th, 1984, 5394 cases had been recorded nationally, 634 of them in San Francisco. New York alone had a higher number of cases than San Francisco (about a third of the total), but its population was ten times as large. San Francisco had by far the highest number per capita, and a great proportion of them came from the Castro and the surrounding neighborhoods; as was not the case in other cities, virtually all of the victims were gay men.

The disease had been identified only three years earlier. In the spring of 1981 health officials at the Centers for Disease Control (CDC) in Atlanta had received reports of an outbreak of an unusual form of pneumonia and a rare form of skin cancer—both of them in these cases deadly. What the victims of the two diseases had in common was that all of them were homosexual men—and their immune systems had broken down. Setting up a task force, CDC officials contacted physicians across the country and in ten weeks found that 108 gay men had been stricken; some had died as long as two years before, their deaths written off to the proximate causes (as, pneumonia) or unexplained. By December 1981, nearly a hundred cases of immune system breakdown had been reported—twenty-four of the total in San Francisco. As the months passed and the number of cases grew, it appeared that the disease struck not only gay men but also drug addicts who used intravenous needles, hemophiliacs, and other blood transfusion recipients; also the sexual partners, and occasionally the children, of AIDS victims. There was also an outbreak among Haitian refugees in the United States. Studying the incidence of these cases, epidemiologists came eventually to believe that the disease was caused by an infectious agent, probably a virus, and was transmitted through blood, semen, and perhaps other bodily fluids. In August 1982, what had been called "the gay cancer" or "the gay plague" CDC researchers now officially dubbed the Acquired Immune Deficiency Syndrome. But the disease itself remained a mystery.

In April 1983 researchers at the Pasteur Institute in Paris announced they had isolated what they supposed to be the AIDS virus. While French researchers identified it as such, the American medical establishment preferred to wait until the National Health Laboratories offered a conclusion; that came a year later when Dr. Robert Gallo of the National Cancer Institute identified the retrovirus HTLV–III as the AIDS virus. It proved to be virtually identical to the one found at the Pasteur Institute. In the meantime, however, epidemiologists learned a good deal more about the disease. They were able to state with some assurance that the disease was infectious rather than contagious: that is, it could be transmitted only through the exchange of bodily fluids and not through the air or by casual contact. The recipients of anal sex were, they thought, particularly at risk probably owing to the delicacy of the rectal tissues; but all forms of sex involving the exchange of bodily fluids (even possibly saliva) carried the risk of transmission. Later, when the virus was isolated, researchers discovered that HTLV–III was associated with another group of infections that were not always deadly; they also found the virus, or rather its antibodies, present in the blood of a large number of people who did not have any disease. It was thought that AIDS itself might strike particularly at those in poor health, or those whose immune systems had already been assaulted by other infections, such as the related hepatitis B virus. But this was not clear. It seemed probable that the virus alone was enough to cause the disease, but if there were any other factors involved, they remained unknown.

Of all the epidemic diseases AIDS was in many respects the most terrible. In the first place, the mean incubation period for it (as was later discovered) was about five years. What this meant was that an individual could have the virus for a few months or possibly up to fourteen years before the first symptoms (such as fatigue, glandular swellings, and weight loss) manifested themselves, and during that time it was altogether possible that he or she could infect others without knowing it. Once AIDS was diagnosed, the victim might have six months, a year, even three or four years to live, but no one had yet survived for more than five years. As there was no cure, the victim had simply to await the onset of one or more diseases that his or her system could not fight off: meningitis, perhaps, or pneumonia, or the rare skin cancer, Kaposi's sarcoma. The appearance of a small purple skin lesion usually heralded the latter—and was in many cases the first sign of AIDS; and as the cancer developed, the lesions spread on and through the body. Kaposi's sarcoma was, in the case of AIDS patients, not only excruciatingly painful but mutilating.

As AIDS moved relatively slowly through the body, so it moved relatively slowly through the population. And in this respect it was also excruciating. Gay men across the country could watch the number of cases grow inexorably month by month, starting with a few, then multiplying into large numbers. In San Francisco, one of the cities where the disease was first noticed, there were 24 cases in December 1981, 61 cases six months later, and 118 cases the following December—and so on. Proportional to the population, the numbers advanced the most rapidly in the close-knit community of Castro. In March 1983 it was estimated that 1 out of every 333 gay men had AIDS; a year or so later, it was 1 out of 100. An epidemiological survey published in 1985 indicated that 37 percent of gay men in San Francisco had been exposed to the AIDS virus; the figure later climbed to over 50 percent. How many men would end up contracting the disease, no one could predict with any certainty, but AIDS researchers thought it possible that the Castro would be literally decimated in the course of the next decade: 1 out of 10 men would die. The gay carnival with its leather masks and ball gowns had thus been the twentieth-century equivalent of the Masque of the Red Death.

In fact the Castro had become something like the Algerian city of Oran that Albert Camus described in The Plague—a city separated from the outside world, where death and the threat of death hung over everyone. By 1984 there were few gay men who did not know someone, or know of someone, who had been struck by AIDS. Most of the victims were in their twenties, thirties, and forties—men in the prime of their lives. Very often they were athletic, ambitious, good-looking men who one day found a purple spot somewhere on their body. The purple spot was the nightmare that haunted the sleep of the Castro. Waking up in the morning, men would search their bodies for it; not finding it, they would search again the next day. Those who found it went on to a new series of nightmares. In the city there was a counseling service, the Shanti Project, where AIDS patients could go to imagine their deaths and take control of their fears in order to live and die as best as possible. Not everyone had the strength for that; not everyone could reconcile themselves to dying while all those around them went on with their lives.

The Castro became a city of moral dramas—dramas that involved not only the victims but their lovers, their parents, and their friends. There were hundreds of stories told. One young man had a lover who deserted him as soon as the news came, saying that he didn't love him anymore—he had found someone else. More often the story was of faithful lovers: one was of a man who nursed his sick friend at home even while he began to suffer from AIDS himself. One young man—so it was said—had parents who had never acknowledged his homosexuality and who, when they heard of his sickness, cut him off and cast him out of the family. Another young man had a mother who moved into his apartment with him to nurse him, and because neither had much money, they lived mostly on gifts of food and money from his friends. A lot of mothers came to San Francisco.

There were stories of landlords who evicted AIDS patients, health workers who would not touch them, and employers who asked them to leave. But most of these stories dated from the early years when the fear of infection was the greatest. In general San Franciscans behaved well. There was no panic, and though some people blamed gay men collectively, people tended to show generosity and compassion to the afflicted men they knew. The city government—led by the mayor—reacted swiftly and generously to the crisis, appropriating $4 million, $5 million, and then $9 million annually for AIDS education, health care, and research. As AIDS patients did not have to be hospitalized for most of the period of their illness, it created an outpatient health care program—a model of its kind and one that could be used in treating victims of other lingering diseases. A network of social-service organizations—the Shanti Project, the San Francisco AIDS Foundation, and Hospice—had city funding to provide emergency housing, counseling, help with medical bills, and home care for AIDS patients. And hundreds of volunteers, both gay and straight, turned out to staff them. San Francisco took care of its AIDS patients better than any other city in the nation and its newspapers, particularly the *Chronicle,* covered the AIDS crisis thoroughly and well. The one ugly note was that incidents of violence against gay people increased measurably. There were stories of juvenile gangs attacking Kaposi's sarcoma patients on the streets, calling them names and beating them.

Most gay men in the Castro, of course, went on with their lives. In the spring of 1984 most of the people I knew there did not talk about AIDS very much. Some of them had already thought themselves through it in some detail. They had decided what they would do with six months or a year to live, and they had imagined how their friends, lovers, and families would react. They had made their wills and settled their accounts. As a result, AIDS no longer preoccupied them. All the same, it was a part of their lives and something they considered before making any long-term commitment. When I told Peter Adair that Armistead was thinking of going to London, Adair replied quickly, "I'm not sure I would do that. I don't think I'd leave San Francisco. If we leave here, we just take the disease with us." Armistead, I explained, was not thinking of going to live in London—he was just planning a few weeks' holiday with a friend. He, too, had considered the responsibility.

The moral drama for gay men in the Castro was something like that for Camus's characters, but it had other dimensions. The plague, after all, threatened everyone in the city—men, women, and children; it struck randomly and killed its victims in a matter of days. Whether people behaved well or badly did not matter in the sense that little or nothing could be done about it. That was Camus's premise: the plague—which was morally meaningless—simply ran its course and subsided. It merely showed how men behaved when faced with a mortal danger they could not affect. Camus's priest, Father Paneloux, who had preached the plague as the wrath of God, abandoned his faith after watching a small child die horribly of it. But AIDS was different. In the first place, it singled out gay men and drug abusers. In San Francisco it struck gay men almost exclusively for the first three or four years. Then one female prostitute came down with it, and it began to appear that heterosexuals could pass it on through sexual contact. Still, its epidemic proportions owed directly to the level of promiscuity within the homosexual population. Fundamentalist ministers who preached God's wrath could thus continue to see the epidemic as God's punishment for the transgression of His law. In addition, all others who harbored negative feelings about homosexuality or sexual promiscuity could now see those feelings as justified. Gay men thus had to face a new form of social condemnation—as well as the disease itself. In the Castro those who had spent a good part of their lives in the struggle against the sexual taboo now had to acknowledge that the sexual liberation they had fought for so strenuously—and on which they had laid their claims of being the avant-garde of a national revolution—had deadly consequences. What was more, they had to face the fact that they were giving the disease to one another.

Quite early on in the epidemic it became clear that gay men could affect the course of the disease: they were responsible for their own lives and for those of others in a way that the citizens of Camus's city were not. But the responsibility was of a strange sort. At least before a test for the AIDS virus was developed and put to use, the responsibility was collective and statistical. That is, an individual gay man could choose to exercise it by forgoing high-risk sex, and it might make no difference to him or to anyone he knew. Even celibacy might not save his life if he had the virus already—though of course it might save the lives of others. On the other hand, it might make no difference if he engaged in high-risk forms of sex with one, two, three, or many other people, since not everyone had the virus and not everyone who had the virus would contract the disease. The only certainty was statistical: if a sufficient number of gay men refrained from high-risk sex with new partners, then the spread of disease would abate. The number of AIDS cases would eventually rise or fall in direct proportion to the choices made. Thus, beyond the individual dramas going on in the Castro, there was also a collective moral drama which involved all of its inhabitants. And because the Castro was an important part of San Francisco, it involved not only gay men but also city officials and to some extent the press and the public at large.

When I returned to San Francisco in June 1984, a battle was raging in the city over public health measures. The struggle had begun about a year before. Until then the gay organizations in San Francisco—as elsewhere—had put all their efforts into obtaining federal government funding for medical research. The federal government had responded sluggishly to the AIDS crisis. The Reagan administration had no sensitivity to gay or inner-city problems, and was in any case attempting to cut back on all forms of social spending. And there were bureaucratic tangles. By the spring of 1983, however, the U.S. Department of Health and Human Services had identified AIDS as the number-one priority, and the Congress, thanks in large part to the California delegation, had appropriated $26 million for AIDS research. In May, Mayor Feinstein had declared an AIDS awareness week, and six thousand people had marched from the Castro to the Civic Center to show their concern and to keep up the pressure for government funding. At that point, however, members of the Harvey Milk club and others raised a new and, as it turned out, bitterly divisive issue.

By the spring of 1983 epidemiologists had produced abundant evidence to show that AIDS could be transmitted through sexual contact involving the exchange of bodily fluids. Their findings had appeared in the regular press, both local and national. Yet a survey made by three gay psychotherapists including Leon McKusick of the University of California, San Francisco, suggested that only a minority of gay men in San Francisco had heeded the implicit warnings. Of the six

hundred men who answered the survey questionnaire, only 30 percent said that they had changed their sexual behavior because of
AIDS; one in fourteen said that they had actually increased their involvement with high-risk sex. The survey was not a statistical sample
of the whole gay population, but it offered some numerical evidence
for what AIDS researchers believed from their experience to be the
case: most gay men had not yet taken the danger seriously enough,
and some did not even know it existed. The responsibility, as far as
AIDS researchers and the Harvey Milk club people were concerned,
lay first and foremost with the city health department and the gay
organizations—neither of which had made any effort to educate the
community on the sexual transmission of the disease.

In the July issue of *California* magazine, reporters Peter Collier and
David Horowitz documented the case for a public health scandal.
Until May, the reporters found, there was not a single piece of health
department literature in the city clinics warning gay men about the
sexual transmission of AIDS. The literature the department put out all
went to reassure the general public that AIDS was not infectious and
could not be transmitted by casual contact. Most gay newspapers in
the city did not print the epidemiological information available in the
regular press, and the gay medical and political organizations, which
had called vociferously for government funding, did little to advertise
the dangers of the epidemic or the ways in which gay men might
protect themselves. Not only that, but they seemed to be engaged in
an attempt to suppress information about the spread of the disease.

In January two researchers from the University of California Medical Center had been ready to release their findings showing that AIDS
had been diagnosed in 1 out of every 333 single men in the Castro
area. They had held a meeting and discussed their findings with
members of the gay doctors' association, the Bay Area Physicians for
Human Rights (BAPHR), and health activists from the Kaposi Sar-
coma/AIDS Foundation and all three gay Democratic clubs. But the
consensus at all the meetings had been against publishing them. Finally, two months later, the report was leaked to Randy Shilts and
published in the *Chronicle*. Before Shilts ran the article, he received
phone calls from a number of gay leaders, including the president of
the Toklas club, who was also the cochair of the Coalition for Human
Rights, asking him to suppress it on the grounds that it would hurt
business in the Castro and reduce the chances for the passage of a
gay rights bill in Sacramento. In *California* magazine Catherine Cusic,
the head of the health services committee for the Harvey Milk club
charged, "There are leaders in this community who don't want people to know the truth. Their attitude is that it is bad for business, bad

for the gay image. Hundreds, perhaps thousands, are going to die because of this attitude. The whole thing borders on the homicidal."

On May 24 the Harvey Milk club voted almost unanimously to put out a pamphlet warning of the sexual transmission of AIDS. Some of the Castro activists in the club—Ron Huberman, its chairman, Bill Kraus, Cleve Jones, Dick Pabich, and Frank Robinson—began to agitate within the 1983 gay community for further measures. In the weeks before the Gay Freedom Day Parade—the event that annually brought 100,000 to 200,000 gay people to San Francisco from elsewhere in the country—they tried to convince the owners of the gay bathhouses to post warnings about high-risk sex. According to Kraus, the bath owners were "totally incensed" by the suggestion. The Toklas club issued a statement disassociating itself from their initiative. Outraged, Kraus, Jones, and Huberman wrote a manifesto and sent it to the largest-circulation gay bar newspaper, *The Bay Area Reporter*; it was printed after a delay of six weeks. "What a peculiar perversion it is of gay liberation," they wrote, "to ignore the overwhelming scientific evidence, to keep quiet, to deny the obvious—when the lives of gay men are at stake." Harry Britt supported the manifesto signers and the drive to post warnings, but many other gay leaders denounced both as treasonous to the cause. "Labeling San Francisco as unsafe for our people is inaccurate and a direct attack on the social and economic viability of our community," the Toklas president wrote.

Just before the parade the mayor asked the city's public health director, Dr. Mervyn Silverman, to close the baths, and gay health activists asked him to pressure the owners into posting warnings. Silverman told the mayor, "It is not the bathhouses that are the problem—it's sex. People who want to have sex will find a way to have it." However, he agreed to ask the bathhouse owners to post warnings. There were further meetings between the owners and the health activists, and eventually a few notices appeared. Most of the gay leaders, however, continued to oppose the initiative. Konstantin Berlandt, the cochair of the Gay Freedom Day Parade, called the proposal to close the baths "genocidal"; his view of the educational effort was that "institutions that have fought against sexual repression for years are being attacked under the guise of medical strategy." For Berlandt, as for the leaders of the Stonewall Gay Democratic Club, the sexual transmission of AIDS was merely a "theory" designed to attack "gay life-styles."

Two or three months later, the health education policies of the city and of most of the gay organizations changed dramatically. By June the city health department had put out risk guidelines on the sexual transmission of AIDS, and the gay health organizations were printing pamphlets discussing safe versus dangerous sex. The Toklas club and other groups that had fought to suppress AIDS information now earnestly did their part to disseminate it. As Catherine Cusic said, "They took the very positions they had trashed a few months before." There were no apologies and no explanations, but they proceeded, and the results were significant. In November 1983, a health department suvey showed that 95 percent of the gay men in the city knew how AIDS was transmitted and knew of the risk guidelines. Attendance at the bathhouses and sex clubs declined—two bathhouses shut down for lack of business—and the VD rate had plummeted. The AIDS Behavior Research Project, a new organization headed by Leon McKusick, instituted a longitudinal study and found that gay men had significantly reduced their participation in high-risk sex.

All the same, a year later, in 1985, as the Gay Freedom Day Parade again approached, a number of health activists felt that the situation still did not warrant optimism. The toll of AIDS victims was still rising at a terrifying rate—the number of cases now doubling every seven or eight months. Roughly a third of the gay male population seemed unpersuaded by the educational campaign, and the indicators of change had come to a stop. Attendance at the baths was up slightly, and the rectal gonorrhea rate had leveled off. Among others, Frank Robinson, who had all but abandoned his science fiction writing in order to study AIDS and what it meant for the Castro, thought the efforts taken thus far were wholly inadequate. "The educational program is crap," he told me. "Look at the new AIDS Foundation posters. There's one with a photograph of two sexy naked men with their asses turned to the camera, and underneath there's a message about the joys of safe sex. Look, I've seen a lot of men with Kaposi's sarcoma. It's a hideous, disfiguring disease. A Hollywood makeup man couldn't duplicate it. There should be pictures of it. But the gay press has never carried a picture, and when *Time* and *Newsweek* did stories on AIDS, the worst they showed were the lesions on a leg."

To Robinson—as to a number of others—it seemed clear that something should be done about the bathhouses, glory holes, and sex clubs. The baths were a big business in San Francisco, far bigger than they were were in most other cities; a lot of openly gay men went to them, as they did not elsewhere, and because of that, they attracted visitors from other cities. The owners asserted that there was no scientifically determined correlation between the bathhouse attendance and AIDS—or even bathhouse attendance and high-risk sex. This was true: a study had never been done. But the baths were facilities for multiple, anonymous sex contacts, and anyone who went to them knew that high-risk sex took place in them. And once the fuss over them had died away, most of the owners had ceased to post the risk guidelines in places where they could be seen. A year before the columnist Herb Caen had reported that a gay doctor had run into three of his AIDS patients in a bathhouse; he had ordered them out but they had refused to leave.

In fact for some months now gay health activists had been asking city officials to take action on the baths. They had given up on the gay organizations, for not even the gay AIDS specialists would make public statements about the dangers posed by the baths. The city, however, was no more responsive. The mayor and the president of the Board of Supervisors, Wendy Nelder, had both let it be known that they favored closing the baths, but both had declined to take action on the grounds that it was not a political matter but a decision for the public health authorities. Silverman, for his part, had said that it would be "inappropriate and, in fact, illegal" for him to close them without the necessary evidence. To Robinson this reasoning was implausible. "They closed the public swimming pools during the polio epidemic when they didn't know any more about polio than they now know about AIDS," Robinson said. "They license the baths—for fire hazards, cleanliness, and so on—so clearly they can close them." In March, Larry Littlejohn, a deputy sheriff and a gay activist of twenty years' standing, had decided to force the issue. Going down to City Hall, he filed a petition to put a proposition on the November ballot requiring the Board of Supervisors to adopt an ordinance prohibiting sex in the bathhouses. Littlejohn knew that if such a proposition were on the ballot, the great majority of San Franciscans would vote yes. (An *Examiner* poll taken in April showed that 80 percent of San Franciscans would vote yes.) He also presumed that the city and the gay organizations would not allow the issue to come to a referendum. There followed a series of events that Robinson, for one, could not wholly account for.

In the two days that followed the Littlejohn initiative, there were gay organization meetings all over the city. The Harvey Milk club held a public debate on the issue. At it, Dr. Marcus Conant, the head of the AIDS Clinical Research Center at the University of California in San Francisco, made his first public statement on the baths. "We have to look at the possibility of closing the bathhouses and bookstores," he said. "I do not say *close* the baths. The word is *discussion*. We must begin the discussion of this problem." Bill Kraus and one of the University of California AIDS researchers spoke in support of Conant's position, but most of the other speakers attacked it. The next day Robinson was at a small gathering of doctors and Milk club people when word came via Dr. Conant that another small meeting was considering asking Dr. Mervyn Silverman to preempt the Littlejohn initiative. It was the consensus at both meetings that if the baths were to be closed, the initiative should come, or appear to come, from the gay community. At Robinson's meeting, several people asked for time to go back to their organizations and discuss the matter with their memberships. But there did not seem to be time. The group drew up a statement requesting Silverman to close the baths, and several people were dispatched to the phones to collect as many signatures as they could for it in twelve hours.

The next day Randy Shilts came out with a story in the *Chronicle* saying that Silverman, who had long resisted closing the baths, was now planning to close them at the request of fifty gay businessmen, physicians, and political leaders. That morning, however, Silverman announced at a press conference that he would defer his decision for a week or two; there were many factors involved, he said, "some of which have nothing to do with medicine." He assured the press that the decision was his alone, and not based on pressure from any group. Clearly, however, he was under a great deal of pressure. According to the Shilts story, he had consulted fifteen gay physicians and political leaders, and the majority had asked him to delay. According to the *Bay Area Reporter* he had spent the previous evening at a gay forum on the issue, where ninety out of a hundred people opposed any action on the baths. In addition, his press conference was attended by several bathhouse owners and a contingent of men dressed only in towels carrying a sign that read, TODAY THE TUBS, TOMORROW YOUR BEDROOMS.

A few days later, according to the press, Silverman called a meeting of AIDS experts on federal and state levels and including the coordinator of the AIDS task force at the Centers for Disease Control. The discussions were held behind closed doors, and the content of them was not disclosed. On April 10 Silverman held another press conference, where, flanked by gay doctors and health activists, he announced that he would draw up regulations banning sex in the bathhouses and sex clubs. The city attorney, he said, had advised him that an order regulating the baths had a better chance of standing up in court than an order to close them. Preparing the order, he added, would take some time partly because the Board of Supervisors would have to clarify the authority of the police and the health departments in the matter.

By June the issue was still not settled—the regulations were still not drawn up. The reason for the delay was not at all clear from press accounts; city officials seemed to be using the press to blame each other. Nelder, the board president, said that she was amazed that Silverman had not done anything about the baths. Mayor Feinstein let it be known that she was "livid" about the delay and wondered aloud why Silverman hadn't "the guts" to close the baths before the Gay Freedom Day Parade. Silverman, however, maintained that he lacked the necessary evidence and that the Board of Supervisors could facilitate the matter by transferring the authority for regulating the baths from the police to the health department. The police chief, Cornelius Murphy, said that he did not want the police to go into the bathhouses—and that seemed entirely reasonable. Harry Britt, for his part, criticized Silverman for not acting "immediately and expeditiously" to close the baths, but on the other hand opposed any regulation of the baths on the grounds that regulation of sexual activity would be a serious violation of civil liberties. He introduced legislation to prevent the city from regulating them; meanwhile a board subcommittee voted to table hearings on the matter of licensing until after the Democratic Convention. (An uproar over the gay bathhouses was the last thing the mayor and the supervisors wanted with the national press in town.) From the press it looked very much as if no one was willing to take responsibility for closing the baths.

In June the nongay San Franciscans I talked to who had followed the controversy were outraged by the delays and by the apparent failure of political will. In April the mayor had candidly said that the issue was politically sensitive, and that she had to be cautious as some gays in the past had dismissed her comments on gay life-styles as patronizing. "I've got to be careful," she said, "and I recognize that." But the mayor—in the view of those I talked to—was not really to blame: the decision to close or regulate the baths was not a political matter, but a public health matter, and should be treated as such. One journalist—a woman now pregnant and soon to go to the hospital for the delivery of her first child—thought the public health authorities had a lot to answer for. "Look," she said, "the doctors and the health department people keep telling us not to worry about AIDS. They told us not to worry about going to restaurants since AIDS isn't contagious. They told us that with great certainty, but now they say saliva might transmit the virus. Then they tell us not to worry about the blood supply in the hospitals because not very much of it has the AIDS virus in it. Well, the one thing they do know is that AIDS can be sexually transmitted. And yet they won't close down the places where all the sex goes on. It's unbelievable."

On my way to an interview with Dr. Silverman, I, too, thought the public health director had a good deal to explain. Why had his department been so slow in putting out literature about the sexual transmission of AIDS? Why had he refused to consider closing the baths a year ago, then temporized in March of this year, then decided to go ahead after meeting with the national AIDS authorities? At the moment he seemed to be lost in a bureaucratic snarl and not at all eager to get out of it. He had said nothing in public about the health hazards of the baths—and nothing whatever to indicate that AIDS might be a health emergency. He seemed extremely sensitive to gay pressures, much more so than the mayor, though he did not hold a political office (the public health director was appointed by the city's chief administrative officer) and he did not seem to be running for anything. Many San Franciscans now blamed him for the fact that the baths were not closed. Even Frank Robinson blamed him, though he knew what the pressures were and knew there were legal problems as well. "In the end I have to fault Silverman," he told me. "In the end you have to act on principle. If you think the baths are a health risk, you have to close them and fight it in court. There is such a thing as a Hippocratic oath."

Silverman surprised me. I had imagined a bland, elderly bureaucrat, and he turned out to be a man in his mid-forties with longish hair and a beard: lively, humorous, direct. A child of the sixties, one would have said. He was, as it turned out, a former Peace Corps physician. His degrees were from Tulane University Medical School and Harvard University's School of Public Health, and he had been in San Francisco since 1977. He was, I discovered, a reflective man but also an activist—a man passionately committed to his work and to the cause of stopping the AIDS epidemic. In two hours he had convinced me not only that he was taking the right approach to the whole question but that it would have been very difficult to second-guess any one of the decisions he had made. "It's an extraordinary situation," he said. "In recent history I don't know that there's been a disease with so many implications. My medical training didn't begin to prepare me for the job I have to do. My job is to change people's behavior—to change their sex practices, for heaven's sakes. That's not a medical problem. It wouldn't be easy with any population, but among gay men the sensitivities are particularly acute. I may look as if I'm responding to political pressures, but what I'm responding to is opposition from the gay community. To succeed I must have their support—I must have their confidence that what I am doing is in their interests. If gays start opposing my decisions—if they start looking on me as a heavy father—then the whole issue of AIDS gets lost. The mayor seems not to understand this."

In fact Silverman—as I began to understand—had one of the most difficult jobs in the country, and one of the loneliest. The beginning of the AIDS crisis had felt like the first tremors of an earthquake; the doctors who watched the mysterious infection bring down new victims week by week had felt a heave of fear, for no one knew what it might do. When epidemiologists found that it was not contagious, Silverman—like his counterpart in New York—had put a great deal of effort into advertising the fact, for there had been a smell of rising panic in the city. There had been terrible incidents—landlords throwing AIDS patients out of their apartments, health workers refusing to touch them—and some talk of taking measures against the gay community. The panic had subsided, but Silverman still got letters asking him to quarantine all gay men—or send them away.

In the gay community the initial reaction had been one of incredulity. "A disease which killed only gay white men? It seemed unbelievable," one gay doctor told me, remembering the period. "I used to teach epidemiology, and I had never heard of a disease that selective. I thought, they are making this up. It can't be true. Or if there is such a disease, it must be the work of some government agency—the FBI or the CIA trying to kill us all." For those who were not doctors it was easier to believe that the medical profession was exaggerating the threat—or would soon have it under control if enough pressure were put. The alternative was accepting a terrible fear and a sense of contamination. While many individuals faced up to it, the gay organizations preferred to deny the scale of the epidemic and the evidence that it was sexually transmitted. (There were still, after all, many medical uncertainties.) At the same time there was a great deal of paranoia going around about the origins of the disease and the role of the government. Such was the outsider mentality in the Castro that a great many gay men took quite seriously the thought that AIDS might be a form of germ warfare targeted on the gay population by the FBI or the CIA. City officials, and indeed all nongay authorities, were suspect as well: if they had not invented the disease, they were probably using it to suppress "the gay life-style." Pat Norman, the city coordinator of lesbian-gay health services, writing an article in the 1983 gay parade program, framed the issue in terms of the government and the medical profession stigmatizing AIDS victims for contracting the disease "because of their *assumed* sexual behavior and/or use of illicit drugs."

Faced with this reaction, Silverman soon realized that if he took a hard line, it would simply rebound against him: he could not force people to believe him or to do what was good for them, and he could not threaten them with the consequences of not doing so. Reining himself in, he formed an advisory committee of gay and nongay physicians and prepared for a gradual, long-term effort. He became grateful for the college course he had once taken in advertising. The first health department literature he was able to put out offered the advice: "Limit your use of recreational drugs" and "Enjoy more time with fewer partners." The appearance of these inadequate warnings represented a victory as they had been booed by gay audiences just months before. Over the months, and then the years, Silverman spent a great deal of time in the Castro going to meetings, discussion groups, benefit dinners, and so on. He got to know the doctors, the political leaders, and others of influence in the community, and gradually they came to trust him. The radicals often disagreed with him, but even they came to believe that he had no motive other than trying to halt the epidemic. Silverman for his part began to have a feel for the situation and for how the community worked. He watched attitudes change as the disease spread and the death toll mounted. The cry of protest from the Harvey Milk club people over city, as well as gay, policies on health education was what he was waiting for. The initiative had to come from the gay community, and in its wake, he could push forward. That the resistance of the other gay organizations had collapsed immediately thereafter was not perhaps so surprising as the leaders had been defending an illusion rather than a calculated policy. After that, Silverman, in cooperation with the gay organizations, had made a great deal of progress: the educational literature had proliferated, the warnings had become gradually blunter, and the community had responded. In the spring of 1984 Silverman decided to take a new step in the educational campaign. "The new literature is just going out," he told me in June. "We can now show pictures of people with AIDS. We couldn't before because people weren't ready for it, and if the receptors aren't there, it does no good. Besides, fear does not seem to have a very long-term effect on people's behavior."

The next stage, however, was going to be more difficult. Virtually all gay men now knew of the dangers, but still evidence suggested that roughly a third of them had not changed their behavior accordingly. Silverman thought that within the remaining third there were probably numbers of people who could never be persuaded to change. There were people for whom sex had become an addiction, like tobacco, alcohol, or drugs. There were people with death wishes and people who thought they would live forever. This was not, in Silverman's view, either remarkable or difficult to understand—certainly not given the number of people in the general population who continued to smoke or to drink and drive. People thought up all kinds of ways to justify their behavior. "Some people tell me they are so anxious about AIDS that they have to go to the bathhouses to relieve stress. Some people say the whole thing is a conspiracy. There are a lot of sexual radicals in this city; in fact there are probably more in San Francisco than anywhere else. San Francisco has always been the place for people who want a little bit more." Nonetheless Silverman thought there was some reason for optimism. Many more people could be persuaded to change their behavior: the proof was that every time there was a flurry of news about AIDS in the press, the indices changed for the better. And in the long run this would have an effect on the epidemic. "The rate of increase in AIDS cases has already tapered slightly, and that's something given the length of the incubation period. I think they could continue to taper down and eventually become flat." For that to happen, however, the public health director would have to have the support of gay organizations—and now the bathhouse issue threatened to destroy all of the credibility he had built up.

Silverman had not chosen the issue. "When I began to think about it eighteen months ago," he said, "I realized that the baths were symbolic facilities. The freedom to have anonymous sex had become associated with gay liberation. The cry was, 'If you close them, we'll go to the barricades.' " No other city had closed its bathhouses, and, as Silverman knew, there was a strong rationale for not closing them. In New York and Los Angeles the working assumption in the public health departments was that if the educational campaigns succeeded, fewer and fewer people would go to the baths; on the other hand, if they did not succeed, and if the baths were closed by fiat, there would be an uproar and dangerous practices would continue anyway. The previous spring Silverman had suggested to the gay activists that they treat the baths as they treated other threats to the community and picket them. His suggestion was much discussed in the Castro, but the pickets did not materialize. With such small support Silverman decided he could not take action himself. But then in March, Larry Littlejohn had forced his hand with the ballot initiative.

From Silverman's perspective what had happened since was this: "After Littlejohn made his announcement, some people got together and said, 'Well, if the baths are going to be closed, better have Silverman do it.' They assured me they would have community support, but when I called around the next day, I found the support wasn't there. So I decided to postpone my decision." (The same people called Randy Shilts to say that they had, or were in the process of getting, fifty signatures on a petition to Silverman. In fact the group got only a dozen people to sign, and some of these took their names off the next day, and the document was never made public.) Now unable to avoid the issue, but uncertain what to do, Silverman called a meeting of AIDS experts. "I thought at the time, maybe I shouldn't worry. We

have a model program for AIDS in this city, and the bath issue has
never even come up elsewhere. But we had a six-hour meeting, and
to my surprise, there was unanimous support for an attempt to regulate sex in the baths. Not on medical grounds. The medical grounds
were clear enough. But on public health grounds. On educational
grounds. So I decided to go ahead. Then I met with gay community
leaders and my advisory board of physicians and I told them what I
was going to do. I promised them that the regulations would involve
only high-risk sex in the baths but that I wasn't going to say that in
making the announcement as I wasn't going to talk about masturba-
tion at a press conference. Well, a number of the physicians and
activists came to the press conference and stood behind me while I
made the announcement. But then seven out of nine of them defected
because I didn't mention 'safe sex.' "

But the die was cast now, and Silverman had to proceed. What he
wanted was an order from the Board of Supervisors transferring the
licensing from the police to the health department. The mayor had
insisted on this in order to spare the police, and her chief, Cornelius
Murphy, from any involvement with the baths. Silverman had gone
along with this—though he thought it would be unnecessary to involve any police in the investigation. But the board seemed disinclined to issue the order. Part of the problem was Harry Britt. Britt,
while criticizing Silverman for not closing the baths, was opposing
any regulation of them. Apparently he was making a distinction in
principle, but in introducing legislation to prevent Silverman from
regulating them, he said that his measures would "kill the issue of
whether the baths should be closed or not." The board subcommittee
responsible for the matter seemed to be leaning in his direction. Apparently its members were under pressure from the gay community,
and the mayor and the board president could not push them into it.
The mayor added to Silverman's difficulties. Silverman had tried to
convince her that the baths were not the heart of the AIDS problem,
but he had not succeeded. As the daughter of one physician and the
widow of another, she looked at the issue in purely medical terms:
the baths were a health hazard and should be closed. "If someone
were trying to commit suicide by jumping out the window, I would
try to stop them. That's the analogy," she said. "The Public Health
Director makes a political argument he should not be making. The
baths are licensed by the city, a lot of young people from all over the
country come here, and there's the possibility of spreading a fatal
disease." She, however, had cancelled the hearings that would have
given Silverman the power to regulate the baths because of their prox-
imity to the Democratic convention. Thus, while to many gay men

Silverman was beginning to look like the patsy of the mayor for trying to regulate the baths after so many refusals to do so, he was also beginning to look to many other San Franciscans like a captive of the gay community.

This latter was a real problem. Before the AIDS crisis most San Franciscans had no notion of what went on in the baths and no idea of the extent of sexual promiscuity in the Castro. Now they were reading the Bell and Weinberg statistics—five hundred, a thousand sexual partners—in the newspapers and coming to the conclusion that gays were different from other people in more ways than one. Under the circumstances the idea that the city would condone the baths seemed quite fantastic. Because the mayor had always favored closing the baths, it was now Silverman who was getting the angry letters. And Silverman could not defend himself. He could not explain gay politics to straight San Franciscans—any more than he could tell the gay community why he had taken so many different positions on the bath issue. Further, he could not publicly attack the mayor or the Board of Supervisors.

Still, the most important issue as far as Silverman was concerned was the reaction of the gay community. Would it eventually accept his position on the bathhouses, or would it go to the barricades? At the moment the barricades seemed a distinct possibility. The Harvey Milk club people generally favored some form of action on the baths, but, once again, they were quite alone in raising their voices. The Stonewall Gay Democratic Club opposed the action. This was hardly surprising since it was in sexual, as in other kinds of politics, the most radical of the three. Two years before it had supported a drive to recall the mayor because its members objected to her veto of legislation introduced by Britt to give "domestic partners" of city employees the same rights to compensation as married partners. But the Toklas club also opposed the regulation of the baths; so did the gay Republican club, the Coalition for Human Rights, the gay doctors' association (BAPHR), the gay newspapers, the gay business association, and just about every other gay organization that could be named.

The opponents of the regulations I talked to explained their position in various ways. They brought up Silverman's own doubts about the effectiveness of such a measure in terms of the whole AIDS prevention program. But they made other arguments as well. Gerry F. Parker, for example, one of the founders of Stonewall and a member of the Castro generation, gave me a long speech on the subject. "I feel very strongly," he said, "that if we lose the battle for the baths, we lose the battle for free expression, free association, and privacy. Along with the church, the government has been the major force for repress-

ing—for terrorizing—gays and lesbians. No scientific evidence definitely proves that there is a correlation between multiple sex partners
and AIDS. If we close the baths, we're back to the fifties again with
nothing but park sex for a certain percentage of the gay population—
largely straight-identified gays. Dianne Feinstein is not just against
the baths, she's against all kinds of things, like bookstores and peep
shows. She wants to take the Wild West image away from San Francisco. She's just using AIDS to do this. She wants us to go back to the
good little fairy days—and we're not going to go."

Jerry E. Berg, a prominent downtown lawyer in his late forties and
a close associate of the mayor's, argued from the opposite end of the
political spectrum. When I asked how the city had responded to the
AIDS crisis, he said, "I'm pleased with what the mayor has done,
both locally and nationally. She truly views it as a community problem." When I asked about the mayor's stand on the baths, he went
on to say, "Well, the mayor knows the seriousness of AIDS and wants
to do something about it and doesn't know what else to do. She sees
the baths as designed for promiscuous sex. Well, I'd like to see them
closed, too. But I take the civil liberties argument very seriously. I
don't think you can legislate morality. And there are economic interests involved. There is no proof that the baths are directly related to
AIDS, and to close them would be a denial of due process. Also, much
of the country looks to San Francisco for leadership on these issues.
There's an enlightened leadership in this city, but not everywhere
else. What if, let us say, Wichita were to close all the gay bars? It could
happen. All kinds of things could happen. Look what happened to
the Japanese in California during World War Two."

I went to see Michael England, the pastor of the Metropolitan Community Church in the Castro, to ask about the impact of AIDS on the
gay community. I had no idea what his position on the baths might
be. When the subject came up, England, a robust, energetic man in
his late thirties or early forties, told me that he had been working
closely with Dr. Silverman on the issue. "I trust Silverman," he said.
"The man is not in any way a homophobe—his sole agenda is to save
lives. If we had only spent the money and energy on it, we ourselves
in the community could have gotten the bathhouses to serve an educational function—they would have been very useful in that way. But
we didn't. Communication was screwed up and people got very paranoid. Now what people are hearing is prohibition and negativism. It
makes them more scared and more ignorant. When Silverman made
his announcement, a lot of people thought he had changed what he
told us and was now trying to restrict all forms of sex. But I didn't
think so. I thought he was simply being too conservative, medically

speaking. The medical experts he called in constructed all kinds of scenarios about how any kind of sex could, under certain circumstances, spread AIDS. They took a much more restrictive approach than the one they would take to, say, drinking or smoking. I think BAPHR has made a lot of sense on this issue; they came out early saying that closing the baths was not the solution."

It occurred to me to say that many gay leaders seemed more concerned about the violation of civil rights than about dying of AIDS. England's reply was: "If I had to go back to living in the closet, I'd have to think very clearly about whether or not I'd rather be dead."

In fact the civil rights argument, as Jerry Berg made it, was not to be dismissed. Given feelings about homosexuality and the opposition to gay rights that still existed in large parts of the country, it was not out of the question that some city might use AIDS as a pretext to close gay bars or otherwise restrict gay men. (Indeed the threat of AIDS was put to service in defeating a gay rights bill in Houston the following January, and Houston City Council members listened to a social psychologist call for the quarantining of all gay men.) Concern for the legal and political precedent the city might create by closing the baths was thus legitimate. This being the case, however, the question was what strategy gay leaders should adopt via-à-vis the baths themselves. Clearly, government regulation was not the best solution from anyone's point of view. San Francisco city officials would have preferred it if bath attendance had simply dropped off to zero of itself— or if the owners had turned their establishments into AIDS education centers. But the bathhouse owners had not done this on their own, and the gay leaders had not exerted enough pressure on them to make them do so. Now these same gay leaders were objecting to government action on the grounds that made little sense to most San Franciscans. The public perception was that gay men were being irresponsible and not taking the most obvious measure to curb the epidemic, and, arguably, this public perception was more of a threat to gay civil liberties than any legal precedent the city might set by regulating the baths. Under the circumstances, it could be argued, gay leaders could best defend their civil liberties by supporting government action on the baths and taking their stand on principle somewhere else. This in any case was the position that many Harvey Milk club people took.

The civil rights argument was debatable politically, but rhetorically speaking, there was something quite suspect about it. In the past, gay liberationists, including Harvey Milk, had permitted themselves frequent recourse to the logic of the slippery slope: that is, if this or that measure was not defeated (the Briggs Initiative or the Anita Bryant campaign in Dade County), the next step was the concentration camps for all gay men and women. It was one thing, of course, to say this for effect in front of a crowd of people, but it was another thing to deploy the logic in serious discussion, for the United States was not Nazi Germany, and there were many redoubts to be defended along the way. In addition, the civil rights argument was almost invariably accompanied by an assertion that there was no proof that the baths were related to the spread of AIDS. Gerry Parker went so far as to say that there was "no conclusive proof of the correlation between multiple sex partners and AIDS." Both statements were literally true in that statistical samples offer probabilities, not proofs—but they were at the same time wholly sophistical. And the very people who made these arguments otherwise acknowledged, implicitly, that there was some correlation between these things. Berg and England said that they thought the baths should be closed, and Parker, after telling me there was no proof of the correlation between multiple partners and AIDS, went on to talk about the sexual "irresponsibility" of the past "for which so many had paid a price."

In fact the arguments gay leaders made against the regulation of the baths seemed to confirm Silverman's view that the baths were "symbolic facilities." These days some small percentage of gay men in San Francisco went to the baths (between 10 and 15 percent according to surveys), and yet for most gay leaders they seemed to stand as synecdoches for gay sexual freedom. They were seen as sanctuaries in a hostile world. They were also perhaps the last defense against the fact that most forms of sex were now mortally dangerous. To read the gay press was to imagine that that was the case, for in speaking to the gay community, opponents of the regulations spoke at a far higher emotional pitch than they did to outsiders. In one issue of *BAR* there was a full account of the public meeting held by the Harvey Milk club at which Larry Littlejohn had announced his ballot initiative. Gerry Parker, according to the article, had gotten up at the meeting and "screamed" at Littlejohn, "What you are doing is going to be a political disaster. You have given the Moral Majority and the right wing the gasoline they have been waiting for to fuel the flames that will annihilate us!" In the next issue of *BAR* there were letters calling Littlejohn an "Uncle Tom," a "quisling," and an "Alice-in-Wonderland do-gooder" who "forced" other people "to behave in a manner deemed for their own good." The editorial in that issue dealt with the statement Robinson, Conant, and others had drawn up asking Silverman to close the baths. The statement was never published, but the editorial said:

The Gay Liberation Movement in San Francisco almost died last Friday morning at 11 a.m. [i.e., the time of Silverman's first press conference].

No, that's not quite it. The Gay Liberation Movement here and then everywhere else was almost killed off by 16 Gay men and one Lesbian last Friday morning.

This group, whose number changed by the hour . . . signed a request or gave their names to give the green light to the annihilation of Gay life. This group would have empowered government forces to enter our private precincts and rule over and regulate our sex lives. . . .

These people would have given away our right to assemble, our right to do with our own bodies what we choose, the few gains we have made over the past 25 years. These 16 people would have killed the movement —glibly handing it all over to the forces that have beaten us down since time immemorial. . . .

The people of the community were quick to see what was being traded off, and have responded in anger and consternation. This office has received more mail on this issue than any other. Not one letter backed the collaborators.

Somewhere in the middle of the editorial was the charge: "The Gay Community should remember those names well, if not etch them into their anger and regret." There followed, in a box and in large type, the names of sixteen people. Among them were Ron Huberman and Carole Migden (the two leaders of the Harvey Milk club), Bill Kraus, Dick Pabich, Dr. Marcus Conant, Frank Robinson, Harry Britt, and "the traitor *extraordinaire*, Larry Littlejohn."

Rhetorical overkill had become something of a convention in the Castro, but I did not remember gay liberationists in the past attacking each other in this vitriolic a fashion. Randy Shilts, however, told me that such attacks had become fairly common ever since the beginning of the AIDS crisis. "There's a whole genre of political leaders who keep saying we're about to be put in concentration camps," he said. "Meanwhile they attack the messengers who bring the bad news about AIDS. Last year I ran a piece about that study on the incidence of AIDS in the Castro, and we at the *Chronicle* made a fuss when the bathhouse owners refused to put AIDS literature in the baths. All of a sudden it was like the McCarthy period. People all over the place were calling me a 'traitor to the gay community' and 'homophobic.' Among gays that's like being called anti-American. The Toklas club passed a resolution calling me the most homophobic person in northern California."

It was impossible to think about AIDS without strong feelings, and in the face of disaster, communities, like emperors, have often preferred to blame messengers rather than to take responsibility—and action. But the form gay anger took still had to be explained. Jerry Berg had suggested an answer to this when I asked him about the impact of AIDS on the community. "Generally speaking," he said, "there was a lack of personal definition of what it meant to be gay. Those who think that what binds us together is sex and not broader human qualities are very threatened by the disease. To them AIDS looks like a great threat to everything gay. Many of these people are quite hysterical, and there is a political craziness around. I have dear friends who are battling over the baths."

Reverend England suggested a further explanation in a roundabout way. England, as I discovered after going to see him, had denounced the attempts made to close the baths in a letter to *BAR* he had written with a fellow pastor of the Metropolitan Community Church. In that letter the pastors gave several reasons for their view that the attempts were "ill-advised." One of them was that ". . . airing of the issue through such a measure may further inflame public panic and give tacit permission to expression of homophobic feelings in repressive legal measures and even violence."

This was the usual slippery slope argument put in psychological terms. The pastors, however, concluded with an argument about gay psychology:

> Finally, we see such a measure as the product, in some minds, of our internalized homophobia, a tendency deep in some of us to see sexuality as evil and to scapegoat non-traditional forms of sexuality, instead of spending the effort to place them in loving and safety-conscious contexts.

The very complexity of the sentence suggested that it touched on a delicate issue. Given the context, England was accusing Littlejohn and the Milk club people of "internalized homophobia." But he had mentioned the same phenomenon to me in a much more general context. When I went to see him in his office, he had just been arranging a funeral service for an AIDS victim at which other AIDS victims would speak. Thinking of Father Paneloux in *The Plague*, I asked what a minister had to say to those living in the shadow of such a catastrophe. His reply followed my thought in that it concerned the Panelouxes of the Christian Right. "The Jerry Falwells of this country," he said, "are trying to tell us that AIDS is God's wrath—that God is punishing us for being homosexuals. As ministers we say that this is not the Christian point of view. God does not punish by disease. Divine love is unconditional, and it will bring good out of evil if we allow it to."

Surprised at the mention of Falwell, I asked him whether any of his parishioners took anything that the Christian Right said seriously.

"There's a lot of internalized homophobia in this community," he said, "and it's very hard to throw off. In the beginning many people believed that AIDS was a punishment. They thought it proved they were bad people or that sex was bad. The immediate reaction was 'I'm never going to have sex again.' But now there's been some turn-around on this. People are active in fund-raising and volunteer activities. But as pastors we still have to deal with the Christian Right. That's our most important task."

England was certainly in a position to understand the psychology of the Castro, and his description of it was wholly plausible. Indeed, some months later, Leon McKusick and three other psychotherapists working with gay men said much the same thing in an interview published in *BAR*. One of the important functions of coming out, after all, was to banish guilt by bringing "the guilty secret" into the plain light of day. The experience, though cathartic, was perhaps not always sufficient to remove every last trace of guilt, and in the face of AIDS, even those not normally in conflict about their sexuality might have this feeling all over again—and see AIDS as a punishment. According to the psychotherapists "AIDS-related stress" could create a crisis in which the individual fell into depression, resorted to defiant acting-out, suffered anxiety, or became paranoiac. In light of England's letter to *BAR*, it occurred to me that this "internalized homophobia" might be the key to the otherwise puzzling response of the community and many of its leaders to the AIDS crisis. England, who understood these feelings (neither he nor the psychotherapists as they were quoted ever used the word "guilt"), had himself tried to deal with them in a variety of ways. One way was to preach the gospel of a loving God who brought good out of evil. Another way was to charge that the message of guilt came from the Christian Right —and not from within. These were his conscious strategies. But he, like many other gay leaders, used other strategies without perhaps knowing it. One was to attribute violent homophobic feelings to the public at large (which would end in "repressive measures and even violence"). Homophobic feelings certainly existed in the public at large, but it was one thing to assess their consequences in a rational manner, as, for example, Berg had, and another to maintain that they would lead to general violence—and concentration camps for gay men. The slippery slope logic began with a projection. Another way was to attribute homophobic feelings to those who brought the bad news about AIDS or who publicly proposed that gay men curb their sexuality. This same form of projection turned the health authorities into punishing fathers. Seen in this light, the gay men who brought the bad news were doubly heroic, for they had first to overcome whatever residue of guilt they themselves felt about their sexuality and then to brave the verbal terrorism leveled at them. It was perhaps no coincidence that those who were able to do so were those who had been closest to the center of gay liberation.

England, when I went to see him, told me that he would be speaking at a panel discussion on the baths the next day in a downtown church. He had not, he said, reached a decision about the regulations, but he would probably defend Silverman's position at the meeting as there would be no one else there to do so. The next day, however, surrounded by opponents of the regulations, he attacked all those who favored government action. "In effect what they're saying is 'We know what's best for you,' " he said. "It's a heavy paternal message, and it caused me to be suspicious right away." This was precisely the reaction Silverman had feared, and coming from someone who had worked with him and trusted him, it boded ill for his move on the bathhouses.

On October 9, just about four months later, Dr. Silverman invoked emergency powers to close the baths and made a statement to the press in which he said that the baths and sex clubs were "fostering disease and death" and "literally playing Russian roulette with the lives of gay men." His move was unexpected. In August, at the request of Harry Britt, a committee of the Board of Supervisors effectively killed legislation transferring the regulating authority over the baths to the health department. Silverman then reconvened his group of AIDS experts to ask them their advice. The group proved divided, but he decided nonetheless to proceed. In September he sent private investigators into thirty establishments (both gay and straight) to report on high-risk sexual activity, and with their report in hand issued an order to close fourteen baths and sex clubs as "public nuisances." The baths closed, but most reopened again after twenty-four hours to test Silverman's order. The mayor, predictably, was furious. Though it was the city attorney who recommended the legal strategy and took the case, she had said that if the choice was hers, she would simply have closed them on her own authority—presumably with a quarantine order. "If I were overturned by a court, so be it," she said. "The important thing is if you save lives, it's worth it, and I'm convinced you will save lives." She added that, "If this were a heterosexual problem, these establishments would have been closed a long time ago. But because this has been involved in politics, they haven't been closed."

On October 15 a Superior Court judge ordered nine baths and sex

clubs closed temporarily pending a hearing on the city's request for
an injunction. (He excepted bookstores and two movie theaters cited
for health violations.) The bath owners prepared to dispute the order,
backed by a number of gay legal groups. The Harvey Milk club, Dr.
Marcus Conant, and Harry Britt came out in favor of Silverman's
initiative, but the other two Democratic clubs, the Republican club,
the Golden Gate Business Association, and the Bay Area Physicians
for Human Rights denounced it. In the community the lines appeared
firmly drawn in the same place they had been drawn in June. But
when a coalition of these groups called a protest rally at Market Street
and Castro on October 29, only three hundred people showed up.
The gay leaders might protest, but the rank and file would not, it
appeared, go to the barricades.

The hearings took place, and on November 29 Judge Roy Wonder
of the Superior Court told the bathhouses they could reopen, but
ordered them to comply with certain regulations, the most important
of which was that they had to hire monitors and expel those of their
patrons who engaged in high-risk sex. Judge Wonder had perhaps
not spent very much time contemplating the working of bathhouses.
In any case, the attorneys for both sides claimed victory. The mayor
was furious that Wonder had allowed the baths to remain open, and
along with the *Chronicle* editorialist, objected that his order would
create a "spying system" repugnant to all. The mayor was perfectly
right, but at the same time it was unthinkable that the baths could
remain open if the order was enforced. The city attorney requested a
clarification of the enforcement procedures, and on December 20,
Judge Wonder gave him the changes of wording he sought. The consequence was that while the bathhouse owners planned an appeal,
all but one of the baths and sex clubs shut down.

What Judge Wonder's order seemed to demonstrate was that had
Silverman simply closed the baths as the mayor had urged, his order
would not have stood up in court. An editorial in the *San Francisco
Examiner* pointed this out and argued that in view of the health emergency the only proper solution was for the Board of Supervisors to
pass an ordinance closing the baths. The supervisors, however, were
disinclined to such a move, and the mayor no more inclined to consider the justice of Silverman's position than she had ever been. The
passage of a proposition she had sponsored on the November ballot
now permitted her to take control of the city health department
through the medium of a new health commission, whose members
she had the right to appoint. In early December she gave Silverman a
clear signal to resign by failing to include him in the planning for the
new commission. Word was put out that the bath issue was not the

only issue between them—earlier in the year, state investigators had found fault with conditions in one of the hospitals under his jurisdiction. But clearly the baths were the main issue, and most of the newspaper articles spoke of her displeasure with his "indecision and foot-dragging" in closing them. On December 11 Dr. Silverman resigned.

By the spring of 1985 there was ample evidence to show that Silverman's initiative on the baths had succeeded in all the ways he had hoped for it. While the bathhouse owners continued to press for an appeal, their case languished in the dockets, and eventually several of them sold off their buildings for very good prices. More important, the gay organizations did not go to the barricades; they did not turn on Silverman or the city government. In November a *BAR* editorialist, Brian Jones, reproached a letter writer for calling people "the enemy" for wanting the baths closed; you might disagree with them, he said, but they are not the enemy. At no time did the protest reach the rhetorical level of the previous June, and as time went on, the issue simply faded away—even from the pages of the gay bar press. That both Superior Court judges involved in the case showed concern for the civil liberties issues involved took the force out of some of the protest. Then when it appeared that no other city would follow San Francisco's lead in closing the baths, most of those uniquely concerned with the consequences dropped their objections. "I opposed government regulations because I worried about the domino effect," one businessman told me. "But now the baths are closed, I'm delighted." Actually, the very day he said that, two bathhouses reopened: their owners were clearly testing the city's enforcement procedures. It made very little difference: the baths had lost their symbolic value. As before, the defenders of the barricades had simply melted away without apology or explanation.

Silverman's main purpose in taking action on the baths had been to move along the whole process of AIDS education. Six months later all the experts in the field I spoke with thought the purpose very well served. "I thought Silverman was wrong," Frank Robinson told me. "I, like the mayor, thought he could simply close the baths and have the order stand up in court. But the way he did it, the baths were closed with a minimum of community objection, and all the right results followed. The fallout was an *extreme* heightening of education. The education program is just about as good as you could get it, and the awareness just about as high as it could be." Leon McKusick of the AIDS Behavioral Research Project thought that the controversy itself had not been helpful but that the months of news coverage that accompanied it had had a significant effect. For two years now McKusick and his colleagues had been doing a study of some four hundred men, sending questionnaires out to them every six months, and the results of his last survey went to show that behavior had changed remarkably. His respondents reported that in November of 1982 they had had an average of six sexual partners in a month; in November 1984, they reported an average of two and a half. In the same period the mean number of unsafe sex acts they reported declined from almost five per month to less than one per month. The decline in both sets of figures had been very gradual in 1983 and very sharp in 1984. In another survey done for the San Francisco AIDS Foundation, 62 percent of the five hundred gay and bisexual men interviewed reported having had no unsafe sex outside a primary relationship in the previous month; nine out of ten reported having altered their high-risk practices in some way because of AIDS.

Though Silverman was now out of office (he remained temporarily as a consultant to the Health Department), his approach to AIDS education had now been taken up by the gay community itself. The San Francisco AIDS Foundation had employed a professional management consultant and engaged the services of a market research firm, the Research & Decisions Corporation. Sam Puckett, the management consultant, told me: "We take a factual, no-nonsense approach that the epidemic is not going away, and we want to solve it ourselves. Here we're not using health educators—there's not a Ph.D. in the place—we're doing market research and advertising. We've just spent a hundred thousand dollars on a market research survey to find out what people know and what they believe. Before, people were working in the dark, and there were so many sensitivities in the community that they were very cautious. But that time is over, and our new ad campaign has been very well received." The leaflets Puckett showed me were very different in tone from those of the year before. There was no coyness anymore. The headline on one of them WAS, THERE IS NO LONGER AN EXCUSE FOR SPREADING AIDS; its message was that the individual bore responsibility not just for his own life but for that of his partner—and for the life of the whole community. Under foundation sponsorship the Research & Decisions Corporation was now moving beyond advertising to start a series of rap groups in which gay men could discuss what AIDS prevention meant in their own lives.

In the space of a year the politics of the Castro had changed even more than the educational programs—though the two were very much related. In the first place, the Milk club people were no longer a besieged minority. In the six months since Silverman had made his move there had been a good deal of internal criticism of "the gay leaders" in the Castro. Randy Shilts had delivered the first broadside in an interview he gave to a gay skin magazine. In the interview, as excerpted in *BAR* in November, he started by attacking both the gay press and the gay leadership for lying to people and telling them only what they wanted to hear. He then called the gay leaders "a bunch of jerks who wrap themselves in silly, dogmatic rhetoric" and went on to say, "Let's not kid ourselves. The local Gay political scene is a looney bin. The community is top-heavy with Chiefs and not an awful lot of Indians. You are not dealing with normal people. These folks are crazy." The reaction to this in *BAR* over the next few weeks was very surprising. The editorial on the subject defended "the gay leaders" solely on the grounds that there had to be leaders in a democracy, and most of the letters praised Shilts for starting a "healthy and much-needed debate." The newspaper did not pursue the subject, but the debate must have gone on elsewhere, for by April a great many people I spoke with were critical, if not contemptuous of "the gay leaders." Jim Foster, the founder of the Toklas club, told me, "The message we've been putting out for years is ghettoization, isolation, and alienation from the larger community. The leaders only know how to lose. They never take responsibility, so it's always someone else's fault." Foster believed that gay politics as such were dead in the climate of the eighties; the solution was now to build philanthropies on the model of Jewish organizations.

Possibly "the gay leaders" represented the community better than Shilts or Foster was ready to admit, for the debate did not lead to personal recriminations, leadership struggles, or new divisions in the Castro. The Castro simply put some distance on politics and on the panicky crowd behavior of the year before. Shouts of "traitor" and "homophobe" were now rarely heard in the streets, and the political craziness surrounding AIDS had all but disappeared. It was not that there were no issues left. Far from it. The newly developed tests for AIDS antibodies in the blood raised civil liberties issues far more serious than the closing of the baths. (Could the test results be kept confidential? If not, should gay men take the tests, as positive results might subject them to discrimination by insurance companies, government agencies, the military, and so on?) But the gay leaders and the gay press generally discussed these issues in a rational manner without discovering "enemies" and building up factions. It was as if a boil had been lanced or a fever had broken. The Castro was at peace.

When I asked Leon McKusick what, as a psychotherapist, he thought had happened to the community, he said, "It's my hypothesis that the community has been going through the stages that individuals are said to go through when faced by a life-threatening disease: denial, rage, bargaining, and acceptance. The community has now accepted AIDS." The leaders had, it seemed, acted out this all-too-human drama and brought its members along with them.

But it was not only political attitudes that had changed, it was attitudes about life in general. There had been signs of this change the previous June—only at that point they had seemed incongruous. Then I had noticed that the gay leaders who most strenuously opposed government action on the baths sometimes talked about the impact of AIDS on the community in a strangely positive way. Gerry Parker, for example, said: "The AIDS crisis has gotten people to come together and look at themselves in the mirror and ask critical questions about their lives. In the seventies this was a very young society, and for the young the dream of the ghetto was a candy store, a romp. In the irresponsible seventies you used to see a lot of refrigerators with drugs in them but no food. Now people are concerned about health; there's a realization that we're all interdependent. It's the 'we' generation, not the 'me' generation anymore. People look for an inner purpose, and there's a lot of interest in Taoism and Buddhism. There was a time when we were cutting the edge of commercialism and fashion—that was a part of our being—but it's no longer true. Now we're into backpacking and wholesome relationships. The lesbian community is far ahead of us in many ways, particularly in its sense of cooperation and interdependence. There's a feminization process going on in the gay community now, and it's very healthy."

Parker had a declamatory style, and while listening to him make this speech, I felt increasingly irritated. In the first place, these sentiments seemed to fit rather badly with his contention that there was no proof of the correlation between multiple sex partners and AIDS. In the second place, much of it was clearly nonsense. Backpacking and Taoism! This was a counterculture fantasy, and one I assumed he was creating in a spirit of boosterism for my benefit. Only later did I begin to think this was not the case. Parker went on to say, "AIDS was a great and profound fear that affected all of us. We know more people who have died of it in the past two years than have died in our lifetimes. I witnessed a number of people going through it, and the encouraging thing is that we found a connection. They were strong people and they had bright outlooks. The political people gave me sage advice on the direction the movement ought to take right up to their last hours."

Parker's description of the AIDS victims rang a bell. The regular San Francisco press had done a number of profiles of AIDS victims, the journalists in every instance choosing admirable young men with wonderful families and fine careers, and generally glossing over the terrible fear and suffering they went through. The gay press usually printed obituaries of the AIDS dead written by their lovers, but in the case of gay activists, the editors themselves would write the obits using much the same language Parker had used: the men had fought and died heroically in the service of their cause. This ennobling of the dead was clearly some form of compensation for the horror or contempt with which the world at large regarded them. Now a similar form of explanation—or mythology—seemed to be growing up around the impact of AIDS on the community as a whole. Right after telling me about the "political craziness" AIDS had engendered, Jerry Berg, for example, said: "My own view is that AIDS is a terrible tragedy, and yet one which offers real opportunities for personal and collective growth. My friends are taking a new look at their relationships, at the meaning of love and intimacy, and they are making choices. It's very positive and exciting. Of course, large numbers will continue to die, but the threat of the disease has given us all a new perspective on life. It's growth-producing, and most people who have had it have grown into grace."

Growth, a new maturity, a new intimacy, a sense of interdependence were phrases I heard again and again in the Castro that year, and often from the very same people engaged in the fratricidal struggle over the baths. Many of my friends satirized this kind of talk. When I asked Larry Glover—now working as a bartender—about the "new intimacy," he said, "It's just like the fifties again: people getting married for all the wrong reasons." Larry did not mean his remark to be taken seriously so much as he meant it to be subversive of the new mythology he saw the community weaving around itself. Larry did not understand people who talked about all the wonderful things that were happening as a result of AIDS.

In the late fall of 1984, however, a McKusick study and the Research & Decisions Corporation survey for the AIDS Foundation came out with some data suggesting that at least some of what Parker and Berg had been saying about community attitudes was, or was becoming, true. The surveys showed that "the new intimacy" had little basis in fact: gay men were not any more involved in "primary relationships" than they had been in the past. About half of them had such relationships and half did not: the figures remained virtually unchanged in two years. According to the Research & Decisions survey, however, respondents in a large majority said they would like to be in a committed relationship—preferably monogamous, and one that would last. Respondents in an equally large majority said they had more concern than formerly about the community as a whole. The studies also indicated that there was a good deal more concern about general health, diet, and exercise in the gay community, and a good deal less drug and alcohol consumption and less interest in impersonal sex. Asked to rate the sentence "Because of AIDS many gay men are changing their lives for the better" on a scale of one to ten, respondents gave it a 7.2 rating, whereas they gave the sentence "AIDS is damaging the gay movement by limiting people's sexual freedom" a rating of only 3.8. Conceivably a number of the respondents told the researchers what they thought they ought to say. All the same, they had created a positive vision for themselves. They had made a decision to focus on the good that might come out of the evil of AIDS. This vision was a consolation, but it was also an antidote to the notion that AIDS was a punishment—a notion that, as Reverend England suggested, lay so deep as to be unavailable to reason. And it helped people act against the threat of AIDS.

By April 1985, the looks of the Castro had changed once again. They had changed so quickly that even its residents pointed it out to me. On a weekday morning or afternoon the people on the main street included numbers of older people and women with children. These people had not just moved into the area; rather, they had taken up doing their shopping and socializing on the main street again. The tourists had vanished, and with them a number of the most expensive gift stores and clothing boutiques. The Castro was a neighborhood once more. The gay bars were still there, and on Saturday mornings the street would fill up with young men. But now the only remarkable thing about these young men was their numbers. Very few—perhaps one or two in a crowd—wore leather or one of the other sexual costumes. Most looked like all other men of their age, and most were clearly doing Saturday errands, having been at work all week. The Castro was still a gay neighborhood, but it had lost its "gender eccentricities." It was a neighborhood much like the other white, middle-class neighborhoods surrounding the downtown.

Sam Puckett, a resident of the Castro, but one slightly older than most of its inhabitants, said something to me which might have been an epitaph for the old Castro: "During the seventies the gay movement here created an almost totalitarian society in the name of promoting sexual freedom. It evolved without any conscious decision, but there was so much peer pressure to conform that it allowed no self-criticism or self-examination. At some point there would have to be less sexual, political, and visual conformity. People grow up and change. But AIDS forced a reexamination in the way that few issues do. What we're seeing now is a revolution. We're seeing a reevaluation of life and relationships and what being gay is all about. We haven't got the answers yet, but at least the questions have been posed."

Puckett's observation about the breakdown of conformity seemed to me to be true on many levels. A sign of the times was a theater piece put on by the major gay theater group in the city, Theatre Rhinoceros. The piece was a series of sketches about the ways that AIDS had entered people's lives, and many of them broke the mold: they are dramatic rather than melodramatic and they explored the nuances of real feeling rather than the sentimental cliché. My friend Peter Adair, who was filming the production for a documentary, told me that the producers had held open casting calls in "the community" and that most of the people involved—actors, writers, and so on— had some experience with the disease. On Peter's film the cast members and others talked about the way AIDS had affected their lives: one man had an AIDS-related condition, and several had lovers or friends die of it; one of the directors was a Shanti volunteer and one actor—a young comedian—was a nurse in the AIDS ward of a hospital. By some extraordinary coincidence the director and the actor-nurse had taken care of the same patient. They remembered him well, for the man had been full of bitterness, rage, and aggressive self-pity. Indeed, he seemed, they said, to have only ugliness inside of him. Profoundly shocked by the patient, the young nurse had gone to the hospital therapist to find out how to cope with the man but also how to deal with his own emotions. The company was now building a sketch around the incident in which the young actor would play himself. "I learned something from it," the actor said gaily on camera. "I learned that just because someone's dying doesn't mean he can't also be an asshole."

Going around to see my friends, I found that many of them were working in one way or another on AIDS. Randy Shilts, of course, had been writing about it for years in the *Chronicle* and now he was writing a book. But Peter Adair had been making a film on nuclear weapons protesters, and Ken Maley's work had for a long time centered on earthquake prevention measures. Now both of them had come back to the disaster closest to them: the real thing as opposed to its substitutes. Adair had made a public-service film for those thinking of taking the AIDS test, and was now involved with the Theatre Rhinoceros production. Maley was, among other things, working on AIDS awareness programs with Jim Rivaldo. Armistead Maupin had returned from England and was traveling around the country talking to gay groups; he would entertain them, but he would also urge people not to deny their homosexuality or to deny the threat of AIDS. Adair told me that gay men in San Francisco probably spent 60 percent of their time thinking about AIDS: after all, about that percentage of them probably had the virus by now. But my friends did not seem obsessed by the subject—and perhaps it helped that they were dealing with it professionally. In any case, life went on.

As Peter, Ken, and Armistead had come back to look the monster in the face, so they, along with many other gay men, had come back in other ways as well. For the past two or three years many people had in one way or another withdrawn from the community: some had actually picked up and left the Castro, or left the city. For some time it had seemed to me possible that "the community" would break up, and that gay institutions—other than those concerned with AIDS— would simply dissolve. But now it seemed that many people had come back—as they told the researchers they would—and the hive was humming again. Armistead, for one, had resumed his duties as Gay Personality and had recently officiated at the ceremony welcoming back to San Francisco the two gay hostages from the June, 1985 TWA hijacking to Beirut. The two hostages, openly gay, had lived in fear that their captors would recognize them as such, for under radical Shi'ite law homosexuality was a crime punishable by death. Their captors, however, had never suspected anything of the sort, for the two men had been dressed in Castro Street gear—olive drab fatigue trousers and tank-top shirts—and the militiamen had taken them for macho toughs. "It was an only-in-San Francisco story," Armistead said. "You couldn't have made it up."

Armistead was, as usual, full of stories, many of them unprintable, about the new gay social institutions and the ingenious ways people had found to have safe but nonetheless impersonal sex. "It's the tribal rites," he said. "People get nostalgic for them." I asked him about the story of the man who bit a policeman. The newspapers had it that a San Francisco policeman had been bitten three times by a man who was resisting arrest; the man had later told the police that he had AIDS. The district attorney then considered changing the charge from assault to felonious assault with a deadly weapon. "Ah, yes," Armistead said, "I heard that, and I was already to get on my high horse and go out and protest police behavior when it came out that the policeman was openly gay. He had gotten his job on the force only after an antidiscrimination suit. No one knows whether the man who bit him was gay or not, and he's refusing to take the AIDS test."

Armistead seemed to me very much back in form. His *Tales of the City* books were selling very well in the bookstores, and now a major production company wanted them for a television series. "They seem serious this time," Armistead said. "But it's a little late. San Francisco isn't at all the place that it was in the mid-seventies—full of odd and unconventional people. Now everyone's so madly dressed for success. But at least they can handle the gay character. After all, every soap opera on television has a gay character in it now. So perhaps we did make some kind of a dent. That's why I go around to places like Texas and Indiana telling people they shouldn't cut themselves off from their heterosexual friends. I tell them it's fun to be an exotic bird."

An era was over, and yet the Castro seemed much as it had been in the very old days when Ken and Armistead and Steve and Daniel had thought of it as their stamping grounds and a small fraternity. The crowds had gone, political enthusiasms had abated, and personal relations—friendships—had come again to the fore. It was now the pattern in the Castro for men, whether they were living with somone or not, to have a number of very close friends with whom they spent the holidays, in whom they could confide, and who would take care of them if necessary. This was the family the Castro had developed, and it was—Armistead's stories notwithstanding—stable and domesticated. But then the people of the Castro had grown up together, and they had a great deal more in common now than the fact of being gay. Indeed, the people they had very little in common with were gay men in their twenties—for whom Harvey Milk was a myth and the clone style as antiquated as high-button shoes. There was only ten years' difference between them, but when men of the Castro generation talked about the younger men, grumbling that they took "gay" for granted and were not pulling their weight, they sounded like codgers talking about the decline of the work ethic. Steve Beery, Armistead's friend, who himself did not look much more than thirty, told me his revelation about the generation gap. Steve still lived on the Filbert Steps opposite Ken and Daniel. One day, when he was at home sick, he looked out on the steps and espied a beautiful young man taking a lunch break with his shirt off in the sun. The young man looked with great interest at Steve, so the next day when he came back at lunch hour and looked in Steve's direction again, Steve invited him up to the apartment. "I was thinking . . . well, you can imagine what I was thinking," Steve said. "But the guy just kept sitting there in the chair talking about one thing and another. As he was leaving, he asked me for a date. A date! I was shocked. He was, I gathered, looking for commitment. He was looking for a lifelong partnership."

Liberty Baptist–
1981

ON October 3, 1980, just a month before his victory in the presidential election, Ronald Reagan stopped in Lynchburg, Virginia, to address a convention of the National Religious Broadcasters, whose host was the Reverend Jerry Falwell, pastor of the Thomas Road Baptist Church in Lynchburg and the president of the Moral Majority. On arriving at the airport, Reagan said, in answer to a question, that he was "quite sure" God heard the prayers of Jews. At the convention, he told an audience of pastors, students, and Lynchburg citizens that he believed in the separation of church and state. He also said that he supported voluntary, nonsectarian prayer in the public schools. "I don't think we should have ever expelled

God from the classroom," he told the cheering audience. Reagan's statements received national news coverage, for there was then some uncertainty about his theological views. In mid-August, at a convention of evangelical pastors in Dallas, he had confessed to having grave doubts about the theory of evolution, and asserted that the Bible contained the answers to all of the world's problems. At that time, he had condemned the use of the separation of church and state as a means of keeping religious values out of government.

About a hundred members of the national press corps had arrived in Lynchburg two days before Reagan's visit, in order to attend the whole of the religious broadcasters' convention. They had hoped to be able to interview a number of the star television evangelists, but they were disappointed, for few of the stars showed up. Pat Robertson and Jim Bakker did not come, although they lived only a few counties away. Even Jerry Falwell was not much in evidence, because he had a son in the hospital and there was a concurrent meeting of the state chairmen of the Moral Majority to attend. Falwell did, however, hold a press conference, at which he denounced abortion, homosexuality, and pornography and called for increased American support to Israel and a stronger national defense. There was nothing much new in it: Falwell's purpose was to assure the press that the Moral Majority was not a sinister organization with a "medieval mentality," as some had alleged. The members of the press went away from the convention with the view that Reagan had moderated his theological position and Falwell had moderated his approach to politics.

About a year before, the press had begun to report on a campaign, already under way, to mold conservative Christians into a political voting bloc. The leaders of the campaign—a number of political organizers for conservative causes and a number of television evangelists—claimed a constituency of fifty million Protestant evangelicals and thirty million "morally conservative" Catholics, as well as a few million Mormons and Orthodox Jews. The political organizers did not, in spite of their public statements, really expect to enlist this whole constituency or to create a Christian political party. What they expected was that a campaign focused on such concerns as abortion, homosexuality, and the proposed Equal Rights Amendment might swing sufficient members of Catholics and Protestant evangelicals to change the normal voting patterns and the election results. And by October of 1980 their expectation seemed a reasonable one. The new organizations—the Moral Majority, the Christian Voice—had grown apace; pastors, working at a local level through the churches, had registered impressive numbers of new voters and had raised money and volunteers for conservative, and against liberal, candidates in a number of states. In Alaska, for example, Moral Majority members had packed the Republican caucuses, and so, at the state convention, Ronald Reagan won all nineteen of Alaska's delegates to the National Convention; they had also campaigned successfully to secure the Republican senatorial nomination for the conservative Frank Murkowski. The Moral Majority had had similar victories in Alabama and Iowa. In many other states, the organizations of evangelicals, in combination with Right to Life groups and conservative political action committees, had defeated liberals and nominated those on the right wing of their party in the Republican primaries. In many states, the relative influence of these various groups was difficult to measure, because the secular and the religious organizations tended to support the same candidates and espouse the same goals. The main issues continued to be abortion and "the family," but the secular conservative groups also spoke out for prayer in the schools, and the pastors increasingly spoke out on the defense and foreign-policy issues of the Right, such as the SALT II and Panama Canal treaties.

By October, the question was whether this conservative alliance might actually come to dominate the Republican party. The Republican platform embodied the views of the alliance on a number of issues, including abortion, school prayer, gun control, and the need for military superiority; the party also dropped its past commitment to the ERA. Though the organizers had initially favored John Connally to win the presidential nomination, Reagan had proved sympathetic to many of their causes. True, he had rejected their candidate for the vice presidency, Senator Jesse Helms, and had chosen a running mate whom they had specifically opposed. But he had selected Robert Billings, the former executive director of the Moral Majority, as his liaison with the religious groups. And after the convention he had taken a number of positions espoused almost exclusively by the pastors and other members of the alliance—such as the desirability of America's reestablishing an official relationship with Taiwan. His appearance at the convention of religious broadcasters in Lynchburg seemed to testify to his accord with the pastors—and to the influence of Jerry Falwell.

Few journalists who visited Lynchburg for the convention had ever heard of Falwell until a few months before. That in itself was a curious fact, for by the summer of 1980 Falwell was well known to millions of Americans through the very media that many of the journalists themselves used: radio and television. On Sunday mornings, his religious television program, "The Old-Time Gospel Hour," was broadcast on network affiliates and other VHF stations across the country; it was, according to Falwell, more widely distributed than the Johnny Carson show. Falwell was not the most popular evangelist on television, but he was one of a handful who in the seventies had developed a nation-wide audience and had been bringing in over $30 million a year in contributions from that audience. As such, he was a part of a phe-nomenon.

In the fifties and early sixties, most religious broadcasters on televi-sion were mainline clergymen—Catholics, Jews, and Protestants—who received free public-service airtime. Billy Graham, Oral Roberts, and Rex Humbard had been on television since the fifties, but by the seventies a host of newcomers had taken over—men in their thirties and forties who created their own organizations to buy time on the air and acquired their own systems of distribution via satellite and cable networks. Some of them were charismatics who preached the power of the Holy Spirit to heal and work miracles; others were con-servative evangelicals or fundamentalists, but virtually all of them (the main exception being Robert Schuller) were on the far right politically. Along with the older evangelists, Pat Robertson, Jim Bakker, James Robison, Jerry Falwell, and others bought up most of the public-ser-vice time on Sunday-morning TV, pushing much of the mainline reli-gious programming off the air and making television evangelism a big business for the first time. In the seventies, the annual expenditure of TV ministries for airtime went from around $50 million to $600 million; by the end of the decade, there were thirty religiously oriented TV stations, more than a thousand religious radio stations, and four reli-gious networks—all of them supported by audience contributions.

The sudden and dramatic success of the so-called electric church resulted in part from changes within the media themselves. Televi-sion had begun as a highly centralized medium: the local stations were controlled by the networks, and the networks by Federal Com-munications Commission regulations. Because the FCC demanded it, all stations had to allocate a certain amount of public-service time for religious programming. Because of network policy, many of the affil-iates could not accept paid religious broadcasting. By the seventies, this situation had changed. The networks no longer dominated their affiliates, and the FCC had ruled that it would consider paid religious broadcasts as satisfying the public-service requirement; therefore, one affiliate after another had begun to sell off its Sunday-morning hours. Since there was—initially—little competition for the "religious ghetto" hours on Sunday morning, the evangelists could buy this time cheaply. The new technology of television—cable systems, com-munications satellites, and UHF stations—made airtime even more available. And it made it even cheaper, too, since many cable stations would pick up the religious broadcasts free to fill their programming schedules. Thus, even in fiscal 1979 it cost Falwell only $9 million a year to broadcast his daily radio and weekly television programs all over the country. In addition, new computer technology (or the new availability of it) permitted independent evangelists to establish sophisticated "feedback loops" through telephone banks and direct-mail services with "personalized" letters and solicitations. These feedback loops were, in a sense, the key to the evangelists' operations, for it took relatively few people giving ten or twenty dollars a month to keep the programs on the air.

The mainline clergy—who worried a great deal about this use of television—insisted upon the minority status of these evangelists, and pointed to ratings showing that Oral Roberts reached only 2 percent of American households each week and that most of them, including Robertson, Bakker, and Falwell, reached less than 1 percent. (National television ratings, however, do not take into account the cable channels, so these figures are in fact significantly higher.) The mainline clergy also pointed out that the audiences for these programs consisted mainly of women over forty-five in relatively low income brackets. They said that while many of the programs of major churches had far larger ratings, this meant nothing to the television stations, since the major churches could not pay for the airtime (and would not solicit contributions). The local stations, by selling off their Sunday-morning airtime, had permitted those evangelists with no scruples about commercializing religion to drive much of the other clergy—Protestant, Catholic, and Jewish—off the air. In 1980, 90 percent of all religion on television was commercial, and almost all of that was controlled by conservative evangelicals. In the view of the mainstream clergy, this represented a distortion of the medium and a great injustice to the majority of Americans.

All the same, the mainstream clergy had to admit that the television evangelists had come along at a time of change in the religious life of the country. During the seventies, they had watched a decline in the membership of liberal churches and a rather dramatic rise in the membership of conservative churches.

In 1976, the year of Jimmy Carter's election, the Gallup organization had found that there were fifty million "born-again Christians" in the country. Probably less than ten million of them were fundamentalists, and a great many of the rest were not politically conservative. (The black churches generally were not, and the largest evangelical body, the Southern Baptist Convention, was split between liberals and conservatives.) Still, just as the political mood of the country was shifting toward the right, so the religious trend was away from liberalism and toward churches preaching social conservatism and moral certainties. The liberal clergy feared that the capture of the media by conservative evangelists had increased this trend, and that in the end the evangelists might succeed in changing the structure of religious life in the country.

Theologically speaking, it was easy to see why conservative evangelists should be attracted to television as a medium: for those who believe that salvation can be achieved by a sudden leap to faith, television served as the equivalent of a vast revival tent, offering immediate mass escape from eternal damnation. But why a mass audience should be attracted to the theology of these evangelists was, in the abstract, less understandable. Both fundamentalism and Pentecostalism, after all, went against much of what has long been assumed to be the American grain: faith in science, faith in the power of human reason, and faith that man can improve the conditions of life on earth. At the core of fundamentalist theology was the doctrine of Biblical inerrancy—the doctrine that held every word in the Bible to be the word of God and literally, historically, true. Thus, Creation occurred in exactly six days some ten thousand years ago. Fundamentalists such as Falwell also believed that the world would end fairly soon with the coming of the Antichrist, and a terrible period of tribulations, followed by the Battle of Armageddon and the return of Christ to earth. Only the Saved would escape these tribulations by joining Christ in the air—the doctrine of premillennialism, or, more precisely, premillennial dispensationalism. Pentecostalists, such as Bakker and Robertson, were a little less specific about this sequence of events, since they believed that God sometimes delivered new prophecies to mankind—some of them in our day, and some of them through the medium of television. All the same, they, like the true fundamentalists, saw the world as one of sin and suffering, and one that even Christians could do very little to improve given the frailty of human nature. In their theology the one important task for a Christian was to bring as many people to Christ as possible.

This dour message was not, however, much in evidence on the television airwaves—and certainly not in the programming of the big-time evangelists. Anyone who turned on the tube of a Sunday morning would see a lot of well-washed, smiling faces and hear the only two pieces of good news in fundamentalist theology: the certainty of salvation for the believer, and the willingness of God to intervene directly in the believer's life. On the "700 Club," sleek, good-looking Pat Robertson would interview a celebrity guest, such as Charles Colson, of Watergate fame, then, minutes later, fall to his knees, lift his hands to heaven, and say, "There's a woman in Philadelphia who has cancer—cancer of the lymph nodes. It hasn't been diagnosed yet, but God has just cured her of it!" On the James Robison show, Robison, who looked like a combination of James Dean and Burt Lancaster, would thunder on about sexual perversion and "secular humanism," then introduce a lovely woman singer—or perhaps the lovely Mr. and Mrs. Cullen Davis, newly brought to Christ. The Oral Roberts show had grand vistas and large multitudes. Standing tall against the skyline of his new hospital and university complex, in Tulsa, Roberts directed banked choirs in inspirational singing or called students out of the huge auditorium to pray over the mountains of mail he received. The message that came through clearest from all these shows was that God pays particular attention to the health and financial prosperity of those who send in contributions to religious TV shows.

Since the days of Billy Sunday, conservative evangelists have preached reverence for the flag, for the armed forces, for the American family, and for the American way of life. Television evangelists thus quite naturally addressed political and social issues. But that they launched themselves into electoral politics was surprising even to their audiences. Of course, not all of them joined the fray. Oral Roberts, a paternal and politically moderate figure, kept out of it altogether—as did Billy Graham and Rex Humbard. It was the younger men who stepped forward: Pat Robertson, the host of a talk show and the director of a religious network in Virginia Beach, Virginia; Jim Bakker, a former protégé of Robertson's, who has duplicated Robertson's success with his own talk show and his own religious network, in North Carolina; James Robison, in Fort Worth; and Jerry Falwell, in Lynchburg. Initially, it was Pat Robertson who showed the greatest enthusiasm for politics. In the fall of 1979, he brought politicians onto his talk show, endorsed candidates all over the map, and told the press, "We have enough votes to run the country." Jim Bakker was not far behind. In November of 1979, he told a reporter, "Our goal is to influence all viable [presidential] candidates on issues important to the church. We want answers. We want appointments in government." In the late spring of 1980, however, both Robertson and Bakker retreated from the political arena, having apparently decided that the risks of political involvement were too great. (Hence, perhaps, their decision not to attend the broadcasters' convention where Reagan would speak.) In the end, only two of the superstars—Robison and Falwell—remained in the fight. Interestingly, unlike Bakker and Robertson, they were not charismatics: Robison was a Southern Baptist, and Falwell the pastor of an independent Baptist church. Falwell was the senior of the two, with the larger television audience, and, as head of the Moral Majority, he took a more active role than Robison.

By the end of the campaign he had become the leading spokesman for the religious Right, and, as far as the press was concerned, the head of the whole movement. "We are fighting a holy war," Falwell had said, "and this time we are going to win."

By comparison with the other evangelists (who were his competitors in what became a fierce and expensive competition for Sunday-morning airtime), Falwell was the most sober and conventional of preachers. His program, "The Old-Time Gospel Hour," was simply a videotape recording of the eleven o'clock service in the Thomas Road Baptist Church. (The tape was edited, and extra footage was occasionally added.) The choir behind him sang traditional Baptist hymns, and he, strong-jawed and portly of figure, wearing a thick three-piece black suit, looked every inch the Baptist preacher of the pretelevision era. True, there was a good deal of showmanship in his services. The female members of one of his singing groups, the Sounds of Liberty, wore Charlie's Angels hairdos and seemed to snuggle up against their virile-looking male counterparts. Don Norman, one of the resident soloists and a pastor of the church, had a distinctly television-era pouf to his silver-gray hair. Another resident soloist, a cherub-faced young man called Robbie Hiner, provided comic relief by joking with Falwell and by wearing, on occasion, a bright-green suit, which contrasted strikingly with the baby-blue carpeting of the church. The "inspirational" singing involved a good deal of heavy breathing and a good many references to heavenly riches. Falwell did not, however, actually say that financial rewards would accrue to those who sent him money. And, unlike many of the evangelists, he quite often mentioned the problems of leading a Christian life in a sinful world.

In a sense, it was not surprising that Falwell decided to go into politics. No otherworldly type of Baptist, he was most characteristically an organizer and a promoter. In 1956, he founded the Thomas Road Baptist Church with thirty-five people in an old factory building. Twenty-five years later, he had by far the biggest church in Lynchburg. It held four thousand people and was jammed for every service on Sundays. He had a school, Lynchburg Christian Academy, from kindergarten through the twelfth grade, for the children of his parishioners; he had a home for alcoholics, a summer camp for children, a Bible institute and correspondence course, a seminary, and Liberty Baptist College, which was accredited and for which he was engaged in building a campus. He had a few wealthy backers, but most of his funds came from small contributors in Lynchburg and around the country. Businessmen in Lynchburg said he was a born leader and the best salesman they had ever seen.

But theologically Falwell had called himself "a separatist, premillennialist, pretribulationist sort of fellow." He believed, as he said, that "this is the terminal generation before Jesus comes," and in 1965 he very eloquently argued the fundamentalist doctrine of separation from the world in a sermon called "Ministers and Marchers":

> As far as the relationship of the church to the world, it can be expressed as simply as the three words which Paul gave to Timothy—"Preach the Word." We have a message of redeeming grace through a crucified and risen Lord. This message is designed to go right to the heart of man and there meet his deep spiritual need. Nowhere are we commissioned to reform the externals. We are not told to wage wars against bootleggers, liquor stores, gamblers, murderers, prostitutes, racketeers, prejudiced persons or institutions, or any other existing evil as such. Our ministry is not reformation but transformation. The gospel does not clean up the outside but rather regenerates the inside. . . .
>
> While we are told to "render unto Caesar the things that are Caesar's," in the true interpretation, we have very few ties on this earth. We pay our taxes, cast our votes as a responsibility of citizenship, obey the laws of the land, and other things demanded of us by the society in which we live. But, at the same time, we are cognizant that our only purpose on this earth is to know Christ and to make Him known. Believing the Bible as I do, I would find it impossible to stop preaching the pure saving gospel of Jesus Christ, and begin doing anything else—including fighting Communism, or participating in civil-rights reforms.

At his press conference at the broadcasters' convention in 1980, Falwell repudiated this sermon as "false prophecy." He had moved 180 degrees from his former position by vowing to undertake civil disobedience if Congress voted to draft women into the armed forces.

Why Falwell changed his mind is an interesting question, and, in view of the fact that great numbers of fundamentalist pastors and lay people around the country went through the same transformation in the seventies, it is also an important one. In the sixties, fundamentalists had been one of the least politicized groups in the country; as Falwell discovered, very few of them were even registered to vote. Whether or not their numbers were on the increase, by the mid-seventies they had begun to make their voices heard. In 1974, for instance, fundamentalist pastors and parents in Kanawha County, West Virginia, had closed the schools down in protest against the introduction of schoolbooks that they said were un-Christian, unpa-

triotic, and destructive of the family and constituted an incitement to
racial violence. A committee of the National Education Association
investigated what became a prolonged series of demonstrations and
concluded that the trouble resulted in part from the cultural gap between the school board and the isolated mountain communities it
served. The Kanawha County incident itself, however, turned out to
be far from isolated. In the mid-seventies, groups of "concerned citizens" in many parts of the country, including the Northeast and the
Midwest, attempted to purge their schools of similar books, protested
against sex education, lobbied for the teaching of "scientific creationism" in biology courses, and called for the return of the old pedagogy
of rote work. In hundreds of other communities—principally but not
exclusively in the South—parents pulled their children out of the
public schools and helped their pastors to build "Christian acade-
mies." According to Falwell, there were fourteen hundred "Christian" schools in the early sixties and sixteen thousand in October of
1980, with new ones going into construction at the rate of one every
seven hours. The same period saw the growth of statewide, then
nationwide, campaigns against abortion, gay rights, and the ERA.
Supported by fundamentalist pastors—such as Falwell—these campaigns had considerable success in state referenda and in state legislatures. Fundamentalists were not the only constituency for these
movements (Anita Bryant is a fundamentalist, while Phyllis Schlafly
is a Catholic), but they were an important one, and their pastors had
influence with other conservative evangelicals. By 1978, a Washington-based group of political organizers on the right—a group that
included Richard Viguerie, the direct-mail specialist; Howard Phillips,
the director of the Conservative Caucus; Terry Dolan, of the National
Conservative Political Action Committee; and Paul Weyrich, of the
Heritage Foundation and the Committee for the Survival of a Free
Congress—had identified the fundamentalist pastors as a strategic
element in the building of a new coalition, which they called the New
Right.

There was something extraordinary about all this. At the time of
the Scopes trial, in 1925, most educated people had considered fundamentalism outmoded and irrelevant—a mere reaction to the advances in science and to modernity in general. Since then, American
historians have tended to neglect the fundamentalist constituency or
to see it as vestigial—the last cry of the still backwaters of the South
against the modern world. But now fundamentalism was the religion
of television and a part of the evangelical revival of the seventies and
the eighties. The oldest Right in America had become the New Right
of 1980. Instead of being typified by a businessman on the golf links,

the Republican party leadership was now looking more and more like William Jennings Bryan in a double knit and television makeup. Pastors who once counseled withdrawal from the world of sin—and specifically the evils of politics—now bargained with politicians in the back rooms of Congress and gave sermons on defense policy.

Falwell's own explanation for these things had, as one might imagine, to do with the increasingly parlous state of the nation and the sense of crisis he and other Americans began to feel in the midseventies. That crisis, he said, now extended across the board, from the 40 percent divorce rate to the growth of the pornography industry to the feminist movement, the widespread use of drugs, social-worker intervention in the family, sex education, abortion on demand, the "abandonment" of Taiwan and the "loss" of the Panama Canal, Internal Revenue Service interference with "Christian" schools, rampant homosexuality, the notion of children's rights, and the spread of "secular humanism." In his view, all these things had corrupted the moral fiber of the country and destroyed its will to resist Communism. In his view, the country was in far worse shape than it was thirty, or even ten, years ago. In his view, moral Americans—Catholics, Protestants, Mormons, and Jews—finally woke up to this fact and realized that they must do something about it.

Public opinion polls and electoral statistics would, of course, suggest that many Americans had turned against some of the liberal reforms of the sixties and that they were worried about the divorce rate, crime in the streets, and other disorders. They would also suggest that many Americans thought the antiwar demonstrations and the "loss" of the Vietnam War weakened the country's military strength and its will to fight Communism. These sentiments might (and in fact did) lead to the election of conservative candidates. But they were not necessarily sufficient reasons for people to flock to fundamentalist churches—or to convince fundamentalist pastors to change their position 180 degrees from "separation" to a holy war. Falwell was leading a radical movement. (One of the questionnaires he sent out to his supporters asked, "Do you approve of the American flags being burned in liberal and radical anti-American demonstrations?" and "Do you approve of the ratification of the ERA, which could well lead to homosexual marriages, unisexual bathrooms, and, of course, the mandatory drafting of women for military combat?") Could the genesis of it be located uniquely in the list of issues—or abominations—he drew up? That, certainly, was Falwell's explanation, and perhaps it was the correct one. But the explanation seemed singularly farfetched in the context of Lynchburg, Virginia, for a more stable, tranquil, and family-oriented city it would be hard to find. Yet

Lynchburg was the city where Falwell grew up and where he founded his first congregation.

Lynchburg lies on the James River, in a country of small farms and wooded, rolling hills at the foot of the Blue Ridge Mountains. A hundred and sixty miles southwest of Washington, it is beyond the gentleman-farming, horse-breeding country and more than halfway to Appalachia. It's a small city—only sixty-seven thousand people— far from any major urban center. All the same, it is enterprising and not wholly provincial. Several large American corporations have plants in Lynchburg, and its nearly two hundred small factories turn out a great variety of goods, including paper products, medical supplies, children's clothing, and shoes. Because of the diversity of its manufactures, business journals sometimes use it for a Middletown or a model of the national economy as a whole. It is an old manufacturing city—one of the oldest in the South, according to its chamber of commerce—but it does not look it, for there are few belching smokestacks. The visita from the top of its one twenty-story building is mainly of trees and a bend in the river. It does not rival Charlottesville—sixty miles to the north—as a cultural center, yet it is perhaps the best known in the South for two women's colleges, Randolph-Macon and Sweet Briar.

Lynchburg was founded—fairly recently, for Virginia—in the late eighteenth century, by John Lynch, an Irish-American tobacco farmer. During the Revolutionary War, John's brother Colonel Charles Lynch set up an informal military court on his property and sentenced Tories to hanging by their thumbs—thus the origin of the word "lynching." Lynchburg began as a tobacco-trading center and an agricultural market town. In the nineteenth century, new settlers —many of them Scotch-Irish Methodists, and Presbyterians—moved in to build grain mills, an iron foundry, and small manufacturing enterprises. During the Civil War, it served as a staging area and hospital center for the Confederate Army of northern Virginia. After the war, its small tobacco farms grew less profitable, but its manufacturers prospered. When the industrial revolution came along, the Lynchburg merchants had the capital to build new foundries, cotton mills, and textile mills and a shoe factory. They used white labor almost exclusively, the blacks remained on small, poor farms in the countryside.

In 1950, Lynchburg was still a mill town, most of its factories old-fashioned and its society hidebound, stratified, and segregated. But in the mid-fifties the town underwent the kind of transformation that was taking place in communities all across the South. A number of major national corporations began to arrive in town, attracted by low property taxes, nonunion labor, and relatively low pay scales. Among them were Babcock & Wilcox, the manufacturer of nuclear reactors; General Electric, which built a radio-assembly plant; and Meredith/ Burda, a printing enterprise. The national corporations stimulated local industry and attracted other large manufacturers from the North and from West Germany. Lynchburg businessmen now point with pride to the healthy diversity of the economy and to high levels of employment, even in recession times. In fact, the unemployment rate is usually lower than the national average; still, the median family income in Lynchburg is below that of Virginia as a whole. But the town has changed in other ways since 1950, for the big industries brought new money into town and new faces into the boardrooms and the country clubs. The colleges flourished. And in the mid-sixties, when the black ministers and their congregations conducted a series of sit-ins and demonstrations, they found that the white community was not immovable. Under pressure, the companies hired black workers, and the city's segregation ordinances were stricken from the books.

Lynchburg calls itself a city, but it is really a collection of suburbs, its population spread out over fifty square miles. In the fifties, its old downtown was supplanted by a series of shopping plazas, leaving it with no real center. There's a good deal of variety to its neighborhoods. Along the James River, in a section called Rivermont, stately nineteenth-century mansions look out over wooded parks and lawns. Behind them are streets of white-shingled Victorian houses and, behind *them*, tracts of comfortable post–World War II developer-built Capes and Colonials. At the edges of town, the developers are still at work, and streets with such names as Crestview and Forest Park run through sections of half-acre lots before dead-ending in the woods. There are poor neighborhoods in Lynchburg—neighborhoods where cocks crow in the backyards of trembling wooden houses—and a part of the old downtown is a depressed area of abandoned factories and boarded-up shops. But there are no real slums. The city has used federal funds to build low-cost housing, and it is now having some success in revitalizing the old downtown.

Lynchburg is not a graceful city. The automobile has cut too many swaths across it, leaving gasoline stations and fast-food places to spring up in parking-lot wastelands. But it is a clean city, full of quiet streets and shade trees. Even the factories are clean; the new ones are windowless buildings with landscaped lawns. It's a safe city and a comfortable place to live. There's not much crime or juvenile delinquency. The medical services are good. The public schools are handsome, well equipped, and good enough to send 63 percent of their students on to college. They are also racially integrated and free of racial tension. As for the things Falwell spends so much time denouncing—pornography, drugs, "the homosexual life-style"—Lynchburg harbors these things quietly if it harbors them at all. You can find *Playboy* in a few magazine racks, but the movie theaters rarely play even an R-rated film. There are a number of bar-restaurants and discos. But the hottest band in town is probably the combo that plays nightly in the lounge of the Sheraton Inn. At night, young people can go to the skating rink or to night games of the New York Mets farm team, held at the Lynchburg Municipal Stadium. If there is a single public nuisance for the young in this town, it is surely boredom.

Lynchburg is a city of churches—it has over a hundred of them—and the first question people ask of new acquaintances is not what they do but what church they attend. At church time on Sunday, the streets are empty and quiet, with almost all the cars in town parked near the churches. Dominated by its churches and by its business community, it is a conservative place in most respects. Traditionally a Byrd Democrat town, it has turned Republican in recent years, voting for Gerald Ford·in 1976—while remaining faithful to Harry Byrd. Still, it has its liberal element. The population is 25 percent black, and the civil rights movement left a well-organized black community. And, besides Liberty Baptist College, Randolph-Macon, and Sweet Briar, it has another liberal-arts college: Lynchburg College, which is coeducational. These colleges do not generate much intellectual ferment or political radicalism, but they and their graduates do provide the city with other voices and a useful degree of political flexibility. The seven-member city council includes at least four moderate liberals, among them a woman and a black man. These liberals now belong. They participate in the humane and amicable consensus that runs the city. When they speak to outsiders, it is in the complacent tone of the chamber of commerce.

Falwell's church, on Thomas Road, is a block or two away from Lynchburg College, in one of the older middle-class sections. From the outside, it is not much to look at: a large, octagonal brick building fronting the street, with a three-story brick school behind it. The parking lot beside it is, however, supermarket-size, and on Sunday the cars jam up the street for blocks trying to fit into it beside the school buses. In summer, many of the cars come from out of state, for families from all over the country like to visit the church they watch on television. In winter, the cars and school buses bring Liberty Baptist

College students and visitors from small rural churches in the area as well as the regular church members.

Winter and summer the congregation consists mainly of couples with two or three children, but there are a number of young adults and a number of elderly people. There is something distinctive about its looks, but at first glance that something is difficult to pin down. The men wear double-knit suits and sport gold wedding bands or heavy brass rings stamped with mottoes; the women, their hair neatly coiffed and lacquered, wear demure print dresses and single-diamond engagement rings. The young women and the high-school girls are far more fashionable. Their flowered print dresses fall to midcalf but are cut low on the bodice and worn with ankle-strap high heels. They wear their hair long, loose, and—almost uniformly—flipped and curled in Charlie's Angels style. Like the boys with their white shirts, narrow-fitted pants, and close-cropped hair, they look fresh-faced and extraordinarily clean. The members of the congregation look, in other words, much like Robbie Hiner, Don Norman, and the other singers who appear on "The Old-Time Gospel Hour." There are proportionately about the same number of blacks in the congregation as there are in the choir—which is to say, very few. (The television cameras tend to pan in on the two black choir members, thus making them more conspicuous to the television audience than they are to the congregation in the church.) What is startling about the congregation—and this is its distinctiveness—is the amount of effort people have put into creating this uniform appearance.

As it turns out, a number of the Thomas Road Church members live in the new, developer-built houses on the edges of town: comfortable suburban-style houses set on half-acre lawns, with central air-conditioning and kitchens like the ones that appear in detergent advertisements on television—and just as clean. To these houses, the Thomas Road families have added shag rugs and wallpaper or chintz curtains. A woman I visited, Nancy James, had just bought a living-room suite, and another, Jackie Gould, had ordered a new set of kitchen cabinets and had them installed without—she said, giggling—consulting her husband. One family had not only a living room but a family room, with a Naugahyde pouf, a twenty-four-inch television set, and a sliding glass door looking out over a stone-paved terrace. On a Sunday evening while I was there, this couple gave a potluck supper for twenty neighbors and fellow church members. The man of the house—resplendent in a fitted white shirt, cream-colored trousers, and white shoes—watched a boxing match on television with the other men while his wife organized the dishes of ham, baked beans, candied squash, and potato salad the other women had brought with them. At dinner, around a lace-covered table, the guests joked, and made small talk about their gardens, the water system in Lynchburg, the problems of giving a Tupperware party, and the advantages of building one's own house. After dinner, the men and women separated, the men going into the living room and the women upstairs for an hour or so of Bible reading and prayers.

In such circumstances, it was difficult to see how Falwell could complain so much about moral decay, sex, drink, drugs, the decline of the family, and so on. Conversely, it was difficult to imagine why such people would be drawn to a preacher who spent so much time denouncing drink and pornography. On the face of it, these people would seem far better suited to a tolerant, easygoing church whose pastor would not make a point—as Falwell once did—of forbidding his congregants to watch "Charlie's Angels." Of course, not all Thomas Road Church members live in such order and comfort. To go with its pastors on their rounds is to see that the Sunday-morning impression of the congregation is to some degree misleading—or in the nature of a Platonic ideal. A number of its members live in government-sponsored housing projects or in neighborhoods of old wooden houses. In one thin-walled apartment, I saw a woman sitting with her head in her hands gazing dejectedly at four squalling children under the age of nine—the baby crawling naked across the linoleum floor. (The pastor prissily told the older girl to put some underpants on the baby.) At a church-sponsored flea market, I found a number of women with worn faces buying and selling children's used clothing while their husbands squatted in a circle under a nearby tree and talked about boot camp and "Nam." According to one pastor, many of the elderly people in the church are single women who live on Social Security allowances of four or five thousand dollars a year. And most of them, according to the pastor, have never traveled outside the state of Virginia.

What is more, to talk to the people who live in the comfortable suburban-style houses is to discover that many of them did not grow up in such middle-class circumstances. William Sheehan, chairman of the church's Division of Prayer, became a lawyer late in life. He ran away from home and a drunken father at the age of eighteen and lived for a year with his grandfather in the boiler room of a school in Montana. He held various jobs, married at the age of twenty-one, and had nine children. His family responsibilities kept him hard at work at manual or clerical jobs. Only when he was in his forties did he have the time to study. He then took night courses in law, passed the state bar exam, apprenticed himself to an older lawyer, and eventually

inherited a practice in a small Montana town. In conversation, Sheehan thanks God in every other sentence and gives the Lord credit for
everything that he has ever done or that has ever happened to him.
He never drank, he said, but he was able to stop cursing when he
accepted Jesus Christ as his Saviour, at the age of nineteen.

Most of Falwell's parishioners came from closer to home, but a lot
of them came from the countryside and the small towns of southern
Virginia and West Virginia. One guest at the potluck supper talked
about his childhood in a narrow coal-mining valley of Appalachia,
where the preachers handled poisonous snakes and spoke in tongues.
He has never got used to the Lynchburg traffic, he said, for where he
had lived the sound of a car on the road meant that you picked up
your shotgun and left by the back door.

To talk to Falwell's parishioners is to see that the geography of
Lynchburg is symbolic in terms of their lives. As the city stands between Appalachia and Washington, D.C., so the arrival of new industry over the past twenty-five years made it the transfer point between
the Old and the New South, between the technologically backward
and the technologically modern parts of the society. Many current
Lynchburg residents, including many Thomas Road members, literally made the journey between the underdeveloped countryside and
the city. Many others, however, made a similar journey without moving at all. In the early fifties, Lynchburg had a relatively unskilled
work force and a very small middle class; today, it was a highly skilled
work force and a much larger middle class. Falwell's parishioners
stand, as it were, on the cusp of this new middle class. They are
clerical workers, technicians, and small businessmen, and skilled and
semiskilled workers in the new factories.

Among the church members and the students at Liberty Baptist are
many who grew up in fundamentalist Christian families and have
never known any other way of life. Those who came from the small
towns of Virginia or West Virginia think of Lynchburg as a sophisticated city; and those who came from big cities like Philadelphia think
of it as a refuge from the anarchy of modern America. Among those
who do not have a fundamentalist background, a high proportion
seem to have had difficult, disorganized childhoods—family histories
of alcoholism, physical violence, or trouble with the law. They had—
or so they say—to struggle out of their families and then to struggle
with themselves. They credit the Lord with their success, and they
date their success from the moment they were, as they say, "saved."

Falwell's parishioners do not give the Thomas Road Baptist Church
—or any other church—credit for the changes in their lives, because
in their theology it is an error (specifically, a Catholic error) to suppose

that institutions stand between man and God. There is some irony in this belief, for the Thomas Road Church is a great deal more than a house for prayers. It is a vast and mighty institution, with some sixty pastors and about a thousand volunteer helpers and trainees. It has Lynchburg Christian Academy, the summer camp, and Liberty Baptist College, whose students worship and work in the church. In addition, it has separate ministries for children, young people, adults, elderly people, the deaf, the retarded, and the imprisoned. Last year, it added a ministry for divorced people and another one for unmarried young adults. On Sundays, the church holds three general services and has Sunday-school classes for children of every age group, from the nursery on up. But it is a center of activity every day of the week. There is a general prayer meeting every Wednesday night. Then, every week each ministry offers a program of activities for its age group, including Bible-study classes, lectures, trips, sports outings, and picnics. The ministries also organize groups of volunteers to visit hospitals, nursing homes, and prisons and to proselytize in the community. The organization is so comprehensive that any Thomas Road member, old or young, could spend all his or her time in church or in church-related activities. In fact, many church members do just that.

Eldridge Dunn, a former tool-and-die maker for General Electric, runs one of the largest and busiest of the church organizations, the Children's Ministry. Dunn explained to me that the purpose of his ministry is to provide a total environment for children—a society apart from the world. "Our philosophy is that children should not have to go into the world," he said. "They should not have to get involved with drugs or Hollywood movies. But you can't just tell kids not to do things. You have to give them something to do. So we try to provide them with everything that's necessary for children. We take the older kids backpacking. We'll rent a skating rink this year. Our idea is to compete with the world." This philosophy, Dunn went on to say, is not unique to the Thomas Road Church; all churches advocating separation from the world engage in a similar competition, however limited their resources—and some churches have far better facilities than Thomas Road. What distinguishes his church is its aggressiveness. "I'd like to build a program for every child in Lynchburg," Dunn said.

On Monday afternoons, Gary Hunt, a ministerial student in his mid-twenties working with the Thomas Road Youth Ministry, collects a dozen or more children from various parts of Lynchburg in a school bus and takes them back to his house for the afternoon. With one exception, the children do not come from Thomas Road families or attend Lynchburg Christian Academy. Hunt, who is tall, blond, and athletic, found them by hanging around a junior high school and playing basketball with the kids coming out of class. Now they gather at his house every week for sports and a Bible-study class, and they have all been, as they say, "saved."

When I arrived at the Hunts' house one Monday afternoon, Hunt was just bringing the boys in from a ball game outside, and his wife, Angie, was showing the girls how to bake chocolate-chip cookies. For a while, the kitchen was a confusion of twelve-year-olds, the girls yelling at each other and the boys wandering around sweatily in search of something to drink. When the kids had quieted down, Gary took the boys to the basement, and Angie settled the girls in the living room. Downstairs, Hunt had the boys sit in a circle around him and passed out small workbooks. Asking them to turn to the chapter on baptism, he read out the text and explained, in a manner that seemed to me perfunctory, the scriptural basis for baptism. He seemed less interested in having them understand the idea of baptism than in having them copy the correct words in the blank spaces of the workbook. But, then, three or four of the boys did not read very well, and all of them seemed to have a hard time sitting still and concentrating on anything for long. When the spaces were filled in, Hunt talked to the boys briefly about their behavior, reminding them that smoking and cursing were sins, and praising them for making progress toward their goal of living as Christ did. He ended by inviting two of them to join the church choir and by asking those who were not baptized to come with him to the church on Sunday and go through the ceremony. The boys agreed with a touching eagerness.

Later, Hunt told me that most of the children came from fairly poor families and that most of them were not Baptists by background. "Some of them are rough kids," he said. "The girls don't know anything about conduct—they yell at each other. Angie shows them how to be ladylike and how to do things they don't do at home, like baking cookies. The boys are tough—used to using their fists. But they've come a long way in a few months. They're less wild. They don't swear like they used to, and they don't fight with the other kids so much."

The pastors and pastoral students at the Thomas Road Baptist Church conceive of their activities in theological terms and could, if called upon, justify any one of them by a Biblical quotation. All the same, to listen to Hunt or to see a pastor remind a little girl to put underpants on her baby brother is to see that they are involved in a world of appearances, social forms, and personal behavior at some remove from Biblical history and at some remove from the direct, mystical experience of Christ. For them, getting "saved" is clearly only the first step. It is true that most clergymen of all faiths are involved with the conduct of daily life, but the Thomas Road pastors —and fundamentalist pastors generally—have a much more specific and detailed set of prescriptions for the conduct of everyday life than do most Protestant churchmen. They have—like many Southern Baptists—absolute prohibitions against drink, tobacco, drugs, cursing, dancing, rock and roll, and extramarital sex, but they also have specific prescriptions for dress, child rearing, and the conduct of a marriage. The Liberty Baptist College student handbook, for instance, decrees that men are to wear ties to all classes. "Hair should be cut in such a way that it does not come over the ear or collar. Beards or mustaches are not permitted. Sideburns should be no longer than the bottom of the ear." As for women, "dresses and skirts . . . shorter than two inches [below] the middle of the knee are unacceptable. Anything tight, scant, backless, and low in the neckline is unacceptable. . . ." These rules are less formally laid down for the members of the Thomas Road Church.

For the proper relations between husband and wife, parents and children, the rules are spelled out in a book called *The Total Family*, written by Edward Hindson, the family-guidance pastor of the church, and endorsed by Falwell. According to Hindson:

> The Bible clearly states that the wife is to submit to her husband's leadership and help him fulfill God's will for his life. . . . She is to submit to him just as she would submit to Christ as her Lord. This places the responsibility of leadership upon the husband where it belongs. In a sense, submission is learning to duck, so God can hit your husband! He will never realize his responsibility to the family as long as you take it. . . .
>
> The same passages that command the wife to obey her husband, command the husband to love his wife! Being a leader is not being a dictator, but a loving motivator, who, in turn, is appreciated and respected by his family. Dad, God wants you to be the loving heartbeat of your home by building the lives of your family through teaching and discipline.

In another chapter, Hindson deals with the parent-child relationship and gives "Five Steps to Effective Discipline." He attacks Dr. Benjamin Spock, modern psychology, and modern public education on the ground that they have encouraged children to challenge their parents. Parents founding their authority on the word of God should, he says, command absolute authority over their children. Spanking, he explains, is Biblically mandated and must be employed if we are not to have another generation of irresponsible, undisciplined adults.

The pastors at Thomas Road would define most relationships outside the family in terms congruent with these. In school, children should not challenge their teachers but should accept instruction and discipline. On the job, a man should work hard, show discipline, and accept the authority of his employer. He should accept the authority of the church and the civil government in the same way. "He does not have the right to break the law, no matter how just his cause may seem," Hindson writes. The pastors would, in fact, make a Confucian equation between the relationships of man to civil government and church and of children to their parents. In Hindson's book, there is an organization chart that depicts these relationships: from "God," at the top, the lines of authority descend to "local church," on the one hand, and "civil authority," on the other; the lines then descend and converge upon "total family"—father first, then mother, then children. The organization chart is entitled "God's Chain of Command."

The pastors at Thomas Road talk about creating a society apart from the world. But when they talk about "the world" in this context what they clearly mean is pornography, drugs, "secular humanism," and so on: the evils of the world as they see them, and not American life in general. It is not, then, really paradoxical that many of their prescriptions for life look very much like tactics for integrating people into society rather than like tactics for separating them from it. Most communities, after all, would be happy to have a clean, hardworking family man who respected authority, obeyed the law, and kept off the welfare rolls. A factory manager, a city official, or a landlord would find such a man an ideal type—particularly if the alternative to him were a drinking, brawling country fellow with no steady job, six runny-nosed kids, and a shotgun he might consider using against a law officer. And, to look at it from another angle, the country fellow would get nowhere with General Electric or the Rotary Club, even if he desperately wanted to. As for the women involved—why, they might have invented this church, so heavily do the prohibitions fall on traditional male vices such as drinking, smoking, running around, and paying no heed to the children. To tell "Dad" that he made all the decisions might be a small price to pay to get the father of your children to become a respectable middle-class citizen.

The pastors at Thomas Road set enormous store by the virtues of sports for young men. And sports, the oldest of Anglo-Saxon prescriptions for the sublimation of male violence and male sexual energies, might stand as a metaphor for the whole social enterprise of the church. Indeed, they ought to so stand, for the pastors often use sports as such a metaphor themselves. At a Lynchburg Christian Academy athletic-awards banquet whose theme was "Steppin' Up to

Victory," Edward Dobson, the good-looking young dean of students at Liberty Baptist College, gave an after-dinner sermon on sports and the Christian life. He said that when he was a soccer player he used to spend hours—sometimes eight hours at a time—practicing one shot; he would give up everything else to do it. Well, he said, success in the Christian life is like success in sports: you have to discipline yourself to give up everything that might interfere or prove an obstacle. What you need is discipline, devotion, and consistency. There are Christians who start up fast, who read the Bible and go to church a lot, but then quit. But you can't quit, because "whenever you quit you become a loser." Keep your eye on the goal, keep running consistently, and "one day you will cross the finish line and stand before Jesus Christ." Later, one of the coaches made another point: "The whole purpose of junior-high-school soccer is to instill a Christlike attitude into young men," he said.

School athletic banquets do tend to call up sports metaphors, but Thomas Road pastors talk about sports on all sorts of occasions. They probably talk about them as much as Anglican schoolmasters—which is a lot—but they talk about them in a different way. Where the Anglican headmaster will go on about how it's not whether you win or lose but how you play the game, Thomas Road pastors will tell kids to get out there and win. Grace under pressure, aristocratic prowess, even fair play are not virtues they are much interested in. "God wants you to be a champion," Falwell once told an assembly of his college students. "He wants you to be a victor for God's glory. A champion is not an individual star but one of a team who knows how to function with others. Men of God are not interested in gaining personal fame. The man of God says, 'I will be the best for God in the place where He puts me.' " Such sports talk does not suggest the manor house or the high commissioner's residence any more than it suggests software and SoHo lofts. It suggests the steel mills and the values of nineteenth-century American capitalism.

Success and how to get it are major themes in Thomas Road preaching. Falwell himself likes to preach from Paul's Epistles to Timothy— from the letters in which the older evangelist gives the younger one some sound practical advice. For one sermon, Falwell chose the text "Let no man despise thy youth; but be thou an example of the believers, in word, in conversation, in charity, in spirit, in faith, in purity." In his commentary, he said he often told younger preachers that "nothing is more important to you than moral purity," and explained to them, "You can survive rumors of a money scandal, you can survive a split in the church . . . but if you break your marriage vows you will never fly so high again." Falwell did not add "if you are caught at it," but the advice is nothing if not a piece of worldly wisdom. In his sermons, his terms of reference often modulate in this fashion from heaven to earth—from how to be a better Christian to how to improve yourself and gain the respect of others. He promises no miracles; his philosophy is simply that material wealth "is God's way of blessing people who put Him first."

When Falwell is addressing his congregation on Wednesday evenings, he often talks about what he has done during the week. He talks about all the important people he has met on his trips around the country. He talks about New York and the narrow escapes he has had among the denizens of Sin City. He talks about his trips abroad —his visits to Israel, Thailand, Taiwan, and southern Africa—picturing himself on the front lines of conflict, and quoting what he said to high officials and heads of state. The obvious inferiority of the natives in these places does not at all appear to dispel the glamour of them for his congregation.

In the summer of 1980, Falwell posed for a *Newsweek* photographer beside his swimming pool on the green lawn in front of the imposing white house he lives in. That the shot might be bad publicity did not occur to him at the time, for his own people know all about that house and the way he lives. At Christmas, Falwell sends out color photographs of himself, his wife, and their three children (whose first names all begin with J) in posh surroundings or posed in formal dress. His own people love to look at these pictures, for they think he deserves everything he has. They love to hear about his travels, for his account of them brings those faraway people and places somehow within their reach. They think themselves fortunate to be in the church with the television cameras where this man broadcasts to the nation. Furthermore, they love to hear him talk about himself, for when he talks about his early life he makes it clear that he is not some pale, prissy, holier-than-thou minister but—underneath his celebrity —someone much like them.

Falwell has said a good deal about his early life, in sermons and in books he distributes as advertisements for himself and his enterprises. As in all official biographies, certain facts have been selected for publication and others left out. According to *Aflame for God*, by Gerald Strober and Ruth Tomczak, Falwell was born, with a twin brother, Gene, to Carey and Helen Falwell on August 11, 1933. ("Although it was impossible to predict at that time, one of the most crucial dates in the history of the town. . . .") The family, which included two children—Virginia and Lewis—considerably older than the twins, lived in a white frame house a mile and a half east of a section of downtown Lynchburg called Fairview Heights. The earliest photograph in the book shows Jerry and Gene aged about two, Jerry in the arms of a man in overalls and a work-stained shirt, with a high-crowned dark hat pulled down over his weather-beaten face. The man is Jerry's grandfather Charles Falwell, and the family resemblance is striking. In later life, Jerry would have the same strong features, the same powerful, confident stance. A photograph of Jerry's father, by contrast, shows a slight man in a three-piece suit with a pained expression on his face. Jerry's older brother and sister are not pictured, but there is a photograph of his mother taken on Mother's Day of 1971 and showing an ample-breasted woman with her hair pulled back beneath a black hat, wearing a printed black silk dress.

This book and other biographical accounts do not say very much about the Falwell family. There is no reason that they should, but the family history does have a certain sociological interest. Charles Falwell was a dairy farmer whose family had settled in the hills east of Lynchburg in the mid-nineteenth century, and had farmed in the narrow bottomland between the steep hills. Around 1900, with the industrialization of Lynchburg, mill hands and factory workers came to settle among the farmers along the railroad line. Fairview Heights—the new settlement—was a poor neighborhood, even in 1920; it had no paved roads and no streetlights, and the houses had no running water. It was also a rough neighborhood. During the Prohibition era, the gentlefolk at Lynchburg used to frighten their daughters with tales of crime, vice, and white slavery in Fairview Heights. The tales were exaggerated but not without foundation, for four or five bootleggers who had sizable operations there had effectively closed it off to the law. "If you didn't live there, you didn't go there," Gene Falwell recalls.

Carey Falwell was the oldest in a family of boys. He had only a sixth-grade education, but he was a shrewd, hard-driving man, and before the twins were born, he had managed to start a succession of small businesses. He financed bootlegging operations, and at various times he owned a service station, an oil dealership, and a small trucking company. The house Jerry was born in was a gentleman's house that Carey had moved piece by piece from Rivermont, the wealthy section of town. He was driven by ambition. In the early thirties, along with his other enterprises, he set up a dance hall called the Merry Garden, with a restaurant and "tourist court" across the street. In 1931, he had shot and killed his brother Garland in the heat of an argument, apparently in self-defense. Around the time the twins were born (their birth, apparently, was not planned for), he went broke and had to sell his businesses to his brother Warren. His reverses and his remorse over the death of his brother drove him to despair and to drink. Eventually, he pulled himself and his family back from the brink of bankruptcy, but he continued to drink, and he died of cirrhosis of the liver in 1948, when Jerry was only fifteen.

Aflame for God says of Jerry's twin brother, Gene, that he "would follow in his father's footsteps and become an aggressive, successful businessman and, along with his older brother Lewis, consolidate and add to the family's extensive commercial interests." The description could be more accurate. Some of the Falwells did very well in life. Calvin and Lawrence, the sons of Carey's more stable brother Warren, took the small businesses they had inherited and built up a series of successful enterprises, including a well-drilling company, a trucking firm, and an aviation company. Genial, hardworking, and civic-minded, Calvin became one of Lynchburg's city fathers; he is a member of the chamber of commerce and the president of the New York Mets farm team. But Jerry is the only real success in his immediate family. His brother Lewis has an excavation company, and Gene, who lives in the "home place," where they grew up, runs a trailer park on the Falwell land. Calvin, an outgoing man with a soft Virginia drawl, speaks affectionately of Gene: "Aggressive? He's the most easygoing kind of guy you'd ever want to meet. Never gets mad. Has all the time in the world for you. I suppose he hasn't worn a tie since his mother's funeral. In fact, I'm sure he hasn't. Like someone once said to me, 'I guess Jerry got the other half.' "

The Falwell "home place" isn't far from the main commercial road, but the white house stands alone in a small pasture between two thickly wooded hills. "Jerry always said he wanted a house up there," Gene told me, pointing to the top of a steep little hill. Gene is in and out of the house all day; he'll go to fix an electric wire in someone's trailer or help a brother-in-law prune a maple tree. A homebody who likes to hunt and fish and to make things grow, he can tell you in detail how to make maple sugar or how people used to make moonshine in a still. An unself-conscious man, he will also tell you how his grandpa used to make fun of the "colored boys" who worked for him. Gene's wife, Jo Ann, who keeps the house, with its shag rugs and its modern kitchen, so neat it looks uninhabited, has clearly not been able to do very much about Gene's clothes or the stubble on his chin. While Jo Ann goes to the Thomas Road Church and Calvin is a charter member of a rather more relaxed Baptist church, Gene stays home on Sunday, like his father and his grandfather before him.

The contrast between the twins became obvious in their early years. The boys entered elementary school together, but after a year Jerry skipped a grade, leaving Gene behind for the rest of their school careers. Jerry was good at schoolwork; he was particularly good at spelling and math, and he used to finish his tests fifteen minutes before the other kids. Since he had an almost photographic memory, he did not have to work hard, yet he did, for he wanted to be the best. In his junior year in high school, he entered the state spelling championship; when he lost because he could not recognize an unfamiliar word, he went back and read through an entire college edition of a dictionary. "He didn't like farm work," Gene recalls. "He'd leave me with the chores. When the time came, he always had something else to do. He never wanted to come out trapping with me, either. He'd have his head in a book or he'd be out playing baseball." Jerry liked the sociable, competitive sports, and he was a good athlete. In his senior year in high school, he was captain of the football team. While Gene dropped out of school in his senior year and soon after joined the Navy, Jerry graduated with a 98.6 percent average and was named class valedictorian.

Jerry was not allowed to give the valedictory speech, however, because school auditors discovered that he had taken cafeteria tickets and for some time had been handing them out to members of the football team. That incident was the last straw for the school authorities. Jerry had been in trouble with them for years. In grade school, he once set a snake loose in the classroom, and another time he put a large rat in a teacher's desk drawer. Later on, in high school, he and some friends tied up the gym teacher and locked him in the basement. Jerry was, as his biography puts it, a prankster. Out of school, he and Gene used to hang around the Royal Café in Fairview Heights with a gang of boys who for fun would do things like piling a family's porch furniture on the roof of the house. They didn't like it when boys from other parts of town tried to date girls from Fairview Heights, so every week or so there would be fights with neighboring gangs. In a recent sermon called "My Testimony," Falwell described these fistfights and said that he and a close friend, Jim Moon (now copastor at the Thomas Road Church), used to spend days and nights away from home, in "places it's not necessary to talk about, doing things it's not necessary to talk about."

Moon recalls that Jerry was always a leader among the Fairview boys, and that he was so in part because he had the only car and he was generous with it. Like so many leaders, Falwell seemed to have need of followers. At the same time, he was different from them, in that he knew what he wanted. "I didn't have any aspirations," Moon said to me. "I don't remember wanting anything or hoping for anything except to grow up. There weren't many opportunities back then. You could go to work at the hosiery mill, the foundry, or the shoe factory. There wasn't much else. When I was sixteen, I was drinking a lot. But Jerry, he always wanted to be an engineer, and he was willing to do whatever was necessary to be the best."

In 1950, Falwell entered Lynchburg College and began to take courses that would lead to a major in mechanical engineering. His plan was to transfer to Virginia Polytechnic Institute in his junior year, and by the end of his sophomore year there seemed to be no reason he should not do it: he had the highest math average in the college that year. But by fall he was enrolled in Baptist Bible College, in Springfield, Missouri, and was on his way to becoming a pastor. Just how he came to this decision is not clear.

The Falwells were not pious people. When Jerry was growing up, the men seemed to regard religion as something that women did. Jerry's mother (described in *Aflame for God* as "a stern disciplinarian, but . . . kind, gracious, and loving") used to take the twins to Sunday school when she went to church; but as soon as she had deposited them they would slip out the back and run to an uncle's house to read the comics until it was time for her to pick them up. According to Falwell's biographies, his only exposure to religion until he was eighteen came from listening—involuntarily—to Charles E. Fuller, a fundamentalist Baptist whose "Old-Fashioned Revival Hour" was the most popular religious radio program of the day. Jerry's mother, so the story goes, would turn the program on every Sunday morning, and he and his brother would be too lazy to get up and turn it off. In January of his sophomore year, Jerry went with a group of friends, including Jim Moon, to the Park Avenue Baptist Church, in Lynchburg, for Sunday-evening services. After the service, he, Moon, and a number of others responded to the altar call and—as he says— accepted Christ. Under the instruction of a youth pastor, Jerry began reading the Bible, attending church services, and participating in church activities. "From January to March . . . I got my salvation established, and then from March to about July, I got my call to full-time service established," Falwell has said.

At least one of the Falwell biographies says that Jerry and his friends went to that initial service at Park Avenue Baptist mainly because they had heard there were some pretty girls in the congregation. The story is wholly plausible, for Jerry later married the pretty young church pianist, Macel Pate, and Moon married the organist. But in *My Testimony* Falwell said that he went not only because of the pretty girls but also because he was already thinking of founding a church of his own. How he would have conceived of such a plan if, as he says, he had not heard the Bible preached in a church before is difficult to imagine. But then, according to Fairview Heights people, he had attended other churches—usually on Sunday nights with his friends. He had simply not been to a fundamentalist church before. In any case, Jerry did not seem to go through any moral or spiritual turmoil when he made his commitment. By his own account, he made a career decision.

Baptist Bible College was little more than a group of Quonset huts with the most Spartan of living arrangements. Falwell says that it was there that he met a number of "great preachers" with churches of three and four thousand people. He would, he says, follow these preachers around and run errands for them, to be near them and to learn as much as he could. He studied hard, but he did not give up his pranks. Once, he drove a motorcycle through the boys' dormitory at midnight. Another time, he ran a garden hose into a friend's room and flooded it. After his friend had spent three hours cleaning the water up, Falwell came in and emptied a five-gallon can of water onto the floor. ("He has an aggressive nature," his biographers comment.) Macel Pate was now engaged to one of his roommates. Falwell managed "to get the other ring off her finger," according to one account, in part by tearing up letters to her that the roommate gave him to mail. Macel, however, did not marry him until he was established in Lynchburg five years later.

According to the biographies, the first real crisis in Falwell's life came during his Bible-college career. He had asked to teach a Sunday-school class of eleven-year-olds in the local Baptist church, but because after some weeks he still had only one student the church superintendent threatened to take away his classbook. Jerry then began to go every afternoon to an unused room on the third floor of the college's administration building, where he would pray for several hours, "crying out to God" for help with the class. On Saturdays, he went through all the parks and playgrounds in the town looking for eleven-year-olds, and by the time the school year was over, in May, he had fifty-six of them in his class.

In 1954, Falwell took a year out of college to work at the Park Avenue Baptist Church. In 1956, he returned to Lynchburg at the end of his senior year and, though he had received an offer to go elsewhere, decided to start a new church there with thirty-five dissident members of Park Avenue Baptist. He and his new congregation found an empty building on Thomas Road—it had recently been vacated by the Donald Duck Bottling Company—and spent several days scrubbing the cola syrup off the walls. A week after the first service in the church, Falwell began a half-hour Sunday broadcast for a new local radio station. Not long afterward, he began a daily radio program and a live Sunday-evening broadcast from a local television station. With these two broadcasts and the morning and evening Sunday services in his church, Falwell was for some time preaching four sermons every Sunday, beginning at 6:30 A.M. and ending around 9:00 P.M. On weekdays, he would go from door to door visiting each house in an ever-expanding radius from the church. In a year, his congregation went from 35 people to 864.

Falwell lays no claim to great originality as a preacher. When he speaks about the sources of his faith, his vocation, or his evangelistic style, he always makes much of Charles E. Fuller and his "Old-Fashioned Revival Hour"; he also speaks of Dwight Moody, Billy Sunday, and the southern preachers he took for mentors at Baptist Bible College. In the fundamentalist tradition, his theology is wholly orthodox; it is the religion of independnt Baptist preachers throughout the Bible Belt. His preaching style is similarly conventional. Falwell does not have the flamboyance of a Billy Sunday—he has no real love for the language—nor does he have the soothing, media-modern style of charismatics like Oral Roberts and Pat Robertson. His is a pithy, old-fashioned preacher—a man who has made himself out of the traditional cloth. What distinguishes him among his peers is his organizational talent and his enormous, driving energy.

In *Church Aflame*, a book he wrote with Elmer Towns, the vice-president of Liberty Baptist College, the authors explain in some detail how Falwell organized the Thomas Road Church and built its membership into the thousands. His method was simply to use every available medium at once—the telephone, the printing press, personal contacts, broadcasting. In the late fifties and early sixties, he devoted himself to building up the church's capacities for what he calls "saturation evangelism." He put his parishioners to work on the phones. He bought a printing press and, with the help of church members, printed announcements, leaflets, and, finally, a newspaper. He then set up a telephone bank and also began to produce tape cassettes for sale. As his congregation increased, he would raise money, build new facilities, and then cast out a larger net for new members. In 1964, he completed the construction of a thousand-seat auditorium for his church services; from that year on, he acquired a new piece of land or built a new building almost every year. In 1967, he founded Lynchburg Christian Academy. In 1972, he brought nineteen thousand people to the Lynchburg Municipal Stadium for a Sunday-school meeting.

For twelve years—from 1956 to 1968—Falwell preached in his own church on Sundays and then went to a television station (first to one in Lynchburg and later to one in Roanoke, sixty miles away) to preach a sermon for broadcast locally. In 1968, he was able to buy black-and-white-television cameras and to tape one of the Sunday services in his church—at once easing his own incredible preaching schedule and providing a format for a television program. Two years later, shortly after the current Thomas Road church building was completed, he bought color-television cameras. Once he was in control of the production of his program, he and his brother-in-law, Sam K. Pate, bought time for the program on local television stations in the East and then throughout the country; following the practice of Oral Roberts, Rex Humbard, and others, they set up a direct-mail funding operation to defray the costs of production and distribution. In 1971, Falwell bought time on two hundred television stations; his revenues that year reached a million dollars.

Church Aflame might serve as a how-to-do-it guide for the ambitious young evangelist if it were not for one important lacuna: money-raising. In this and other books, Falwell discusses the tithing of the local congregation, but he is silent on how to raise money from a television audience. On this subject, he has said, "We try to do everything that General Motors does to sell automobiles. Except that we do it better, maybe"—a statement that is not only too general to be helpful but also not quite accurate.

Falwell's fund-raising pitches on television (he makes them himself —an uncommon practice among television evangelists) suggest not General Motors ads but cereal-box-top offers. Send in nine ninety-five and you will receive, in addition to your own special volume of inspirational literature, a perfectly free gratis Jesus First pin. Or: Become a Faith Partner—send in ten dollars a month and receive our four-color magazine of faith, *Faith Aflame*. Alternatively, here are two free Jesus First pins—wear them always—and send fifteen, twenty-five, a hundred dollars a month to help our Liberty Baptist students or our crusade against sin. You will receive our Crusader's Passport. Call Jerry Falwell toll-free and share your need with one of our counselors.

Some of the pitches are more sophisticated. In the spring of 1980, Falwell was offering seven volumes of inspirational literature—the package, wrapped in silver paper with ribbon tied in a bow, looked extraordinarily like a gift-wrapped package from a liquor store. Celebrate the twenty-fifth anniversary of the Thomas Road Church, Falwell said, and send in a hundred dollars now, or twenty-five dollars for four months, to help with the construction of much-needed buildings at Liberty Baptist. He explained that the package contained the books that, apart from the Bible, had most influenced his spiritual life.

One can only assume that these books were out of print and so reissued for the anniversary—which was in fact the church's twenty-fourth.

Falwell himself dreams up a good many of these pitches, but, as this particular appeal suggests, there are also a number of professionals at work on his fund-raising. Since 1973, he has employed an advertising agency and a Massachusettes computer-consulting firm called Epsilon Data Management, both of which have what they call "inputs on the creative side." The main job of Epsilon Data Management is to help coordinate the mailings. Through this firm, Falwell can make appeals to a variety of different constituencies with a series of computer-printed letters appropriate to each. One set of appeals, for example, stresses patriotism, another missionary work, another the menace of pornography and homosexuality. Through Epsilon, Falwell manages four different "clubs," whose members contribute to his various ministries monthly sums averaging about twenty dollars. His 170,000 Faith Partners and the 40,000 members of his I Love America Club contribute to the general "Gospel Hour" fund; the members of his Founders Club and his 15,000 Club give money for buildings and for scholarships, respectively, at Liberty Baptist College. Falwell's televised appeals alternate among these various constituencies.

On occasion, Falwell will make appeals for causes outside his own ministries, but the giver must beware. At one point, Falwell flew to Thailand to visit a refugee camp, where he was photographed in a bush jacket holding a Cambodian child in his arms. Thereafter, he made a series of appeals on television for the Indo-Chinese refugees. In March of 1980, he sent out an urgent letter describing in heart-rending detail the plight of the Vietnamese boat people and appealing for emergency funds to buy food and medical supplies. On page 2 of the letter, the recipient would discover that the first hundred thousand dollars from that appeal would go to the boat people and the balance would go to "The Old-Time Gospel Hour." (In the spring of 1981, two similar appeals were made on behalf of refugees in Somalia.) A special newsletter sent out around the same period included photographs of starving Cambodian refugees and a description of their plight. In this newsletter, Falwell asked for twenty-five, fifty, or a hundred dollars from each recipient to help start the Liberty Missionary Society, "which will reach out to lost, hurting, and hungry souls around the world." To examine the budget for the society in the newsletter was, however, to see that the appeal would bring the starving Cambodians no food and no medicine at all. The budget—$2 million—showed, for instance, $450,000 to support Liberty Baptist students on short-term missionary service in eighteen countries, $37,500 to buy airtime for "The Old-Time Gospel Hour" in countries outside the United States and Canada, and $450,000 for capital expenditures on Liberty Baptist College. And $100,000 was promised for "foreign Bible distribution."

These fund-raising techniques have proved remarkably successful. In fiscal 1979, "The Old-Time Gospel Hour" raised $35 million from the two and a half million people on its mailing lists. The financial management of the church has been rather less than successful, though, and over the years Falwell has had his troubles with it. In the early seventies, his organization floated bond issues worth $6.5 million. In 1973, the Securities and Exchange Commission sued the combined ministries for "fraud and deceit," charging that the church was insolvent and could not redeem the bonds when they came due. In court, the judge absolved the church of intentional wrongdoing, and the SEC lawyers dropped the words "fraud and deceit" from their complaint. Falwell thereupon declared a great victory. The church, however, had admitted in the course of the trial that one of its bond prospectuses was inaccurate and that its general ledgers were incomplete. The financial affairs of the church were put in the hands of five prominent Lynchburg businessmen; that is, into what was for a nonprofit institution the equivalent of receivership.

On assuming responsibility for the finances of the Thomas Road ministries, the businessmen found that the scant records the church did have were in a state of confusion. In the next three years, they instituted proper accounting procedures, cut overhead costs, let a number of "Gospel Hour" administrators go (including Falwell's brother-in-law), and, perhaps most important, adopted a cost-effective system for buying radio and television time. "The Old-Time Gospel Hour" had been buying "packages" of airtime almost at random from brokers, when the tried-and-true system for evangelists was to persuade a local group to finance the purchase of airtime on a local station for thirteen weeks and drop it if contributions did not then cover the cost. Between 1973 and 1977, "Gospel Hour" revenues rose from $7 million a year to $22 million, and in May of 1977 the committee of businessmen was able to retire most of the church's unsecured indebtedness and hand the management back to Falwell and his staff.

Three years later, the church was again in financial trouble. Its balance sheet for the fiscal year ending in June of 1980 showed that it had assets of $41 million, of which $36 million were sunk into property, plant, and equipment; it showed mortgages and liabilities amounting to $19 million. In August of 1980, the church borrowed

$3.5 million more through a bond issue. Its ability to service its debt depended entirely on Falwell's ability to bring in money, particularly through "The Old-Time Gospel Hour." In the fiscal year 1979, he had brought in $6.7 million above operating expenses—sufficient funds to service the debt. But in the fiscal year 1980, "Gospel Hour" income did not increase as much as expected, and the operating expenses rose, giving the whole organization a net of only $3.8 million. Since the church had few assets apart from its own buildings and grounds, the whole enterprise of the Thomas Road Church began to look shaky.

How the church could have got into such debt when its total revenues had continued to rise each year—from $22.2 million in fiscal 1977 to $51 million in fiscal 1980—was an interesting question. In 1973, when the businessmen took over the organization they made an extensive investigation of its bank accounts—personal and institutional—and found no evidence of hanky-panky. What they did find —in addition to a lack of any financial management—was deficit spending, on the one hand, and a great deal of waste and inefficiency, on the other. Some in Lynchburg therefore concluded that the organization had simply fallen back into its old ways. "Jerry's always criticizing the government for overspending," a businessman close to him said. "But he is the biggest deficit spender of them all. There's no end to what he would like to do, and he doesn't know how to say no to anyone."

The theory concerning deficit spending bears some examination, for Falwell is clearly an ambitious man, who is always out ahead of himself, his vision always exceeding his present possibilities. He himself has rather proudly said that he has never had the money to complete any project that he began. He founded Liberty Baptist College in 1971, when the church was millions of dollars in debt; and the summer of 1980, when it was in the throes of a new financial crisis, he was talking about putting up a new church building for ten thousand people, a college for fifty thousand students, and apartments for thousands of elderly people. Clearly, Falwell would like to do everything at once. But what he actually does with his money is the real point at issue.

Figures from Falwell's organization show that "The Old-Time Gospel Hour" raised about $115 million in four years—fiscal 1977 through fiscal 1980—and that virtually none of this money went toward the operating expenses of the Thomas Road Church; the local congregation paid for most of the church's expenses with tithes. In those four years, Falwell put a total of $16 million into the construction of the LBC campus, and each year he put about $2 million into the operating expenses of the college. The bulk of the revenues, however, went back into "The Old-Time Gospel Hour," for its own operations.

So in the scheme of things Falwell gave a rather high priority to "The Old-Time Gospel Hour" and a rather low one to the comfort and education of his college students. As the businessmen who took over his organization found out, although "The Old-Time Gospel Hour" is the fund-raising arm and the vehicle for further expansion, it was the college that attracted a sizable percentage of the contributions. The businessmen had wanted to close the college for prudential reasons but had found that, for the same prudential reasons, they could not. As a result, the college had two entirely independent existences for its first six years—one on paper, the other in reality—and the students fell into the gap between the two. Falwell advertised the college on television. He sent out a catalog with a picture of what seemed to be a bosky campus; one of his books of the period pictures students playing basketball in a gymnasium. When the students came to Lynchburg—first three hundred, then a thousand, then two thousand strong—what they found was a series of dilapidated rented buildings scattered around the city. There was no campus (the catalog photo was of a city park), no gymnasium (the college used gyms belonging to a public high school and Lynchburg Christian Academy), and, for the first few years, no library. (Falwell's students used the Randolph-Macon and Lynchburg College libraries until there were complaints about their attempts to proselytize other students.) Some of the students took pride in their ability to survive these hardships, but others left. Finally, in 1977, Falwell was able to begin the construction of the campus, and the students were finally installed on it. In the summer of 1980, however, the campus consisted mainly of a collection of prefabs made of cinder block and metal sheeting. Those students who lived on campus slept on bunk beds, four to each tiny room.

Whether one judges the "Gospel Hour" to be an efficient operation or not depends on whether one categorizes it as a direct-mail business or as a church. In fiscal 1979, for example, when its receipts were $35 million, its operating expenses were nearly $26 million. The fund-raising vehicle itself spent more than $5.00 for every $7.00 it earned. Of course, many of those who send in money are contributing to the program itself. Thus, the cost of airtime—$9 million in fiscal 1979—and the cost of production are the very objects of their charity. But in fiscal 1979 "The Old-Time Gospel Hour" spent nearly $11 million for direct mail and promotion. It had other administrative costs, which included the payroll and employee benefits for some eight hundred people. Falwell himself makes only $42,500 a year in salary, but his organization pays a number of his expenses—including the maintenance of his twelve-room house (deeded to the church by a wealthy businessman) and the cost of a private jet. Therefore, Falwell's contributors, in 1979, paid roughly forty cents of every dollar they gave for administrative costs.

There is no evidence of any illegality in these practices. Still, Falwell's organization has engaged in certain transactions that most businesses and nonprofit institutions would avoid. In the fiscal year 1980, it bought $1.5 million worth of gift offers and other materials from a company whose president was a member of its own board, and it borrowed $1 million from a board member. It also employed an agency run by Falwell's brother-in-law to buy its media time. All these transactions may have worked to the advantage of "The Old-Time Gospel Hour"; there is some evidence in each case that they have. But that is surely not true of a decision made in the summer of 1979 to transfer all the health-insurance policies for "Gospel Hour" employees from Blue Cross/Blue Shield to a "Christian" company that turned out to be inadequately financed and had been legally barred from doing business in another state. Another company now handles those policies.

On top of these questionable transactions, there is very often a disquieting difference between what Falwell says is happening and what is actually going on. In October of 1979, for instance, Falwell informed his supporters through his newspaper and by direct mail that he would have to take "The Old-Time Gospel Hour" off the air "unless God definitely shows me that he wants us to continue in this media." Therefore, he wrote, "I am putting out the fleece." (He carefully explained that the reference was to Gideon and the salvation of Israel.) He asked for fasting and prayer and six and a half million dollars. When a reporter questioned him about the announcement, Falwell said, in effect, that he had exaggerated a bit—that he did not intend to take the program off the air but merely to reduce the number of stations from which he bought airtime; and that the $6.5 million represented only $1 million more than "The Old-Time Gospel Hour" had brought in the previous October. In November, Falwell announced that he had raised the $6.5 million and the crisis was over.

Whether or not Falwell actually raised all of that money, the crisis was not over; it was just beginning. He had called a moratorium on further construction of the LBC campus in October—at the time of the crisis call—and it remained in effect until July of 1980. Yet in 1980 —and this was yet another indication of his priorities—his expenditure for airtime actually increased. "The Old-Time Gospel Hour" picked up some fifty television stations, and in addition Falwell produced three television specials and bought airtime for them on two hundred stations around the country. Also, in the spring of 1980 he spent $2 million to buy the entire shopping plaza in which the "Gospel Hour" offices were situated.

In June of 1980, Falwell refused to pay $67,000 in local real-estate taxes owed on the land occupied by LBC but owned by "The Old-Time Gospel Hour"—which was not, for these purposes, tax-exempt. When the city dunned him for the unpaid real-estate taxes, he told his congregation that the city was discriminating against the Thomas Road Church and that he would not pay "until all churches and colleges in Lynchburg pay taxes"—a phrase suggesting that the land belonged to the college or the church. Around the same time, the chief executive officer of "The Old-Time Gospel Hour" told the local press that the church owned no property or enterprise in Lynchburg not "involved in the ministry of the Gospel of Jesus Christ." At that time, however, "The Old-Time Gospel Hour" was leasing space to a supermarket, a gift shop, and a restaurant-bar in the shopping plaza that contained its offices.

Falwell's financial troubles—and the confusion that he creates around them—can be understood only in the context of the relationships that exist between him and his congregation and between that congregation and the outside world. In 1979, the dean of the Liberty Baptist Seminary resigned after a doctrinal dispute with Falwell. When, in the course of the dispute, Falwell questioned his administrative abilities, the dean angrily responded that it was Falwell who was the poor manager, creating financial crisis after financial crisis. He also accused Falwell of running a dictatorship. The last accusation was a curious one for the dean to make, since fundamentalist churches are generically dictatorships. Most Baptist churches—including most of those which belong to the Southern Baptist Convention—are governed by their lay members; they have deacons or committees of laymen to oversee the finances of the church and to hire and fire the pastors. But independent Baptist churches are run by their pastors. Falwell has always run the Thomas Road Church, and he has always insisted on his own absolute rule. In a sermon titled "The Day of Great Men Has Not Passed," he said, "God's plan is that His flock is to be led by shepherds, not run by a board or a committee." He explained:

> God never intended for a committee nor a board of deacons nor any other group to dominate a church or control a pastor. The pastor is God's

man, God's servant, God's leader. When you tie the hands of God's man, when you keep him from acting as the Holy Spirit leads him, you have murdered his initiative, you have killed his spirit.

This system of governance might seem out of place in a church that democratically assumes that anyone can attain salvation without the intervention of the pastor. But just as fundamentalist theology posits the absolute authority of the Bible, fundamentalist moral doctrines posit the absolute authority of pastors, teachers, fathers, "civil authority," and so on. In "God's chain of command," there are no relationships of equality but only superiors and inferiors, authority and obedience. While fundamentalist theology exists quite independent of individual pastors, individual pastors do tend to impose their own personal authority.

"This Jim Jones thing haunts everyone," Jackie Gould told me. She was the second person in Falwell's congregation to bring Jones's name up to me. The first was a professor who worked with the Moral Majority. "Imagine a spectrum that runs from a Jim Jones cult on the one hand to the most arid of liberal churches on the other," the professor said. "Well, some of the big fundamentalist churches in the South would fall close—dangerously close—to the Jim Jones end of the spectrum. I know because I used to belong to one of them. I got out, but it was a terrible culture shock. The question is, of course, where Dr. Falwell's church would fit in this spectrum. It is one of the religious kingdoms of the South. But in my view it is one of the most liberal and progressive of them."

It is true that Falwell's church is nothing like a Jim Jones cult. Lynchburg people outside the church do not even make the association, for they can see perfectly well that the congregation runs too much to Tupperware and to careers in Babcock & Wilcox or the military. Among the thousands who come to visit the Thomas Road Church each year, there are a few Flannery O'Connor guilt-ridden crazies with stones in their boots (Falwell has concrete walls around his house and a guard) and a few sweet-Jesus people who arrive at the welfare office saying that God has sent them and will the state please get them home. But most of the visitors are families in big Chevys or couples on Super-Saver fares who have come East to see an aunt and, incidentally, to drop in on the church that they watch on television. Among the resident church members are some who moved to Lynchburg just to join the Thomas Road Church. But these people also came to go to college, to train in church work, or to send their children to a "Christian" school. They came to live and work within a big, well-organized church.

All the same, there is something a bit exotic about Falwell's congregation. The LBC women, with their midcalf dresses, and the LBC men, with their clipped hair and white shirts, present an obvious contrast to all the other college students in Lynchburg. But it is not just a matter of appearances. If you ask a Thomas Road member "What brought you to Lynchburg?" or "How did you find this house?" the answer will be "God brought me here" or "God found this house for us"—and only after that will come some mention of the family's desire for a warmer climate or the intervention of a real-estate agent. Such answers might indicate passivity or a sense of helplessness if it were not that Thomas Road people always seem to know exactly what God wants. This moon-child quality is far more pronounced in some people that in others, but all the Thomas Road people seem to have the same opinions about what God wants for society at large. As an outsider soon discovers, there is no real point in talking to more than one of them on a topic of general interest, for there is a right answer to every question, and Nancy James or William Sheehan can give it to you as well as any of the pastors. Or, if that particular person can't, it's simply because he or she lacks the specific information. "I'm totally against the ERA," Nancy James told me during a visit I paid to her house. When, for the purposes of discussion, I recited some of the pro-ERA arguments, she listened seriously and apologized for being so uninformed on the subject. I thought at the time that the arguments had made some impression on her, but later, as I was leaving, she came out after me to apologize again and to say, "I will find out more about the ERA. I know I'm against it. I'm just not sure exactly why."

For Thomas Road people, education—in the broad sense of the word—is not a moral and intellectual quest that involves struggle and uncertainty. It is simply the process of learning, or teaching, the right answers. The idea that an individual should collect evidence and decide for himself is anathema. Once Falwell told his congregation that to read anything but the Bible and certain prescribed works of interpretation was at best a waste of time. He said that he himself read all the national magazines, just to keep up with what others were saying, but that there was no reason for others to do so. (His church members seem to follow this advice faithfully; their weakness, when they have any, is in the realm of television watching.) He and his fellow pastors attack the public schools for teaching "immorality," "secular humanism," and other evils. But what bothers the most pious members of his congregation is not just that the schools teach the wrong answers; it is that the schools do not protect children from information that might call their beliefs into question. When I asked Jackie Gould whether she would consider sending her children to something other than a Bible college, she said, "No, because our eternal destiny is all-important, so you can't take a chance. College so often throws kids into confusion." The purpose of education, then, is progress in one direction, to the exclusion of all others.

As a result, book learning in the Liberty Baptist schools is severely limited. The entire library of Lynchburg Christian Academy would fit inside a few telephone booths; it contains one volume by Dickens but no Thackeray, no Melville, and no novels by any modernist writer. Liberty Baptist College has a library that was bought from a defunct college. It also has a tiny bookstore, and this displays books by LBC faculty members, books by Billy Graham, books about Winston Churchill, and not much else, next to banks of taped sermons, boxes of stationery, and piles of T-shirts. In a Western-civilization class I attended at the summer school, the professor managed to get through the political, economic, cultural, and intellectual history of nineteenth-century Europe in two hours. While he dictated an outline of European history, the students obediently took notes, asking questions when they had not heard exactly what he said. Nationalism, utopian socialism, scientific socialism, Marxism, the professor said. Finally, a young man interrupted to ask, with a laugh, if there were really ever people who believed in socialism. Fourier, Blanqui, the professor answered, and then he wrote "thesis, antithesis, synthesis" on the blackboard. A little later, a young woman raised her hand and asked who those people were. "Thesis, antithesis, synthesis," the professor explained, adding that this represented the dictatorship of the proletariat.

At the Liberty Baptist schools, students are protected both from information and from most logical processes. There is no formal ban on logic, but since analytical reasoning might lead to skepticism, and skepticism to the questioning of Biblical truth, it is simply not encouraged except in disciplines like engineering, where it could be expected to yield a single correct answer. (Not coincidentally, some of the brightest people I met at Thomas Road, including Falwell himself, had studied engineering.) In anything resembling human affairs, the intellectual discipline consists of moving word sticks and fact sticks from one pile to another with the minimum coefficient of friction ("Could I put down 'an end to oppression' instead of 'civil liberties' on your exam?" one student asked the Western-civ professor. The professor said yes, he could.) Irony, ambiguity, and contradiction are treated somewhat like pornography: they should not exist, but if they do they should be avoided, or contagious diseases will follow. Casuistry is not unknown among fundamentalists, but for lack of

intellectual exercise even pastors at Thomas Road sometimes cannot
explain their own philosophy. I asked a pastor, a teacher, and a professor, in turn, what was meant by "situation ethics"—a term that
fundamentalists use in excoriating the public schools—and none of
them could define it. All three gave me examples not of situation
ethics but of moral dilemmas. And they did so with great conviction,
since in their world moral dilemmas do not exist. People familiar with
fundamentalist colleges in the South would not find this intellectual
rigidity surprising. On the contrary, they would be struck by the
relative liberality of LBC. For example, Bob Jones University, in
Greenville, South Carolina, which is the biggest of the fundamentalist
colleges-cum-seminaries, takes the doctrine of withdrawal and separation far more seriously. The college has a fence around it, literally
and figuratively. Until their senior year, female students are not allowed to go out without a chaperone, even for a visit to the dentist.
By contrast with such strict-constructionist schools, LBC is a worldly,
sophisticated place, fraught with intellectual tension. For an outsider
the tension is difficult to appreciate, but what Falwell has said about
the status of the college makes the contradictions clear.

Speaking to the incoming freshman class in the fall of 1980, Falwell
promised that LBC would become an accredited college, with a degree
that would stand on a par with a degree from Harvard or Yale. In the
next breath, he said that the church would continue to control the
college, and promised that the students would find no differences of
opinion among faculty members. In the fall, he made good on his first
promise. His administrators reluctantly spent the money to have the
library moved up to the campus from downtown, and the college was
accredited. Now, according to his administrators, the fear is that LBC
will eventually follow a lot of other religious colleges down the slippery slope toward academic freedom. It is for this reason, they explain, that "The Old-Time Gospel Hour" owns the land that LBC
stands on (and hence the fight over real-estate taxes). It is also for this
reason that Falwell, speaking of the LBC faculty, says things like
"Any time they start teaching something we don't like, we cut the
money off. It's amazing how that changes philosophy."

The status of LBC as an accredited, sectarian college points to the
duality of Falwell's own ambitions and to the paradox of his whole
community. While Thomas Road people want separation, authority,
and certainty, they also want career advancement, some worldly
goods, and a little power in the society. The conflicting aims go a long
way toward explaining the confusion of fundamentalist politics in the
1980 election. "Fundamentalists are evolving," one Moral Majority
administrator told me. "I know you must think that a strange word

or me to use. But so be it. It's the effect of television, the effect of education." But then he added, "Of course, you won't find many people who have been educated outside of Bible colleges, as I have." And, in fact, the tensions and contradictions within the Thomas Road community are lost on most Lynchburg people, for what the church turns outward to the city is its hard shell.

In sheer size, the Thomas Road Church, with its related ministries, ranks as one of the most important institutions in Lynchburg. Its congregation is by far the city's largest. However, of the eighteen thousand people Falwell numbers in his congregation, many are students or people who live outside the city limits. The congregation thus probably does not, as its pastors have sometimes claimed, comprise a quarter of the population of the city. With some thousand employees, the combined ministries are the fourth-largest private employer in town. LBC now has three thousand students, many of whom live off campus. The church brings thousands of visitors t Lynchburg annually, and over the years it has brought the cit hundreds of new residents. (Falwell's administrators say that ten ne members arrive in Lynchburg every week, but how many came town just because of the Thomas Road Church is not certain. As f the number who leave town every week, that is not a statistic th anyone collects.) Because of its size, the church has created tra problems in the neighborhood and a few other low-level commun frictions, but they are offset by the welcome business it has brou to the motels, taxi services, shops, and other establishments.

Other than the movement of people, however, the Thomas R Church has had almost no impact on the life of the city. Since 1 Falwell and his people have stood apart from city politics and f community projects of all sorts. The Thomas Road pastors do belong to the local ministers' organization; they take no part in menical efforts, and are not known to make contributions to cha supported by other churches. Even the lay people tended to ta part in local politics or civic organizations until 1980, when, fo first time, Thomas Road members voted in some numbers. In L burg, this constitutes odd behavior, for the city is an excepti tight-knit, civic-minded place. Except for the Thomas Road p the local politicians, businessmen, ministers, and college prof all know one another and, whatever their ideological or party ences, cooperate with one another on local affairs. While the re ship between Thomas Road and the city government has hist been correct, and even amicable, the civic leaders talk ab church as if it were a foreign country in the middle of their tow in Lynchburg, but it's not of it," one of them remarked.

For all the distance the Thomas Road Church has kept, t.   (
great many people in Lynchburg who do not like Falwe,
church. The dislike is so general that it takes new member:
congregation very little time to experience it. The source of the
tion for most people is not political but personal: it is the attitud
Thomas Road members take toward those outside the church—
attitude that they themselves are always right and everyone els
always wrong. "Look how they park!" one householder on Thom,
Road exclaimed, pointing to two cars carelessly pulled up on the law1
of a neighbor's house one Sunday morning. "They think they're justified in doing anything they want to do."

The way most Lynchburg people meet Thomas Road members (or
realize they have met them) is through the members' proselytizing
efforts. A number of Lynchburg churches engage in door-to-door
evangelism, but the Thomas Road Church is by far the most aggressive of them. Not only the pastors but many parishioners as well
spend a good deal of their time trying to convert others. Church
members of all ages will evangelize at checkout counters, baseball
games, and dinner parties—some requiring only the briefest of con-
versational openings before asking whether or not their interlocutor
is "saved." In addition, the church organizes groups to witness in
hospitals, nursing homes, and neighborhoods across the city. Every
Saturday morning, groups of ten to fifty Thomas Road people go out
on campaigns, gathering first at the school for breakfast, prayers, and
a briefing session.

One Saturday morning, I went out with a busload of seventh-grade
girls to the Madison Heights section of town and walked with three
of them from door to door up and down a suburban-looking street.
Before the girls left on their mission, Lee Simmons, a teacher at
Lynchburg Christian Academy, had read to them from the Bible and
asked them to remember the wonderful experience they had when as
children they accepted Christ into their lives. The three girls I accompanied did not, however, radiate much Christian compassion as they
went about their task. When someone opened a door, they would
settle their young faces into stern, adult expressions and start reading
off questions from a little pink card they carried: "We are doing a
religious survey. Are you a member of a religious group? . . . Do you
attend its functions weekly, monthly, never? . . . How do you think
a person gets to Heaven?" In the midst of this catechism, their interlocutors would usually plea another appointment and disappear into
the house. But at one house the girls found a girl of about their own
age out in the backyard. Cornering her, they asked, "If you were to
die in the next instant, do you know that you would go to Heaven?"

The girl, who had been quietly sunbathing in the backyard, looked down and scraped her feet in embarrassment. "Well, yeah, I dunno, I *guess* I would, but I dunno exactly."

The three girls fixed her with hawklike stares. "Well, wouldn't you like to know?"

"Well, yeah, sure, but—well, how would anyone know exactly?" The girl brightened.

"Well, *I* know," the leader of the team said, tossing her hair back proudly. "*I've* been saved. Wouldn't you like to know?"

Now defenseless, the girl looked around for help, but found none. "Well, yeah, sure, I guess."

The three seventh graders accepted her submission with icy detachment. "Are you now ready to accept Christ into your life?" one asked in a tone appropriate to the question "Are you ready to be blindfolded and shot?"

The girl never answered the question, for at that moment her older sister appeared from around the corner of the house, allowing her to beat a retreat.

The three girls lost their composure only once that morning, and that was when a woman who had recognized them as coming from "Jerry's church" answered their questions forthrightly but treated the girls with the amused condescension that adults show when they buy lemonade from a little kid's roadside stand. Later, walking away from her house, the girls regained their adult expressions and began to discuss the woman as if she were a problem case.

I said, "But surely she was 'saved.' She said that she had taken Christ into her heart many times."

"She wasn't saved," one of the girls replied in a cold, superior voice. "You can take Christ into your heart only once." And as she thought about the ignorance my remark revealed she looked at me with amazement and then with hostility.

Such aggressive evangelism must succeed with certain people, but it annoys a lot of others. The pastors are always preparing their flock to deal with negative reaction. Tim Setliff, a young pastor (formerly the driver of a beer truck), told a large group of people at the next breakfast briefing session that they should prepare for those many people in Lynchburg who would say they hated Jerry Falwell and the church. "But they don't know Jerry Falwell," he explained. "And you can't hate someone you don't know. These people don't hate Falwell, and they don't hate you, personally. They hate the Lord Jesus Christ."

Setliff was not speaking out of turn, for Falwell preaches the same message in one form or another nearly every Sunday. This past sum-

mer, he told his congregation, "The war is not between fundamentalists and liberals but between those who love Jesus Christ and those
who hate Him." To Falwell, it is axiomatic that his kind of people are
the only righteous ones and that they will therefore face nothing but
hostility from the rest of the world. Even when he is speaking in
sports metaphors, he will say, "Learn to pay the price. If you're going
to be a champion for Christ, learn to endure hardness. . . . You won't
always have the applause of men." Then, dropping the sports metaphor, he will continue, "You will have Satan as your archenemy. The
moment you entered the family of God, Satan declared war on you.
The Christian life is to be a competitive, combative life. . . ."

Though Falwell frequently makes allusions to sports, it is the military analogy that is central to his view of the church and its role in the
world. "The local church is an organized army equipped for battle,
ready to charge the enemy," he has said. "The Sunday school is the
attacking squad." And, elsewhere, "The church should be a disciplined, charging army. . . . Christians, like slaves and soldiers, ask
no questions." Many evangelists see their enterprise as one of spreading the Good News and sharing the love of Christ with fellow human
beings. But for Falwell evangelism is, quite simply, war. In one sermon on the role of the evangelist, he said, speaking of his own experience:

> Radio became the artillery that broke up my fallow ground and set me
> to thinking and searching, but the local church became the occupation
> force that finished the job and completed the task the artillery had begun.
> It is important to bombard our territory, to move out near the coast and
> shell the enemy. It is important to send in the literature. It is important to
> send that radio broadcast and to use that dial-a-prayer telephone. It is
> important to have all those external forces being set loose on the enemy's
> stronghold.
> But ultimately some Marines have to march in, encounter the enemy
> face-to-face, and put the flag up, that is, build the local church. . . .
> I am speaking to Marines who have been called of God to move in past
> the shelling, the bombing and the foxholes and, with bayonet in hand,
> encounter the enemy face-to-face and one-on-one bring them under sub-
> mission to the Gospel of Christ, move them into the household of God,
> put up the flag and call it secured. You and I are called to occupy until He
> comes.

Nowhere in this sermon does Falwell mention Satan. The enemy
here is quite clearly human; it is quite clearly everyone who does not
subscribe to his own particular brand of fundamentalism.

Like many military men, Falwell loves numbers. To journalists, he

likes to quote dollar figures, listener statistics, and poll percentages—
often with some exaggeration in his favor. To his congregation, he
quotes the soul counts of his missionary legions on long-range pa-
trols. "In London, two thousand souls were saved for Christ this
week. In New York, Liberty Baptist students saved forty-two souls in
a twenty-four-hour period." Occasionally, Falwell paints his enterprise as old-fashioned territorial imperialism. Every pastor, he said in
one sermon, has a divine mandate to "capture our Jerusalem for
Christ," then "capture our surrounding province, or state, our Judaea
for Christ," then "capture the adjacent nations, our Samarias," and,
finally, "touch the uttermost part of the earth and likewise capture it
for Christ." Usually, however, he makes a more modern analogy:
America is "the only logical launching pad for world evangelization."

In the context of Lynchburg, Virginia, Falwell's military metaphors
sound less remarkable than they might elsewhere, for Virginia has a
strong military tradition, and over the years the counties around
Lynchburg have sent more than their fair share of volunteers and
recruits into the armed forces. In Falwell's own congregation, military
service is probably the rule rather than the exception. (At the start of
one service, Falwell announced that someone in the congregation was
looking for helmets, an M-16, and other military gear "for photographic purposes." A man in the balcony signaled that he could lend
the equipment.) But to speak of a tradition is to raise a chicken-or-egg
dilemma, for Falwell's militarized theology is hardly original with
him. His particular brand of fundamentalism has always proposed a
Manichean universe and identified believers with soldiers, slaves,
and early Christian martyrs. It is precisely the tradition of Flannery
O'Connor's Hazel Motes, who went off to war and who came back to
martyr himself because he could not find anyone else to do it.

Of course, most Thomas Road people probably do not see themselves as bayonet-wielding marines except at the moments when they
are listening to such sermons. Still, there was something of that gung-
ho spirit in the seventh-grade girls out on their evangelistic mission.
And there is definitely some of it in the LBC students training to be
pastors and church workers. Those LBC students refer to their college
as "boot camp" and look upon their education as training in discipline
and hardship. This past summer, fifty of them spent two and a half
months in New York City working for the pastor of a fledgling Bible
church in upper Manhattan and living in dormitories that were somewhat more crowded and somewhat less comfortable than the usual
boot-camp barracks. The fifty—forty young men and ten young
women—would get up at 6 A.M. every day to play two hours of team
sports before breakfast; after breakfast, they would have a period of

study and devotions; then, while the young women prepared meals or did secretarial tasks, the young men would walk the streets for five, six, or seven hours, going from door to door and proselytizing for the church. In their two and a half months, they went downtown only once, and then not to sightsee but to hold an evangelistic meeting in Times Square. One of the students told me he had seen the face of Satan in that Forty-second Street crowd—the Devil in this case having appeared in the guise of a punk rocker.

When I asked Thomas Road people what they most liked about Falwell, the reply was very often "He is such a loving man" or "He has such a big heart." I found the reply puzzling. True, Falwell did not attack members of his own congregation, and a number of them told me of his acts of kindness and generosity to individuals. Still, I could not understand how they could ignore the hostility he so often gives vent to from the pulpit. Then it occurred to me that they had not ignored it. The Reverend Carl McIntire, a preacher of Falwell's own brand of fundamentalism, has written, "Separation involves hard, grueling controversy. It involves attacks, personal attacks, even violent attacks. . . . Satan preaches brotherly love in order to hold men in apostasy." Thus, he concluded, aggression "is an expression of Christian love."

When Falwell talks about himself as a young man, he paints a picture of the toughest kid on the block—football captain, gang fighter, and prankster, who would take the steering wheel off a car going sixty miles an hour. Such super masculinity is a quality he attributes also to Christ. In one sermon last year, he denounced the tradition of portraying Chirst as a thin man with long hair and flowing robes. "Christ wasn't effeminate. . . . The man who lived on this earth was a man with muscles. . . . Christ was a he-man!" he concluded triumphantly, and loud "Amens" went up from the congregation. The men in that congregation seemed to see love as emanating from strength—from dominion and power rather than from the Lamb. For them, Falwell's aggressiveness might seem to be a promise of protection both from outside enemies and from the anarchic and rebellious spirit within. Rather than the shepherd, Falwell might be the ram guarding his flock. When he is not on the offensive, he takes a paternal tone. "The Love of a Big Man" is the title of a chapter in one of his self-promoting books. Like the younger television evangelist James Robison, he can put on a threatening display; but also—and better than most media-cool personalities—he can be the stern but genial and caring father.

In other words, Falwell secures his own authority by maintaining the tension between his congregation and the society at large. His

Christians may be martyrs or conquering marines, but they are always in danger. Often, he seems to go out of his way to fabricate enemies for the church. One Sunday, the enemy was a local reporter who identified Falwell as "right-wing." "Isn't that reporter on the other side if she calls us 'right- wing'?" Falwell asked—though in one of his books he had identified himself as more right-wing than anybody else. Another day, he accused the "liberal media" of conspiring to raise the price of airtime on Sunday mornings, although, as he well knew, the price rise was a result of inflation and of competition from television evangelists attempting to follow in his footsteps. Yet another day, the enemy was the people in City Hall who "discriminated against" the church by asking the "Gospel Hour" to pay real-estate taxes: "Somebody down there doesn't like the message we preach." In the next breath, he compared himself to an exiled Russian Baptist preacher who had spoken to his congregation two weeks before: "Did Georgi Vins stop preaching when they put him in prison?" Life "isn't going to get easier for Christians," he continued. "There will be ever-increasing pressures from the socialists and humanists."

To what extent Falwell shares the sense of danger he creates is not certain. He often seems quite comfortable in the company of "liberals" and others he has proclaimed enemies of the church. In 1973, a Roanoke reporter covering the SEC trial noticed that while the Thomas Road congregants who were packed into the courtroom regarded the SEC lawyers with open hostility (or, in the case of a black lawyer, contempt), Falwell chatted with the lawyers between sessions, and even seemed to become friendly with them. A few years later, he seemed absolutely at ease with Bob Guccione, the publisher of *Penthouse*, when both men appeared on Tom Snyder's "Tomorrow" show. Yet I have seen him stiff with tension in the face of a single journalist. Then, too, he has a habit of talking about the prospect of his own violent death.

So, in spite of all the washer-dryers and the living-room suites, there is a kind of cultishness about Falwell's congregation. To a stranger who shows a sympathetic interest, Thomas Road people can display great generosity and an almost painful openness. But when they are challenged the same people will shut the gates and look upon the outsider as the enemy—an enemy with whom they have no way to negotiate. To anyone who criticizes the church they will attribute the worst possible motives, at once dismissing the criticism and dehumanizing the critic. For questioning church policies, people in Lynchburg have received threats of "God's vengeance."

Some of the Thomas Road people I talked to—such as William Sheehan and Nancy James—had clearly waged impressive moral struggles for their own lives and those of the members of their families. One woman told me in touching detail about the breakup of her marriage, and her long and finally successful struggle to establish a new relationship with her husband and children. But for people outside the compass of the family and the church she—and others like her—seemed to have no moral imagination, and not even much sympathy. This terrifying hardness conceals an equally terrifying vulnerability, because as a result of their lack of sympathy these people know very little about the outside world.

People who have worked with Falwell's organization give the impression that it is this innocence, this vulnerability, that, more than anything else, explains the disarray of Falwell's finances. Most Thomas Road people have not been educated outside Bible colleges; they know little about finance or the law. And many of them have a "God will provide" attitude toward money. The few rich people among them are generally self-made men who have no patience with bureaucratic and lawyerly restrictions, and believe this large nonprofit institution can be run the way they run their own companies. They trust few people outside the church, so they seldom get good advice. And yet the cultishness within the organization prevents anyone from calling anyone else to account in a rational manner for bad decisions or bumbling. The we-they barrier could shield incompetents, and it could also shield crooks and con men, for those within the organization are easily manipulated by anyone who professes to be a "Christian" and a Falwell supporter. In the late seventies, a man named Frank William Menge appeared on the scene professing devotion to Falwell and offering him a number of harebrained schemes. Because he said he was a fundamentalist and because he was married to the daughter of a tycoon, Falwell put him on the board of "The Old-Time Gospel Hour" and did not discover for some time what seemed patent to outsiders—that the man was a swindler, and a rather poor one at that. This blind trust works both ways, and Thomas Road people—it need hardly be said—have never called Falwell to account for any of his decisions.

In a sense, it was only natural that Falwell and his people should go into politics. They had, after all, detailed and comprehensive views about the organization of society. And they had absolutely no doubt that their way was the correct one. Aggressive proselytizers, they had set themselves to convert everyone in the society itself. Add to this missionary movement a man with leadership qualities and you hve the elements of a powerful political organization. The question, then, might seem to be not why Falwell went into politics but what took him so long. The answer would seem to be the one that he gave in 1965: the doctrine of separation between the church and "the world." The doctrine has a long history in American Protestantism—the longest, in fact, since it provided the motive for the Pilgrims' voyage to the New World. But in the twentieth century it has been exclusively a fundamentalist doctrine, and one that even fundamentalists have often observed in the breach. At the time of the great theological controversies in the twenties, fundamentalist theologians and evengelists preached not only against the social gospel but also against the Bolsheviks, the League of Nations, and the "garlic-eating immigrants." Fundamentalist pastors across the country campaigned, along with many other Protestants, for Prohibition and for the defeat of Al Smith, the first Catholic to run for president. In the fifties, there was another burst of fundamentalist activism. Among others, the radio evangelists Carl McIntire and Billy James Hargis used their pulpits for right-wing political crusades. Then, too, Billy Graham, the most popular evangelist of all, came out for Nixon in 1960, 1968, and 1972, and expressed himself freely on such subjects as defense appropriations, arms-control treaties, and the Vietnam War.

Among fundamentalists, it was really only the southern pastors who observed the doctrine of separation with any consistency. Some of them were strict about it—to the point of forbidding their followers to associate with nonfundamentalists. Others preached that the church should not interfere in politics except on "moral issues," such as the blue laws, the prohibition of alcohol, and the teaching of evolution in the schools. But then, even without a doctrine of separation, the pastors of most conservative southern churches took the same position: that is, they rejected the social gospel.

The difference between northern and southern churches was not, by and large, doctrinal but rooted in history and in the different social and economic conditions of the two regions. In the case of certain fundamentalist churches, the withdrawal into personal piety seems to have been a reflection of the poverty and sense of despair in the South after the Civil War. The churches of the poor—particularly the Pentecostal and Holiness churches—rejected the material world altogether for spiritual discipline and chiliastic speculation. For the poor, these churches offered an internal migration from life as it was on earth. But not all the conservative churches were so withdrawn from worldly concerns. The Southern Baptist Convention, after all, split off from the Northern Baptist churches before the Civil War on the very material issue of slavery: the all-white denomination opposed church interference with it. Many church historians therefore maintain that the many white churches continued to reject "politics" after the Civil War because their congregations were more or less content with things as they were. Their withdrawal from all but "moral issues" was, one writer has said, an "existential amnesia"—a denial of responsibility for the past of slavery and for the present of racial injustice.

As a matter of theology, Falwell belongs to this southern tradition of pietistic withdrawal. But as a matter of circumstance he and his people belong to the New South and its economic success story. Even in the early years, he never interpreted the doctrine of separation to mean withdrawal from commerce and industry. His sermons were often lessons in wordly success—how-to-do-it manuals in the mainstream tradition of Billy Graham and Norman Vincent Peale. Instead of urging retreat from the social order, he urged participation in it. His failure to criticize the social status quo—except on the "moral issues" of alcohol and others—thus had to be interpreted as support for it.

In the early years of his ministry, Falwell—like many people in Lynchburg, and like many white ministers across the South—was a segregationist. When several black high-school students conducted a kneel-in at the Thomas Road Church, in the early sixties, they were evicted by the police. He founded the Lynchburg Christian Academy as an all-white school for his all-white church. In his 1965 sermon "Ministers and Marchers," he invoked the doctrine of separation in order to make a frontal attack on the civil rights movement. Falwell began that sermon by questioning "the sincerity and nonviolent intentions of some civil rights leaders such as Dr. Martin Luther King, Jr., Mr. James Farmer, and others, who are known to have left-wing associations." He went on to say that the Communists were obviously exploiting this tense situation, and that the demonstrations and marches "have done more to damage race relations and to gender hate than to help!" Toward the end, he talked about the involvement of church leaders with "the alleged discrimination against Negroes in the South" and asked why they did not concern themselves instead with the problem of alcoholism, since "there are almost as many alcoholics as there are Negroes."

Falwell now says he changed his mind about the role of preachers in politics because of such issues as abortion and school prayer. But it was the civil rights movement that prompted that first political speech. In October of 1980, just before Reagan's visit to Lynchburg, when he called the 1965 sermon "false prophecy," he asserted that he and his fellow ministers were now doing exactly what King and his fellows had done. His repudiation of the sermon makes it clear that his change of position was little more than a political change from support of the status quo to attack upon it. The civil rights movement was the turning point. It showed Falwell that preachers could be politically effective and removed one important reason for his support of the status quo. Ironically, it may have benefited Falwell and other white fundamentalists as much as or more than it benefited the blacks in the South. If the fundamentalists had felt any guilt about the plight of their fellow human beings, the civil rights movement relieved them of it. It gave them moral absolution, and it gave them the vote; it gave them their civil rights at no cost to themselves.

At no cost because the civil rights movement actually changed very little at the Thomas Road Church. Falwell and his pastors have brought a few blacks into the church and into the Liberty Baptist Schools. But the congregation remains more than 90 percent white, and with the unwritten law against interracial dating, white parents can still see the school and the college as alternatives to the fully integrated public schools. The Thomas Road pastors say that they don't make much of an attempt to evangelize the black population of Lynchburg. When I asked Falwell why they did not, he said that the black pastors would resent it—they would resent him for taking the "leading people" away from their churches. The Reverend Jim Moon gave a slightly different answer to the question: "I don't think the white man will ever reach the black population. They don't trust us and never will. We have to train black pastors to reach them. We are a white church and will always be that way."

Falwell does not any longer speak ill of civil rights leaders. In a sermon shortly after his repudiation of "Ministers and Marchers," he described the efforts of Martin Luther King, Jr., as "noble." He does not attack black politicians in Lynchburg. A year ago, he took M. W. Thornhill, Jr., the black city councilman, out to lunch and offered the equivalent of an apology for past actions. Falwell has, in other words, accommodated himself to the change of attitude in the country and in Lynchburg. Now, like many politicians, he refers to racial issues by other names. On television, he has pushed all the coded buttons: "welfare chiselers," "urban rioters," "crime in the streets." On his return from a trip to southern Africa in 1979, he declared support for the government installed by whites in what was then called Zimbabwe Rhodesia and criticized those governments and organizations which were giving aid to the guerrilla forces and the black refugees. In his subsequent book, *Listen, America!* he praised the apartheid regime in South Africa for its support of religious freedoms and attacked "Comrade Mugabe, the new Marxist dictator" by suggesting that he would suppress Christian freedoms in Zimbabwe.

Politically, Falwell clearly stands for a reaction against all the pressures for integration and social justice brought by the liberal coalition in the sixties and seventies. Then, many of his church members clearly do fear the consequences of integration, if it means that their children's schools must include large numbers of poor black students. But on a personal level I found no sign of racial hostility in the Thomas Road congregation. At Liberty Baptist College, I saw a good deal of camaraderie between black and white male students, and nowhere did I hear a racial slur as such. What I did hear was anti-Semitism.

In a Bible-study class at Liberty Baptist summer school, a student answering a question about Biblical history said, "Well, if Jews are anything like they are today, they're richer than anybody else, so . . ." and he went on with his answer. That the professor made no comment on the remark was surprising as well as shocking. Religious tolerance is, of course, not the forte of the Thomas Road Church. (The pastors use the word "Christian" to mean "fundamentalist," as in this sentence pronounced by a college administrator: "We're going to have a Christian football team equal to that of Notre Dame.") Still, Falwell and his pastors seemed to have left behind some of the Know-Nothing attitudes of the Protestant countryside—their anti-Catholicism, at least, having been rendered down to the bone of doctrine on which Sunday-school students cut their theological teeth. For fundamentalists, the Jews have been less theological enemies than precursors—the Chosen of God, who will in the end return to Israel and be saved. Falwell has visited Israel, given money for the planting of a forest there, and shaken hands with Prime Minister Menachem Begin; and has lunched with the leaders of the Jewish National Fund in New York City. He has made Israel one of his causes. "To stand against Israel is to stand against God," he has said repeatedly, and, in a more directly political vein, he defended the Begin government's settlement policy on the West Bank. He has invited Orthodox Jews to join the Moral Majority. Yet he has a Moral Majority director in New York State who recently said that Jews have "almost a supernatural ability to make money," and claimed to number among his followers "a full-blooded Jewish man." When a reporter asked Falwell about the remark concerning money, he said that he himself did not believe in stereotyping. But a few months before Falwell had said on the steps of the Virginia state capitol, "A few of you here today don't like Jews. And I know why. He can make more money accidentally than you can make on purpose."

In Falwell's congregation, the traditional anti-Semitism of those who have never consciously met a Jew in their lives seems to have met and matched up with a newer kind of reaction. The Dyba family, of Pearl River, New York, had recently moved to Lynchburg to join the Falwell congregation. Stanley Dyba, a retired officer in the New York City prison system, complained for two solid hours about the deterioration of the suburban town they had lived in. With enthusiastic assistance from his wife and children, he described the increase in crime, the corruption of the school system, the drugs, the lack of patriotism, and the lack of respect for authority, attributing all these things to the predominance of "one ethnic group." This ethnic group turned out to be not the blacks (as I had anticipated) but the Jews. As he saw it, the liberal Jews—not the Orthodox Jews, he was careful to say—had destroyed the community by introducing disruptive notions of rights: children's rights, teachers' rights, prisoners' rights, and so on.

Falwell identifies "the liberals" as both the political and the spiritual enemy. At various times, he has denounced all the rights movements of the sixties and seventies. During the 1980 presidential campaign, he took to describing himself to the members of "the liberal press" as a conservative. In the past—the fairly recent past—that was not how he had sounded and not how he had described himself. In 1977, he called for a return to "the McCarthy era, where we register all Communists," and added, "Not only should we register them but we should stamp it on their foreheads and send them back to Russia." In *American Can Be Saved*, a book published in 1979, he wrote, "If you would like to know where I am politically, I am to the right of wherever you are. I thought Goldwater was too liberal!" Falwell's political definition of a "liberal" would fit anyone to the left of Senator Jesse Helms; his theological definition would fit any Protestant who is not a fundamentalist. "The liberal churches are not only the enemy of God but the enemy of the nation," Falwell has said. He would describe as "liberal" anyone who teaches evolution and anyone who does the fox-trot. ("I don't know why every one of our Presidents thinks he has to wine and dine every drunk who comes over here from some other country and dance with his wife. It seems to me that if a President is a Christian, he can offer that foreign head of state some orange juice or tomato juice, have a good minister come in and read a few verses of scripture, and if he doesn't like that, put him on the next plane back home!" Falwell said this during the Carter administration.)

Under the circumstances, what is surprising is the cordiality that has always existed between Falwell and the conservative, largely Episcopalian business establishment of Lynchburg. To be sure, Falwell himself is a big business these days—someone to be reckoned with in Lynchburg—but this was not always the case. It was not the case in

1973, when the five Lynchburg business leaders volunteered to help save his church, and gave him several hours of their time every week for several years without recompense. These men still approve of Falwell, and they are not the only ones. In 1978, Thomas Glass, then the publisher of the city's two newspapers, told a Roanoke reporter, "Lynchburg is a conservative community. People here appreciate the things Jerry stands for—God and country and the basic things in life." An Episcopalian, Glass called Falwell "A wonderful man of God."

Many Lynchburg businessmen who admire Falwell do not hear what he says when he addresses his own people. And when he talks to a group like the Rotary Club he will pick an issue, such as gay rights legislation, that everyone can agree on. (He told the Lynchburg Rotary Club last spring that such legislation would force every business to hire a quota of homosexuals.) Still, those in the business community who have worked with Falwell have a fairly exact idea of where he stands; at least, they know enough to know that they do not go along with everything he does. They believe, for example, that it is tacky, at best, to raise money by offering American flags from the pulpit, as Falwell does. And they consider "the people around Jerry" a bit fanatical and very naive. Some would, as one of them put it, "buy into school prayers," but none of them would consider joining the Moral Majority, any more than they would consider joining the Thomas Road Church.

When these businessmen are asked what they like about Falwell, they tend to talk about the institutions he has built for his own people: the home for alcoholics, the summer camp for children, the school and the college, with their "surprisingly high academic levels." One corporate vice president said, "What impresses me is the behavior and appearance of the LBC students. They look to me like the ideal American youth—though my wife doesn't think so, and they make my kids sick." In general, the wives and children of these men take a far more jaundiced view of Falwell and his students. But then the kids who are going to other colleges do not have the perspective their fathers achieve. "It's a laboring church," said one of the five businessmen who had been on the committee to straighten out the church's finances—the president of the First Colony Life Insurance Company. "There's no participation in it by community leaders, and that is probably why it is so successful. The nonachievers have to have something to be proud of, and they are proud of their church and contribute handsomely." Even those establishment people who are close to Falwell tend to talk sociology, and even those who are not see the church as being good for others. Joan Jones, a member of the Virginia state legislature from Lynchburg, a Democrat, and an ERA supporter, said,

"These are disquieting times for the average person. To have some-one like Jerry around, who is positive, who creates an identity for them, is very comforting. In this mobile society, there is a need for support. It's very comforting to build one's whole life around an in-stitution like the Thomas Road Church."

To listen to the people of the Lynchburg establishment talk is to wonder whether it is not, finally, they who are the real targets of Falwell's wrath. "You can't hate people you don't know," Tim Setliff says. Falwell does not know those people he so often singles out for attack—Jane Fonda, Gloria Steinem, Hugh Hefner—but he knows the business elite of Lynchburg and its privileged children, who go to ivy-covered colleges and learn to believe in women's rights and envi-ronmentalism. And no country-club member is more conscious than he of the class divisions in the town. "Lynchburg used to be a cliquish place," he told me. "But no longer." In a sermon, he said that just after his conversion, in 1952, he drove around Lynchburg in his car, stopping by the wayside to pray. "I began praying for the Rivermont section, the elite section where our wealthy people live, because I knew that not one of them was hearing the Gospel." After that, he prayed for the poorer sections of the city. The anti-Semitism of Fal-well's followers has very little to do with religion and a great deal to do with their feelings of resentment against the rich.

But Lynchburg establishment people tend to discount a good deal of Falwell's rhetoric, for, with all his apparent aggressiveness, he has never challenged them directly. Instead, he has in many ways tried to identify himself and his church with the traditions of the Virginia aristocracy. In his political TV special "America . . . You're Too Young to Die," Falwell posed himself against a gentleman-farmer backdrop of rolling green fields, fine wooden fences, and a handsome old barn with a wooden cask in it. His LBC publicity brochures often speak of "heritage." There is some pathos in this, for Falwell appar-ently wanted a redbrick campus at LBC. His present church is red brick, and, according to his brochures, was build from a design by Thomas Jefferson. In his sermons, Falwell often identifies the tradi-tions of the Founding Fathers with those of his spiritual ancestors the Puritans—a confusion that Jefferson would have objected to most strenuously.

Falwell has attacked "the liberal churches," but seldom any local church or local minister by name. He has never tried to upset the political consensus in the city—with the result that most establish-ment people think he couldn't do it if he wanted to. He has also rarely attacked any form of business enterprise in Lynchburg. In 1978, he, along with many other Protestant ministers, opposed the legalization of pari-mutuel betting in Virginia, and in 1979 he called for a boycott of Swedish goods, on the ground that the Swedish government was giving aid to guerrilla forces in Zimbabwe Rhodesia. But he has never campaigned against discotheques, against the selling of wine and beer in the local supermarkets, against the showing of Hollywood films in the local theaters—or, indeed, against any form of business enterprise. In his various fund-raising letters, he has launched tirades against those who manufacture and profit from pornography, but he has never once attacked the Lynchburg plant of Meredith/Burda, which, until two years ago, printed *Penthouse* magazine.

The businessmen who know Falwell say that all this can be explained by the fact that Jerry is really a live-and-let-live kind of guy. "You have to know Jerry," they say. "You'd know he was no fanatic." Those who have worked with him over long periods say that he has never tried to convert them. He would talk business, not theology, and he wouldn't mind a fellow having a drink or a smoke in his presence. A lawyer who describes himself—accurately—as a "cigar-chewing Episcopalian with a mustache" remembers that once Jerry invited him to go ahead and have a drink when they were seated together in a restaurant. He refused, he said, because he did not want to risk any public embarrassment to Falwell. "You have to know Jerry. In person, he's a wonderful guy, really."

M. W. Thornhill, Jr., also thinks that Falwell can be charming. He was personally touched by Falwell's gesture of reconciliation to him. "But look," he said. "When he tries to get his people to vote for Reagan, I consider that he's on my back and on the backs of all poor people in this city. And, let me tell you, many of his people are just as poor as we are."

Falwell has always had an economic philosophy of rugged individualism and laissez-faire enterprise. In his view, "the free-enterprise system is clearly outlined in the Book of Proverbs." He is antiunion and against almost all forms of government assistance to the poor. In *Listen, America!* he produces flourishes of quotations from Milton Friedman and then denounces the food-stamp program and welfare for all but the sick, the aged, and the unemployed during a depression. His economic philosophy is not as sophisticated as that of the Lynchburg business establishment, but, over all, it coincides with the interests of the local business owners and managers far better than it does with those of most people in his own congregation—for his church is, as the insurance-company president pointed out, a laboring church. Not only that, but many people in his congregation depend on government assistance in one form or another. Some of them live in government-built housing; some of them live on food stamps; some use the health services that the city provides to those who cannot pay; a number—residents and transients alike—apply to the federally funded Lynchburg Community Action Group for emergency money to pay a month's rent or to cover their transportation back home. What is more, LBC as an institution depends on government assistance. Not only does it have a tax-exempt status—as does "The Old-Time Gospel Hour" federally—but it depends rather heavily on the city's free health services. Many of the LBC students are married and have children. According to a spokesman for the Lynchburg Health Department, so many of them bring their families in for free medical care that they strain the city's capacity for looking after its own residents.

Falwell's economics—like his flag-waving superpatriotism—derives from the fundamentalist program of the twenties. It is no less—and no more—traditional. In the late nineteenth century, the rural "Bible-believing" Protestants had supported the free-silver campaign and the populist anti-big-business crusades of William Jennings Bryan. When World War I broke out, they campaigned against American military preparedness, and until the United States entered the war they opposed American participation in it. By 1920, however, the populist movement was dead, Bryan himself had left politics, and the great theological controversies had arisen, pitting conservative scriptural literalists against modernists and advocates of the social gospel. The fundamentalists, as the former group then began to call itself, saw Christian civilization threatened by an array of frightening new forces: German rationalism, the social gospel, socialism, Bolshevism, Catholicism, sexual permissiveness, and Darwinism. While the theologians erected doctrinal walls against all these new tendencies, the evangelists thundered out against the "Reds" in this country, the liberal immigration laws, the Catholics, the Jews, the "garlic-eating immigrants," and the teaching of evolution in the schools. Rural populism did not, it appeared, translate into a labor populism, and the evangelists in the newly industrialized cities made common cause with business against the labor unions. Billy Sunday told his audiences of Protestant workers—newly arrived from the countryside—to work hard, live clean, and pray to Jesus for the life to come. "We've had enough of this godless social-service nonsense," he said to a reporter in 1915. A number of his revival campaigns—including a draft-registration campaign in 1917 and a subsequent crusade among striking West Virginia coal miners—were paid for by industrial magnates like John D. Rockefeller, Jr. Out of this alliance between big business and the nativist Protestants came the Prohibition amendment and Republican administrations that curbed the labor unions and gave free rein to big business.

When members of the press have asked Falwell what made him change his mind about the role of preachers in politics, he has usually responded by listing four or five events. Last June, his list consisted of the Supreme Court decision on abortion, the "pornography explosion," the federal government's attempt to interfere with "Christian" schools, and the FCC's application of the "fairness doctrine" to remarks about homosexuals. This January, the list included the 1962 Supreme Court decision on school prayer but not the fairness doctrine. Last June, he said that the abortion decision of 1973 was a turning point for him, but this January he said that evangelicals (among whom he included himself) had not paid much attention to the abortion issue until three to five years ago. Just when Falwell changed his mind and just which issues weighed most heavily with him are not at all clear.

Falwell did not announce his decision to go into politics until 1979, but he had begun to move in the direction of the political arena some years earlier. According to former associates, the impetus came from the demands of his television ministry; his trips around the country seemed to convince him that he could reach a far wider audience by talking about "family" issues than by talking theology. In any case, around the mid-seventies the emphasis of his preaching changed; instead of attacking other religious creeds and the evils of drink, he now attacked pornography, homosexuality, abortion, and the ERA. In the Bicentennial year of 1976, he began a series of I Love America rallies—elaborate, choreographed affairs with singers and choruses—on the steps of state capitols around the country. During the presidential campaign, he attacked Jimmy Carter—the one evangelical candidate—for giving an interview to *Playboy*, and declared that "as a private citizen" he would vote for President Ford. In 1977, he associated himself with the campaigns led by Anita Bryant and Phyllis Schlafly, and a year later he launched a Clean Up America campaign. The campaign was designed as another fund-raising mechanism for "The Old-Time Gospel Hour," but along with the fund-raising letters he included ballots posing questions like "Do you approve of known practicing homosexuals teaching in public schools?" and promised to send the answers on to the president and to Congress. He put out booklets containing advice on how to form organizations to put pressure on local politicians, and that year he himself campaigned around the country. At the end of 1978, he claimed credit for the defeat of a gay rights ordinance and a state version of the ERA in Florida and the defeat of the proposal to legalize pari-mutuel betting in Virginia.

In 1979, Falwell resumed his I Love America rallies. According to one associate, these rallies and a new fund-raiser, the I Love America Club, had their origins in his desire to do something with Bicentennial Bibles he had left over after 1976. Be that as it may, the rallies plunged him into politics. In each state, he would invite local politicians to join him in speaking before an audience of pastors and their congregations. A politician—for instance, Senator Paul Laxalt, of Nevada; Governor John Dalton, of Virginia; Governor James Rhodes, of Ohio; or former Governor Julian Carroll, of Kentucky—would appear and talk about school prayer or national defense and affirm what a great American Jerry Falwell was, and Falwell would reciprocate by affirming the politician's morality. In North Carolina, he held Senator Jesse Helms up as an exemplary politician, and told his audience to support such "Christian gentlemen" as I. Beverly Lake, the Republican candidate for governor that year. Up to that point, Falwell had claimed to be involved in a purely moral campaign on the moral issues. It was not until the formation of the Moral Majority, in the summer of 1979, that he admitted to political involvement—the distinction between moral and political clearly having something to do with tax status.

It was during this period, when Falwell was moving into politics step by step, that he came into contact with the Washington-based group of professional political organizers and lay activists for conservative causes: Richard Viguerie, the direct-mail expert, who had raised money for a number of right-wing candidates, including George Wallace; Howard Phillips, who had been brought into the Nixon administration to dismantle the Office of Economic Opportunity; Paul Weyrich, a former journalist who had worked as an aide to two Republican senators; Robert Billings, the former president of Hyles-Anderson College, in Crown Point, Indiana, and president of the National Christian Action Coalition, which was leading a campaign to keep the IRS from taxing "Christian" schools; and Ed McAteer, a former salesman and the field director for the Christian Freedom Foundation. During the years of the Carter administration, these men had set up a network of think tanks, education lobbies, and political action groups, including the Heritage Foundation, Phillips's Conservative Caucus, Weyrich's Committee for the Survival of a Free Congress, and Billings's National Christian Action Coalition. In preparation for the next election, they met not only with Falwell but also with James Robison, Pat Robertson, and a number of other evangelists. Out of their discussions came three new organizations:

the Religious Roundtable, directed by McAteer, with James Robison as its vice president; the Christian Voice, headed by the Reverend Robert Grant, with its political action committee directed by Gary Jarmin (a former legislative director of the American Conservative Union); and the Moral Majority, whose first executive director was Billings. (He left in mid-1980 to work as Reagan's religious liaison.)

Falwell's staff members have maintained that Falwell alone conceived and created the Moral Majority. But that organization clearly shows the influence of Weyrich and others in the so-called Kingston Group. It was, for example, Weyrich's idea that if the blue-collar Catholics were mobilized around abortion and other social issues they could be "the Achilles heel of the liberal Democrats." The Moral Majority was set up as an ecumenical organization for conservative Catholics, Mormons, and Orthodox Jews as well as Protestants ("reverse ecumenism," Weyrich called it)—though Falwell never had much success in organizing the clergy from these other faiths. During the 1980 campaign, he stressed abortion above other issues. Then, too, the Moral Majority was set up in a sophisticated fashion as three organizations: the Moral Majority, Inc., a legislative lobby; the Moral Majority Foundation, an educational group; and the Moral Majority political action committee. Falwell ended by using only the Moral Majority, Inc., during the presidential campaign, and created a series of state organizations headed by pastors which were neither controlled nor financed by the national organization. It was these pastors who on a local level organized campaigns and individually endorsed candidates. Falwell supported Ronald Reagan "only as a private citizen"—and this rather late in the day. Like Richard Viguerie, he initially supported John Connally, and switched his allegiance when Connally began to lose and Reagan to win in the primaries.

By the summer of 1980, the activities of the Moral Majority and similar groups had brought forth a chorus of protest from mainline clergymen, liberal politicians, and commentators. Many of these critics, objecting strenuously to the issuing of moral report cards on congressmen and the endorsement of candidates from the pulpit, claimed that Falwell was violating the principle of separation of church and state. Falwell, however, argued that the pastors were acting well within their rights: They were not breaking any law (their lawyers had informed them that only if the churches as institutions lobbied or endorsed candidates would their tax status be endangered). And by endorsing candidates on matters of principle they were only doing what the liberal clergy had done in the sixties and seventies. Falwell was right on these points, but the issue had another dimension as well—one never fully explored by his critics.

The doctrine of separation between the church and the world had been erected by certain Puritan groups in Europe as a means of protecting the church from the state, and not vice versa. In the New World, however, the Puritans had arrogated the right to impose their moral code upon society by enshrining it in the law. Their descendants, both liberal and conservative Protestants, had continued to claim that right as a voting majority in spite of the Enlightenment tradition of the Founding Fathers and in spite of the increasing religious diversity of American society. In this century, they had voted in Prohibition and had had the words "under God" inserted in the Pledge of Allegiance. As the twentieth century progressed, the courts and the legislatures overturned a number of religiously based laws, beginning with Prohibition, and then, in the sixties and seventies, mandatory school prayer, laws against abortion, antisodomy laws, and laws against cohabitation. They had apparently redefined the private spheres, asserting in these matters the individual's right to freedom of choice and conscience. The Moral Majority and other groups, such as the Right to Life movement, were now insisting that the state should claim competence in these "moral issues" and relinquish its competence in the areas of aid to the poor, affirmative action, and other issues—issues that the liberal clergy, among others, saw as based upon moral principles. (On the Phil Donahue show, Falwell said it was the churches that should feed the poor, and not the state, with its food-stamp program.) The line along which the church should separate itself from the state has thus never been precisely or immutably established in constitutional law, and it is not now a matter of consensus among Americans; the same goes for the point at which one man's religion begins to interfere with another's. It was Falwell's contention that separation between church and state did not mean separation of God and government.

When talking to fundamentalist audiences during the campaign, Falwell and the other politically active pastors justified their political activity—their abandonment of the separationist doctrine—in this fashion: The nation is now in the most serious crisis in its history. Pornography, abortion, divorce, militant homosexuality, drugs, crime, and atheistic humanism are corrupting the moral fiber of the country and destroying its will to resist Communism. America, like the Roman Empire, is on the decline. This decline began long ago (the thirties is the period that Falwell looks back to with nostalgia), but the real plunge came in the seventies. Christians must act now, for civilization itself is at stake. America is the last launching pad for world evangelism, and if it falls to Communism—as a result of its own moral decay—that will mean the end of Christianity.

To the nonfundamentalist ear, the explanation must suggest rhetorical inflation and casuistry; and yet perhaps it is a more exact account of fundamentalist political thinking than the list of single-issue grievances that Falwell so often gives the press. The picketing of the schools of Kanawha County was, after all, not a single-issue protest but a reaction to the changes that had taken place in American society over fifteen years. What is more, all the great outbreaks of fundamentalist fervor in the past have been motivated by a similar sense of crisis and cultural breakdown. According to Sidney Ahlstrom, author of *A Religious History of the American People,* many church historians place the beginning of the fundamentalist movement with a group of evangelical ministers from several denominations, primarily Presbyterian and Baptist, who after 1876 organized annual meetings for Bible study in the conviction that the United States—indeed, the whole Christian world—was "sinking so deeply and so decisively into apostasy and heresy that it could only mean the approach of the Last Days." The movement did not coalesce until the twenties, but when it did those conservative evangelicals who called themselves fundamentalists shared a belief that the world was in crisis—a fear that as a result of modern thinking in all its forms the collapse of Christian civilization was imminent. A minority entertained theories that this collapse would come as a result of Zionist, Bolshevik, or Catholic conspiracies. Of course, most fundamentalists cannot concentrate on global concerns any better than anyone else, with the result that much of the time they are, like the rest of us, preoccupied with the problems of everyday life. But fundamentalists who have addressed the state of the world have always done so in apocalyptic terms. If America was not Israel—the City on the Hill—then it must be Babylon. In the fifties, Carl McIntire and Billy James Hargis were preaching the imminent coming of Satan in the shape of a worldwide Communist conspiracy that would end civilization by destroying the American family. True, these were the radicals—what one writer had called the "ultrafundamentalists." But the moderates had their own sense of crisis. Billy Graham, for example, preached quite regularly between 1950 and 1970 that the nation was in its worst state of spiritual decline. And quite regularly during that period he preached that the world would end soon.

This sense of crisis is quite natural, given the doctrine of premillennialism—the scenario that many fundamentalists have for the end of the world. In rough outline, the scenario, drawn mainly from the books of Daniel and Revelation, goes this way: At a time of confusion in the world, a false prophet, the Antichrist, will appear and will be supported by the apostate churches; simultaneously, the Beast will appear, in the form of a powerful political leader—a leader who will build a new Roman Empire and for a while bring peace to the world. The Jews will return to Israel, and some will be converted. Then the Beast and the Antichrist will together unleash the upheavals of the final three and a half years, or "great tribulation," in which the Jews will once again suffer persecution.

Finally, Christ will come with an army of saints to defeat the combined forces of the Beast and the Antichrist at the Battle of Armageddon and to install His millennial reign on earth. The whole tribulation period will last for seven years, and only the true Christians—the "saved"—will not have to suffer them, for at the outset they will be pulled up from the earth in "the secret rapture" and will "meet Christ in the air." (Theologically, the rapture marks the end of the Church age or "dispensation" in which God worked on earth through Christians. Thus the whole doctrine is called "premillennial dispensationalism.")

Since the Second Coming succeeds the tribulation, fundamentalists have always devoutly hoped for the onset of this period, unpleasant though it will be for everyone else on earth. And since they regard the Biblical prophecies as the literal truth, they have always looked to current events for signs of the beginning of this drama and for characters to cast in it. Since 1917, many have been convinced that the Beast will arise in Russia; the Bolshevik Revolution confirmed for them an earlier prophecy that Russia would play a major role in the tribulation. And since 1917 many have been certain that America would supply the armies of the saints. The creation of the state of Israel in 1948 fitted in perfectly with the prophecy of the return of the Jews to Palestine; many fundamentalists have been certain ever since that the tribulation will begin with a Russian attack on Israel.

The literalness of this interpretation of the Bible—born, as it is, of hope—has brought fundamentalists, in contrary fashion, to an otherworldly view of current events. The translation, after all, works both ways: If the Beast is—as prophesied—to be found in Communist Russia, then the Russian Communist leadership may well have powers not limited by the ordinary laws of nature. In the fifties, Billy Graham said, "My own theory about Communism is that it is masterminded by Satan. I think there is no other explanation for the tremendous gains of Communism in which they seem to outwit us at every turn, unless they have supernatural powers and wisdom and intelligence given them." Thus equipped, of course, the Communist leaders would have the ability to project their power in all kinds of mysterious ways. In the fifties some number of fundamentalists saw the introduction of fluorides into the water system as Communist subversion. This being the case, foreign policy will not stay foreign, or domestic policy domestic: the divorce rate might well bear a direct relationship to America's ability to resist Communism, as the world is a single battlefield between good and evil.

Fundamentalists, whatever their level of sophistication or escatological abstraction, have always seen danger ahead for the Christian world. This is as true today as it was in the 1890s. What has changed is merely the nature of the threat—or the precise indicators of the coming tribulation. In the 1890s, when fundamentalists were focused mainly on theological issues, they saw the new Biblical scholarship as the apostasy inaugurating the reign of the Antichrist. In the twenties they saw a host of threats from German rationalism to social dancing —with the emphasis differing between theologians and country pastors. In the fifties they became preoccupied by Communism. In the view of preachers like Carl McIntyre and Billy James Hargis, Communism was the root cause of all evils, and its influence was seen in the liberal churches, in permissive child-rearing practices, and in all else that was corrupting American society. In the seventies, however, Jerry Falwell, James Robison, and others reversed this causal sequence: the feminists, the pornographers, and the militant homosexuals were destroying the American family, and its destruction would (in Confucian sequence) lead to the destruction of the nation by Communist armies.

A true premillennialist might, of course, see this destruction as inevitable—and indeed, much to be hoped for, since it would lead, eventually, to the Second Coming. Yet the fundamentalist ministers involved in the New Right apparently believe that this particular form of destruction can, and should, be averted. On the other hand, they have not shed their eschatology. Both Falwell and his close associate, Reverend Tim LaHaye, have written books on the prophecies, and LaHaye has described the rapture as more or less imminent. ("There will be airplane, bus and train wrecks throughout the world. Who can imagine the chaos on the freeways when automobile drivers are snatched out of their cars!") But their politics indicate that they believe reform is possible in the United States. Falwell has never commented on the contradiction, but LaHaye has—theoretically—reconciled his politics and his escatology by a "pretribulation tribulation" that is not predestined and therefore can be averted: the reign of liberal humanists in America. Such theoretical problems aside, however, it is quite clear that when Falwell and LaHaye talk about FCC rulings, Supreme Court decisions, or IRS regulations, they are talking mere politics: the affairs of this world. On foreign-policy issues, however, they seem to lose their grip on the mundane and go into an uneasy existential wobble.

In the summer of 1980, Falwell broadcast a series of six sermons on prophecy to his television congregation. In one of them, he described the tribulation and the Battle of Armageddon in some detail. The tribulation, he said, is possibly already upon us, for the world is, as has been prophesied, chaotic and leaderless. Russia will soon attack Israel, but it will eventually be defeated, and then the Antichrist will move into the Middle East and unleash the great tribulation, which will culminate in the Battle of Armageddon on a field two hundred miles long and a hundred miles wide, with Jerusalem at its center. (Here Falwell showed the television audience pictures of himself in Israel inspecting the proposed battlefield.) The four hundred million who it is prophesied will die there will surely include large numbers of Red Chinese.

During this broadcast, Falwell advertised a new booklet of his called *Armageddon: The Coming War with Russia,* pitching it as upbeat. "I believe that America can win that war," he said. Earlier that summer, however, his optimism on that score seemed to be severely qualified. In an interview then, he told me that American military power was inadequate even to defend the country. "The Russians could walk right in and take over without firing a shot," he said. "They could do that any time between now and the mid-eighties—and long after that if we continue with the Carter administration's nondefense policy. In the nineteen fifties and sixties, we had military superiority over the Russians, and that's what we need again. Not military equality but military superiority." When he was asked how the Russians would "walk in," he answered, "Across the Mexican border." He then said that his information came from "leaders of the defense industry" and military men such as retired Admiral Thomas R. Moorer, retired Lieu-tenant-General Daniel Graham, and former Navy Secretary J. William Middendorf.

The coupling of Russia with Biblical prophecy poses problems that even the most experienced military men might not feel competent to deal with. The identification of the United States with Christian civi-lization poses problems of another sort. This year, Billy Graham said that he had changed his mind about a lot of things since the fifties. "It was a mistake to identify the Kingdom of God with the American way of life," he said. "I've come to see that other cultures have their own way that may be of just as great a value." (Graham's change of heart apparently came during one of the many crusades he had led in other countries since the fall of Richard Nixon.) Falwell persists in that identification, and he has run up against one of the many difficulties involved with it.

In August of 1980, Falwell told the *Washington Post*, "I am not one of those who use the phrase 'Christianizing America.' " He had not used that phrase, but just a year before the same paper had quoted him as saying that he wanted to "turn this into a Christian nation." Since then, he has learned better than to equate "Christian" with "moral": the Moral Majority was, after all, an organization for Christians and Jews. His postion now was that he was an advocate of separation theologically but was ecumenical in matters of politics. This he explained to the press and to his hard-line separatist critics, such as Bob Jones, Jr. He could see nothing wrong with this position, even after all the furor over the remark made by the president of the Southern Baptist Convention, the Reverend Bailey Smith: "God Almighty does not hear the prayer of a Jew." It was thus that on the eve of Ronald Reagan's visit to Lynchburg in October of 1980 Falwell said, in answer to a question from the press, "I believe that God answers the prayer of any redeemed Jew or Gentile, and I do not believe that God answers the prayer of any unredeemed Gentile or Jew." He explained that it was a fundamental tenet of his faith that man comes to God only through Christ, but that this was merely a theological argument he had with his rabbi friends, and that it implied no anti-Semitism. A few days after Reagan's visit, however, Falwell met with Rabbi Marc Tanenbaum, of the American Jewish Committee, and later said, in a statement issued by Tanenbaum, "It grieves me that I have been quoted as saying that God does not hear the prayer of a Jew. . . . God is a respecter of all persons. He loves everyone alike. He hears the heart cry of any sincere person who calls on Him." The price of ecumenical politics was apparently the renunciation of a fundamental tenet of faith. Alternatively, it was the maintenance of two separate audiences. While Falwell was talking with Rabbi Tanenbaum, he was—through "The Old-Time Gospel Hour"—running ads in magazines around the country asking "Christians everywhere" to sign his "Christian Bill of Rights," so that he could present it with their signatures to the next president of the United States.

Haywood Robinson, the head of the federally funded antipoverty program in Lynchburg and the pastor of a church that had been deeply involved in the civil rights movement, posed the problem of political involvement for preachers in this way: "I believe most profoundly that churches should concern themselves with the affairs of this world—and therefore with politics. But there is a thin line separating the legitimate, gospel-mandated expression of Christian responsibility to promote the Kingdom of God on earth and knee-deep involvement in the political process. It is important to uphold principles, such as human dignity, but once you start endorsing candidates right and left and addressing questions like how many tanks we should have, you cross that line. Instead of a monitor of the political process, you become a participant sharing the goals of politicians. The principles become lost, and the political rewards become self-justifying."

For Robinson, as for most clergymen, the issue of the clergy's role in politics raises only a tactical question: How deeply can they become involved while remaining true to their principles? For fundamentalists, however, it raises another sort of difficulty, since in fundamentalist theology there are no general principles but only scriptural dicta on discrete issues. These dicta cannot be compromised, nor can anything be added to them, for they are literally the Word of God. Fundamentalists, therefore, have a hard theological row to hoe when they attempt to deal with a pluralistic society and the art of the possible.

In October of 1980, Moral Majority staff members were describing Falwell as a conservative and pointing to recent interviews with him to demonstrate how moderate his approach really was. Those interviews indeed suggested that he had moderated his views on a number of subjects in the course of the campaign. Falwell had always denounced drinking, but in October, the week that Ronald Reagan came to Lynchburg, he denounced "excessive" drinking. Earlier, he had told the *Washington Post*, "I have no objection to a homosexual teaching in the public classroom as long as that homosexual is not flaunting his life style or soliciting students." And he added that heterosexual teachers should act with the same propriety. This statement was rather different from one that was going out with his fundraising letters for the Moral Majority: "Is our grand old flag going down the drain? . . . Just look at what's happening here in America: Known, practicing homosexual teachers have invaded the classrooms."

What had happened over the summer was that Falwell had developed an entirely different public from the one he was used to. Newsmagazines and newspapers around the country gave him extensive coverage, and the major television interviewers asked him to be on their shows. Having sought this audience, he found a new set of interlocutors, and he learned a good deal from them. That, at least, was the opinion of Rabbi Tanenbaum, who said after his meeting with Falwell, "I gathered that this was the first time he'd had that kind of [theological] discussion with a rabbi. He appeared to agree with almost everything we talked about." In his *Washington Post* interview, Falwell had said, "It looks like we're coming on like religious crusaders of the Dark Ages, rule or ruin. That is the last thing the people I work with have on their minds, but we've got to prove that by action. . . . I think we have a P. R. job on our hands to prove that we are human beings who love people but who have convictions about what is right and wrong." This was said less than a year after Falwell had remarked, "We are fighting a holy war."

The difficulty was that this new audience would not go away when he talked to his old audience in the old tone of voice. Last summer, at a rally in the Shriners' temple in Harrisburg, Pennsylvania, he presented a slide show that featured, according to *The New York Times,* "repeated images of Charles Manson, Times Square sex-film marquees, atom bombs exploding, young men with their arms around each other, and unbreathing fetuses lying in bloody, white ceramic hospital pans," and a quote attributed to the head of the American Communist party: "I dream of the hour when the last Congressman is strangled to death on the guts of the last preacher." And in an introduction to a book by Richard Viguerie, Falwell talked about "the godless minority of treacherous individuals who have been permitted to formulate national policy." Earlier in the year, he told an audience in Alaska that he had challenged President Carter about the homosexuals on his staff and that the president had replied that his staff had to represent the American people. When the White House produced a transcript of Falwell's own tape proving that no such exchange had taken place, Falwell had to explain that he had not meant the story to be taken literally.

The period of the campaign was a difficult time for Falwell, because there were so many conflicting demands on him. His own people were asking for the old truths and the old ferocities; the Republican politicians were asking him to look like a tolerant, conservative sort of fellow; and the press was asking him to be consistent and accusing him of breaking the commandment against bearing false witness when he was not consistent. Then, too, the contributions to "The Old-Time Gospel Hour" seemed to be declining. In October, he preached a sermon on a text from Matthew 26, "And Jesus went a little further," comparing himself to Jesus, who "always went a little further." The moral of his sermon was that all Christians had to show the courage and dedication of Jesus in doing more than it seemed safe to do. But, that being the moral, it was an odd text to take, since in that verse Jesus goes on further—ahead of his disciples—to pray, "if it be possible, let this cup pass from me." By the end of the campaign, Falwell seemed really frightened by the criticism. One Sunday, he brought a full box of press clippings to the rostrum and complained bitterly about the lies and the calumnies of the reporters. In a fundraising letter dated October 10, he wrote:

> I have become the victim of a vicious, orchestrated attack by the liberal politicians, bureaucrats, and amoralists. . . .
> The liberals and amoral secular humanists have tried to destroy my character and my integrity.
> And sadly enough, some of my friends who once supported the Old-Time Gospel Hour have believed some of these false reports and charges made in the Press. . . .
> I have burned the bridge behind me. You will never read it in the newspaper that Jerry Falwell quit. You may read that someone killed me—but that is the only way I can be stopped. . . . Opposition is becoming more and more violent. Our enemies are hitting us from every side.
> And we are certain that right now there are key individuals in our country who are plotting to close down this ministry.

There was one familiar note in the letter:

> In fact, if I am not able to raise 5 million dollars within the next thirty days . . . I may be forced to begin taking the Old-Time Gospel Hour off the air, city by city.

But this was the first time that Falwell had requested funds for his religious program on the ground of his political martyrdom.

The election results cheered up Falwell a good deal. "It was my finest hour," he said apropos of President Carter's early concession speech to Reagan. On behalf of the Moral Majority, he took credit for a number of Republican victories across the country, and he delightedly told his congregation about all the "important people" who had been calling to congratulate him. He became conciliatory toward the press, telling his congregation that he was slowly winning over "hostile" reporters through Christian love, and that it was good for reporters to come to the Thomas Road Church, since they would hear the gospel "for the first time in their lives."

The Republican victories, however, presented Falwell with a continuation of the dilemma he had faced during the campaign. The road in front of him forked. In one direction lay the rugged narrow valleys of the old-time religion, with its absolute truths, its puritanism, and its ferocities, where he could be the King of the Outsiders. In the other lay the broad plains where the majority of Americans lived, with all their liberal uncertainties, and where he might have some influence if he joined the general, confusing din. That he would have such a choice had perhaps not occurred to him, for his own people—his own congregation in Lynchburg had never confronted him with such a clear division of the ways. They, too, thought that there was a compromise—or they wanted it both ways. They had left the coal-mining valleys of Appalachia and come into the city to work for Babcock & Wilcox or the Dairy Queen. They would not for anything give up their cars or their television sets; they liked their freedom; but much of what they saw in this new world either scared or offended them. With this ambivalence, they looked to Falwell for all the old certainties done up in glossy packages. They looked to church for a haven of security—but a haven with windows on the wide world. They sent their children to LBC to train as Marines for Christ—and to get a degree that would be useful in civilian life. Some of them were far more hard-core, hard-shell Baptists than others, but the differences among them merely paralleled the divisions in the minds of most of them. The ambivalence of the congregation also paralleled the ambivalence in Falwell's own personality: at times he could be a genial, tolerant, easygoing sort of fellow, and at other times he could be as rough as any boot-camp sergeant. On his own home ground, he had no need to choose, for both sides had proved useful, and indeed, without both of them he could not have done what he did.

Now, however, there was a parting of the ways. The issue was posed most concretely when, less than a month after the Inauguration, a coalition of fundamentalist groups in California announced that it would spend three million dollars on a media campaign against homosexuals, and a spokesman for one of the groups, the Santa Clara chapter of the Moral Majority, said, "I agree with capital punishment, and I believe homosexuality is one of those that could be coupled with murder and other sins." The Moral Majority spokesman in Lynchburg denied any knowledge of this but said that Falwell was against protecting homosexuals as a minority group through gay rights legislation.

In the long term, Falwell could become a tolerant, conservative kind of preacher with influence in Washington. Billy Graham's career pointed the way. It also provided a warning. Graham had wound himself so tightly around Nixon that he came to seem responsible for the man and all the expletives deleted. The Moral Majority had backed so many candidates in 1980 that there was at least a statistical risk that one of them would be caught with a hand in the till or, alternatively, would take to drink or to liberalism.

Figuratively speaking, the choice for Falwell lay between the genial Republican businessmen and his "disciplined, charging army." That army was his strength, but it was also his weakness, since not even his own pastors in Lynchburg understood the big, polyglot world. They had not been trained for it, and if Falwell tried to explain it to them he would risk having them charge off under the command of some other general. He might succeed in bringing them along with him, of course, but then they would no longer by very good marines. They would no longer be people like Mark Totten and Lester Bledsoe.

Mark Totten, Lester Bledsoe, and I walked for three and a half hours one afternoon in July on blistering New York City pavements. We walked south from the Manhattan Bible Church, in Inwood, to the mixed Jewish and Hispanic neighborhood of Washington Heights. "This is the Jew—Jewish—section of town," Lester said. And then, with amazement, "You know, there are no Jews or Catholics in my town at all, and now I'm working only with Jews and Catholics."

Lester, a slow-talking, rangy young man from a tiny town in southwestern Virginia, had gone to LBC directly from high school. Mark, who came from West Virginia, had, like Falwell, studied engineering before deciding to become a pastor. They wore white short-sleeved shirts and pressed pants when they went on their rounds. They had been in New York almost a month with the LBC contingent, and now they were trying to make a second contact with the people they had "witnessed to" before; they were also handing out leaflets titled *Let's Get the Worm Out of the Big Apple!* The Jewish community of Washington Heights puzzled them. "There's no drug problem here," Mark said. "The kids are taking all kinds of drugs in my hometown." The students had been prepared for Sin City and for people with a desperate desire to reform. The Jews seemed—well, unavailable. A month before, Lester and Mark had attracted the attention of a crowd of kids in a park playground with their Bible reading. But then a group of parents saw them as Moonies and accused them of trying to kidnap their kids, and the school principal had the police evict them from the park. Then, said Mark, amazed, all the children in the neighborhood went away to camp. Mark and Lester had tried to ring doorbells and talk to the adults, but the apartment buildings all had security systems, and it had proved very difficult to witness to people through intercoms. The people they met on the streets told them they were happy to see nice clean boys like them helping out the Christian churches. Mark and Lester had no follow-up addresses in the Jewish part of the neighborhood. "Well, I'll say this for them," Mark said. "They keep their streets clean."

We walked on into the Hispanic area of Washington Heights. Here Lester had some addresses, but half of them turned out to refer to nonexistent buildings. We walked on and on, Lester occasionally passing out a leaflet and saying in a commanding voice, "You be sure to read it, now." Three of the addresses were right, but there was no one home in the first apartment and only small children in the second one, which we climbed five flights to get to. In the third apartment, a girl of fifteen or sixteen in shorts rolled well up on her plump thighs welcomed us to a blast of rock and roll. Lester lectured her about missing the Wednesday-night youth meeting. She thanked him gaily for coming around and said maybe she would come next Wednesday and bring her girlfriends. As we left the building, I asked Mark whether they had told her that the church did not permit dancing. Mark answered judiciously to the effect that everything comes in its time.

We walked on. At the ramp to the George Washington Bridge, where their territory ended, we paused to look at the vast cityscape of lower Manhattan. Mark said that he was thinking of coming back to New York to work as a pastor. "Just look out there," he said. "One and a half million people in twenty-two square miles. Why, there aren't five thousand people in the twelve miles between my home-town and the next one. Think of all the souls to be saved." He also said that he would like to visit the Union Theological Seminary, since he'd heard that it was full of Communists and liberals. We walked back the way we had come. In the middle of one block, Lester stooped down and reached for something on the ground. He came up with a baby sparrow—he had somehow seen the tiny gray thing fluttering on a gray grating. Cradling the sparrow in his large hands, he gently moved it to a bush near the entranceway to an apartment building.

At the edge of Fort Tryon Park, we had our longest conversation of the day—with a man called Jack, who lived in the park. Jack was quite drunk—not an unusual condition for him—but very clean, since he had just finished washing himself and his clothes in water stream-ing out of a nearby hydrant. Lester and Mark knew a lot about Jack; they had talked to him many times before, witnessing to him and trying to persuade him to come to the Manhattan Bible Church. They had been unsuccessful. Jack said he had done many years in prison but many more in college and graduate school. At one point, he had had a wife and a house in the suburbs; now he was, he said, engaged in his own metaphysical exercise of living in the open on what he could cadge from people in passing cars. (Never, never, he said, from the walkers, since that wasn't fair to the neighborhood.) When Mark began to lecture him on scriptural inerrancy, Jack interrupted to give a long, rambling discourse on early church history, the Greek philo-sophical tradition versus the Hebrew, and the problems often faced by Protestant theologians. He had flashes of great coherence, and he quoted—if I understood him correctly—Aristotle, Saint Augustine, and Karl Barth.

"Jack is very arrogant about his education," Mark said.

"These are nice kids," Jack said. "But they don't know anything. They don't know church history, and they have no philosophical grounding. I could become a Catholic, but not this." Waving his beer can, Jack went off into another ramble about the early church. Mark and Lester listened patiently, and when he had finished Mark recommenced his own monologue, about the Bible and the path it showed to salvation. Jack was clearly glad to have someone to talk to, but whether Mark and Lester stayed there out of interest or out of sheer doggedness I could not tell. And I could not ask them, for the word "interest" does not figure in their vocabulary.

After more than half an hour of this inconsequence, I said that I had to go. We walked back to Manhattan Bible Church through the sweltering streets of a Hispanic neighborhood—now, in the evening, coming alive with people and the din of radios and the smell of garlic and hot chilies. "I didn't think there could be so many people who don't speak English," Mark said. No one on the streets paid any attention to us or to Lester's leaflets, yet Mark and Lester did not seem to be discouraged. They looked as fresh and clean and energetic as they had when they started out at midday.

LIBERTY BAPTIST—1986

By 1985 Falwell was a successful and much sought-after figure in "the world." That year the *U.S. News & World Report* poll of leaders in twenty-nine fields ranked Falwell as the fourteenth most influential person in the country (just after Vice President George Bush and just before Attorney General Edwin Meese) and the third most influential person in the private sector (after Lee Iacocca and Dan Rather). In Washington, Falwell moved quite freely in establishment circles, for many Republican legislators and administration officials felt they needed him politically, or sympathized broadly with his views. He visited the White House frequently. Then, too, the press maintained its interest in him, and as he was a formidable debater, so he continued to appear regularly on national talk shows ("The Donahue Show," "CBS Morning News," "Nightline," and others). Then, also, in 1985 he started his own television call-in show on one of Ted Turner's Cable Network News stations. Press interviewers were no longer a challenge to Falwell. His genial side was usually in the ascendent, and he retracted few, if any, statements he made. To amuse himself —or so it seemed—he reached way over into the liberal camp for debating partners. He invited Senator Edward Kennedy to speak at Liberty Baptist College and debated Reverend Jesse Jackson on "Nightline." His star turn, however, was his appearance at the Oxford University Student Union, where, clad in a dinner jacket and black tie, he debated the prime minister of New Zealand, David Lange, on the morality of nuclear weapons. The Oxford Union debate was so formal and so hoary with British tradition that it appeared only on the Public Broadcasting System in the United States.

The American public's reaction to Falwell was not, as it turned out, wholly favorable. Indeed, the greater his public exposure, the more he seemed to polarize his audience. On one hand, the Moral Majority grew apace and proved even more successful as an organization than Falwell himself had anticipated; also revenues from "The Old-Time Gospel Hour" and other religious money-making ventures continued to mount, reaching $100 million in 1985. On the other hand, many voters reacted quite strongly against him. Even Republican voters did not embrace him as the administration did. (According to one poll of a thousand Reagan voters, 29 percent viewed him favorably and 44 percent unfavorably.) In his home state of Virginia politicians now believed that a Falwell endorsement brought a net loss of votes. In an interview with a *New York Times* reporter, Falwell did not exactly deny this. "It would," he said, "be a net loss only if we said, 'This is our candidate—elect him.' But we do it differently. We tell them, 'We'll organize and we'll get out our vote. Where you feel it better to say "Jerry who," do it that way. If you feel it's best to denounce us in certain quarters, do it that way.' " Falwell was quite frank about his counsel of subterfuge.

Falwell's own politics did not change very much—at least in the sense that he continued to denounce abortion, godlessness in the public schools, homosexuality, and other social evils as he saw them. In 1985 his solution to the AIDS epidemic was legal documentation of all those who carried the AIDS antibody and the preferring of manslaughter charges against any AIDS carrier who knowingly infected another person. He did not, however, attack the Reagan administration for failing to put its weight behind antiabortion legislation or for failing to give priority to the "moral" or "family" issues of the New Right—as, school prayer or tax tuition credits for religious schools. In fact he did not attack the Reagan administration on any issue at all. In 1986 he gave George Bush, a man known to be of two minds on the abortion issue, what amounted to his endorsement for a future presidential candidacy. (This while the Reverend Pat Robertson publicly considered running himself.) But then Falwell was publicly and organizationally engaged in changing his own priorities. In January 1986 he created The Liberty Federation as a successor to the Moral Majority —announcing that his purpose was to broaden the base of issues he and his supporters could address. The Moral Majority, he said, "means fighting pornography, abortion, and homosexuality," but The Liberty Federation "gives us the right to address economic, social, and political issues." The issues he specifically mentioned were national defense spending, the Strategic Defense Initiative, and "Soviet/Cuban expansionism." George Bush spoke at the first convention of The Liberty Federation, and, rather than to take the way out Falwell offered Virginia candidates, he endorsed Falwell's efforts enthusiastically. "America," he said, "is in crying need of the moral vision that The Liberty Federation has brought and that it will bring for our political life."

Falwell's interest in economic and defense policy was not new. His endorsement of John Connally for president in 1979 suggested a personal tropism for these issues; his endorsement of Bush, as opposed to Congressman Jack Kemp of New York, suggested the same. In any case, he took a great many trips abroad between 1980 and 1985, and, the "Moral Majority" rubric notwithstanding, made plain his views on a number of foreign-policy issues. In December 1985, for example, he visited the Philippines and expressed strong support for the Marcos government. He was, however, most concerned with Israel,

South Africa, and Central America. He spoke out for aid to Israel, and so passionate was his support for the white South African regime that he called Bishop Desmond Tutu, the best known of its opponents and the winner of the 1984 Nobel Peace Prize, "a phony." (This was the one statement he was forced to amend.) He campaigned vigorously for aid to the contras in Nicaragua, and on this issue he seemed to have some influence on the president. The general perspectives of the two men on Central America, were the same to begin with, but in 1986 President Reagan, campaigning for aid to the *contras,* discussed Central America in precisely the same way Falwell had discussed it in 1979, the vision being of Communists pouring into the United States over the Mexican border. On Central America, on the Strategic Defense Initiative, or "Star Wars," on the need for more defense spending, and on tax policy, the views of Falwell and Reagan were almost indistinguishable. It was perhaps this that made Falwell more of an establishment figure and less of an outsider than he otherwise might have been.

Falwell's public stance—and certainly the public's perception of him—changed only slightly in five years, but in the same period great changes took place within his own community and his own institutions. In the first place Liberty Baptist College grew enormously in half a decade. As far as his "Old-Time Gospel Hour" audience was concerned, Falwell made his college the first priority, raising millions for it—and pouring those millions directly into the college. Thirty-seven buildings sprang up on Liberty Mountain, and students flooded in. By the fall of 1985 he had at least 4500 students on the campus and, counting the various extension courses, 7000 students in all. So many students now went to the Thomas Road Church each Sunday that even with two or three services there was hardly room for anyone else, and many of the older members of the Lynchburg congregation joined new fundamentalist churches founded by graduates from the Liberty Baptist theological school. The training of fundamentalist preachers and teachers remained important functions of the institution. But now the college had other functions as well. In 1984 the existing schools of religion and education were supplemented by a school of arts and sciences, a school of business and government, and a school of communications. There were still not very many teachers: only 207 of them for 7000 students, and only 45 percent of them had Ph.D.'s. But in the spring of 1985 Liberty Baptist College became Liberty University.

According to administrators, the goal of Liberty University was to train fundamentalist students to become business executives, government officials, professors, journalists, television producers, and so on;

the goal was to send them out into the world, salting the whole society with them. This was an old dream of Falwell's, but it was a dream much elaborated by his experience of the world and much grander in scale than it used to be. By the year 2000 Falwell's projections were that Liberty University would have numerous other graduate schools, including schools of engineering, law, and medicine, and a student body of 50,000. In the end fundamentalists would be distributed through the State Department, the banks, the American Bar Association, the American Medical Association, the media, and the public universities. That was the plan in any case, and it was a daring one. In terms of the radical Right of the fifties it marked a giant step forward. Instead of trying to read the professional and technical intelligentsia out of the society by calling its members disloyal or "un-American" (as the Birchers and the McCarthyites did), Falwell was putting on an ambitious effort to beat them at their own game. The great existential question was whether Falwell's students could become members of the ruling intelligentsia—the Dan Rathers and George Schultzes of their day—and remain fundamentalists.

The question would not be settled for years to come, and perhaps would never be settled in any precise fashion. In the meantime, however, Professor Susan Harding, an anthropologist from the University of Michigan at Ann Arbor, studying Falwell's community, discovered a number of interesting problems cropping up within the university —and a number of even more interesting solutions. The most concrete problem was how to teach biology. The American Civil Liberties Union had challenged the teaching of creationism at LBC, and a federal court in the South had ruled in another case that creationism was religion. The Virginia Board of Education therefore decided that the college must take creationism out of its science curriculum and teach evolutionary biology. The ruling presented Falwell with a real dilemma, for to fundamentalists evolution was anathema—almost literally. But Falwell and his people figured out a way to obey the letter, if not the spirit, of the law, and the Virginia board accepted it. The compromise was that biology professors would teach evolution in courses appearing under the rubric of science—and the very same professors would teach creationism as a required course for all students under the rubric of philosophy. A fact sheet about biology education at LBC (later LU) stated that all eight biology professors were born-again fundamentalists who annually signed a statement of faith, and that "no professor was ever asked to teach anything as a proven fact that violated his or her religious convictions." Evidently the idea was that biology professors should teach evolution as a fiction— which the world in its error demanded—and then teach the truth somewhere else. In the Shi'ite world a maneuver of this sort is known as divine dissimulation." In one way it had every chance of success. From my observation of LBC professors, at least, there was little risk that their teaching of evolution would be persuasive enough to destroy the students' faith in creationism. In another way, however, the compromise was something of a gamble, for it was a deception, and consciously or unconsciously, students might ponder it and wonder what other compromises were to be made with "the world."

Actually there were other secular humanist snares in the university. Though none were quite as blatant as the teaching of evolution, some were more insidious. Liberty University (the word "Baptist" having significantly disappeared) was, for example, setting up an anthropology department. When Professor Harding asked an LU philosopher how the university would manage this, given anthropology's commitment to cultural relativism, the philosopher's answer was that fundamentalists could investigate other cultures as well as secular anthropologists. They could, he said, gather ethnographic data and think how social change occurred without ever assuming that all moral systems were equal; they could describe other cultures while always knowing "in the back of their minds" that Christianity was the one true religion. The answer was a fascinating one. Just in saying this the philosopher was abandoning the central tenet of fundamentalist pedagogy: the idea that mere exposure to other ideas or ways of living can totally corrupt the young mind and lead students to the worst kind of abominations. He had abandoned the entire fundamentalist rationale for demanding that public schools withdraw textbooks and course materials that fundamentalist parents did not approve. Beyond that he was proposing that students could keep two entirely different systems of thought in their minds at once without suffering from the balancing act. Further, he was saying that students could transcend the secular discipline with the theological one without having their faith changed by the very act of transcendence. This was surely hubris in the precise, original sense of the word. And it was the philosophy of Liberty U.

In addition to taking certain steps away from intellectual, or doctrinal, orthodoxy, the LU community was engaged in revising its views on matters of sex and the family. In 1985 freshmen and sophomores were still forbidden to date, and premarital sex was out of the question. But now, according to Harding, family counselors were discussing sex quite openly. Taking the tack that sex within marriage was sacred and that it deepened relationships, counselors now went so far as to discuss sexual techniques as a means of giving pleasure. This was a radical departure, for if sex was for pleasure as well as for propagation, then birth control had to be discussed—and the next step might be sex education for all. Then, too, Falwell had come to the conclusion that abortion could be condoned in the case of rape or incest. What his exceptions showed was that the taboo against abortion had not really to do with the taking of a human life (since children born of rape and incest are, after all, still humans) but rather with the maintenance of other sexual taboos (as premarital sex). Falwell did not suggest this line of thinking, but he did at least make abortion a possible subject for discussion among fundamentalists. More important perhaps than the airing of these issues was the fact that women at Liberty University were going to work outside the home—the married as well as the unmarried. According to one professor, 70 to 75 percent of the wives of male LU professors and graduate students worked outside the home. Then, too, women undergraduates were being encouraged to train not just for jobs but for lifelong careers. In 1985 a special supplement of the *Moral Majority Report* on the graduates of the college featured two women along with the men—one of them a tax specialist and the other a microbiologist studying at a state university. Falwell and his pastors had for some time condoned divorce under certain circumstances; now, with women working, they were going to have a much more difficult time explaining "the traditional family."

In sum, Falwell had by 1985 set his course quite firmly in the direction of "the world." Not only that but in the space of five years he had sailed so far away from the rock of doctrinal purity as to come quite perilously close to the opposite shore and the shoals of postmillennialism. He and his pastors maintained that the Last Days were nigh, but they were also training students and planning for the year 2000. Falwell's theological position was that of despair for the future and despair about human nature; all the same, he seemed to have a good deal of hope for the future of the United States under the leadership of the Republican party and his own Liberty University students. It had been a long time since he had talked about subversives in Washington destroying the moral fiber of the country. Satan still existed in the world, but to listen to Falwell was to believe that he had gone abroad—to gather strength in the Soviet Union and Central America. It was in the area of foreign policy that Falwell's eschatology meshed most closely with his temporal positions. And, oddly enough, it was precisely in this area (Falwell always referred to it as defense policy) that he had the greatest influence in Washington. In five years he had failed to obtain major legislative victories for the Moral Majority issues, but he could point with pride to the administration's position on Central America and to the Star Wars program. On educational and Moral Majority issues fundamentalists under his aegis were moving toward the rest of the country; on foreign-policy and defense issues the country had moved toward him.

Sun City–
1983

ON Route 301 south of Tampa, billboards advertising Sun City Center crop up every few miles, with pictures of Cesar Romero and slogans that read FLORIDA'S RETIREMENT COMMUNITY OF THE YEAR, 87 HOLES OF GOLF, THE TOWN TOO BUSY TO RETIRE. According to a real-estate brochure, the town is "sensibly located . . . comfortably removed from the crowded downtown areas, the highway clutter, the tourists and the traffic." It is twenty-five miles from Tampa, thirty miles from Bradenton, thirty-five miles from Sarasota, and eleven miles from the nearest beach on the Gulf Coast. Route 301, an inland route—to be taken in preference to the coast road, with its lines of trucks from the phosphate plants—passes through a lot of swampland, some scraggly pinewoods, and acre upon acre of straw-berry beds covered with sheets of black plastic. There are fields where hairy, tough-looking cattle snatch at the grass between the palmettos. There are aluminum warehouses, cinder-block stores, and trailer homes in patches of dirt with laundry sailing out behind. There are Pentecostal churches and run-down cafés and bars with rows of pickup trucks parked out front.

Turn right with the billboards onto Route 674, and there is a green-and-white suburban-looking resort town. Off the main road, white asphalt boulevards with avenues of palm trees give onto streets that curve pleasingly around golf courses and small lakes. White ranch-style houses sit back from the streets on small, impeccably manicured lawns. A glossy four-color map of the town put out by a real-estate company shows cartoon figures of golfers on the fairways and boats on the lakes, along with drawings of churches, clubhouses, and curly green trees. The map is a necessity for the visitor, since the streets curve around in maze fashion, ending in culs-de-sac or doubling back on themselves. There is no way in or out of Sun City Center except by the main road bisecting the town. The map, which looks like a child's board game (Snakes and Ladders or Uncle Wiggily), shows a vague area—a kind of no-man's-land—surrounding the town. As the map suggests, there is nothing natural about Sun City Center. The lakes are artificial, and there is hardly a tree or a shrub or a blade of grass that has any correspondence in the world just beyond it. At the edges of the development, there are houses under construction, with the seams still showing in the transplanted lawns. From there, you can look out at a flat brown plain that used to be a cattle ranch. The developer simply scraped the surface off the land and started over again.

Sun City Center is an unincorporated town of about eighty-five hundred people, almost all of whom are over the age of sixty. It is a self-contained community, with stores, banks, restaurants, and doc-tors' offices. It has the advertised eighty-seven holes of golf; it also has tennis courts, shuffleboard courts, swimming pools, and lawn-bowling greens. In addition to the regular housing, it has a "life-care facility"—a six-story apartment building with a nursing home in one wing. "It's a strange town," a clinical psychologist at the University of South Florida, in Tampa, told me before I went. "It's out there in the middle of nowhere. It has a section of private houses, where people go when they retire. Then it has a section of condos and apartments, where people go when they can't keep up their houses. Then it has a nursing home. Then it has a cemetery." In fact, there is no cemetery in Sun City Center, but the doctor was otherwise correct.

In his social history of the family in Europe, *Centuries of Childhood*, the French historian Philippe Ariès shows us that "childhood" is a social construct. In medieval France, the concept did not exist, for children were not differentiated from other people. In the twelfth century, children out of swaddling clothes would be dressed as adults, and as soon as they could get about independently they would join the world of adults, participating in their work and their social life as fully as their physical capacities permitted. (The painters of the period depicted children as dwarf adults, ignoring their distinctive physiognomy.) The notion of "childhood" developed very slowly over the centuries. Only gradually did children become specialized people, with their own dress, their own work (schooling), their own manners and games. To travel around Florida these days—and particularly to visit a retirement community such as Sun City Center—is to suspect that a similar kind of specialization is taking place at the other end of the age spectrum: that American society is creating a new category of people, called "the aging" or "senior citizens," with their own distinctive habits and customs. (That the name for these people has not yet been agreed upon shows that their status is still transitional.)

In a sense, the residents of Sun City Center and their peers across the United States are living on a frontier. Not a geographical frontier but a chronological one. Old age is nothing new, of course, but for an entire generation to reach old age with its membership almost intact is something new. Until this century, death had no more relation to old age than it had to any other period of life. In fact, it had less. In seventeenth-century France, for example, a quarter of all human beings died before the age of one, another quarter died before the age of twenty, and a third quarter before the age of forty-five; only ten out of a hundred people reached the age of sixty. In France from the seventeenth century to the nineteenth, the percentage of the population over sixty remained almost constant, at 8.8 percent. In America during the same period, life was probably even shorter for most people, and the population as a whole was much younger. But then in the twentieth century the demographics turned around; they changed more than they had in the six previous centuries. In 1900, the average life expectancy for children born in the United States was 47.3 years. In 1980, it was 73.6 years. This startling increase was due mainly to medical success in reducing the rates of infant, childhood, and maternal mortality. But there was—also as a result of medical advances—some increase in longevity as well. In 1900, white men aged sixty could expect an average of 14.4 more years of life. In 1978, they could expect an average of 17.2 more. (And women could expect to do better than that.) As a result of these and other demographic changes, the number of people sixty or sixty-five and over increased both absolutely and relative to the population of the United States as a whole. In 1900, people sixty-five and over represented 4 percent of the population. In 1980, they represented 11.3 percent of it, and there were 25.5 million of them.

The younger generation in this country has grown up with the notion that people should reach the age of sixty-five, and reach it in good health. But Americans now over sixty belong to the first generation to do that. Modern medicine has increased longevity to some degree, but, just as important, it has alleviated some of the persistent, nonfatal maladies of the body. Throughout history, of course, some people have reached their eighties in excellent health, but until this century the majority of Europeans and Americans aged as many people still do in the poorest countries of the world—suffering irreversible physical decay in their forties and fifties. Philippe Ariès reminds us that until recently chronological age had very little meaning in European society; the world "old" was associated with the loss of teeth, eyesight, and so on. The very novelty of health and physical vigor in those past sixty-five is reflected in the current struggle over nomenclature. Since the passage of the Social Security Act, in 1935, demographers have used the age of sixty-five as a benchmark and labeled those at or over it as "the old" or "the elderly." The terms are meant to be objective, but because of their connotations they have proved unacceptable to those designated by them. Sensitive to their audience, gerontologists and government agencies have substituted "older people," "the aging," or "senior citizens." These terms, being relative, could apply to anyone of almost any age, but, by a kind of linguistic somersault, they have come to denote a precise chronological category.

People now over sixty-five live on a frontier also in the sense that the territory is fast filling up behind them. By the end of the century, if current demographic trends hold, one in eight Americans, or slightly more than 12 percent of the population, will be sixty-five or over. The increase will at first be relatively small, because the number of children born in the thirties was a relatively small one; but then, barring catastrophe or large-scale immigration, the numbers will start to climb. In the years between 2020 and 2030, after the baby-boom generation reaches its seniority, some fifty-five million Americans, or nearly 20 percent of the projected population, will be sixty-five or over. How the society will support these people is a problem that

Americans are just beginning to think about. Politicians have been considering the implications for Social Security and federal retirement benefits, but they have not yet begun to imagine all the consequences in other realms.

The younger generation assumes that at sixty-five people leave their jobs and spend five, ten, or fifteen years of their lives in a condition called retirement. But here, too, the generation now around sixty-five has broken new ground. Historically speaking, the very notion of retirement—on a mass scale, at any rate—is new, and dates only from the industrial revolution, from the time when a majority of workers (and not just a few professionals) became replaceable parts in organizations outside the family. The possibility of retirement for large numbers of people depended, of course, on the establishment of adequate social-insurance systems, and these were not created until long after the building of industry. In this country, whose industrial revolution lagged behind that of Western Europe, the possibility came only with the New Deal. The Social Security Act of 1935 created an economic floor for those who could not work. More important, it created the presumption that American workers had a right to retire —a right to live without working after the age of sixty-five. This presumption led, in turn, to the establishment of government, corporate, and union pension plans that allowed workers to retire without a disastrous loss of income. But these pension plans did not cover very many people until some time after the World War II. Even in 1950, 46 percent of all American men sixty-five and over were still working or looking for work. In 1980, only 20 percent were.

In *The Coming of Age*, published in 1970, Simone de Beauvoir called the treatment of the elderly in Western societies a scandal. Citing 1957 statistics, she pointed out that in the United States a quarter of all couples over sixty-five had incomes below the poverty level; the scandal was far worse in the case of single people, since 33 percent of elderly men and 50 percent of elderly women had less than poverty-level incomes. The de Beauvoir analysis is now way out of date, however. Since the late fifties, the economic situation of older people in this country has improved dramatically. In 1978, only 14 percent of all noninstitutionalized elderly people had incomes below the poverty line—or about the same percentage that existed throughout the society. (Between 1959 and 1978, the numbers of the elderly poor actually declined, not only relatively but absolutely, from 5.5 million people to 3.3 million.) Elderly single women fared far worse than couples or single men (21 percent had incomes below the poverty level), and the older people fared worse than the younger "elderly." But everyone went up with the rising tide. Between 1965 and 1976, the median

income for families headed by an elderly person increased by 38 percent in real dollars. In 1960, outlays for the elderly constituted 13
percent of the federal budget. In 1980, the figure was 27.5 percent.
This rise reflected not only a growth in the number of elderly people
but also a real increase in Social Security and federal-pension benefits.
In addition, Social Security benefits and pensions (from the government and also from a few corporations) have been adjusted to the
Consumer Price Index. The result is that for the past ten years—the
years of high inflation—the economic situation of older people has
improved both absolutely and relative to that of younger people. In
the seventies, the average Social Security benefit shot up 55 percent
faster than the price index, while the average income of wage earners
rose less than 2 percent in real terms. Between 1970 and 1976, the
median income for younger people increased by only 4 percent,
whereas it increased by around 20 percent for those sixty-five and
over. Thus, the present generation of people in their sixties and seventies may be the most privileged generation of elderly people in
history.

Simone de Beauvoir complained in her book that older people were
looked upon mainly as a social problem. In the sense that she was
correct at the time, she would be correct today—except that the
"problem" has largely reversed itself. In the sixties and seventies,
American parents worried about the kids of the Woodstock generation "dropping out of the system"; in fact, as we now discover, it was
their fathers who were dropping out, in droves. In 1981, only 68
percent of all men between the ages of fifty-five and fifty-nine had
year-round, full-time jobs; of those between sixty and sixty-four, only
49 percent did. By the end of 1981, more than half of all male retirees
—57.1 percent—had gone on Social Security pensions before they
were sixty-five. The fact that the median age of retirement rose
slightly after the economic downturn of 1974–75 suggests that not all
these men were victims of unemployment or of mandatory-retirement
policies. According to a Louis Harris poll conducted in 1981, 60 percent of all retirements were voluntary; of the remaining 40 percent the
great majority resulted from ill health or disability, with mandatory-
retirement policies accounting for only a fifth. What all these statistics
indicate is that people are living longer, and are also retiring earlier
by choice and maintaining something closer to their old standard of
living. The question is whether the society will continue to be able to
support this unemployed population in addition to its children. Pro-
jecting current trends into the future, demographers calculate that by
the year 2000 there will be only three active working people to support
every person over sixty-five; in the year 2030, the ratio will be only

two to one. Government planners, adding up the cost of federal benefits for these future generations of retirees, estimate that at current
rates expenditures for Social Security, government pensions, and
other programs benefiting the elderly would claim 35 percent of the
federal budget in the year 2000 and 65 percent of it in 2025. Given
these statistical projections, a number of commentators have announced the imminent outbreak of a war between the old and the
young.

Americans now in their sixties and seventies are surely the first
generation of healthy, economically independent retired people in
history—and, in the absence of significant economic growth, they
may well be the last one. But, whatever the economic arrangements
of the future, this generation remains the cultural avant-garde for the
increasingly large generations of the elderly which are to follow them.
Already, its members have broken with many of the traditions of the
past, shattering the conventions of what older people should look like
and do. And in the process they have changed the shape of American
society. The census statistics describe a part of this transformation.
They tell us, for one thing, that this generation has used its economic
independence to get out of the house—or to get its children out. In
1900, some 60 percent of all Americans sixty-five and over lived with
an adult child. Today, only about 17 percent live with one. The figures
do not tell us who initiated the move, but they correlate very well
with the increasing wealth of the elderly. Today, a majority of Americans over sixty-five live in the same community as at least one of their
children, and live in the place in which they spent most of their lives.
However, a significant minority of them have altered the traditional
pattern by moving away from their families and out of their hometowns to make new lives for themselves elsewhere. Retired people—
so the census shows—have contributed greatly to the general American migration to the Sun Belt; indeed, they have gone in such numbers as to make a distinct impression on the demographics of certain
states. New Mexico, Arizona, and Southern California now have large
populations of retirees, but it is Florida that has the highest proportion of them. People over sixty-five constitute 17.3 percent of the
population of Florida—as opposed to the national average of 11.3
percent. These elderly migrants have not distributed themselves
evenly around the state but have concentrated themselves on the
coasts and in the area of Orlando. As a result, there are three counties
on the west coast where the median age is between fifty and sixty,
and eleven counties around the state where it is between forty and
fifty.

Before World War II, there was, broadly speaking, no such thing as an age-segregated community and no such concept as "retirement living." Until the mid-fifties, in fact, "housing for the elderly" generally meant church-run homes for the very poor. In 1956, the federal government began to subsidize housing for the elderly in a number of ways—by direct loans to nonprofit developers, by mortgage insurance, by rent subsidies—and the funds translated largely into age-segregated apartment complexes. Around the same time, private developers began to build housing for middle-income retirees. In the early sixties, when credit and housing materials were still relatively cheap, huge developers, such as the Del E. Webb Development Corporation, of Phoenix, began to construct entire new towns for the retired. In the mid-seventies, when housing costs doubled and tripled, the developers grew leery of such grand schemes, but by that time there were—according to one estimate—sixty-nine retirement villages, a number of which had populations of over ten thousand. The sixties and seventies saw a proliferation of mobile-home parks for the elderly—in 1975, one survey indicates, there were 700 of them, housing some 300,000 people—and the creation of various other forms of age-segregated housing, from retirement hotels to luxury condominiums. The most original of these forms was the so-called life-care facility. This offers the buyer a small house or a private apartment, maid service, nursing care, and meals in a common dining room; in addition, it offers nursing-home care when or if it was necessary. Such institutions are expensive, but by the mid-seventies, according to one estimate, some 85,000 Americans were living in them. Gerontologists struggling to create a taxonomy for all these new forms of retirement housing estimate that about 5 percent of Americans sixty-five and over live in age-segregated housing and another unknown but significant percentage live in neighborhoods that are more or less age-segregated.

The twenty-five-year increase in life expectancy, the expansion and growing length of retirement, the migration of elderly people away from their children and hometowns, and the development of age-segregated housing are phenomena that have occurred on a mass scale in such a short time that they are difficult to comprehend, much less to analyze. As Ronald Blythe wrote in the introduction to *The View in Winter*, his book on the elderly in England, "the economics of national longevity apart, the ordinariness of living to be old is too novel a thing at the moment to appreciate." Of course, there are experts, but these experts—the social gerontologists—do not claim to have much information. Social scientists in general have some propensity to conclude articles in academic journals with the announcement that more research on the subject is needed. Social gerontologists often begin and end their articles with this declaration. Robert Atchley, the author of one of the best-known texts on gerontology, concludes his book with the thought that "there is not a single area of social gerontology that does not need more answers to crucial questions."

In the early sixties, the late Professor Arnold M. Rose, a sociologist at the University of Minnesota, published a paper entitled "The Subculture of the Aging: A Framework for Research in Social Gerontology." In it, he listed all the changes in the status and condition of the elderly—greater longevity, improved standards of living, better health, better education, and so on—and deduced from them the growth of a "subculture of the aging." This subculture, according to Rose, would have its own distinctive attitudes toward death and toward marriage, its own style of "interpersonal relationships," its own argot, its own leisure activities, and its own rituals. There was, he said, an "almost complete absence of empirical data" on most aspects of this subculture. But there was evidence that older people were developing "group consciousness" based on "self-conception and mutual identification"; that is, they were beginning to think of themselves as a group and to contemplate group action in social life and in politics. Otherwise, the subculture remained hypothetical.

Since Rose's paper was published, a number of social gerontologists have attacked his thesis, on the ground that race, class, and even generational culture mean a great deal more to people than age, and create more profound divisions in the society. These objections make sense—certainly on a national level. True, organizations representing the elderly—the American Association of Retired Persons, the National Council of Senior Citizens, the National Retired Teachers Association, and others—have combined to fight for Social Security and other federal benefits, and do so most effectively. But these organizations do not always make common cause—and most of them do not take stands—on social, cultural, or political issues. And their lobbying groups do not always speak with a single voice. In St. Petersburg, for example, the oldest retirement town in America, and therefore presumably the most age-conscious, the retired people who live in the old downtown hotels and rooming houses vote differently from those who live in the new high-rise condos on the beach. The first tend to vote Democratic and for government-aid programs; the second vote Republican and against government spending. (Both, however, vote against local bond issues for the schools—this is their only real area of agreement.) Though about three-fifths of the registered voters in

St. Petersburg are over sixty, the city has no united "senior citizen" lobby, and it has only one city council member over sixty-five. Furthermore, in all the years that retired people have dominated the city they have not developed a distinctive single "culture." The blacks in St. Petersburg live in neighborhoods segregated by color, not by age, and the white retirees from the North inhabit a variety of different worlds. In St. Petersburg, I met a spry ninety-six-year-old man who was lobbying the city council to build a new auditorium where the state societies could put on dances and minstrel shows without interference from "the coloreds or the kids." There also, I met a sixty-five-year-old woman who divided her time between teaching holistic health care to the elderly, tutoring disturbed children, and growing organic vegetables and herbs in a garden of a house she shared with her ex-husband. "I'm an aging hippie," she told me brightly. And when I asked her about Sun City Center she said, "I wouldn't think of going to a place like that. What, and live with all those old people? I'm sure it's not good for anyone."

To say that there is no national subculture of "the aging" is not, therefore, to say that subcultures don't exist. Even those gerontologists who have registered objections to Rose's thesis would admit that in certain communities retired people are inventing new kinds of relationships, new ways of spending their time, and new ways of dealing with death. The Sun Cities and Leisure Worlds are without precedent; no society recorded in history has ever had whole villages —whole cities—composed exclusively of elderly people. These communities are not just places where the elderly happen to find each other, as they do in certain rural communities and certain inner-city neighborhoods after everyone else has moved out. They are deliberate creations—places where retired people have gone by choice to live with each other. Most of them, founded in the early sixties, are now old enough to have evolved from mere developers' tracts into communities with traditions of their own. Oddly, however, they remain almost a terra incognita to gerontologists, despite all the research devoted to them.

The appearance of developer-built retirement villages occasioned a great debate in gerontological circles—indeed, one of the greatest debates ever conducted in that field. In the early sixties, opinion was generally ranged against them. Both professionals and laymen—city planners, journalists, and the like—attacked them as ghettos for ill-adjusted, alienated people or as playgrounds that "trivialized" old age. But there were some who heralded them as an exciting new solution to the problems of physical incapacity and social isolation which so often plagued the elderly. All these early opinions tended to be a priori judgments, by those who had spent little or no time in retirement communities. Then, in the mid-sixties, a number of gerontologists went out to the retirement villages with scientific sampling methods and attitudinal charts. Their investigations produced a new welter of articles in the professional journals. One study showed that the inhabitants of a certain retirement village were better educated and better off than the average retired person—a fact that could have been deduced from the price of houses in that development. Another study showed that the residents of Leisure World, in Laguna Hills, California, had gone there because of the golf; their desire for an "easy-maintenance dwelling unit"; the smog in Los Angeles; and the invasion of their old neighborhood by "minority groups." They had, in other words, gone there for all the reasons overtly and subliminally advertised in the real-estate brochures. The gerontologists had so far discovered what the developers already knew. Measuring the attitudes of residents by "life satisfaction" scales and other tests of their own devising, the researchers also found that the inhabitants of retirement communities were generally satisfied with their communities. This discovery was also less than a scientific breakthrough, since the householders clearly had the option of moving out if they were dissatisfied. One of the last of these studies, conducted by Gordon L. Bultena and Vivian Wood and published in 1969, reached the conclusion that these communities provided life satisfaction to that self-selected group of people which chose to live in them. This redundancy has become the final considered opinion of most gerontologists today.

The interesting thing about these studies was the near-exclusive concern of the researchers about the happiness of retirement-community residents. "Are you happy?" the researchers would ask in a dozen different ways, and in a dozen different ways the residents would answer, "Yes." More recently, the gerontologists have got around to asking themselves what they mean by happiness. In *Aging in the 1980s*, a new textbook put out by the American Psychological Association, Dr. Joyce Parr writes of "an increasing awareness of the problem of confusion associated with such global concepts [as] life satisfaction, morale, adjustment, and developmental task accomplishment." Dr. Parr continues:

George (1979) expressed the need for reexamining the concept of life satisfaction and the psychometric characteristics of the available instruments. Cutler (1979) demonstrated both the multi-dimensionality of the concept of life satisfaction and that the dimensionality differs substantially across age groups. Larson (1978) presented a review of a variety of measures used to investigate the well-being of older persons. [He] cautions that such measures tell us little about individual informants and notes that "we have little idea how the construct permeates ongoing daily experience."

These are the "crucial questions" that are likely to lack answers for some time to come. Or, as Dr. Parr puts it, "there is an increasing recognition that characteristics of environments interact with characteristics of persons to produce behavior. It is also recognized, however, that much work is needed to develop meaningful ways to describe this interaction." The gerontologists may next begin to ask themselves what they mean by "meaningful."

Among developer-built retirement villages, Sun City Center is middle-sized, conventionally organized, and remarkable only for its isolation. It was founded by the Del E. Webb Development Corporation in 1960. Initial plans called for a development of private houses with communally owned public buildings and recreation centers. That same year, Del Webb also began the development of Sun City, Arizona, near Phoenix. But while Sun City, Arizona, expanded to city size and extends almost to the suburbs of Phoenix, Sun City Center grew slowly and experienced a number of difficulties along the way. The first difficulty was its name. Del Webb wanted to call it Sun City, but a tiny town a few miles away already had the name and refused to give it up, claiming to be the chrysanthemum center of the nation. In 1972, Sun City Center had only about three thousand residents, and Del Webb decided to sell. The purchaser, a Tampa real-estate consortium, formed a new management company for the town, the W-G Development Corporation. Impatient with the pace of sales, W-G broke with the original plan and allowed another development company to build condominiums right next to the housing tract. When it was just under way, the 1974–75 recession hit, the Florida condo market collapsed, and the new development came to a dead stop. W-G and the new development company reverted to their mortgage holders. In 1981, both companies were bought by a partnership supported by corporate pension funds and managed by Victor Palmieri and Company, a large assets-management firm. (Palmieri had been an ambassador-at-large and the Coordinator for Refugee Affairs under the Carter administration.) Sun City Center now comprises the original housing development, with a population of fifty-five hundred (I shall call it Sun City), and the newer condominium development, called Kings Point, with a population of about twelve hundred per-

manent and eighteen hundred seasonal residents. According to
W-G. Both developments are now doing very well, and the town has
been growing more rapidly in recent years than it grew in the past.
The changes of ownership do not seem to have affected the residents
adversely, and while some move out after spending some time there,
it is usually for reasons of their own; most residents consider W-G a
satisfactory landlord.

Twenty-five miles from Tampa, the nearest city, Sun City Center
has become a world unto itself. Over the years, the town attracted a
supermarket and all the stores and services necessary to the maintenance of daily life. Now, in addition, it has a golf-cart dealer, two
banks, three savings and loan associations, four restaurants, and a
brokerage firm. For visitors, there is the Sun City Center Inn. The
town has a post office. Five churches have been built by the residents,
and a sixth is under construction. A number of doctors have set up
offices in the town, and a Bradenton hospital recently opened a satellite hospital with 112 beds. There is no school, of course. The commercial establishments all front on the state road running through the
center of town, but, because most of them are more expensive than
those in the neighboring towns, the people from the surrounding area
patronize only the supermarket, the laundromat, and one or two
others. The local farmers and the migrant workers they employ, many
of whom are Mexican, have little relationship to golf courses or to
dinner dances with organ music. Conversely, Sun Citians are not the
sort of people who would go to bean suppers in the Pentecostal
churches or hang out at raunchy bars where gravel-voiced women
sing "Satin Sheets and Satin Pillows." The result is that Sun Citians
see very little of their Florida neighbors. They take trips to Tampa,
Bradenton, and Sarasota, but otherwise they rarely leave the green-
and-white developments, with their palm-lined avenues and artificial
lakes. In the normal course of a week, they rarely see anyone under
sixty.

Bess Melvin, a resident of Sun City who works part time in public
relations for W-G, took me on a tour the first day of a visit I made to
Sun City Center. Our first stop was the Town Hall recreation complex
—a group of handsomely designed buildings with white columns and
low red-tiled roofs. In front were shuffleboard courts and lawn-bowling greens, and in the center was a large, round swimming pool,
surrounded by deck chairs and tables with gaily colored umbrellas.
The buildings housed a glass-roofed indoor swimming pool, an exercise room, billiard rooms, card rooms, and studios with all the equipment for woodworking, weaving, pottery-making, ceramics, and
decoupage. There were shops displaying lapidary work and shell dec-

orations made by the residents, and there was an auditorium with brass chandeliers, and chairs that could be rearranged for a meeting or a formal dance. That morning, there were three or four people working in each of the studios and several people doing laps in the indoor swimming pool.

"Sun City Center isn't like the stereotype of a retirement community," Bess Melvin explained. "The usual thought is that you lose your usefulness. You sit back and rock in your rocking chair, and life slows to a stop. But the people here aren't looking for that. Sun City Center has a hundred and thirty clubs and activities. We've got a stamp club, a poetry club, a softball club, a garden club—I could go on and on—as well as active branches of the Rotary, the Kiwanis, the Woman's Club, and that sort of thing. The residents form their own clubs and run the Civic Association, so if you've got a particular talent or social concern you can always find an opportunity to develop it. Many people take up painting, and we have some really fine artists here."

Possibly some people still imagine retirement communities as boardinghouses with rocking chairs, but, thanks to Del Webb and a few other pioneer developers, the notion of "active retirement" has become entirely familiar; indeed, since the sixties it has been the guilding principle of retirement-home builders across the country. Almost all developers now advertise recreational facilities and print glossy brochures with photos of gray-haired people playing golf, tennis, and shuffleboard. The "activity centers" in the various developments differ, but the differences have largely to do with the economics of the community.

According to the W-G real-estate agents, a new two-bedroom house in Sun City costs from $60,000 to $90,000. Some of the older houses—the ones on the prettiest of the lakes—now resell for $100,000 or more, though they cost only $20,000 or $30,000 in the mid-sixties. A homeowner can buy membership in the Civic Association for fifty dollars a year and have the use of all the communal facilities. Golf is extra—$850 a year for a couple—and golf is clearly the main attraction of Sun City Center. W-G not only advertises the town's eighty-seven holes of golf prominently but sponsors national golfing tournaments and offers weeks of golfing instruction for seniors across the country. At Kings Point, the arrangements and the economics are somewhat different. In the early seventies, the developer put up small, flat-roofed buildings with condos costing only about $12,000 each. After the Florida condo bust, however, W-G found that the real market for Kings Point lay among higher-income people. The new condos are thus more luxurious, and cost $40,000 to $60,000 each. Here also golf is the main attraction—that and the huge white Kings Point club-house, with indoor and outdoor pools, card rooms, exercise rooms, and so on. The facilities are just as clean and handsome as those in Sun City, but there are certain stylistic differences, in part because many condo owners only winter in Florida. Whereas at Sun City the residents' Civic Association owns and runs the recreational center, at Kings Point these things are owned by W-G and run by a social director. Whereas Sun City has dance clubs and sports clubs, Kings Point has dance and exercise classes.

Bess Melvin took me to the library in the Town Hall complex at Sun City. The small, bright rooms contained displays of periodicals and a collection heavy on histories, biographies, and novels. Her task there was to photograph the president of the Sun City DAR presenting a book on Early American costumes to the library. A svelte woman in her sixties, the DAR representative had for the occasion dressed in a white jersey dress, stockings, heels, and gloves. She seemed to have no further appointments that morning. I wandered outside to watch the parade of golf carts, bicycles, three-wheelers, and wide American cars proceeding rather slowly along the central boulevard. The traffic was heaviest near the entrance to the golf club. Behind the club, twosomes and foursomes were embarking on the course, the women in golf skirts, the men in Bermuda shorts, Lacoste shirts, and narrow-brimmed straw hats.

Anyone visiting a retirement community for the first time would expect to be impressed by a uniformity of age. But Sun Citians have so much else in common in the realm of appearance that age seems the least of it. On the streets, most people wear golf clothes whether they are golfing or not. At home, the women uniformly wear slacks, with blouses hanging loose outside them. At church on Sunday, it's difficult to recognize a female acquaintance from the back, since all the women have the same neat permanent wave; and in the winter about half of them will have on identical blond fur coats. At Sun City Center Inn on a Saturday night, the women lined up at the well-stocked buffet or dancing to organ music with their husbands wear flowered dresses in pink and green, pearls, and low-heeled sandals. On such occasions, the men—all close-cropped and clean-shaven—dress even more colorfully, in checked trousers and white shoes, red or green linen slacks, pink shirts with blue blazers, madras ties, and the occasional madras jacket.

According to W-G statistics, the people now buying houses in Sun City Center have incomes of between $21,000 and $29,000 a year. ("Some of them are millionaires," Bess Melvin assured me.) The income level of Sun Citians has shifted upward over the past ten years along with the price of the houses. Still, Sun Citians are a remarkably homogeneous group; in particular, those who live in Sun City proper occupy a far narrower band on the spectrum of American society than economics would dictate. To look at the Sun City membership directory is to see that the men are by and large retired professionals, middle-management executives with large corporations, or small businessmen. Among the professionals, there are some retired doctors and lawyers, but these are far outnumbered by school administrators, colonels, and engineers. Most of the women were housewives, but a surprisingly large number were schoolteachers or registered nurses. Most Sun Citians are Protestants—Episcopalians, Presbyterians, Methodists, Baptists, and Lutherans—but there are some Catholics as well, and a very few Jews. Politically, they are conservative and vote Republican. (The two most prominent visitors to Sun City in recent years were Ronald Reagan and Malcolm Muggeridge. The former came to give a speech in the early days of his 1980 primary campaign, and the latter, unbeknownst to most Sun Citians, stayed almost a month.) A great number of them are Masons or members of such organizations as the Kiwanis, the Shriners, and the Woman's Club. They come from the Northeast and the Midwest, and none of them—it is hardly necessary to say—are black.

One of the earliest settlers in the town, Erna Krauch, a retired schoolteacher, explained the homogeneity of the community by the fact that many Sun Citians came here through personal recommendations. Mrs. Krauch and her husband, being one of the first couples to come, found Sun City Center through an advertisement. They had spent winter vacations in Sarasota for a number of years, but when they came to Sun City, in March 1962, they bought immediately. By October of that year, Mr. Krauch had sold his business, a pharmacy in Brentwood, Long Island, and by Thanksgiving the house was finished and they had moved in. "He wanted a warm climate," Mrs. Krauch said. "And a place to play golf. He never worried, as I did, about leaving everything and coming here. He lived only two years after that. I think he knew."

Most of the Sun Citians I talked to had come here in much the same way. They had wintered in Florida for some years. Around the time of the husband's retirement, they had visited Sun City Center—often on the recommendation of a friend or acquaintance—and had made a snap decision to buy. A few months later, they had sold their house in the North and moved in, with all their belongings. The men had initiated the move, and the women had been less than sanguine about it at first. "In the beginning, the people who came were mostly retired schoolteachers and businessmen looking for summer homes," Mrs.

Krauch said. "They were people who didn't put on airs, people you could be quite natural with." She dropped the subject, but came back to it later, saying, "They were doctors, lawyers, and professors—that sort of thing—people you didn't have to prove anything to. The people who buy the houses now are financially better off than we were when we came. They are more affluent. They can afford to retire. Whereas for us it was a kind of summer home." Technically, what Mrs. Krauch meant was a winter home, but she was at that moment waving a hand toward her chairs and tables, of white rattan and her sofas, covered in flowered chintz. Still, the distinction she was making was a curious one, since she and her husband had never had a second house. They had sold their house on Long Island before moving here. Mrs. Krauch had lived in her "summer home" continuously for over twenty years.

When I asked why they chose Sun City Center, most of the men I talked to said, "The golf." Ronald Smith, an engineer retired from Western Electric, told me that he had always wanted to live on a golf course but had not been able to afford it while the kids were going to school. When he and his wife, Lora, first arrived here, they had dropped everything—had not even bothered to unpack—and had played golf solidly for two months. Now, fourteen years later, Ronald Smith was still playing every day, and Lora was recovering from a knee operation she had undergone in order to be able to play again.

But for Lora Smith, as for most of the other women I talked to, the main attraction of Sun City was the people. "It's the people who sell the houses, not the real-estate agents," Mrs. Smith said. The Smiths had come at the suggestion of a couple they had met in Florida—he was a banker, Mrs. Smith remembered, and his wife was a schoolteacher, like her. "When I arrived, I looked at all the manicured lawns, and I thought perhaps Sun Citians were a lot of conformists," she said. "But then I knocked at five doors, and five different kinds of people came out—all very generous, very pleasant. I could not believe that everybody was that kind of person. There's such a variety of people here—people of achievement, people who talk about ideas, not about their ailments, because that's the kind of minds they have." Lively and gregarious people themselves, the Smiths had no difficulty finding friends. "No one gives a hang here what you did or where you came from," Mrs. Smith said. "It's what you are now that matters." Later, in a different context, her husband said much the same thing, adding that the colonels refused to be called "Colonel."

Sun City Center has age restrictions, of course. For a family to be eligible to live in Sun City, at least one member must be fifty, and neither there nor in Kings Point can residents have children under eighteen. But with one exception no Sun Citian I talked to said he or she had chosen the town because of the age restrictions. When I asked Mrs. Krauch why she and her husband had chosen an age-segregated community she looked startled. "Oh, I didn't feel I would just be with a lot of older people," she said. "And Sun City Center isn't like that!" Sun Citians would certainly be horrified to know that some retirees in St. Petersburg and Tampa look upon their town as an old-age ghetto. When Sun Citians speak of a "retirement community," what they usually mean is a life-care center or a nursing home. They came to Sun City Center for all the amenities spelled out in the advertising brochures and for a homogeneity that had little to do with age. In a country where class is rarely discussed, they had found their own niche like homing pigeons. And once they were home they were happy. "Lots of fine people," one resident told the community newspaper. "This is a cross section of the better people in the nation."

The notion that Sun Citians do not care about past professional status is a thought often articulated in Sun City. Sun City boosters— and most Sun Citians are boosters when they talk to an outsider—say it almost as regularly as they say that they are always active and on the go. The fact that the Sun City membership directory—it is actually the phone book—lists the residents' past professions along with their addresses suggests, however, that the notion is less a description of the community than a doctrine belonging to it. (Some people list the company or service they worked for, others their calling—"educator," say—and a very few put nothing at all.) Most people, like Mrs. Krauch and Mrs. Smith, have a fairly exact idea of the professional standing of their neighbors. The less exacting say, "We have some doctors and lawyers. We have some millionaires, too." Sun Citians will very often praise the company they are in by saying, "They're people of achievement—people with prestige." That most Sun Citians have the same set of achievements and the same sort of prestige does not seem to worry them; indeed, the contrary is true.

A curious thing about the Sun City Center complex is the lack of parallelism in the rules governing the communal facilities at Sun City and at Kings Point. The Kings Point club—owned by the developer— is open to anyone (or anyone within reason) who wishes to purchase membership. The Sun City Civic Association buildings—owned by the residents—are closed to anyone who does not live in that particular development. More than one resident explained to me that the tax laws were responsible for this restriction. But a community-relations executive for W-G told me that the tax laws had nothing to do with it: the restriction was an arbitrary one, made by Sun City residents. Asking around among Sun Citians, I discovered that when Kings Point was founded, in 1972, a number of Sun Citians had objected to the development, arguing that the cheap condos would attract a new element and ruin the community. Failing to stop it, they had refused to open the Civic Association to Kings Pointers. "It's really foolish," Lora Smith told me. "Sun City has all these clubs established—an Audubon Society Chapter, music groups, and that kind of thing—but the people from over there can't join them if they meet on Civic Association property. I mean, a really good musician from over there wouldn't be able to join a chorus or chamber-music group. There's a sort of a wall between us. People here feel—Well, they feel they arrived a little sooner than people over there. It's a matter of snob appeal, you see."

When I asked Kings Point residents what the people there used to do for a living, the answer was initially "We've got some doctors and lawyers—some millionaires, too." But when I pressed them about the differences between the two developments they said, "Well, they're more affluent over there." The fact is that Kings Point has a much greater variety of people than Sun City. It has former doctors and lawyers and perhaps some millionaries, but it also has retired policemen, retired door-to-door salesmen, and at least one retired commercial fisherman. It used to be impossible to discover the extent of the professional variety, since the Kings Point directory did not list the former employment of its residents. One resident told me he considered the Sun City directory a form of boasting. However, professions are now listed in the Kings Point book. Kings Point also has some Democrats, some Catholics, and some Jews. There are not many Jews—only two hundred in a population of three thousand—but there are more than the handful who live in Sun City. And that is another source of anti–Kings Point feeling. Asked to explain the restriction made by the Civic Association, one long-term resident of Sun City said, "Well, you know, at the beginning some people over there bought six or eight condominiums for speculative purposes, and they rent them out." This woman had told me that she speculated in land elsewhere in Florida, so I thought her objection an odd one to make. But she continued, "I know a lot of Jews I don't think of as being Jewish. But there are just some people I think of as Jewish, because of certain qualities they have."

Dr. Robert Gingery, the pastor of the interdenominational Protestant church in Sun City Center, told me that anti-Semitism was a serious problem in the community. "I do all I can to fight against it," he said. At his invitation, the Jewish congregation holds services and

Hebrew classes in the chapel of his church. The Sunday I attended his services, he made a point in his sermon of praising the rectitude and courage of the Jewish people after the Diaspora. "We in the church try to act as a bridge," he said, "but a lot of people were brought up with these attitudes." The Jews in the community are naturally quite conscious of these attitudes, but most of them are anxious to play the issue down. The head of the Jewish congregation said that at Kings Point anti-Semitism was "no worse than it is any-where in the society"; but he and others admitted that it was one of the reasons for the exclusion of Kings Point people from the Sun City Civic Association.

Kings Point people—Christians as well as Jews—are well aware of Sun City attitudes, and resent them. "There's a strong sense that this is the wrong side of the tracks," one man said. What is more, the Kings Point people retaliate systematically. While I was there, the development voted against sending money and volunteers to the Sun City Emergency Squad, even though the contributions would have meant free ambulance service for Kings Point. Kings Pointers habit-ually refuse to go along with civic projects initiated by Sun Citians. But they have another, more insidious form of retaliation. At the entrance to Kings Point, there is a large white double archway through which all vehicles must pass. The guards at the gate—some of whom are retired policemen living in Kings Point—will not let anyone through the gate who does not have a sticker or a visitor's pass. The gateway does seem to enhance security in the development. But because the guards are so punctilious about their job, refusing to let even the oldest citizens through without a pass, one function that the gateway serves in the course of a day is to keep Sun Citians out.

What most Kings Point people do not realize is that Sun Citians make distinctions among themselves that are finer but no less finely understood than those between the two developments. Sun Citians are not uniformly "affluent," and people like Mrs. Krauch know ex-actly where the richer people live and what their houses cost. The newer people have, on the average, higher incomes than those who retired on the Social Security and pension benefits of between ten and twenty years ago. The older people resent this inequity, not only for its own sake but because it makes it seem that the younger people had better jobs than they did. Struggling to make me understand this injustice, one of the older residents said, "No, it's not that the new people are *richer*—it's that they had larger pensions when they re-tired." There is thus some friction between age groups. But age does not completely determine status; Sun Citians make other distinctions as well. "The golfers are the elite of the community," one man told me. "They're the ones who give the cocktail parties." According to Sun Citians, there are, generally speaking, three social groups: the golfers, the "cultural set," and the people who take craft classes and go to potluck suppers at the Town Hall. The golfers don't mix much with the others. "I went to a party the other day," one of the older residents told me, "and there was a golfer there. He didn't have anyone to talk to. I happened to know him, so finally he came up to me and said, 'I guess golfers are different people.' I'd like to have said, 'Yes, they're the biggest bunch of snobs!' " While the nongolfers tend to categorize all the golfers as "stuffed shirts," the golfers make their own internal distinctions. In 1980, a group of them got together and put up the money for the developer to build a private golf course on the edge of town. Now completed, the Caloosa Club is a private country club inside a semiprivate country club.

In Sun City Center, a few people make serious efforts to break down some of these social barriers. One of them is Lou Ellen Wilson, an attractive and competent woman of forty-four, who is in charge of community relations for W-G. The company has an interest in keeping peace between the developments, and Mrs. Wilson often manages to make them cooperate in spite of themselves. Because of her, the Sun City ambulances do react to emergencies at Kings Point—the fact is simply not advertised. Another such person is Jackie Fenzau, the social director of the Kings Point club. A striking-looking woman of generous enthusiasms, Mrs. Fenzau, who is in her early fifties, has since the beginning organized everything that goes on at the club, including bus trips, classes, and entertainments. She is proudest of her monthly "theme dances," at which people wear costumes and do skits or sing songs. ("You should see the cutups we have!") Her goal is to make people happy with the club and with each other, and in her view the people who are the least happy are the ones who dwell on their past achievements. "Some people are still in competition when they come here," she told me. "A few of the men are very insecure, so they brag about what they have done in their lives. But that doesn't make them any friends. One couple I am thinking about had a terrible time adjusting. He came in here all the time to complain, telling me he was a lawyer. He had a very negative attitude toward everything. With most people, though, you wouldn't know what they did unless you happened to be involved in some activity where their backgrounds could be useful. Most people have reached a time in life when they don't want to worry about what Mr. So-and-So did."

Dr. Gingery has much the same attitude, though he, of course, addresses the problem of community in more global terms. He has served in Sun City Center for over ten years; his church, affiliated with the United Church of Christ, now has over sixteen hundred members and is one of the fastest-growing churches in the denomination. This is something of a personal triumph for Gingery, since there are four other Protestant churches in town and his views are not wholly orthodox for the community. A Methodist by training, he is both a theological liberal, as most Sun Citians are, and a political liberal, as most of them definitely are not. A tall, handsome man of sixty-three, he gives a stylish sermon and could probably get away on charm. But he and his three assistant pastors work very hard. He spends a great deal of time on pastoral work, and he has made his church the cultural and civic center of the town. The most important piece of neutral ground between the two developments, the church has music groups, writing groups, and a "college," which brings in speakers to talk about subjects ranging from medical advances to foreign policy; the "college" also has a weekly forum for the discussion of community affairs. Dr. Gingery worries a good deal about the fact that Sun City Center is an island of wealth in the midst of rural poverty. Recently, he persuaded his church members to put up seed money for a government housing loan so that forty or so very poor families in the area could build houses with indoor plumbing. He is possibly the social conscience of the town. He also likes Sun Citians. "There's a great deal of camaraderie here," he told me. "People know they are in the same boat. When I talk with new arrivals in town, I like to compare them to the Pilgrims crossing the ocean to take up a new life. They have to put their best foot forward, and they do. They work at making friends, and they know what didn't work before."

Dr. Gingery's simile is a powerful one. The story of the Pilgrims' crossing—the creation myth for the United States—suggests an ideal of community, a brotherhood transcending all social distinctions. It evokes the egalitarian strain in the American tradition and the optimism about making a radical break with the past. In the context of Sun City, however, the image is somewhat disturbing, for if Sun Citians were to cast off their past, who or what would they be? They have no jobs, no families around them, and not very much future. Furthermore, the community they have chosen is already so homogeneous as to threaten the boundaries of the self. Writing of the United States in the 1830s, Alexis de Tocqueville as much as predicted the reaction of Sun Citians:

In democracies where the members of the community never differ much from each other and naturally stand so near that they may at any time be fused in one general mass, numerous artificial and arbitrary distinctions spring up by means of which every man hopes to keep himself aloof lest he should be carried away against his will into the crowd.

This can never fail to be the case, for human institutions can be changed, but man cannot; whatever may be the general endeavor of a community to render its members equal and alike, the personal pride of individuals will always be to rise above the line and to form somewhere an inequality to their own advantage.

Dr. Gingery and Jackie Fenzau would surely consider this a gloomy view of human nature. But Tocqueville did not see it that way at all. His concern was for the integrity of the individual. What worried him about egalitarian systems was their tendency to destroy individual differences, dismantle identity, submerge the individual within the crowd. Had he been able to visit Sun City, he might have felt that by making social distinctions Sun Citians were in an existential sense protecting themselves.

Certainly it is fortunate that Sun Citians can discern the differences between the houses in their development, for an outsider walking or driving around Sun City finds the experience akin to sensory deprivation. The curving white streets—with names like La Jolla Avenue and Pebble Beach Boulevard—lead only back upon themselves, and since the land is flat they give no vistas on the outside world. Turning through the points of the compass, the visitor comes to another lake, another golf course, another series of white houses. The houses are not identical—the developer always gives buyers several models to choose from—but they are all variations on the same theme: white ranch house. Then, too, the whole town looks as if it had been landscaped by the same landscape gardener. Every house has a Bermuda-grass lawn, a tree surrounded by white gravel, and a shrubbery border set off by white stones. Some owners have put white plaster statues of cupids or wading birds in the shrubs. In the newer sections, each house has a wrought-iron fixture with a carriage lamp and a sign reading THE JONESES or THE SMITHS (there are twenty-eight Smiths in Sun City Center, and fifteen Joneses), and, under that, "Bob and Betty" or "Bill and Marge." No toys litter the pathways. The streets and the sidewalks are so clean they look scrubbed.

The developers have created this world, but they have made no mistakes. Sun Citians maintain it, and they like it as it is. One woman told me that she had come there at least in part because of the neatness of the lawns. "But I'm afraid I don't take as good care of my lawn as I should," she said. "When the wind blows hard, a palm frond will often blow down, and the next day my neighbor will be angry at me for not picking it up. He wants me to cut the tree down. I don't think

I will." Kings Point people often sit outside their houses; Sun City people rarely do, perhaps because they require more privacy, perhaps because they're loath to disturb such perfection.

Sun Citians keep their houses with the same fanatical tidiness: the fibers in the carpets are stiff from vacuuming; the tables reflect one's face. One woman I visited had put a plastic runner across her new white carpeting; another apologized for the mess in her workroom when there was only a pencil and a sheet of paper out of place. But the interiors of Sun City houses are not anonymous, for Sun Citians are collectors; their houses are showcases for family treasures and the bric-a-brac collected over a lifetime. On the walls are oil paintings of bucolic landscapes, pastel portraits of children, Thai rubbings, or Chinese lacquer panels inlaid with cherry blossoms. Almost every living room has a cabinet filled with pieces of antique china and gold-rimmed glass. On the tables are ship models, sports trophies, carved animals, china figurines, or trees made of semiprecious stones. In a week in Sun City, I visited only one house where there was no bric-a-brac to speak of and where the owners lived in a comfortable disarray of newspapers, usable ashtrays, and paperback books. In most Sun City living rooms, the objects seem to rule. China birds, wooden horses, or ivory elephants parade resolutely across coffee tables and seem to have an independent life and purpose of their own.

For all this cleanliness and order, there is something childlike about Sun City. In part, it's that so many people have collections of puppets, animals, pillows, or dolls. In part, it's that everyone is so talkative, so pleasant, so eager to please. The impression also comes from the warm air, the pastel colors, the arbitrary curving of the streets, the white plaster ducks on the lawns and the real ducks that parade undisturbed among them on their way from lake to lake. The very absence of children contributes to this atmosphere, since the people riding around on three-wheelers or golf carts seems to have no parents. Then, too, one associates uniformity of age with camp or school.

The rhythm of life in Sun City comes in some measure from the weekly schedule of events set by the Civic Association. On Mondays from nine to noon, Sun Citians can choose yoga classes, the Table Tennis Club, the Shuffleboard Club, the Lawn Bowlers' Club, or the Men's and Women's Golf Association matches. The studios for the shell-crafters, needlepointers, weavers, and so on are open most weekday mornings and afternoons. On Tuesdays, the Men's Chorus meets from nine to eleven, and the Duplicate Bridge Association meets at one. On Wednesdays and Fridays, the Potter's Wheel

Club meets in the mornings, and there is volleyball at two. The decoupage group meets on Thursday mornings, and the Men's Card Club plays gin rummy at twelve-thirty. Most days, a regular bus leaves for Tampa or Bradenton at ten, but there are special trips for dinner theaters once a week in the winter. The Woman's Club has a luncheon once a month, and so do the Investment Club and the Shriners; the Kiwanis Club meets every week. Most of the card clubs—Ladies' Penny Ante Poker, Men's Bridge, and so on—meet at one o'clock or in the evenings from six-thirty to ten. On Tuesday evenings, there is square dancing, on Wednesday evenings there is ballroom dancing, and on Saturday afternoons Sun Citians can practice their rumbas, waltzes, and cha-cha-chas.

To talk with Sun Citians is—necessarily—to hear a great deal about their schedules. With one or two exceptions, all the Sun Citians I met went on at length about the activities, clubs, civic groups, and cultural events in the town. Not just the public relations people but more than one of the residents reminded me that this was "the town too busy to retire." It was not sheer boosterism, for the same people would go on to tell me what activities they participated in and what busy schedules they had. In preparation for an interview, one man went to the trouble of writing out a list of his activities: Emergency Squad, travel abroad, gardening, bicycling, Photo Club, Radio Club. He also wrote out a list of his wife's activities: library, bicycling, cleaning.

So strongly do Sun Citians insist on their activities that after a while the visitor must begin to imagine that there is some unspoken second term of people who are not active at all. And, of course, such people exist. Sun City has its sick and feeble elderly people. It also has some alcoholics—how many it is impossible to tell. Dr. Gingery's pastors counsel only a handful of them, but one of the pastors, Dr. Mark Strickland, believes that there are many more, who go untreated, since their circumstances permit them to live as alcoholics undetected. (A doctor at the University of South Florida who has researched the subject believes that alcoholism is more prevalent among the elderly than is generally supposed.) In addition, there are people who after the loss of a spouse have simply turned their faces to the wall. There are also people who don't know what to do with themselves, and watch an inordinate amount of daytime TV. And there are a great many people who, while active, are not really very busy. When a golf cart breaks down in some public place, a dozen men will collect around it to kick the tires and trade theories about the electrical connections.

But the fact that this second term of people exists does not, perhaps, provide an explanation for Sun City's insistence on busyness.

For to stay around Sun City Center for any length of time is to see that some large proportion of the Sun Citians do lead active lives. The Sun City Town Hall and the Kings Point clubhouse are busy places all day long. The craft studios are perhaps not quite as popular as Sun Citians advertise, but there are usually a few people in every one of them. The organized activities—the bingo games, the bus trips, the dances—are well subscribed, and a lot of people swim, play shuffleboard, and work out in the exercise rooms. The golf courses have players on every hole from morning until dusk, and at the Caloosa Club at midday there are sometimes three dozen women playing bridge and gin.

Not all the activities go on at the clubs; many people have private pursuits. The Neubergers, a former meteorologist and his wife, collect replicas of musical instruments of the Renaissance and invite their friends in for musical evenings. (The Neubergers also swim a half mile a day in the lake behind their house. They continue to do this even though Mr. Neuberger was once rather severely bitten by an alligator.) The George Richardses have a dachshund named Gretel who has won numerous prizes for tracking and obedience. Ronald Smith works a ham radio and collects golf balls. (He now has nine hundred golf balls of different makes and markings.) Mrs. Evelyn Schultz swims competitively in the over-seventies division. Colonel Lyle Thomas grows orchids; James Morris carves animals and birds out of wood; and Louis Goodrich collects and rebuilds wall and grandfather clocks. These people are known around town for the interesting hobbies they have.

Frank Minninger is known as the best decoupage artist in Sun City Center. A tall, bronzed, good-looking man in his late seventies, he was wearing, when I met him, red linen slacks and an open shirt. He came here fourteen years ago, when he retired from the Connecticut General Life Insurance Company. Since then, he has made fifty decoupage handbags, half of which he gave away to friends and half of which he could show me, since he had given them to his wife. He had also built five ship models and grown a border of prize red begonias. He had, he said, always loved hobbies. When his boys were growing up, he had built model trains for them. And for some time he was quite serious about photography. He did a series of wildflower photographs which was exhibited around the country. Kodak bought a series of Christmas cards that he and his wife did over the years with pictures of their youngest son and their dogs dressed in costume and posed around the fireplace. His wife raised German shepherds, he said, and he was very keen on bird-watching. Minninger described all his hobbies to me in great detail and with enormous pride and enthusiasm. "There's an awful lot of people here who don't do anything," he said. "But if you're not happy it's really your own fault." Frank Minninger seemed to be a happy man. He seemed to be doing what he had wanted to do all his life—and what in fact he might have done for a living if he had not had a certain vision of himself. When I asked why he had chosen Sun City, he said he had come for the golf and the duplicate bridge. "I have all these hobbies," he told me gaily, "but golf is my business."

That many Sun Citians do lead active lives is perhaps not very surprising. Many of them, like Frank Minninger, are not old except by a demographer's measure, and some of the more recent settlers are not old even by that. In the beginning—that is, in the early sixties —most of the people who bought houses were around sixty-five years old. But in recent years people have been coming here in their early sixties and in their late fifties. In 1980, nearly a quarter of the population was under sixty-five. Many of the younger men had been military officers—people who had taken their pensions after twenty years and then worked at another job for a few years before retiring. Some of them had been civil servants with similar pension schedules, and some had been executives of companies that, for diverse reasons, encourage retirement before the age of sixty-five. Theodore Peck, for example, a former Air Force Reserve officer and sales manager for a carpet company, bought his house here when he was forty-six and moved in when he reached fifty. (Peck, exceptionally, still works. He deals in local real estate.) Betty Cooper Pierce, the wife of an Air Force officer, has been here almost nine years and is only fifty-nine. To these people, Sun City is certainly not a home for the elderly but, rather, a community desirable for its well-kept grounds, its golf, and its complement of successful people. Furthermore, many of those who are chronologically older have the same attitude. Ronald Smith, for example, plays golf every day, and in the evenings he still has too much energy to sit still for very long. He and his wife told me that they had looked forward to retirement—looked forward to all the things they could do when they were no longer tied down by children and jobs. Now, fourteen years later, they were still enjoying themselves. "It seems as if we'd always been here," Lora Smith said. "It's the long vacation we wished we'd always had."

What surprised me most about Sun Citians was how few of the men seemed to regret leaving their jobs. Civil servants, corporate executives, schoolteachers, independent businessmen—indeed, many of the same people who talked with such pride about the professional success they had had—told me that they had planned their retirement years in advance. A number said they would have retired earlier if they had been able to afford it. One man who had traveled all over the world for the Department of Agriculture, and who appeared enviably fit, said that he had retired at fifty-five, because he was "sick of working." Another man said that he had sold his chemical company "in order to get out of the rat race" and in order to fish and play golf. "I miss the competitiveness of business," he told me. "But I'd hate to go back to work. Pressure, pressure, pressure—I don't want to get involved." He now plays golf five times a week and says, "Don't know what I do but I'm busy all day long." A third man said he had retired from a management position at Kodak. He and his wife had traveled for a year and were now staying in a rented house while deciding whether or not to move to Sun City. "Maybe I shouldn't have retired so early," he said. "But I paid my dues. You work for industry, you work for x years, and you retire."

Some Sun Citians told me that they had liked their jobs, and, quite possibly, some who spoke as if they did not miss them were justifying choices that had been made for them. But for many of the men their careers, their professions, seemed only a means of achieving a satisfactory private life—a "life-style," as some put it. And even those who said they had liked their jobs seemed curiously detached from them: they had had jobs, but they had no work in the sense of lifelong interests. There are exceptions. Dr. Harry Skornia, for example, a former professor of communications, is now in his early seventies and continues to read what is being published in his field and to write articles when his health permits. Fred Russell, formerly the president of a construction company and a former city commissioner of public works, has become involved in public works and other civic affairs in Sun City. Then, too, there are some people, such as the Neubergers, who have artistic pursuits or hobbies they care passionately about. But these exceptions were strikingly exceptional. With regard to work, most Sun Citians seemed like castaways on an island of plenty.

Sun Citians' insistence on busyness—and the slightly defensive tone of their town boosterism—came, I began to imagine, from the fact that their philosophies, and, presumably, the beliefs they had grown up with, did not really support them in this enterprise of retirement. Sun Citians are, after all, conservatives and vigorous exponents of the work ethic. They believe that the country is going soft because most Americans don't work hard enough. They complain about the younger generations, and, according to Dr. Gingery, a few of them have threatened to disinherit their grandchildren because "these kids don't know the value of a dollar." Though many of them are former government employees or former executives of large corporations, they believe in free enterprise and rugged individualism.

The businessmen quite naturally complain of the "double and triple dippers" in the community, but some of the former government employees—living on indexed pensions—also complain that the government is too big and too paternalistic. A schoolteacher who had taken early retirement in order to move here with her husband told me that she and her friends had backed President Reagan's economic program enthusiastically. "We're old enough and conservative enough to believe that all this spending has to come to a screeching halt," she said. "There are so many boondoggles, so much cheating and crookedness as a result of it. Much of it can be blamed on Johnson and his printing of money. We're just mopping up now after that binge of spending. I can't for the life of me see what's wrong with cutting out the school-lunch program. What's wrong with having a bag lunch from home? We're losing the stuff of which this country was made in the beginning. We want things given to us. We want cradle-to-grave care."

Sun Citians believe in good citizenship, in charity, and in the virtue of volunteer work. They are by temperament joiners, and Sun City has, as Bess Melvin pointed out, a vast array of social, charitable, and civic organizations. Every week, the Sun City Center newspaper announces meetings, fund-raising drives, awards ceremonies, and so forth, held by the Rotary Club, the Woman's Club, the Kiwanis, the Civic and Home Owners associations. The women's groups and national fraternal organizations do raise money for scholarships and other charities; the Shellcrafters and Sawdust Engineers make things to give to the children of the area, or to sell for their benefit. Of course, there is a lot of busywork in these organizations, and a lot of meetings are held for purely social reasons. That is true everywhere. And, as is the case in most volunteer organizations, a few people do the lion's share of the work. What is interesting is that Sun Citians seem to feel somewhat less of a social obligation than they did before they retired. Harry Skornia, who has long been active in community affairs, estimated that only 10 or 20 percent of the Sun Citians took an active role in the various civic organizations. "The rest play golf and bridge, watch TV, and drink at cocktail parties," he said. "They don't come here to be active, they come here to retire." Skornia, being one of the few liberals in the community, had, I imagined, a rather jaundiced view of his fellow citizens. But then Ted Peck, a former president of the Sun City Center Republican Club, told me much the same thing. The club has over six hundred members, but very few of the members are active; they vote in elections but do not otherwise participate. "People are so busy going to cocktail parties," Peck said. "Most of them don't want to work. They feel they've done it all their lives—they feel they've made a contribution." Mrs. Krauch, also a former president of the club and now the head of a cancer drive, gave a similar analysis. "No one wants to take responsibility. They're people who have participated so much that they feel they don't have to anymore. 'I've had it' is what people say. 'I'll help, but I don't want the job.'"

Sun Citians are not Puritans—Dr. Gingery was, in a sense, taking too long a leap with his analogy. "They've never thought their work was socially necessary," Skornia observed. They are private people who enjoy their houses, their friends, their families, and their games. Many of them look upon Sun City as the reward for which they have worked and made sacrifices. Sun City boosters—and there are a lot of them—describe their town as an ideal place to live. But to look upon Sun City Center as an ideal world is to discover something new about the people who live there. Their political philosophy, after all, assumes the wide-open spaces; it is one of unbridled competition, of freedom from social restriction, and even from society itself. Their pleasures, however, are golf and bridge—games for people who love competition but also love rules. They are games for problem-solvers —orderly, conservative people who like to know where the limits are. The harmonious, man-made landscape of a golf course is like a board game writ large—or like Sun City itself. It's not for loners or rugged individualists but for sociable people who value traditions, conventions, and etiquette. It's not "the rat race." There's an aesthetic to it, but it's not that of the open range. Sun Citians think of themselves as quintessentially American, and so, perhaps, they are. But, like President Reagan, they imagine cowboys and live in a world of country clubs. What they value they might themselves associate with the European tradition. What they want is security within a fixed social order. Asked why so many Sun Citians were Republicans, Ted Peck said, "The same reason we feel so comfortable here. It's middle to middle upper class here. There are people who have worked and have prestige. There's comfort in the social status here." The irony is that their golf courses have been carved out for them from Florida swampland, their artificial lakes have alligators in them, and they live in a town without any history on the edge of a social frontier, inventing a world for themselves.

Art Rescorla knows this, but he is an exception, and the organization he heads is also exceptional. The Sun City Emergency Squad is the most important cooperative organization in the town, and the one Sun Citians take most seriously. All those in the housing development contribute to it, and, unlike the Civic and Home Owners associations, it was started by the residents rather than the developers, and has no paid staff. With its fleet of three ambulances, the squad responds to calls for emergency help and drives people to the hospital. For its volunteers—and for many people in the community—the squad has an aura of glamour about it. One woman squad member described it to me in terms of midnight emergencies: a woman with a heart attack, the squad unit responding in five minutes, the victim and her shocked husband being hurried into the ambulance, the rendezvous on the highway with the county paramedical unit, the return home in the middle of the night. And, indeed, the squad does respond to the one real threat to the community—the one thing that bursts through the cocoon of comfort and security.

Art Rescorla spends most of his days in the squad office. When I first went to see him, he was doing the accounts. Excited volunteers kept running in and out of his office with what I first assumed to be emergency business but turned out to be routine bookkeeping questions. Rescorla first referred them to the team head for the day, but they reappeared with the same questions, and then he patiently answered them himself. He described the work of the squad to me in a businesslike fashion. Its main work was transport, he said; only one out of ten calls was an emergency. The squad has 150 volunteers, who go through a twenty-one-hour first-aid course and, in some cases, a driving course; they are then on call for a twenty-four-hour period.

Rescorla had been described to me as "not a very gregarious man," but we talked, initially, for two hours, and he seemed to me to be merely a man who cared less than some others about pleasing. He did not wear resort clothes, and when I went to his house I noticed that he and his wife did not have a collection of animals or dolls. Also, he spoke quite bluntly about the subjects other Sun Citians skirted: illness, old age, and death. He was in many ways the odd man out. He said he had been forced to retire from his job at the American Petroleum Institute when he reached sixty-five. That was in 1975, and he had, he told me, been very resentful—not at the loss of his salary but at the loss of his work. He had taken a volunteer job at the Smithsonian Institution doing research projects, and he had worked without pay for the Virginia town he lived in. But he found that in both places the younger people passed over his ideas and his projects in favor of their own. When I asked him whether this had to do with a lack of respect for age, he said that it had more to do with the fact that younger people were still in the competition—still concerned with furthering their own careers. He could not blame them for that —that was how it was. He had moved to Florida in 1978 because of arthritis. When his doctor told him to go south, he had written away to sixty retirement centers and gone to visit ten or twelve of them. Most of them, he said, were simply apartment complexes or housing tracts built by a promoter and then abandoned with nothing but a sales office. But Sun City Center was a real town, and Rescorla had seen it as an alternative community, a place where he could find work and be useful among his peers.

Rescorla had found work for himself: he served as the managing editor of a publication of the American Chemical Society, he was the academic dean of Dr. Gingery's "college," and he was involved in a number of community projects besides the Emergency Squad. But he had also been in some degree frustrated, because few Sun Citians seemed to share his vision of what a retirement community could be. "What bothers me is that we are losing the brainpower of older people. There's a lot of it around in this area waiting to be tapped. In this job, I look for people with special backgrounds. I found a man who had worked for a telephone company, so I grabbed him, and he helped make a radio hookup for us. He's got the abilities, so I say use them. The trouble is that we push people into senility. A lot of people come here when they're at their peak, and then they drop off." He still, however, believed in the potential of age-segregated communities. "We should put people into areas like this, where they can use their talents. If they're in competition with younger people all the time, they just give up." In his view, what the town needed was a government. It was not likely to get one in the near future, since incorporation would probably mean a rise in the real-estate taxes, but it would have to get one in order to be heard. "When we talk to the country or the state now, we sound like an old-age home," he said.

Rescorla's view of Sun City corresponded to the attitude that the sociologist Arnold Rose labeled "aging-group consciousness." Rose had observed that certain older people were far more conscious than others of their peers; they saw "the aging" as a subsociety and identified with it; they believed that the elderly should organize and demand more rights. These people came from a great variety of backgrounds, but what they had in common was forced retirement. They had not jumped out of the working world and the larger society —they had been pushed.

With the exception of Rescorla, the Sun Citians I talked to had not come here because the town was for older people. On the other hand, they did not seem to object to the age restrictions. When I asked people how they liked living in an age-segregated community, a few said they missed seeing children around. (Some of them then went on to explain that they meant this quite literally: What they missed was seeing children—they didn't miss having them around all the time.) Interestingly, these questions always elicited answers about children—almost never about any other age group. Many Sun Citians, it became clear to me, had simply lost their consciousness of other age groups. They had come to Sun City not to be old but to be young. To put it another way, they were attempting to despecialize old age. "Look at the way we dress," one Sun Citian, a retired minister, said, indicating his own madras shirt. "At a cocktail party the other day, I saw a woman in a miniskirt. She had very nice legs, but she must have been sixty-five or seventy. Her mother would have turned over in her grave!" Paradoxically, the effort at despecialization seemed to work better in an age-segregated community.

On Thursday nights, the Kings Point club holds an informal dance, with music from an amplified sound system. The night I went, about a hundred people had come. I found a seat at a table with three couples. The men were wearing Western shirts with string ties, the women slacks and flowered cotton blouses. The men handed around drinks from bottles they had brought, and all of them were laughing loudly at each other's jokes. When the music started, the women went to the dance floor to join a half dozen other women, some of whom were certainly in their eighties. Led by a tall woman in a tent-like muumuu, they formed a line and did a kick-step routine to a number called "Bad, Bad, Leroy Brown." They had learned the routine in dance class, and now they were completely relaxed about performing it in front of an audience. When the dance ended, the men got up, and a few minutes later the floor was filled with couples doing the fox-trot. Through the crowd I could see two diminutive elderly women dancing together.

Actually, there are many ages in Sun City Center. In twenty-some years, the age spectrum has grown almost as large as it is in most new suburban communities: it encompasses four decades, and two generations of certain families. One seventy-three-year-old woman I met had a mother in her nineties living in a house a block away from her. Families with two generations of retired people living in Florida are no longer uncommon; the families tend to consist of a daughter, married or widowed, taking care of her elderly mother. In twenty-odd years, Sun City Center has developed its own life cycle, beginning with people in their fifties and ending with those in their nineties. Carolyn Tuttle, for example, used to be the youngest person on her street when she and her husband moved in, a dozen years ago; now in her seventies, she is, as it were, middle-aged, since some of the earliest settlers are still there and some younger people have moved in. The median age in the whole town is now seventy. When I asked Mrs. Tuttle about age segregation, she told me that she did not miss having young people around. "I love children dearly," she said, "but I don't crave to fall over tricycles on my lawn or see young couples mooning over each other." Later, she said, "When Sun City Center was founded, almost everyone was about sixty-five. Now some of the people are well into their eighties. I know a number of people who are losing their sight, and others who can hardly get about. The next step is the life-care center. I've lost so many friends to retirement homes. It's almost as bad as losing them to death."

Carolyn Tuttle has a bright little dog, a schnauzer, who appears to understand much of what she says. She herself is a greyhound of a woman—tall, lean, attractive, and full of nervous energy. A former English teacher, she uses the language with a playful elegance. Her husband died three and a half years ago. Since then, she has become a member of the Emergency Squad and a vice president of the Civic Association. She does church work, and she directs a poetry workshop, and she belongs to the Woman's Club. A couple of years ago, she took a trip to Australia and the South Pacific with a group. "It's a very fulfilling life here," she said. "Of course, there are people who do nothing but play bridge and golf, but that's their privilege." Though she is a Sun City booster, she finds it difficult to control her irony when she describes the provincial theater groups that come through and the tea-and-cookie meetings of the Woman's Club. She is as demanding of herself as she is of others, and she is also, very obviously, lonely.

In the early sixties, Sun City was a community of couples. The development company pitched its advertisement to couples and built its houses for two. People put up signs that read WORDEN—DOT AND HOW or THE SMITHS—BILL AND MARGE, and the signs signified a good deal. Like many Americans of their generation, Sun Citians had long, stable marriages. On the average, perhaps, their marriages were happier than most, since unhappy couples usually do not decide to pull up roots and leave for a permanent vacation together in a strange town composed of other couples. Then Sun City was a test of these marriages. For social purposes, each couple had to become a united front, an entity. And there were no distractions—no children, no office to go to, no compelling reason for one person to "get out of the house" without the other. Added to that, retirement gradually erased the difference between a man's sphere of activity and a woman's. ("My husband is always the man," one woman told me. "A lot of other men become just people.") Couples that survived these tests grew closer; they became single units, husband and wife joined together like Siamese twins.

But now Sun City is composed of couples and widows. Just how many widows there are it is impossible for a visitor to tell, since most widows do not take down the DOT AND HOW signs or take their husbands' names out of the residents' directory. The 1980 census, however, shows that almost a third of the women in Sun City then were widows living alone. This is about the national average for people their age, since women lived an average of 7.7 years longer than men. In Sun City, there are five widows for every widower, which is about the national ratio.

"How," in fact, died three and a half years ago. "Dot"—Dorothy Worden, who is in her seventies and full of life—says she would consider remarrying if she found the right man. But she doubts she ever will, since there are so few men her age around. Of course, she says, some men do lose their wives, and they generally want to remarry, but then there are so many widows with the same thing in mind. "When a man's wife dies, all the widows come around the next day with casseroles," Dot told me. "Some women I know even make a practice of going to funerals. If they like the look of the bereaved husband, they'll go home and make him a casserole even though they've never met him before. Well, it works sometimes. Men aren't very good at living alone. You saw the furniture-sale right down the block? That was put out by a man who just married the widow of a close friend. His wife hasn't been dead a year. That's a fact, but no one really objects. He needed her, and, besides, none of us have all that much time left."

In St. Petersburg, there's a dance hall, called the Coliseum, where for over fifty years retired people have gone to dance to combos and the big bands every Wednesday and Saturday night. Some are couples, but others are single people. The women sit at the tables in groups of four or six with briefcases that open out into bars. The single men stand in a line at the back of the hall, like high-school boys at a prom, passing comments and looking for the prettiest woman to dance with. If a man dances with a woman, and she likes him, she'll invite him for a drink at her table, and sometimes that will be the beginning of something. I asked one man in the line why he came back there night after night, year after year, and he said, "The widows." I said he surely might have found one by then. He turned away slightly and said, "Oh, no, I'm not looking for anything permanent."

At the Kings Point dance, I sat next to a dark-haired woman with dangling silver earrings who seemed to be having a wonderful time. I asked if she and her partner were married, and she said they were not. "My husband died when he was very young," she told me. "He was only fifty-nine years old, but we had been married for thirty-three years. It was shattering. Your friends ask you out, but you're always a fifth wheel. I have children—my oldest son's a doctor in Boston—but I don't want to be a burden to them, so I came to Florida. I met Harry three years ago—his wife had just died, and I adopted him, because I'd been through the same thing. It's like a new life for me. We haven't gotten married, though, because of taxes."

At Kings Point, everyone knows couples like this one, who are not married, and knows the reason for it: if a woman remarries, it is widely (and often erroneously) believed she stands to lose her late husband's pension. Then, too, a couple filing a joint tax return may have to pay more in income tax. The laws are straightforward, but in Florida—particularly in Florida—they have created some strange social circumstances. They have led the most respectable people to the most unconventional behavior. "You can't tell who's married and who's not," a friend of Dot's who lives at Kings Point told me. "People sometimes say they are married, and the woman goes by the man's name. It doesn't matter to us if they're not married, but it seems to bother their children. So sometimes we know and their children don't. Either they tell their children they're married or one of them moves out of the house when the children come down."

Remarriages seem to be more common in Sun City. But then many Sun Citians have enough money to be able to afford the higher taxes. Perhaps for that reason, Sun Citians are far less tolerant than Kings Point people of unconventional living arrangements. Dot, who has lived in Sun City for a decade, knows of only one unmarried couple openly living together there. She does not know of any couples who simply pretend to be married.

Most widows in Sun City Center do not find new partners. The statistics are not in their favor in this town any more than they are nationally. But the statistics are so new that when their husbands die many women face a situation they never anticipated and are not in any way prepared for. According to Dr. Gingery, there are in general two kinds of widows: the dependent ones, who go to life-care centers, and the independent ones, who make a life for themselves. Both Dot and Dr. Gingery know women who actually flourished after their husbands died—who made their own friends for the first time and took up activities they hadn't thought of before. They also know women who do well enough but simply feel that their life has been diminished. Widows at Kings Point seem to be able to have an extensive social life: the neighbors are close, and they can go to dances or on expeditions in groups. Sun City is more of a private place, and thus widows seem to spend more time alone in their houses.

Mrs. Carl Kietzman, who is in her early seventies, has lived alone since her husband died more than three years ago. Formerly an officer in the DAR, she was married to an Army Reserve officer who worked for the automobile insurance division of General Motors. They came here from Ohio, but they had moved around the country a good deal in the course of their lives. A big-boned, strong-looking woman, Mrs. Kietzman has decided opinions on most matters but not on what to do with the stretch of life in front of her. "It's no fun to be alone," she remarked at one point in our conversation, out of the blue. She said it quite simply, and stopped, looking down at her hands. At another point, she said, "This is the first time in my life I've ever lived alone. My family had a big house in Houston. I married young, and I had a happy marriage." When I asked Mrs. Kietzman if she thought of marrying again, she said, "I live on pensions, which would stop if I were married. And I just couldn't live with someone—it's against my principles." Then she said, "But I wouldn't meet anyone here. I don't even see the couples we used to see—or not a lot. You feel like a fifth wheel. I'm in one bridge game because someone's husband died. I miss the company of men. I miss dancing. One night, I went to the singletons thing they have, but I didn't meet any men there. There were so many women. So I ate dinner and I played bridge and I went home." A year after her husband died, Mrs. Kietzman thought of leaving Sun City and going to live with a woman friend who had a big house in Ohio. She liked the woman—she even liked her eight dogs—but in the end she decided against it, because it would have meant selling most of her furniture, and she couldn't bear to do that.

Mrs. Kietzman took me on a tour of her house, pointing out a handsome walnut four-poster bed and a walnut chest of drawers. "They came from Texas," she said, "and they've been in my family for a hundred years." In the study, she apologized for the terrible mess, though the study was almost as painfully neat at the rest of the house. "I don't like to cook," she said as we went though the small kitchen. "My husband always used to do the cooking after he had his heart trouble." The dining table had a lace tablecloth over it and a set of china angels playing around the centerpiece; it looked as though it was never used. "I swim, and I work on committees," she said as we sat down again. "But there isn't much to do at night. There's a bridge game two or three times a month, and sometimes I go out with my girlfriends. If he'd lived, I might have been better integrated into the community. But it isn't good for widows. My neighbors are kind to me, though. They come over when I need something. The man next door says I should lock the door when I go outside through the carport to the utility room to do the laundry."

Security is something of a preoccupation in Sun City, though the town is safe by the standards of most cities and towns. (There are occasional burglaries, mostly of empty houses, and some years ago there was, very exceptionally, a rape.) Sun Citians discuss crime a great deal. A woman in her seventies told me, "I have a gun, and I would use it." In January of 1982, a committee of residents announced plans to create a security patrol, with volunteers driving two radio cars through the streets from dusk to dawn. Major General Joseph (Smokey) Caldara (U.S. Air Force, retired) was selected to head up the patrol. At the time, there was some feeling that elderly vigilantes driving cars would be more of a hazard than a safeguard, but between three and four hundred people volunteered for service, and General Caldara began the operation in April. By July, there had been six burglaries (making a total of eleven for the year), and there had been one patrol-car crack-up. The patrol continues, but the most effective security system in Sun City is still the neighbors. There are Neighborhood Watch Committees in every section of town, but, more important, the residents all notice what goes on in the streets around them. If something looks amiss at a neighbor's house, a Sun Citian will always go and investigate—particularly if the neighbor is a single person with a health problem. This mutual concern often has nothing to do with friendship; it is impersonal, though unsystematic, and it is generally welcomed, because all Sun Citians feel that one day they may require help of some kind. Art Rescorla came to Sun City to find work, but there was another reason he and his wife chose this particular town. "I liked the idea that Trinity Lakes"—the life-care center— "was here," he told me. "It was a place to go if we got into trouble. And if things got real bad, this is a place where people work together. So my wife would always have some companionship."

The developers who built Sun City made no provision for sickness or incapacity. Like builders of retirement villages all over the country, they built recreation facilities, not clinics or nursing homes. (The real-estate people are still reluctant to discuss the problems of extreme age. One man told me that the average age in Sun City Center was sixty-two or sixty-three.) But as the years passed and the first Sun City settlers grew older, medical services were established. Doctors set up offices in the town, the Emergency Squad was organized, and in 1975 an independent developer began to build Trinity Lakes. Residents of Sun City worked on the feasibility study for the facility, and when it was finished a number of them moved in. Trinity Lakes eventually had 152 apartments and had 60 beds in the nursing home

—almost all of both filled with Sun Citians. In a sense, it completed the community, for it offered residents a place to go when they could no longer take care of their houses, and it meant they could stay in Sun City Center or keep their relatives there for as long as they lived.

Recently, however, Trinity Lakes changed hands, after it was alleged in a lawsuit that several million dollars in membership fees had been used improperly. The suit was eventually dropped, but it shook the faith of Sun Citians not only in Trinity Lakes but in all life-care centers that require a large capital investment in return for lifetime guarantees. There are several such institutions in the Tampa–Bradenton areas, and Sun Citians had heard rumors of financial scandals about some of them. As a result, many Sun Citians, including Art Rescorla, are looking for institutions that do not require an irrevocable commitment of capital. The security they sought has proved elusive.

The fact that many Sun Citians have gone to Trinity Lakes and other such centers in Florida says a good deal about their relationships with their children. Of course, some Sun Citians have no children. (Their age cohort—Americans who came of childbearing age during the Depression—had relatively few children, and the Sun Citians probably have even fewer than the average.) And some do rely on their children when they become ill or cannot cope for themselves. But many Sun Citians have made the decision not to depend on their children in sickness any more than in health. In this decision, they are not untypical of middle-class Americans of their generation, and here their generation has broken new ground. Many, perhaps most, Sun Citians took care of their own parents (some of them are still doing so)—and had them living in their houses for years. Art Rescorla was one. "I took care of my mother for fifteen years," he said. "In the end, I had to put her in a nursing home, because it was either her or my wife. My mother took in her sister, and my father his brother. My kids would take care of me if they had to, but I wouldn't impose that on them."

Whether Sun Citians make this decision for their own sake or for the sake of their children is not at all clear, because they tend to describe it in a perfectly ambiguous manner. Art Rescorla, who has thought about the subject a great deal, said, "If I had a heart condition, I wouldn't want to impose it on my kids—at least, as long as I could afford not to. Why hold children down? It would be an interference. I'm not resentful—they have their own lives to lead. Other people—Negroes and Cubans—all live together, but we've reached the point where we don't have to do it." Rescorla had nonetheless imagined what it would be like to live with his children. "Our lifestyles are so different it would be difficult to adjust. I wouldn't have any freedom except in my own room, so in practice I'd be confined there. I might just as well go to a nursing home." He spoke without bitterness—indeed, without any particular emotion. "It's heartbreaking to see people here—terminal cases—put into Trinity Lakes to stay until they die. But it doesn't upset their whole families, and they get better service there."

At the bar in the Sun City Center Inn one night, a man sat alone drinking stingers. He said his name was Lewis Fisher. Sixty-three years old and just retired, he had come down to Sun City with his wife to rent a house for the winter months. His wife was sick in bed with a virus, so he had come out alone—suffering, he said, from "cabin fever." He and his wife were trying to decide whether or not to retire to Sun City. "We have two places up north, but we'd like to move to a warmer climate," he said. "We've thought about it for a long time." When I asked if it would be difficult to leave his family, he replied, "My kids have done well, but there are no strings attached. We are as free as birds now." Later, he said, "Do you want to sacrifice five months of good weather for three days—Thanksgiving, Christmas, and Easter? They have a right to their own lives." Fisher seemed glad to find someone younger—myself—to talk to, explaining, "The youngest person I've talked to in months is the bartender. I look at my wife and I say, 'Are we ready for this?' " Turning away, he continued, "Don't like to admit I'm growing old."

Sun Citians often speak of their children with a great deal of respect and affection, but they do not speak as if their lives and their children's were entwined. A sociologist studying retirement communities found that their members had a marked tendency to disinherit their children in favor of friends in the communities. Because these people did not appear to dislike or disapprove of their children, he called this phenomenon "benevolent disinheritance." Sun Citians do not seem to disinherit their children. Rather, they put up with the distance; they exchange visits with their children, but they often make do without family gatherings on the holidays. (Dr. Gingery now has a breakfast party for his parishioners on Christmas morning, because, as one widow told me, "it is the bluest day of the year.") They make their own independence a virtue. "Our children treat us as friends," Lora Smith said. "They see what full lives we have, and they say we're models for them." Similarly, dependence on children is treated as a weakness. A woman going north to be with her children and grandchildren is said to have "gramma-itis." For many, perhaps, the distance is not entirely unwelcome, since it obviates the inevitable tensions between parents and their grown children. "I've noticed that some people here visit their kids out of charity," Rescorla said. "They think they should, because they're blood relations, but they breathe a sigh of relief when they get back here. People don't dislike younger people, but they don't want to depend on them. They have more confidence in people their own age—they trust them more." Dr. Gingery also thought there had been a general loosening of family ties, but he had a different view of the causes and consequences. "All this moving around since the Second World War has had its deleterious effects. This age group couldn't follow their children, so the kids lose their grandparents. But it's more than that. Kids lose a sense of responsibility to the extended family—not just their grandparents. And they lose a sense of responsibility to the community."

Sun Citians have taken some steps to create a substitute for the extended family. Neighbors do take care of each other in all kinds of emergencies; when someone falls ill they help out by doing errands, bringing food, or just dropping in for a chat. Sun City Center has its own Meals on Wheels unit; it has a blood bank; and it has oxygen tanks strategically placed around the town. Dr. Gingery's church has a guardianship program to take care of those who cannot make decisions for themselves. (The weakness of the program is that people must sign up for it in advance, and not many are willing to do that.) Professional home nursing is readily available, and the churches have volunteers who take care of shut-ins. Sun City is probably one of the best towns in America in which to be sick. Still, the system of caring for the ill and the feeble is far from perfect, and many people worry what they will do when, as Dorothy Worden said, "this nice interlude is over." Rescorla told me that the squad had recently taken a couple to the hospital because the woman had fallen ill and could no longer take care of her husband, who was blind. The hospital, however, could not keep them, and if their son had not come down to put them in a nursing home, they would have had nowhere to go. Rescorla's immediate ambition is to create a cooperative nursing service for the community—a group of volunteers who would do the housekeeping, get the groceries, and so on, at least on a temporary basis. He and other community activists in town believe in extending the network of volunteer organizations, but they worry that the town is getting too big for that, and they worry that the new arrivals do not understand the problems of the very old—or are so well off that they prefer to have things done for them rather than do the work themselves. "We often bring people back from the hospital who can't take care of themselves," Rescorla said. "It's very sad in most cases. People who can't manage and who haven't prepared for this—they're buried, they just die."

Sun City Center has never had a cemetery. The developers of retirement villages make a point of keeping graveyards at a distance. Not long after Del Webb founded Sun City, Arizona, a speculator bought some land near the development and threatened to turn it into a cemetery. Del Webb bought him out at several times the price he had paid. As usual, the developer seems to have understood the trend. At any rate, funeral customs have changed a good deal in Sun City over the past ten years. "When I first came here," Dr. Gingery said, "ninety percent of the people wanted a funeral service with a casket, viewing of the body, and burial in a cemetery. Now ninety percent are cremated and have memorial services."

In shifting from burial to cremation, Sun Citians are a part of a nationwide trend—only, they are in the avant-garde. Dr. Gingery told me that the preference for cremation in the Sun City was a sign of growing maturity about death. Dr. Strickland explained, more bluntly, that it reflected the decline of pagan thinking about physical resurrection, and this quite naturally took place first among people of a certain class and education. As the ministers suggest, the nationwide trend is in large part a function of changing religious attitudes, particulaly among liberal Protestants. It is also, in some part, a judgment on the funeral industry. But Sun Citians have other reasons as well. "I never thought I'd believe in cremation," Verle Modeweg told me. "I'm a Baptist, after all. But we began going to the Presbyterian church down here before the Baptist church was built, and the minister convinced me." Then she said, "Burial is so expensive and such a waste. I'd rather give my money to the church." Cremation is the final act of tidiness, and as such it has appeal for Sun Citians. But it is also quite clearly a function of mobility, of rootlessness. "I don't have anyone," Mrs. Modeweg continued. "And my husband doesn't either, so there's no one to keep up the graves." Many Sun Citians have no hometowns, and their children, if they have any, live in places where they have no attachments. These people ask that their ashes be scattered over the Gulf, or they buy a place for them at Mansion Memorial Park, a cemetery some miles away. Mrs. Modeweg said. "We bought a place at Mansion Memorial, and now friends come up to me and say, 'I've just found out that I'm going to be right next to you!' It seems very neighborly."

Dr. Gingerly believes that in ten years Sun Citians have become much more aware of the aging process and much more accustomed to the idea of death than people in general. In this, he is surely correct. Death occurs more frequently in Sun City than it does in most other communities. Yet it is much like death in a wartime army: it is expected, and it happens to comrades, but not (except in the case of a husband or a wife) to somebody one has known all one's life. Sun Citians don't celebrate it with elaborate rituals; they don't talk about it very much, or worry about it in the way they worry about prolonged sickness or incapacity. They are stoics, and they have, in a sense, tamed it.

"Death is less of a tragedy when you're past sixty," Bess Melvin said. She was in her office, but not in her public relations role. "I think people here do have a different attitude toward death from people in a mixed community. There's a greater sense of acceptance. People don't dwell on it so much. They think about how to have fulfilling lives. They say to themselves, 'I enjoy having a big car. I've always wanted a Caddy or a Lincoln. Death—there it is. I'm ready. But in the meantime I'm going to lead the most enjoyable life possible.' "

Rajneeshpuram

IN January 1983, Bhagwan Shree Rajneesh took to driving fifty miles to Madras, Oregon, every afternoon in one of his Rolls-Royces accompanied by armed disciples in an escort Jeep. He would turn around at the weigh station just outside of town or go to the nearest supermarket, where his companion, a young woman with long dark hair and a china-white face, would get out and buy him a soda; then the convoy would turn and drive the fifty miles back to Rajneeshpuram. Every afternoon around the same time Reverend Mardo Jimenez of the Madras Conservative Baptist Church would look out of his office window and see the convoy turning at the weigh station. Finally he could stand it no longer; he decided to demonstrate.

The first demonstration was not very big: just Jimenez and a handful of parishioners standing on the roadside opposite the weigh station, praying and shouting such things as "Bhagwan out of Madras," "Repent your sins," and "America will be free." But Jimenez persisted, and day after day the knot of people around him grew bigger and the shouting louder. One day a group of Rajneeshee disciples showed up in a bus; arriving at the weigh station ahead of their Master, the young people stood in a semicircle singing Christmas carols to drown out the noise of the shouting across the way. In the days following, the double demonstration began to attract all kinds of people: curiosity seekers, families from other churches, and tough-looking guys in sweat caps hitching up their blue jeans. Jimenez stood on the top of a car holding a Bible in one hand and in the other, an American flag so big it threatened to drag him away in high winds. "I love you," he called, wind-tears streaming down his cheeks, and "Believe in Jesus." Day by day the numbers of Rajneeshee increased until there were four busloads of them at the weigh station. Then the truckers began coming, the drivers tooting their horns and waving V signs as they pulled their rigs off to the Jimenez side of the road.

What motorists coming over the hill on Route 97 into Madras would have seen was this: a hundred-mile vista of open Oregon rangeland flanked by the spectacular snow-covered peaks of the Cascade range; then, at the beginning of the first large human settlement they had seen in seventy-odd miles, two groups of people standing on either side of the highway amid an assortment of vehicles. Passing by them, they would see on one side a group of people with banners reading JESUS IS LORD gathered around a car on which a preacher was holding down an American flag like the figure on the Iwo Jima monument. On the other side they would see a crowd of young men and women all dressed in shades of red—red down jackets and red jeans or cords—playing guitars and singing. Through the car window, they might hear a few bars of "Joy to the World" or "Love Is a Beautiful Feeling." Then they might continue on their way through town into the open rangeland and see no other human being for the next twenty-five miles.

In fact, were the drivers from Oregon, they probably would have been able to interpret the sight they had seen, for by January 1983, most Oregonians had heard of Bhagwan Shree Rajneesh, the Indian guru with his red-clad followers and his twenty-one Rolls-Royces. A year and a half before, "the red people" had paid $6 million for one of the biggest ranches in central Oregon: a hundred square miles of dry hills and canyons sloping down to the John Day River. They had come from Poona, India, via Montclair, New Jersey. At first just a few of them came to farm the land; then more and more arrived. Now there were six hundred "red people" living on the Big Muddy Ranch, and the town they incorporated, Rajneeshpuram, was the largest in the area next to Madras (population 2260). The Rajneeshee had also taken over the tiny town of Antelope twenty miles away from them, buying up most of the properties, electing their own city council, and creating a good deal of ill-feeling in the process. In addition they had bought a hotel and restaurant-nightclub in Portland. Many people thought they were some kind of sex cult, but this was not clear. The guru did not speak in public anymore. The ranch was run by a thirty-three-year-old Indian woman called Ma Anand Sheela, but most of the disciples were Westerners, Americans, and Europeans, with a great deal of money and the best lawyers in the state.

I first heard of the Rajneeshee in March 1983, while visiting at a university in the Willamette Valley near Salem. Several of the professors were fascinated by them, and one had taken an eight-hour bus trip out and back to visit the ranch. The Rajneeshee gave guided tours, and otherwise they did not seem to fit any of the usual patterns. In the first place, they were not kids but adults, and many of them well-educated professional people: accountants, doctors, lawyers, even professors. In the beginning they were thought to be dirt farmers, but now they seemed to be building a model city for themselves out on the range. Already they were farming some hundreds of acres of land with modern equipment, and they were building housing for themselves, roads, and an airstrip. The scale of the enterprise was extraordinary. They said they had already put some $30 million into the development—and that, apparently, was only the beginning. They had seriously alienated their neighbors in the process, but that—in the professors' view—was perhaps inevitable, as there were a lot of fundamentalists in central Oregon who couldn't be expected to take to an Indian guru. On the other hand, they seemed to go out of their way to create publicity and to make trouble for themselves. For example, they had given the press a photograph of the twenty-one Rolls-Royces lined up all in a row. Then the guru's secretary, Sheela, had given an invocation at the state legislature, and that, naturally, had stirred some people up. It was not at all clear why they did such things.

Controversy, as I later discovered, had surrounded the Rajneeshee ever since their arrival in the state. The main point of contention was Antelope. Just three months after they moved onto the ranch, 1000 Friends of Oregon, a public interest group dedicated to maintaining the strict Oregon land-use laws, had told them they would fight any effort to construct buildings not intended for farm use on agricultural land. The Rajneeshee had responded by buying up properties in the nearest township (or "city" in Oregon law), for residential and commercial use. The forty residents of Antelope, most of them retired people, had refused to give permits for commercial development. Sued by the Rajneeshee, they had tried to disincorporate the town, but the Rajneeshee had outmaneuvered them by bringing in enough of their own people to outvote them in an election. The disputes continued until in the next election the Rajneeshee voted all but one of the older residents off the town council and replaced them with their own people. The Rajneeshee had acted legally—they were well within their rights—but what many people in the area saw was a large and powerful group imposing its will on a few elderly people without the money or the legal sophistication to fight back.

The drama had not ended there. Since Antelope the Rajneeshee had been engaged in a new series of legal struggles. Wasco County had given them permission to incorporate a "city" on the ranch, but the local ranchers and 1000 Friends were now challenging the incorporation on the grounds that the county had not submitted it to state land-use planning goals. If the Rajneeshee lost, they might have to tear their city down. Then in January 1983, the Portland office of the U.S. Immigration and Naturalization Service had issued orders denying Bhagwan Shree Rajneesh permanent resident status. His disciples were now fighting his deportation back to India. In addition they were preparing for a suit, now visible on the horizon, on the issue of whether the municipal status of their commune violated the religious-establishment clause of the constitution. The Rajneeshee lawyers, for their part, were suing two of their neighbors for libel and the former Antelope town council for discrimination. All in all, there were fifteen lawsuits extant.

After Antelope, too, the Rajneeshee had become a major political issue of the state. In another state—New York or California—even six hundred red-clad people might disappear into the variegated human landscape, and the fate of forty householders might be a day's story. But Oregon, for all of its size, has only three million in population and a very well-developed sense of its own identity. Public spirited and relatively homogeneous, Oregonians behave in many ways like the citizens of a single town—or two towns, really, one in the Willamette Valley with its green fields and its string of universities, and the other in the dry wheat and rangeland east of the Cascades. In the spring of 1983 every state legislator had to have some position on the Rajneeshee. They had many defenders, particularly in the universities, but their Antelope victory had turned many people against them. In the Willamette Valley they provoked interest and concern; but in Wasco and Jefferson counties, across whose borders the ranch lay, they were fighting the nearest thing to a range war.

Strangely enough, in spite of all this controversy, the Rajneeshee remained quite mysterious to Oregonians. When I returned to Oregon in May to visit the ranch, the press was running two or three stories a week on them. Yet with all this coverage and all the time they had to make up their minds, journalists had not yet come up with a formula to describe the Rajneeshee. And when the stories were put together, they yielded rather little information about the nature of the group or the substance of Rajneeshee beliefs. The guru apparently had many followers all over the world. (Ma Anand Sheela gave figures ranging between two and three hundred thousand worldwide.) In India he had had an ashram, but not a conventional one. A documentary film about it distributed in Oregon showed orange-robed figures around the feet of the guru behaving like a lot of highly charged Pentecostalists. It also showed groups of naked Westerners in "therapy" sessions, shaking uncontrollably, hitting each other, and engaging in various forms of group sex. When the film had appeared in Oregon theaters, journalists had quoted Sheela as saying that these therapies were not practiced anymore. No one had apparently asked what these therapies had to do with Hinduism—or any other kind of Indian religion. "Bhagwan" meant "God" or "The Blessed One," depending on the translation. All the disciples had Hindi or Sanskrit names, but the ranch settlement was called a commune, not an ashram: the Rajneesh Neo-Sannyas International Commune. The Rajneeshee said it was a "Buddhafield" in which a special energy flowed. Since coming to Oregon the only thing the guru had said for publication was that a nuclear war would break out in the nineties and that only the commune would survive, its members finding shelter in caves in the hills.

Talking to journalists, politicians, and officials in Portland and Salem, I found that there were not just two views of the Rajneeshee but an extraordinary variety of opinions crisscrossing the political lines. Not only did the fundamentalists view the Rajneeshee with hostility, but there were liberals who thought them a powerful and dangerous group who would stop at nothing to achieve their own, possibly sinister, ends. At the other end of the spectrum there were people who saw the Rajneeshee as spiritual pioneers attempting to create a model cooperative society—and running afoul of religious bigotry. Between these extremes there were liberals and conservatives who thought of the Rajneeshee as an original and interesting group with something to contribute to Oregon (though you wouldn't want to live there) and others who saw them as a laughable gathering of aging sixties dropouts who were making themselves a pain in the neck. Even those people who had visited the ranch (and by now there were quite a few of them) could not agree on the nature of the enterprise—or even sometimes on what they had seen. Two agricultural experts, for instance, had visited the ranch on separate occasions, and one had seen a productive farm and a model of environmental planning, while the other had seen a farm that would never pay for itself and a potential threat to the ecology of the region. Most journalists now visited it as they would a Chinese commune, hesitating, weighing one thing against another, reporting the information given to them by their guides, and then expressing some skepticism. All in all, it was as if the state had swallowed a large foreign body and were ruminating on it, wondering if it would be digestible or not.

Of course, in the context of central Oregon, Rajneeshpuram was somewhat outlandish. Even the name was outlandish since Madras, pronounced *Mad*-ris, had lost whatever association it once had with the Indian city. Then, too, the settlement lay in cowboy country and the landscape of Hollywood Westerns. Ninety miles south of the Columbia River the foothills of the Blue Mountains rear up out of the wheatland, and from there on it is open range where deer and elk and even antelope roam. The rivers, cutting their way through the soft volcanic rock, have left dramatic, towering cliffs, buttes, and tabletops. The dry hills are covered with sage and juniper, and the slanting afternoon light turns them purple and blue. The ranchers irrigate the land along the rivers, but it takes perhaps a hundred acres to feed a single head of cattle in the hills. On the main road through this country there are signs for Shaniko, Antelope, Fossil, and Horse Heaven —towns that flourished during the Gold Rush and the short, ill-fated period of homesteading that followed. In the nineteenth century the ranchers used to ride an hour and a half in to their feedstores, general stores, and blacksmith shops. Now that the ranchers can drive an hour and a half to the supermarkets and trucking depots of Madras, these towns are ghost towns, or near ghost towns.

Antelope, I discovered, lay fifty miles from Madras in a small oasis of green trees. It was just two streets of frame houses with lawns in front, two churches, a school, a café. A horse in a back pasture was switching his tail against the flies, and cattle were moving slowly over a far hillside. Otherwise there wasn't much activity. The café, a low white frame building with an ancient gas pump beside it, looked like a study in Western realism except that it had a sign over the window reading RAJNEESH ZORBA THE BUDDHA RESTAURANT. Inside there were hanging plants and little handmade wooden tables around the old café bar; on the walls were shelves of herbal teas and organic preserves, shelves of mystical literature, and pictures of Bhagwan Shree Rajneesh, a man with large liquid eyes and a long white beard. The day I went in to ask directions for Rajneeshpuram, a young woman in a pink sweat suit was standing behind the counter making an avocado and alfalfa sprout sandwich, while another young woman in red denims waited tables. Both had long strings of wooden beads around their necks with wooden-framed pictures of the guru hanging from them. Two brawny men in jeans and work shirts were sitting rather uncomfortably at one of the tiny lacquered tables talking in low voices; they had come, I guessed, because there wasn't another café for twenty-five miles. When I asked for directions, one of the young women walked outside the café with me and pointed at a road winding up the hillside across the valley: "Four miles up there on the macadam, then take the dirt road to your right—you'll see the sign. Then go ten miles and make a left and keep on that road." She paused and then said darkly, "The signs have bullet holes in them."

Rajneeshpuram turned out to be a full forty minutes' drive from Antelope across a three-thousand-foot range of hills, four miles on macadam and another fifteen on dirt roads. There were, I noticed, no bullet holes in the signs for Rajneeshpuram, but plenty in the stop signs, where they usually are in this part of the country. At the crest of the range were two pillars with inscriptions on them, one in English, the other in Sanskrit. The English inscription read:

I go to the feet of the Awakened One
I go to the feet of the Commune of the Awakened One
I go to the feet of the Ultimate Truth of the Awakened One.

A little farther on was a sign reading WELCOME TO RANCHO RAJNEESH —VISITORS WELCOME, and above it, two flags flew, one American and one Rajneeshee—two doves on a white background. A young man in a pink police uniform waved me on past a flatbed truck carrying a Caterpillar tractor. The road wound down the hill under a series of extraordinary volcanic rock formations—thin pillars of lava with heavy, overhangs that looked like mushrooms sliced in half. The road narrowed and another sign read ESSENTIALLY A ONE-LANE ROAD. Circumnavigating a man-made lake, it came at last to the head of a large canyon—a valley, really—completely hidden away in the hills.

The valley was an astonishing sight in the midst of that empty rangeland. From some slight elevation above it I could see two big Caterpillar bulldozers and a backhoe at work, and beyond them a

stream of traffic—yellow school buses, trucks, and automobiles—
moving around a system of roads. Driving down the canyon, I passed
a dirt airstrip with a hangar and five aircraft sitting out in front of it: a
DC3, a Mitsubishi executive jet, and three light propeller planes. Beyond that was a machine shop and next to that a small factory under
a shed roof with a big pile of lumber beside it. Red-clad figures were
carrying lumber, stacking wooden platforms, and lifting what looked
like a small A-frame house onto the back of a flatbed truck. The roads
converged on an old farmhouse and two big gray barns—clearly the
original ranch buildings. The barns now fronted on what looked like
the main street of a Gold Rush town. There were people everywhere
and a near traffic jam of vehicles, their transmissions straining, plow-
ing their way through the viscous mud. Bearded men in denims and
women in jeans and parkas were rocking one of the trucks out of a
rut. Down the street, past some trailers, there were new wooden
buildings in various stages of construction. A group of red-clad people were pouring concrete for a floor of a building; another group was
putting up roof beams, and a third was nailing shingles onto a roof.

I stopped at a trailer marked MIRDAD—INFORMATION and found
Veena, a sun-frosted blonde with big blue eyes and a soft English
voice. I had talked with Veena on the phone before coming and she
had sent me a press packet with slickly printed brochures and copies
of newspaper articles favorable to the Rajneeshee. She and four or
five other attractive young women known as the "Twinkies" dealt
with the press and the stream of visitors coming to the ranch. She
offered me a tour—her fourth, as it turned out, of the day. Before me
there had been two busloads of senior citizens and a busload of college students doing "in depth" studies on the Rajneeshee. She had a
phone call, and I waited while she told a journalist on the other end
of the line that Bhagwan never said there would be ten thousand
people on the ranch by 1990; he did not speak, she said, so there was
no way he could have said that. She repeated this very patiently four
times.

"This is Jesus Grove," Veena said, negotiating her big Escort Jeep
through the crowds on the main street. "Each part of the ranch is
named after a saint. There's Buddha Grove, the Magdalena, Siddhar-
tha, Zarathustra Drive, Alan Watts, and here's Walt Whitman Grove.
We had some trouble finding an American saint." She explained that
the old ranch house was now a vegetarian restaurant for visitors and
disciples—or *sannyasins*, as she called them, using the Hindi name.
The settlement had begun just around it with trailers and mobile
homes. Now that there were eight hundred sannyasins on the ranch,
and more to come shortly, they were building out into the canyons—

on the nonarable land within the city limits. "Most of the building you see going on here now is for the festival. We're expecting fifteen thousand people for Bhagwan's *darshan* in the first week of July."

Veena pointed out the post office and trailers housing the planning office and the city hall. At the end of the main street another canyon opened up, its entire floor covered with construction. Four long wooden buildings were near completion, and foundations were being laid for two more; beyond them a tent city was going up for the festival visitors. Sannyasins, perhaps a hundred of them, were digging postholes, pouring concrete, fitting windows, and laying out platforms for the tents. Most of them appeared to be in their thirties, but there were a few in their twenties and some older people as well —all of them dressed in various shades of red, with wooden prayer beads, or *malas*, around their necks. The men were bronzed and bearded, the women rosy-cheeked with their hair flying. Handsome and healthy-looking, they appeared to work in a kind of good-humored chaos. Couples here and there were hugging each other and joking; a woman ran across the road and leaped, laughing, into the arms of a man on the other side. "There's one of the architects," Veena said, pointing to a bearded man in jeans pounding a nail into the roof of one of the unfinished buildings. "We've got a lot of extraordinary people here. That one"—she indicated a man carrying boards over his shoulder—"was a professor of literature. And that one over there with the notebook makes the most beautiful dulcimers."

Veena's tour of the ranch began with the water conservation projects. The lake I had seen on the way down turned out to be a forty-five-acre reservoir held by a four-hundred-foot earth dam. In the summer, Veena said, the lake would be used for swimming and boating—there was so much water around. Up in a nearby canyon was a series of open pits built as a natural sewage treatment plant. Because the canyon lay in Jefferson County, county officials would permit them to use it only for the festival and not the year round. "Bureaucratic snarls," Veena said. "So stupid. It would allow us to save hundreds of thousands of gallons of water for irrigation." Looking up from one of the pits, she waved her hand at a distant hilltop. "Over there we'll put our crematorium. Wasco County has just given us permission to build it."

We drove down the main canyon alongside a creek, Veena pointing out the check dams they had built to slow the course of the water and the juniper cuttings they had put in to fortify the eroded banks. In many places the banks were now thick with vegetation. "You'd be amazed," Veena said, "how much greener it's gotten in two years."

Past the center of Rajneeshpuram the canyon opened out into an expanse of irrigated fields along the John Day River. We passed several greenhouses and stopped at a dairy where a row of sleek holsteins stood in a concrete-floored milking shed; across the road was a poultry farm with the same expensive, well-cared-for look. A large airy shed housed two thousand Rhode Island Reds, and in the A-frame chicken coops beside it there was a variety of exotic fowl, including several peacocks and two emus. The emus, Veena explained, were used to keep off the coyotes. Down the road on the riverbank was a fifty-acre market garden laid out in neatly plowed furrows. Like the dairy and poultry farms, it looked like something conceived and maintained by an agricultural school. In the distance I could see several sannyasins working with a truck and a tractor; nearby, where the rows were already green with lettuces and spinach, several more were raking and weeding. "Work is our worship. We sannyasins work twelve to sixteen hours a day," Veena said. "But it doesn't seem like work. It's our meditation. And Bhagwan taught us that work is play."

Veena did not speak about the spiritual aspect of the ranch very often on our trip—possibly because visitors found the material achievements easier to assimilate and certainly because water and land use were now the main issues for the commune in state politics. Most of her remarks, I later discovered, fit into the Rajneeshee counterargument against charges from the local ranchers and 1000 Friends of Oregon. Veena did, however, point out where the guru lived: it was a compound with several buildings in a grove of juniper and newly planted deciduous trees. "We've built an indoor swimming pool for him so he can exercise his back. He has asthma and allergies and a disc problem, so we try to keep him comfortable." In front of the compound was a long, low aluminum building with its doors closed and locked: the garage for the twenty-one Rolls-Royces.

Our next stop was one of the new housing developments for the sannyasins: a group of very small A-frames set into the hillsides of a subsidiary canyon. With floor space for just two beds, each A-frame was neatly made with a window, a heater, air-conditioning, and carpeting on the floors. The structures, Veena explained, were an invention of a Rajneeshee designer. After last year's festival, they had hundreds of tent platforms, but no housing for the new permanent residents, so someone had figured out how to put three tent platforms together to make a house. In this complex the A-frames had electricity but no water, so here there were bath and toilet facilities in a central building at the mouth of the canyon. In the new complexes the designers had put four A-frames together on a single platform and had added two bathrooms in the middle to serve the four.

We next went to the Magdalena, a big building housing the communal kitchen and dining room for those who worked on the ranch. Commune members took all three meals there, coming in from their sleeping or workplaces in the yellow school buses which plied regular routes around the ranch. When we arrived, the twenty-odd sannyasin-cooks were setting out the evening meal: a ratatouille, meatless lasagna, fresh asparagus, tofu, cheese, homemade bread, and a variety of salads. The head chef, an ebullient young woman with a mass of curly blond hair, said that the asparagus had been bought from a local supplier but that all other vegetables were home-grown. She showed us around the kitchen, pointing out the creamery and the professional bakers' oven. "We make everything," she said. "Brioches, croissants, cheesecake—you name it." Opening the oven, she showed us dozens of finished loaves of bread—nutbread, oatmeal bread, whole wheat bread, and one particularly good-looking loaf that had a ticket on it marked BHAGWAN. As we left, the sannyasins were just beginning to come in for dinner. Leaving their coats and shoes in the mudroom outside, they joined the chow line and then took their plastic trays to the long Formica refectory tables in the dining room. A young woman served three kinds of draft beer, and against the wall there were containers full of coffee, tea, and fruit juices. On one wall was a shelf with a few dog-eared magazines and a bulletin board with recent newspaper clippings on Rajneeshpuram. There was also something that looked like a suggestion box, but which, Veena explained, was a mailbox where sannyasins could drop their letters for Bhagwan. Did they get answers? I asked. Yes, she said, often they did.

Back on the main street we went into a new building with a wood-paneled interior. In one part of it was a boutique with fashionable and fairly expensive sports clothes: jumpsuits, jogging suits, parkas, sundresses, and so on—all of them, of course, in shades of red. "Sannyasins love to dress well," Veena said, fingering a delicate little jersey. Now that she mentioned it, I remembered seeing a fairly high incidence of designer jeans on the sannyasins. Just outside the boutique was a gift shop with postcards of the ranch and trinkets of various kinds, most of them decorated with the Rajneeshee symbol—two doves—or pictures of the guru. "We call Him Bhagwan, not *the* Bhagwan," Veena corrected me. There was also a windfall of books for sale —almost all of them by Bhagwan Shree Rajneesh. On the other side of the building was a large, handsomely appointed room with a bar and a dance floor. In the daytime it served as a lounge and snack bar; at night it was a discotheque. "Visitors always ask me what we do for entertainment up here," Veena said. "They mostly want to know what we do without television. I tell them that we don't have any leisure time—and it's true. If you work twelve, fourteen, sixteen hours a day, all you want to do is go to bed. But now that we have this disco, it's full almost every night. Sannyasins love to dance, and there's a lot of energy here. You can just feel it."

There were at that moment only two other people in the room: a man and a woman drinking Perriers together and playing with tarot cards.

In the next ten days I commuted back and forth between Rajneesh-puram and Madras, talking both with the Rajneeshee and with their neighbors in central Oregon. The state of hostilities between the two was now such that it was like commuting across Belfast.

The face-off between the Rajneeshee and the Jimenez group had not ended in violence, but in the opinion of Michael C. Sullivan, the district attorney of Jefferson County, it had come very close to doing so. For four days the police had watched the truckers gather and the pickup-truck cowboys stalk about, spoiling for a fight. Finally the Rajneeshee leaders had come to Sullivan for help, and he had negotiated a settlement: the Conservative Baptists would stop demonstrating if Bhagwan Shree Rajneesh would stop driving to the weigh station every afternoon. Sullivan, a graduate of Washington University in St. Louis, and a man of unusual intellectual detachment, could find no humor in the situation even now. The Jimenez group, he said, did not speak for most people in Madras. A Methodist minister and a Catholic monsignor had spoken out against violence and religious intolerance while the trouble was going on. All the same, the demonstration testified to the state of emotion in the two counties. Since then there had been no violence, but the opposition had taken shape politically. Three separate citizens' committees had formed to organize against the Rajneeshee, and one of these had brought a thousand people to a protest meeting. Most of the local politicians had turned against the Rajneeshee, and in Jefferson County, the smaller and more rural of the two, Sullivan was now the only elected official who kept the lines of communication open with them, always in the hope of averting trouble.

The Rajneeshee explained this welling-up of hostility toward them as "mere bigotry," and there was no doubt that religious intolerance played a part in it. One of the citizens' groups was circulating a petition for a ballot initiative asking state officials to drive this "alien cult" from the state. Reverend Mardo Jimenez, when I went to see him, told me he thought the guru was possessed by the devil. Jimenez, a Honduran by birth, who came to Oregon to minister to Hispanic

migrant workers and gained citizenship—the status so much desired
by the guru—just the year before, however, told me that this was a
purely theological formulation which he did not expect everyone to
accept. He had other objections as well. In the first place, he said, the
Rajneeshee were immoral people who engaged in orgies and wanted
to destroy the institution of marriage; in the second place, they were
cultists who surrendered their personalities and mental powers to a
man they called "God"; thirdly, they had political and territorial ambitions in the two counties, and perhaps the state.

As Jimenez suggested, there were more than religious objections to
the Rajneeshee in the area. The Rajneeshee city plan now projected a
population of 3700 by 1995. That was a lot of people, given the fact
that there were only 12,000 people in all of Jefferson County and only
22,000 in Wasco County. The ranchers would have objected to the
creation of any settlement that size: water was scarce in the rangeland, and they liked the country the way it was. But with the Rajneeshee there were political problems as well. Almost all of the disciples
were of voting age, and in the last election their three hundred voters
had voted en bloc for all candidates. With three thousand-odd voters,
they could influence, if not dictate, the result of any election in one,
or perhaps two, counties.

A number of the ranchers told me that they couldn't care less what
the Rajneeshee believed in, but now, after two years, they did not
trust them and they did not like them. In the beginning the Rajneeshee had said that they were a rural commune, and all they wanted
was to farm the land. Then they said they would not move their
people into Antelope; then they said they had no interest in staying
there. Now you had to wonder whether they did not want to bring
more than 3700 people to live at the Big Muddy Ranch. There were a
lot of broken promises, but beyond that, they had treated the Antelope people badly, insulting them—calling them "rednecks" and "ignorant old people"—and harassing them in all kinds of ways. They
had photographed them, videotaped their meetings, taken down the
license plate numbers of every car that came into town. They said
these were precautions against election fraud, but you wouldn't treat
older people like that, unless you meant to drive them away.

Mike Sullivan told me that he got along very well with the Rajneeshee he had met, and would defend their rights to the end, but that
he did not approve of their tactics. He had advised them not to sue
their neighbors for libel, and he had advised them to make some
gesture of goodwill toward the community. But they had not followed
his advice. Instead, he said, they kept making aggressive demands
and acting like big-city people and getting everyone's back up. "Their

style is to come in and bang on the table and say, 'If you don't do what we want, we'll sue you.' Well, the county judges here are in their seventies. They're tough old birds who've been through World War II and their attitude is, 'So perhaps you confuse me with someone who cares.' "

A few days later in a Madras restaurant, I ran into one of the judges Sullivan had talked about. A big man, Helmer Wallan had powerful arms that hung at some distance from his torso. One of his hands was bandaged, and there were small unbandaged wounds on his arms and face. Of the Rajneeshee he said: "They think they can do anything, and so far they have. But we'll find a way to beat them, don't worry." It seemed reasonable to believe him. A propane gas tank had just blown up his truck, and he had walked away from the explosion like Popeye.

The brochures Veena had sent me about Rajneeshpuram were quite specific on certain subjects, such as agricultural production, and quite vague on others, such as the purpose of the whole enterprise. In one of them Ma Anand Sheela had written:

> Rajneeshpuram is our attempt to give expression to the religious vision of our beloved Master, Bhagwan Shree Rajneesh. It is our offering to Him, and also a reflection of the love and wisdom which He showers on us.
> . . . The work that we are doing here is a united effort by those who love Him to create a beautiful oasis—both material and spiritual—where anyone can come and drink from the fountain of His love and quench their thirst forever.

The brochure also quoted the guru as saying:

> The idea of the commune is beautiful: people living together in a nonpossessive way, neither possessing things nor possessing persons; people living together, creating together, celebrating together and still allowing each one his own space; people creating a certain climate of meditativeness, of love, of living in that climate.

The prose reared up like the bright wall of a glacier without a single handhold. The only two suggestive details were Sheela's capitalization of the *H* in "Him" and "His" and the guru's Californian use of the word "space." When Veena tried to explain the commune—steering her Jeep between potholes or picking her way through the mud by the dairy barn—the same reflecting glass appeared. "The ranch is a Buddhafield," she said. "You can just feel the energy here." And, "He teaches us to be conscious, to be aware. How do we feel about

Him? Well, it's like falling in love with someone, only more so."
When I asked her how decisions were made on the ranch, she said,
"There's no system, really. We work together and things happen
spontaneously."

The odd thing about it was that Veena was otherwise wholly articulate and down to earth. Furthermore, the ranch was anything but a
spaced-out flower-child operation. Indeed, it bore rather more resemblance to Camranh Bay in the mid-sixties than to any hippie commune
of the same date. Small wonder there had been rumors of missile
testing by a foreign power. The Rajneeshee had achieved an extraordinary amount in less than two years—and with very little outside
labor. They had begun with 64,000 acres and some federal land, most
of it of very poor quality; overgrazed by sheep in the decades past,
the ranch had not been worked profitably for twenty years. (For the
past ten years it had belonged to a series of real-estate trusts.) Since
July of 1981, the Rajneeshee had—they said—cleared 3000 acres of
land and planted them with winter wheat, sunflowers, vegetables,
vines, and fruit trees. They had built a 350-million-gallon reservoir, 14
irrigation systems with underground pipes taking the water to the
fields, and several artesian wells for drinking water. Their truck farm
now provided some 90 percent of all the vegetables consumed on the
ranch; their poultry farm and dairy produced all the necessary milk
and eggs. The infrastructure for the city now included a ten-megawatt
electrical power substation, an urban-use sewer system, a telephone
and computer communications center, and 85 school buses—or the
fourth largest public transportation system in the state of Oregon.
Starting with a single farmhouse, they now had 250,000 square feet of
building. With 38 new residential quadriplexes they could now house
1000 people over the coming winter. The tent city they were now
building would accommodate 15,000 people for the week of the Master's Day festival.

With all the speed of this development, the Rajneeshee had clearly
done a good deal of careful environmental planning. One of the main
worries of the local ranchers was that the Rajneeshee would use up
so much water they would lower the water table throughout the region. According to the Oregon State Water Resources Department,
however, the ranch had its own aquifer—independent from those of
the neighboring ranches—and the Rajneeshee had done enough
water conservation work so that it would be adequate to their needs
for the foreseeable future. In addition to the big dam, the Rajneeshee
had constructed 150 small check dams on the major creeks and built
up their eroded banks so that vegetation and wildlife were returning
to the canyons. On their farm the Rajneeshee were experimenting

with crop rotation to minimize the use of chemical fertilizers; they had brought eight new types of legumes from the agriculture school at the University of Idaho to rotate with the winter wheat. In their truck farm they were alternating rows of plants and flowers to reduce the need for pesticides. They had also put a good deal of effort into waste disposal. Every day teams would make a tour of all the buildings and collect bottles, aluminum cans, paper, and other waste materials and take them to a recycling plant. And in spite of the fact that all the construction made the city alternately a mudhole or a dust bowl, the Rajneeshee kept all the buildings and the equipment remarkably clean. In the first year, the buildings had been makeshift and the housing crowded and uncomfortable. But now the Rajneeshee were giving more attention to the amenities: the new buildings were carpeted and their varnished wood paneling and furniture gave them the look of new ski lodge condos.

According to the Rajneeshee, the total cost of their operations in Oregon now hovered somewhere around $50 million. Where all this money came from was, of course, the question. Ma Prem Savita, the head accountant for the ranch, told me that the Rajneeshee had a financial structure consisting of three major elements: the Rajneesh Foundation International—the "church" of which Sheela was the president; the Rajneesh Investment Corporation, a wholly owned subsidiary of the foundation, run by Sheela's husband, Jayananda; and the Rajneesh Neo-Sannyas International Commune, whose officers were all commune members. According to Savita, only the foundation was tax exempt, but it had few assets; its main economic activity was the sale of Rajneeshee books and tapes. On this it had grossed a million dollars in the past year. The investment corporation owned all the long-term assets, including the Portland hotel and the ranch, and paid taxes on them. The commune was a uniquely American cooperative structure created initially for the Shakers and used by groups whose members were not employed elsewhere and did not make profits. Though nonprofit at the corporate level, it was taxable through its members—something like a partnership. The commune ran all the business on and off the ranch and paid for the running expenses, including the lease of the ranch from the investment corporation. The commune was now bringing in some money, Savita said, but most of the $50 million had come from non-tax-exempt loans to the investment corporation and non-tax-exempt donations to the foundation and the commune. The donations, she said, were usually between $5000 and $25,000, but some were much larger.

Savita, who had created this rather elegant structure, was an accountant by training. But then, I discovered, most of the Rajneeshee managers were professionals in their fields. The city planner, for example, Swami Deva Wadud, had been a successful practicing psychic for six years before coming to the ranch; before that, however, he had been a city planner in San Mateo, California, and San Luis Obispo. He had a B.A. from the architecture school of the University of Michigan and an M.A. from the Harvard Graduate School of Design. The farm coordinator, Neehar, was an Australian with a Ph.D. in linguistic philosophy. He had run a farm in Australia for a number of years and along the way had picked up a working knowledge of plant biology and riparian ecology—among other things. The head of the dairy farm was a former dairy farmer from Wales, and the head of the kitchen, a professional nutritionist. The coordinator of the water systems, Swami Anand Videh, told me he was strictly an amateur at what he did: he had had to learn what he knew about sewer systems on the ranch. But he had a degree from Harvard in visual and environmental studies, and his office was staffed by professional geologists and engineers. Ma Yoga Vidya, the president of the commune, was a former systems analyst for IBM and Univac. A South African, she had graduated from the University of South Africa with honors in math and then had studied computer sciences at the University of London.

The other departments on the ranch—legal, publications, and so on—were staffed with people of equally impressive credentials. Swami Prem Niren, who headed the legal team, had been a partner of the influential California firm of Manatt, Phelps, Rothenberg and Tunney. Now thirty-eight years old, charming, and very bright, he was teaching himself to be a constitutional lawyer. His wife, Ma Prem Isabel, who ran the public relations department might, most journalists agreed, have done PR for any large corporation. A Chilean of French extraction, she had gone to university and then worked her way around the world, spending two years in Tahiti with the Polynesian tourist bureau. The chief lobbyist for the group, Ma Mary Catherine, was an ebullient Oregonian with a Ph.D. from Yale and a decade of experience in Portland city politics.

That the Rajneeshee were a fairly rarefied group of people might have been deduced by any visitor from the sign ESSENTIALLY A ONE-LANE ROAD. Just how rarefied they were, Krishna Deva, the mayor of Rajneeshpuram, gave me to understand the first time I talked with him. A tall, handsome man in his mid-thirties, with a trimmed black beard, Krishna Deva, known as K.D., was the former David Knapp of Santa Monica, California. He was, he told me, a clinical psychologist by training; he had an M.A. from Lone Mountain College in San Francisco and had worked with handicapped students at Santa Monica City College. For his Ph.D. dissertation at the Fielding Institute in Santa Barbara he had done a study on three hundred American Rajneesh disciples in Poona. "There are various myths about us," K.D. said. "People think that a master-disciple relationship is like a master-slave relationship. They think we are dependent types, avoiding life, avoiding stress and decisions. But I studied three hundred sannyasins using Abraham Maslow's criteria for the self-actualizing person, and the group rated very high on the independence scale. By and large, the people here on the ranch are people who have had success in worldly terms, and who see themselves as successes. When they came to Bhagwan, they were people in transition. There was some change involved—some openness happened. But they're not dropouts. They're what I call 'dropups.' "

K.D. went on to explain that this was only natural. "Bhagwan says, 'Religion is a luxury.' That means that your stomach must be full and you must have a sense of self-worth and self-esteem before you can be a truly religious person. Otherwise prayer is only a plea. To Bhagwan, Mother Teresa is a hoax. The priests and the politicians create the poor."

K.D. did not exaggerate the "worldly success" of the sannyasins. While I was at the ranch two psychologists from the University of Oregon were completing a survey preparatory to a study they would be doing on the Rajneeshee in Oregon. The results of their survey matched the results of the survey K.D. had done three years before. Then the average age of the disciples was just over thirty; now it was about thirty-four; 54 percent were women and 46 percent men. According to both surveys, 80 percent of the disciples came from middle- or upper-middle-class backgrounds; their fathers were, overwhelmingly, professionals or businessmen. Some 83 percent of the Rajneeshee had attended college, two thirds had bachelor's degrees, and 12 percent had doctorates. Before coming to Rajneeshpuram, their median income had been $20,000 (a sum that might have been greater had the survey excluded those who were working without pay for the guru in Poona). In addition K.D.'s survey showed that a quarter of the American sannyasins were Jewish, a quarter were Catholic, and the rest Protestant by background. Almost all of them were white and two thirds of them had been living on the West Coast.

Making my own informal survey during my first week on the ranch, I gathered that the Rajneeshee included a few former businessmen—notably Sheela's husband, Jayananda, the former John Shelfer of New Jersey—but proportionately fewer of them than one might find on, say, the Los Angeles–San Francisco shuttle. There seemed, on the other hand, to be a fair number of professional people—doctors, lawyers, architects, and the like. One doctor I met was a specialist in pediatric allergies who had taught at the Stanford Medical School. When I asked Veena to introduce me to someone who had recently joined the Rajneeshee, she found me a lawyer who had just quit the William Morris Agency. A lot of people seemed to have come from the so-called "caring professions": social work, psychotherapy, and so on. The mayor of Antelope, Ma Prem Karuna, had a Ph.D. in adult education from Boston University. The group included a number of musicians (there was a rock band and a country-and-western band on the ranch), some dancers, some theater people, and a good many craftspeople: potters, weavers, silversmiths. The editor of the *Rajneesh Times* was a former Fleet Street journalist, and one of his office mates was a professor of literature from Brandeis University. But it seemed to me there were fewer literary people than visual artists and designers. One afternoon in the wake of the guru's daily drive through the city, a woman came up and introduced herself as the former art editor of *Ramparts* magazine. Then there was, I discovered, a large contingent from the world of fashion. One of the few black Americans on the ranch was a young man of striking height and beauty who had been a successful male model in New York.

While the backgrounds of the sannyasins went some way to accounting for the caliber of Rajneeshee operations, they only magnified the larger question of what these people were doing in the wilds of Oregon with a silent guru and twenty-one Rolls-Royces. In fact the sannyasins never saw the guru except when he sallied forth from his house in one of the Rolls-Royces for a drive—which he did punctually every day at two in the afternoon. For these pass-bys the sannyasins would line up along the roads and greet him with palms pressed together and beatific expressions on their faces. During my first few days on the ranch I met the parents of three sannyasins who were visiting the ranch and clearly wondering the same thing I was.

One couple, whom I met touring the ranch in a Jeep with Isabel, were on their way back home to Westchester, New York, after a trip to China. The man wore a formfitting white shirt, white slacks, and natty white shoes. A retired businessman, he asked Isabel a good many questions requiring numbers for answers: the cost of the farming operations, the yield of the dairy cows, and so on. Isabel gave him the numbers, and he fell silent. His wife said nothing. Finally he made a remark about China, but when no one took it up, he lapsed into silence again. Isabel, undaunted, rattled on about water tables and the way so many parents complained about their children gaining weight on vegetarian food. The son, age twenty or so, looked like a prospective yeshiva student; squenched down in the backseat and sweaty with embarrassment, he said nothing for the entire trip.

The second couple I met in the parking lot in front of the information trailer; they had just taken the tour and were on their way to dinner at the ranch's Zorba the Buddha restaurant. They were from Cleveland; the man was a banker—very WASP, very old school tie. Their son was the water coordinator, Videh, who had joined the Rajneeshee just after graduating from Harvard. They talked with nervous enthusiasm about what they had seen on the ranch: wasn't it amazing what they'd done in so short a time? The woman showed me a pretty purple stole she had bought at the boutique "just so I'll fit in a little bit better." But they seemed not at all anxious to leave the only other person on the ranch who was not wearing pink, purple or red head to toe.

The other parent I talked with was the chairman of the board of a large metropolitan newspaper; she came and went rather tight-lipped with a member of the board of 1000 Friends of Oregon.

Oddly enough, it was Veena, my first guide to the ranch, who began to make some sense of the Rajneeshee for me. The indefatigable Veena told me the story of her life just as she had told it to all the other journalists and tourists who had ever asked it of her. Born in England, she had been brought up in South Africa by her divorced mother in Church of England, Sunday-school style. She had worked her way through college as a fashion model and then left for England to work on and off as a teacher and an educational psychologist for disturbed kids. Since this was the late sixties, she hung around with rock groups and fashion people and smoked some dope. "Actually," she said, "I was always a little rebel. There were always a lot of boys, a lot of parties. But otherwise I kept the lid on tight. Finally I just quit." A boyfriend asked her to go to India with him, so she packed her jeans and went; only she dropped him somewhere along the way and hitchhiked by herself through Afghanistan. She didn't much like India (there were so many poor people, so many beggars), but found another boyfriend and stayed. She was sitting on a beach in Goa— her hair now down to her waist—when an Italian film crew came by and asked her to be in a film about hippies in India. "I could have told them about hippies," she said. "They didn't know very much." One of the women in the crew wore a mala around her neck, and Veena had found her extremely nice. "She told me about this extraordinary guru. I didn't pay much attention because India seemed full of weird gurus and Westerners on strange trips of one sort or another. But sometime later my boyfriend and I were in Bombay on our way back to London with an afternoon off, and he persuaded me to go and see this one. I didn't especially want to go. We went to this high-rise apartment, and I thought, gurus don't live in high-rises, but then, there he was: the most fascinating, the most compelling, man I'd ever met."

The guru had asked Veena to come to a meditation camp he was holding in a hill station above Bombay a few weeks later. She debated the offer and said no. But later on the train to New Delhi with her boyfriend, she reconsidered and turned back. She didn't like the meditation camp initially. "There were about two hundred Indians there and about thirty white people, and in the meditations people were dancing around doing all this shouting." She was on her way to the station when the guru sent a messenger after her asking her to come back. She went back and tried again, but it was no good. Again she tried to leave, and again the guru sent a messenger after her. He talked to her, and urged her to take *sannyas*, or accept disciplehood. She resisted, but he was so compelling, and he offered her a new name, Veena, or "the instrument the gods play on." She had never liked her own name, Sheila Fisher, so eventually she accepted. That was January 1972. In March she went back to England at the guru's request to set up a Rajneeshee meditation center. She had worked for him since then and never looked back.

Veena's story recalled a time and place—or perhaps a space—far removed from the Oregon rangeland in 1983. In the late sixties an Afghan rifleman standing on the heights above the Khyber Pass would have seen the beginning of a decade-long procession of Westerners on their way to the East. The hippies and flower children came first, hitchhiking and backpacking their way to the hills of Nepal, where the sacred monkeys played around the stupas and where the pungent herbs grew within the sound of temple bells. Having passed through Tibetan Buddhist realms, they turned in a caravan south to the subcontinent, where yogis sat naked on hillsides and by the rivers smoke from the funeral pyres blew around monks chanting the Vedas. After the hippies came the photographers and the models, the designers and the rock stars, the filmmakers, the priests and the psychoanalysts, and behind them the whole parade of middle-class drifters and *Luftmenschen*, losing or finding themselves in the dense, luxurious exotica. Americans, Germans, Italians, Australians turned up wearing *dhotis* and flowers in their long hair. These magical mystery tourists discovered sitar music, yogic asanas, and Zen koans; they learned sutras, mantras, and the Upanishads; they developed tastes for mandalas and cultivated the Third Eye. The subcontinent was a vast spiritual marketplace; with its thousands upon thousands of gods, saints, and holy men, it had something for everyone. Austere Freudian analysts found ashrams where they could fast, remain celibate, and sit still for six hours at a time. Jungians found shamans exorcising technicolor demons from women writhing on the floors of temples. Arica graduates found Sufi masters, neo-Reichians found the Tantra, and hippies found blind holy men with begging bowls. A Time-Life photographer found a descendant of Sai Baba to materialize a roll of color film unavailable in India. The tour was largely unmapped, and for all practical purposes endless, but there were some well-marked stations along the way: the beaches of Goa, the American Express offices, hospitals that specialized in intestinal disorders, and several large, prestigious ashrams.

The new Western invasion of India was remarkable both for its duration and for the size of its forces. In the mid-seventies the French consul in New Delhi estimated the number of French in India at a quarter of a million; the consulate, so the writer, Gita Mehta, reported, had a permanent staff of doctors and psychiatrists to pick up the casualties and fly them back to France. How many Americans went could be calculated roughly by the booty they returned with: the joss sticks, the wind chimes, the chakra diagrams, the vegetable curries, and the books of occult lore. Of course, whole sectors of American society remain quite innocent of even the hatha yoga asanas. Karmic calculations are rarely made in Rotary Clubs, the Council on Foreign Relations, and the Southern Baptist Conference. But *kundalini* and *zazen* are common parlance elsewhere, and the Bhagavad-Gita is more familiar to most college students than *Beowulf.*

What was puzzling about the Rajneeshee—and what had made them so difficult to place—was that their commune bore no resemblance to a monastery or an ashram. American adepts of Eastern religions tend to be particular about the authenticity of their appearance and their practices. In Zen centers, for instance, loose-robed figures would pad about, their eyes downcast, their legs slightly bowed from long hours in the lotus position. But the Rajneeshee all had the rugged, healthy allure of California skiers. True, they all wore shades of red and orange—"sunset colors," they called them—but their down coats, their jumpsuits, and velour sweatshirts could have walked out of any Marin County boutique: there was a kind of hitouch sensuality about the clothing. Then, instead of meditating in any formal sense, they were building, and building, among other things, data processing systems, boutiques, and discotheques.

The work schedule at the ranch was a rigorous one. Sannyasins went to breakfast at the Magdalena between six and seven in the morning; they then went to their workplaces, returning for lunch at midday and for dinner at seven in the evening. In addition to the meal breaks there were tea breaks, morning and afternoon, during which tea, juices, fruit, and cake would be served in tents near each work site. Then at two in the afternoon the sannyasins would line up along the roadside to watch the guru drive by in one of his Rolls-Royces. Apart from that, they worked all day long, and there were no holidays in the week—Sunday being the day for meetings. The system was that each person had a job to do, and the commune took care of the rest. A kitchen staff prepared the meals each day; and there were people assigned to clean the A-frames and trailers, and people who washed and ironed clothes. A farm worker or posthole digger could thus come back each night to a clean room with clean clothes— and no errands. Toothpaste, soap, and other toiletries were provided; so also, I was told, was clothing—jeans, T-shirts, and so on—for those who needed it. Anyone going off the ranch on business could take a commune car and pick out clothes from a special public relations wardrobe.

The fact that each sannyasin had only one job made the work schedule somewhat less onerous than it sounded. Still, sannyasins had very little time to themselves, and as the number of people moving in always seemed to run ahead of the housing available, most of them had little privacy. The commune had movies every week or so, and during the year a variety of entertainments. But there was no television on the ranch, and as yet no library. Sannyasins could order newspapers, magazines, or books by mail, but most of them read very little, if at all. Apart from Bhagwan Shree Rajneesh, the most popular author on the ranch was Louis L'Amour.

In the beginning virtually all the commune members had done manual labor on the farm or on construction sites. Now that the commune was larger and its functions more diverse, a number practiced the professions they had been trained for: lawyers worked as lawyers, art editors as art editors. But because there were rather more professors than, say, plumbers among the sannyasins, many people still had to do jobs they had not done before. Another psychic—Wadud's wife—was air traffic controller for the ranch, and an acupuncturist was coordinating the truck depot. The ranch now had a riding stable with a dozen head of horses for rent to visitors. The wrangler, who sat his horse as well as any local cowboy, told me that he had been a martial arts instructor, and before that a novitiate at a Catholic seminary in New York State. (He had, he said, spent an intermediate year studying philosophy and literature at the Sorbonne.) Another New Yorker I met, a former Marxist historian, now spent most of his time on the ranch operating one or another of the earth-moving machines.

He preferred that, he said, to teaching school—his first assignment at Rajneeshpuram—and was getting pretty good at it; but so, too, were his six women colleagues, one of whom also worked as a belly dancer in the Portland nightclub.

While most sannyasins picked up their new tasks quite quickly, a few of them had to go to some lengths to learn the skills required by the commune-city. When it was decided that a police force was needed to protect the ranch, six young men and women went for a ten-month training course at the Oregon Police Academy. All of the recruits graduated in the top 10 percent of their class, and one of them, a droll young man named Swami Deva Sangeet, was picked out as the best of seven hundred Oregon police trainees. Rajneesh-puram now had a police force—or a Peace Force, as it was known—sporting pink uniforms and police revolvers.

What surprised me, given the apparent egalitarianism of the commune, was that there was no system of job rotation. Dishwashing was the one exception: sannyasins took turns washing dishes according to a monthly schedule. Sannyasins did change jobs, and now that the commune had indoor as well as outdoor work, many changed jobs temporarily: office workers, for example, would spend a day a week cutting junipers or would fill in at a construction site for a week or two. But there was no question of right involved and no democratic practice. The personnel department headed by Ma Yoga Vidya assigned the jobs, and sannyasins took what they got. When I asked Isabel whether people assigned to menial jobs—say, cleaning—did not get bored and resentful after a bit, she laughed and said, "Of course not. Here all work is play and all work is meditation." She went on to explain that having a cleaning job in the commune was not like having the same job outside, since one's job—one's worship—had nothing to do with money or status. When I persisted, she introduced me to two women in their thirties, both of whom had been cleaners for eight years, first in Poona and then here. One of them, a South American married to another sannyasin, was ironing a jacket for Krishna Deva when I met her. She told me she loved her work, and there was no doubting her, for as she went about the trailer picking up clothes, she seemed to glow with a deep and serene enthusiasm. The other woman, formerly a dancer, had just left her cleaning job—after eight years—to join Veena and Isabel in the public relations department. But she, too, said she had loved her work. "When I was cleaning a room, or clothes, I felt I was cleaning myself as well." She laughed. "It could be that I got a bit too attached to my cleaning. It will probably be good for me to do something quite different."

Changing jobs, or doing a job other than that for which one was trained, had, I gathered, a spiritual or psychological value for the individual (in addition to whatever practical value it had for the commune). Before going to the ranch I had visited the Rajneeshee hotel in Portland—formerly the Martha Washington residential hotel for women. The manager, a sleek young man in wide-wale corduroys, a button-down shirt, and a tie, could have been the manager of any hanging-plant restaurant in the city, even with his mala on. He turned out to be a former student at the Union Theological Seminary in New York and a massage therapist who for a period in the seventies had practiced the Alexander technique out of the Chelsea Hotel. He had worked, he said, at many different jobs in the ashram, and all of them had been "great opportunities" for him. "My main concern now," he said, "is getting rid of this YMCA furniture and finding something a little less tacky." By the by he told me that a former architect was working in the kitchen of the hotel "because he needed it." The architect had not been consulted on his current project.

Swami Anand Subhuti, the editor of the *Rajneesh Times*, explained this concept of "need" to me. "Awareness," he said, paraphrasing the guru, "requires spiritual detachment. The attachments of the ego to role, status, and achievement must be dropped, for like all other kinds of programming, they stand in the way, they are obstacles." At one point, he said, he himself had become too attached to his own creation, the *Rajneesh Times*. "I had a powerful claim on it, and my possessiveness became apparent. So someone came to me and said, 'Do A-frames for a bit.' So we are going to have an untogether paper for a while. So what? So I did A-frames for a week." Apparently a week had sufficed to detach him, for he was back on the job. How long it took the architect to get out of the kitchen I did not discover. But for some people, I was told, it took a long time to drop their programming.

The doctrine of nonpossessiveness also, I discovered, applied to love and marriage in Rajneeshpuram. The guru, Subhuti said, did not object to marriages per se, though the press would never understand this, but only to marriages that were institutional structures without meaning, and the product of social conditioning alone. In practice many sannyasins were married (and Subhuti was one of them), but the idea was that if one partner were not happy, the marriage should be ended. A lot of marriages, so the guru said, involved only guilt, pretense, and neurotic dependency; thus faithfulness was not a virtue to be cultivated for its own sake. The one who was left might feel miserable or jealous, and that person should not suppress those feelings but rather watch them and come to detach himself or herself from them. As for sex, there were no fixed rules about it. There were certainly no rules about celibacy, for Bhagwan believed that the truly detached might transcend sex, but enforced celibacy led only to frustration and obsessive thoughts of it, rather than to detachment and awareness.

What these doctrines meant as a matter of practice was difficult to tell, for the Rajneeshee were making a deliberate effort to rebut charges by Reverend Jimenez and others that they were a "sex commune." These doctrines, however, had their own intrinsic interest. Communes, and particularly religious communes, tend to have rather strict rules about sex and marriage. But these doctrines were entirely permissive in matters of behavior—so much so that they might have been invented to accommodate people of the Rajneeshee's age and background all over the country. They were matters of attitude, principally, and as such, they seemed to provide a psychological solution to the problems so many people seemed to be having with "relationships." The idea, it seemed, was simply to reduce the coefficient of emotional friction between people by an act of transcendence—a detachment from self.

Among the various suspicions harbored by the local ranchers was that the commune separated children from their parents. The suspicions were justified in some degree, as in respect to children the commune operated much like a kibbutz. The babies lived with their parents, but children over five—or so I was told—lived with other children in the same housing complex with their parents. The ranch had a day-care center, where some of the mothers worked, and a school, kindergarten through twelfth grade. The children spent half of each day in school and the other half playing or working in different parts of the commune. In the afternoon the littlest kids would go to help feed the cows and the chickens; the eight- and nine-year-olds would run messages, paint signs, or help on the construction sites. The older children would spend somewhat more time with the working adults, helping out and learning carpentry, accounting, or whatever interested them. They would also do an hour a day of dance, theater, or mime. They would see their parents at mealtimes and after dinner before bed. The children I met were a pink-cheeked, rambunctious lot, not at all shy of adults. The only strange thing about them was how few of them there were: only fifty children among eight hundred or a thousand adults. Given the average age of the sannyasins, the number would seem to testify to an almost Shakerite restraint or, since this was not the case, to an antiprocreation policy such as the Oneida Community had for its first twenty years. The Rajneeshee, however, said that there was no such policy.

What the Rajneeshee were teaching their children seemed to me an important point. But on visiting the school, I found that the Rajnee-shee had not put very much thought into it. Anabodhi, the sweet and slightly diffident woman who taught the younger children (she had taught adult education and worked with disturbed children in Los Angeles), told me that she and the other teachers were following the guidelines laid down by Bhagwan. These guidelines were remarks the guru had made on the subject in the course of his lectures to sannyasins in India, and most of them were rather general observa-tions about "education" in the largest sense of that word. More spe-cifically he had once said that universal education was criminal and undemocratic, since not all children wanted academic training: some wanted to be carpenters or fishermen. He had advocated education in practical things, and he had quoted Ivan Illich, without attribution, to the effect that man can be saved "only if society is deschooled." The only curricular guidance he had given was that children should learn math and languages but not history since "history is meaning-less bunk" (no attribution to Henry Ford). The schoolteachers were thus working out a curriculum on their own, and for the moment it was still an informal one. They were teaching the younger children basic skills using the commercial textbooks; and they were teaching the older children science, environmental studies, math, and social studies—the latter with an emphasis on comparative cultures. They were also tutoring one older boy to pass his SATs for college and looking for books to put another teenager (there were only a few of them) through a business English course. What made their system of education different, they said, was the opportunity children had to work on the ranch with adults, learning sculpture or computer pro-gramming by apprenticeship. The following year, when Rajneesh-puram joined the public-school system, they would, they said, set up a formal curriculum in accordance with state guidelines and incorpo-rate the work-study program into it.

The Rajneeshee education program struck me as surprisingly unin-tellectual given the number of Ph.D.'s in the community. (Later one professor told me he saw no reason why his children should go to college—they had so many accomplished people on the ranch to learn from.) It also seemed relatively undoctrinaire. But the same was true of the Rajneeshee approach to urban planning and agriculture as well. With all the efforts in the direction of environmentalism, Rajneesh-puram was no Findhorn: the cabbages were manured, not talked to. On the question of pesticides Neehar, the farm coordinator, told a wildlife biologist: "I have no philosophical problem with the killing of millions of aphids, but we want what's here to live in harmony. We want to find out where the balance lies." Videh, the young water projects coordinator, told me that a rough balance existed on the commune between those who worried about the detrimental effects of technology and those who thought about economics and practicality. The technology was eclectic as a result: the ranch had a natural sand-filter sewage-treatment plant, but it also had a big electrical power substation. Videh told me about the efforts he was making to determine what effect the detergent they were using had on the streams. Then he said, "But you know, a lot of New Age technology-ecology people are a bit neurotic. We're more interested in consciousness than in those kinds of priorities."

Rajneeshee spokesmen and Rajneeshee literature proclaimed "love, lightness and laughter" as the theme of the commune. This self-advertisement struck a discordant note to the local ranchers, but any short-term visitor to Rajneeshpuram would notice a remarkably high level of good humor among the sannyasins. On the streets people called out to each other gaily and walked with their arms about one another's shoulders. In an office you might find one staff member teasing another and the whole group howling with laughter. Also a great deal of hugging went on. Tourists looking out of the smoky windows of their buses would see people embracing in the tea tents, in the vegetable garden, and behind the trash mashers and wonder what was going on. In the three weeks I spent in Rajneeshpuram I heard very few cross words exchanged and very few downbeat remarks. People tended to be positive about everything, including the unpredictable weather, and, as hard as they were working, they made the work look like fun.

The most obvious explanation for all of this good humor was that that work on the ranch was fun; it was play in the ordinary sense of that word. Where else, after all, could a professor (or a belly dancer for that matter) get to tool around on a bulldozer and build a road? Where else could a young architect design a housing project and then get to bang in the nails? Picking lettuces and digging postholes had undeniable satisfactions if you weren't doing it for a living and if you were doing it with a lot of attractive people your own age. The work was hard, but there were no bills, no phone calls, and no child-care responsibilities. "It's like a second childhood," the pediatric allergist from Stanford told me. "It's like a big game. Even treating patients is like that, since you're treating the people you live with. I never used to see my patients. Here it's much more flowing. Plus you can be alone with yourself when you want to be. All the old connections just aren't here." What was more, the commune did not have to subsist on what it could grow. If a bulldozer broke down, there was money enough for another one; if the tomato crop failed, tomatoes would be bought. And where else could you find such a high concentration of attractive, well-educated young adults with an ideology of nonpossessiveness and sexual laissez-faire? Guru or no guru, the ranch was a year-round summer camp for young urban professionals.

But it was something else as well. Visitors to the ranch noticed a good deal of hugging, but what they would notice if they stared was that there were two kinds of hugs in Rajneeshpuram. One was of the spontaneous, affectionate sort and the other a long, studied embrace followed by deep eye contact: the Growth Movement hug. Isabel and her colleagues did not mention this aspect of the commune in their briefings, and indeed they rather steered visitors away from it, but the ranch was awash in the Human Potential Movement. Walking around the ranch I found, after a week or so, former Gestalt therapists working tractors, Laingians in the kitchen crew, Reichians digging ditches, and post-Reichians in the A-frame factory. According to the Oregon University survey, 11 percent of the commune members had postgraduate degrees in psychology or psychiatry and another 11 percent had B.A.'s in the field. But with all the years of academic training represented, there was not, as far as I could determine, a single straight Freudian or straight behaviorist on the ranch. The sannyasin-psychologists had done their university work and then gone off to study with such people as Fritz Perls, Alexander Lowen, and Carl Rogers. In addition to the qualified psychologists there were a number of other people on the ranch who practiced Growth Movement therapies: rolfing, primal screaming, bioenergetics, and encounter therapies. Added to these were practitioners of every kind of New Age specialty from shiatsu to acupuncture to past-life readings.

A number of the therapists were now giving courses at the Rajneesh Institue for Therapy and the Rajneesh Institute for Meditation and Inner Growth. These institutes were new to the ranch—in May a new building was just going up to house them in time for the influx of summer visitors. The catalog distributed to Rajneesh centers around the world advertised such therapies as: Rajneesh Bodywork ("This one-month intensive emphasizes enhanced aliveness and awareness of the body, and includes intuitive bodywork, sensory awareness, work with the breath and bio-energy movement, dance and touch"); Rajneesh Energywork ("An exploration of our unrealized potential for consciousness"); and Rajneesh Dehypnotherapy (". . . ways of opening up the unconscious parts of our minds to see and then drop patterns formed in childhood and which restrict our development in the present"). The institutes also offered instruction in various forms of meditation—kundalini to zazen—and practical courses such as Buddhafield Construction and Buddhafield Business.

These courses were not for the Rajneeshee living and working on the ranch; they were moneymaking programs designed for visitors. Growth Movement therapies, however, played a fairly central role in the life of the group. The ashram in Poona had offered all kinds of therapies, and virtually all sannyasins on the ranch had been through at least one of them—there or at Rajneeshee centers elsewhere. Now that the guru was no longer speaking, and no longer giving *sannyas* himself, the Rajneeshee required all prospective sannyasins to go through courses of therapy and meditation before joining the group. On the ranch most sannyasins continued to practice Growth Movement techniques among themselves. Each workplace, for example, was also an informal encounter group where people helped each other to work out their problems. If someone came to work in the morning depressed over a love affair, or just depressed, his or her co-workers would try to get to the source of the depression by whatever means at hand: head massages, psychic healing, or simply talk. If two people in a department did not get along, they would, with the help of others, try to figure out why not. One woman told me that while working in the laundry she had helped one co-worker get over a bad love affair and had been helped by another who "mirrored me and showed me how to drop my garbage and programming." (The two had apparently fought.) The Rajneeshee were thus not just having a good time, they were working at it.

Curious about these therapies and how they fit into the spiritual enterprise of the ranch, I went to see Swami Prem Siddha, a senior therapist at the institute. Siddha was, he told me, a graduate of UCLA School of Medicine and the UCLA Neuro-Psychiatric Institute. He had had a private practice and done consulting work for a number of organizations, including the American Dental Association and the National Institute of Mental Health. In the sixties he had become involved with the Growth Movement and had studied Gestalt with Fritz Perls, bioenergetics with Alexander Lowen, and rolfing with Ida Rolf. "I feel like I live in the maddest city in the world," he said when I asked him about the therapies. "It's mad because it supports joy and happiness. You have to work at being unhappy here—and that's the reverse of the way the rest of the world is. It's a mad city in that people bow down to earth twice a day in the name of truth, and to each other, in recognition of a common interest in learning the art of living, in learning that life is beautiful." Siddha under his given name of Leonard Zunin had written a pop psychology book called *Contact: The First Four Minutes* on how to meet people. "It's a mad city because people bow down every day to the Enlightened One—to a self-realized being. It's mad because people work twelve to eighteen hours a day for someone they love, and they call their work worship and meditation." He had met the guru when he had gone to India to learn about Tibetan Buddhism. "It's a mad city because people are letting go of their conditioned beliefs, all their programming about right and wrong, all their conditioning about how the world should be. They're helping each other experience life. They're learning how to *be*, not how to become."

Siddha might have puzzled the people of Antelope, but he would have been an altogether recognizable type in Los Angeles. "I'm flashing on something," he said at one point. When I asked him whether he was not bothered by the elite nature of the enterprise and by its withdrawal from the larger society, he responded, as Krishna Deva had, by quoting the guru. "Rich people are seekers. The poor are merely survivors. True religion is a luxury which can come only after one's survival needs are met." Then he said, "We're a community of seekers, not of Enlightened beings. We have to learn—to go to school. Society doesn't consider school a waste of time, but when someone takes the time to find themselves, to find the true nature of joy—*that* they find a waste of time."

Clearly, I thought after leaving Siddha, the ranch was some form of hybrid between an Indian ashram and the Esalen Institute. It was a place—to put the matter bluntly—where the privileged few could work on Enlightenment and their relationships without at the same time giving up any of the ordinary pleasures of life. It was the ultimate me-generation boarding school, and also, in view of the guru's recent pronouncement, a rather exclusive bomb shelter where the chosen few would survive the holocaust to come. This I thought until I met Wadud, the city planner.

"People say we change our minds every six months," Wadud said when I asked him why the Rajneeshee had first represented themselves as building a "rural commune." "And that's pretty much the case. When we came here, Sheela didn't know what she wanted of this place. That fall we hadn't even thought of a religious festival. If we'd said we wanted eight hundred people when we came here, people would have freaked. Anyway, the whole argument is irrelevant. There's a perception that we deceived people in the beginning, but the fact is that we simply grew much faster than even we could imagine. Now we have a comprehensive plan quite as detailed as the plan for Portland—and we put it together in three months."

Wadud had come to the ranch a year ago with his wife and his two-year-old daughter, giving up his own successful New Age center in Berkeley and leaving the house with the hot tub and the Mercedes-Benz. Now he was wholly engaged in his new work and full of enthusiasm. Lean and wiry, he spoke quickly with a hint of impatience, as though he were already two or three thoughts ahead. "There's the plan over there," he said, pointing to three large paperback volumes. "What it says is that we'll have a population of three thousand seven hundred sometime between now and 1995. We could grow faster, of course, but then we'd have to amend it. The major economic development will be in resort and education facilities, but there will be some light industries—mostly crafts. Right now we're planning a hotel for religious education and education in general."

Wadud drove me up into the hills to the proposed site for the hotel and university; it was near the entrance to the ranch at a height of three thousand feet with an extraordinary view of three ranges of hills. He described the buildings he planned in some detail—luxurious materials, low buildings following the contours of the land. When I asked whether the hotel would be for Rajneeshee disciples only, he said, "No, I suspect many others will be coming. Some will come for the education, others will come as tourists because of the unique social experiment going on here. One of our purposes is to be studied —already two professors from the University of Oregon are doing a study on us. Eventually this city should become something like the new Disneyland in Florida. Epcot is a model of the technological future; this will be a model for humankind's social potential. We're perceived as being self-centered, but our concern is to create an alternative model of society for mankind."

This, I thought, would come as yet another shock to the local ranchers. Most of them had read Wadud's plan and knew the projected population figures. But they assumed the Rajneeshee were building a town for themselves; the notion that they might be constructing a type of Disneyland out there on the range had not yet occurred to them. What occurred to me was the reaction a friend of mine had had when he read in his tenth-anniversary Harvard yearbook that a classmate had joined the Jesus people and was speaking in tongues. "There's a Harvard man for you," he said. "He joins the group one day, and the next day he's in the front row with glossolalia."

Even after I had spent ten days at the ranch, however, the nature of the Rajneeshee social experiment remained somewhat mysterious to me. To ask how the ranch was organized was to elicit answers having to do with spontaneity and awareness. When I asked Videh, the water manager, how decisions were made in his department, he said, "Technical decisions are made by technical people and whoever else is concerned. It's a personal thing. It's how it feels to you. If you're clear about something, you're usually right. It's a matter of intuition. Here a tone is set, a flavor, that affects the work we do.

There are no rules or rituals. From time to time we get pep talks to remind us of why we're here—to remind us we're a family again. Yesterday, for example, someone on the pipe crew accidentally cut through a major phone line. So we had a meeting, and he was criticized—but in good spirit, the point being that we can all screw up. We all have to watch for carelessness and be aware of what we're doing." How policy disputes were resolved and whether the rank-and-file sannyasins had any say in them were not questions Videh or any of the other managers answered with any clarity.

What they did say was that Ma Anand Sheela, the president of the Rajneeshee Foundation International and the personal secretary to Bhagwan, was the "mother" of their family and made the major policy decisions in consultation with Bhagwan. So much was clear enough. Sheela was—observably—the queen of Rajneeshpuram. She and her second husband, Jayananda, lived at the very center of the commune in a luxurious prefab house that served as the headquarters of the foundation. All day long a procession of sannyasins would file through her house; ranch managers, lawyers, and so on would come to discuss their work and ask her advice while a young male sannyasin served meals or prepared fresh fruit juices and tea. Sheela, dressed in a pink or red velour sweat suit, would curl up on the couch like a little cat, shake the bangles on her wrist prettily, and laugh and laugh. "It's not good to be serious," she would say, making a seductive little moue. Over the main couch was a map of the world with numerous red and white pins stuck into it. "They're the Rajneeshee centers around the world," she said once of the pins. "I put them there in a housewifely way, but then I never finished. I have no idea how many there are." Sheela preferred flippancy to "dreary" discussions about numbers, and she liked to create impromptu little dramas about herself.

The second time I met her she told me a bit about her background, She was, she said, born in Baroda in the region of Gujarat and had been brought up there and on the family farm in Madhya Pradesh; her father belonged to one of the great industrial families of the region and, as a young man, had been a close supporter of Mahatma Gandhi. At Gandhi's suggestion he had gone to Oxford and returned to make a fortune in cotton ginning and real estate. This was, I later discovered, not quite the case. Her father was a relatively small businessman and a farmer (he had managed the farm in Madhya Pradesh); as a young man he had fought for Indian independence and had traveled to England, but had then returned to live quitely in Baroda. Sheela was the youngest of six children and, so she said, "the spoiled child of the family." Two of her older brothers and a sister emigrated to the

United States, and at the age of seventeen Sheela followed them. She enrolled in Montclair State College in New Jersey, and there met and married a young American, who died some years later of Hodgkin's disease. On a trip home she was taken by her father—an admirer of Krishnamurti and Kahlil Gibran—to see Rajneesh, and a month or so later became a sannyasin. Her husband followed her to India and both of them joined the ashram in early 1973. Gradually she rose to positions of more and more responsibility in the ashram, but she continued to visit the United States and in 1975 she incorporated a Rajneesh meditation center, Chidvilas, in Montclair. In June 1981, she accompanied the guru to the United States as his secretary, putting him up at the Montclair center; a month later she put down a million and a half dollars as down payment for the ranch in Oregon.

"I looked in many different states—Arizona, Texas. I was looking for somewhere dry for Bhagwan's health, and I came on this by chance. Once I saw it, I knew it was right. I just knew." Sheela believed in her own womanly intuition; she also believed in the stars. "Just by chance I found it a year to the day after my husband's death. And then, quite by chance, I signed the lease on the day of his birth." In addition Sheela believed in acting on impulse. She was given to impulsive gestures. She would give a sudden gift, delay an airplane others were waiting for, change her mind about a project, and express her anger on national television. "I think you need to shut up for awhile," she told the former mayor of Antelope, Margaret Hill, on ABC's "Nightline." Only thirty-three years old, she seemed an unlikely sort of person to be running a commune full of psychotherapists and Ph.D.'s.

The commune, I gathered, had no formal hierarchy, but it had, along with the department heads, a group of people called "coordinators" who met with Sheela once a week and made the major decisions for the commune. These coordinators then passed the decisions along through departmental meetings. Anyone could criticize or object, but there were no votes taken at any meeting. Within the departments the job of the coordinators was to act as personnel managers in a rather extended sense; their charge was not only to see that their departments were properly staffed but that people worked well, individually and as a group. If someone was unhappy or careless or if two people fought over turf, the coordinator would try to work out the problem—often by group criticism sessions. Most of the coordinators were women because the guru apparently thought that women were more motherly, more intuitive, and less attached to roles, status, and their own ideas than men. In a commune where such values were paramount, the difference between the coordinators and the department heads seemed to be analogous to that of "red" and "expert" in Mao's China.

The system, as it was described to me, seemed very original and hi-tech: Maslovian management several generations beyond the original. But how it actually worked for the individual and where final authority lay I found difficult to pin down. The head coordinator and president of the commune, Ma Yoga Vidya, told me that she had just taken over the legal department because two lawyers were not communicating. "We advised them to do something about it," she said, "but finally they seemed to need a stronger person, so I moved in. One of the lawyers blew up at another, saying that something was his idea and he hadn't been given credit. I said, who cares whose idea it is. It's been OK since then." A tall blonde of striking good looks, Vidya seemed to me a very strong person—someone you would hesitate to cross. "I work by intuition. Sometimes I roam around the commune. I look at faces, and I can see when someone's unhappy. I saw a young woman last night looking very down, so I asked her coordinator what the trouble was. She'd had a fight with her boyfriend. Occasionally people get very caught up in themselves." In certain cases, Vidya said, she would ask people to change the kind of worship they did, or recommend meditation and therapy courses. No one had ever refused—they were always grateful in the end—and she had never thrown anyone out of the commune. "We just ask people if they really fit in, and people are honest." This was worrying. Previously I had asked Wadud whether coordinators could be criticized, and he had said they could—and they were always grateful in the end. But neither he nor Vidya could or would describe what would happen if they were not. "We're always watching for factions and cronyism and trying to stop them—or rather to unlearn these old patterns," Wadud said. "We're developing a very loving and beautiful way of dealing with each other. This is the Buddhafield, and one of its qualities is that we don't become ingrown and institutionalized."

Watching the guru drive through the ranch, his sannyasins lined up on the roadside greeting him with a *namaste*, the Hindu greeting which looks like prayer, I supposed that one of the keys to the Rajnee-shee social experiment lay in the philosophical connection between the guru and the Growth Movement. Siddha, along with the other therapists I met, however, convinced me that there was no way they could explain this syncretism analytically. There was yogic "energy" and Growth Movement "energy"; the two notions were vague enough to begin with, but in Rajneeshee philosophy, they seemed to have melted and fused beyond recovery (and the same went for "con-sciousness" and "awareness"). The only solution, therefore, seemed

to be to trace the historical connection between the two and to discover what the therapists and the guru had in mind when they met.

Siddha had been one of the first therapists to meet Rajneesh, but
the very first was Teertha, an Englishman with a Birmingham accent,
now the head therapist on the ranch. Tall, gray-haired, and slightly
stooped, Teertha spoke slowly and would fall into silence when he
felt the question too alien. When I asked him about the guru's prediction of nuclear war, he said that the planet earth was working off its
karma, but that in the end it would surely be saved by immaterial
beings from another planet. He had, he said, no academic training in
psychology; he had studied at Warwickshire University and worked
at a variety of jobs, one of them in photo advertising. On a trip to the
United States he had wound up, somewhat by accident, at the Esalen
Institute at Big Sur—then the center of the Growth Movement. He
spent a year there and then returned to London to set up his own
growth center, the first in England, at the request of the Esalen directors. His center had flourished, but after a while, he said, his therapists had "ceilinged and gotten stuck." They had tried meditation but
found most of the Eastern techniques unsuitable, since people just
couldn't sit still that long. Then one day in the process of looking for
a new acupuncturist, he ran across an Indian who told him about a
system of "dynamic meditation" taught by a man who called himself
Bhagwan Shree Rajneesh. Shortly afterward, in the spring of 1972,
Teertha—then Paul Graham Lowe—went to Bombay to see Rajneesh.
He found the guru's "dynamic meditation"—which involved a great
deal of physical activity before the sitting—well suited to his purposes. But beyond that, he found an Enlightened Master. He became
a disciple and went back to London to turn his center into a Rajneesh
meditation center. A year later he moved his entire center down to
Bombay.

After Paul Lowe came Leonard Zunin and Michael Barnett, another
English therapist and the author of a book called *People Not Psychiatry;*
and after them a steady flow of Growth Movement therapists found
its way to Rajneesh. Because of Teertha's connections with Esalen, a
lot of Californians came, and from Esalen the word spread to various
of the other movement circles: to the Reichians, to the group around
R. D. Laing, and so on. Then, as the movement itself spread from
England to the Continent, the talk of Rajneesh followed it. Eventually
hundreds of therapists and other movement enthusiasts came, many
of them to go home in red clothes and malas with new names and
new identities. Of these some stayed permanently with Rajneesh, or
went home at his request to found Rajneeshee centers, giving up their

independent practices and putting the money they made into the movement.

In a sense this rush of therapists to Rajneesh was not so difficult to account for. In the seventies Esalen and the other big Growth Movement centers were periodically swept by enthusiasms for one or another exotic religion or technique. One year it was Sufi dancing, another year, Soviet experiments in parapsychology; one year it was Arica, a mind control system invented in Chile, and another year it was Tibetan Buddhism. Why not, then, one year Bhagwan Shree Rajneesh? In another sense, however, the attraction of the therapists to the guru required some explanation—as did their attraction to Arica, tarot cards, and the like. Psychology was, after all, a science, and Freudian psychology, the tradition from which they came, harbored the most thoroughgoing suspicions of such enthusiasms. While psychotherapists as a group might be no less spiritually inclined than, say, lawyers or architects, their profession gave them solid grounds for skepticism about any system that demanded the shedding of identity and the surrender of the ego to someone else. The Growth Movement therapists were, however, a special case; the spiritual ferment at Esalen merely showed what had been a tendency in the movement since its inception.

In the forties and fifties a number of psychologists in the United States broke with Freudian and behavioral psychology to form what they called the Humanistic, or Third Force, Psychology. They were rather a mixed group of people ranging from Gestalt therapists to "sensitivity trainers" to neo-Reichians, and the awkward name they took betrayed the awkwardness of gathering them all together under one rubric. But it did identify the belief they held in common: the belief that psychology had the potential not just for curing the sick but for improving humankind. Freud, they complained, saw all human beings as more or less neurotic and more or less hoist on the petard of their—inevitably—neurotic civilization. Such pessimism about the perfectibility of human nature was unacceptable to them. It was intuitively alien, and they did not so much reject it as brush it off. Idealists and romantics, they had something in common with Rousseau, for they could imagine man outside the context of any particular civilization. They believed that by stripping off the repressions layered upon him, man would come to his full flowering in something like the state of nature. Social institutions did not much concern them—that was not their field. But then, rather than intellectuals, they were in the main practitioners—hands-on people, uninterested in theory. What they did was to create a series of powerful new techniques and approaches which had immediate, observable results. What the observable results meant was not clear at all, for typically, they were people in a hurry. (One of the things that drove them to invention was their impatience with the slow, archeological methods of Freudian analysis.) Thus none of them bothered to give their techniques a theoretical foundation. The books written by such as Arthur Janov (father of Primal Scream Therapy) or Alexander Lowen (creator of bioenergetics) were more or less pop psychology marked by carelessness and lack of concern for the scientific method. This lack of concern, however, lurked in the very nature of the enterprise, for in their view "humanistic psychology" stood in opposition to "scientific psychology." But if psychology was not a science—or based on the scientific method—then what was it? The question went unanswered.

The difficulty is most readily apparent in the works of Abraham Maslow, the only one to make any sustained attempt to define "humanistic psychology." A research psychologist, rather than a therapist, Maslow found in the course of writing a book on abnormal psychology that what interested him were not the sick but the very healthy: not mental illness but mental health. His idea was to study people who were exceptionally healthy, people who made "the full use of their talents, capacities and potentialities," or those he dubbed "self-actualized people." His method was this: He made a list of people he considered self-actualized: Jefferson, Schweitzer, and Spinoza (but not, for some reason, Washington, Goethe, or Bach). He then made a list of the characteristics he thought these people had in common: courage, humility, creativity, altruism, and so on. After that he constructed a series of tests to determine who among the living was "self-actualizing" and who was not. He started first with students at Brandeis University, since that was where he taught. Among his tests was one K.D. had used on the sannyasins—a test for "inner-directedness." The enterprise was rather less scientific than many party games, and the results were predictably solipsistic: the "self-actualizing person" was someone Maslow happened to think highly of, for one reason or another. His next enterprise was a "theory of basic needs." His theory proposed a hierarchy of "needs" beginning (at the bottom) with physiological needs, such as food and shelter, and ending (at the top) with "growth needs," such as truth, beauty, and "meaningfulness." According to his theory, human beings had generally to satisfy each level of needs before graduating to the next one. That is, they had to fulfill, say, "belongingness needs" before they could graduate to "esteem needs," and above that to "growth needs." Now much quoted in business management texts, this theory would, among other things, rule out the possibility that someone could be a fine mathematician, or for that matter, an interior decorator, without a healthy love relationship and high self-esteem. K.D.'s statement that only the rich could be truly religious was a quote from Rajneesh, but it was also pure Maslow.

Such vagaries went largely unnoticed. The academic psychologists and the members of the great analytic institutes found such Growth Movement musings too far beneath their intellectual dignity to criticize. And the Growth Movement people weren't interested. One result was that practice ran so far ahead of theory as to become quite independent of it. Another was that, while the movement grew like Topsy, it split and went off in different directions. Some of its practitioners moved into mainstream psychotherapy; others went into business management, and still others went into pop psychology, spreading the language and adapting the therapies so that entrepreneurs like Werner Erhard could package and mass-market them. The purists—those around Esalen and the newer Growth centers—continued to experiment and to venture along the paths indicated by the first generation. These people, the real inheritors of the movement, were distressed by the popularizers and the accommodationists. Idealists, they came into the movement not to learn more sophisticated forms of life adjustment, but to seek higher forms of consciousness. They were radicals, but radicals of a different sort from their neighbors in Berkeley. While the political radicals denounced "elitism," distrusted all forms of authority, and paralyzed themselves trying to make their organizations perfectly democratic, the Growth Movement radicals looked for teachers and sought an elite of "the self-actualized." They went to sit at the feet of Fritz Perls, Carl Rogers, Ida Rolf, and the other star therapists. (They had to: since there was no theory, they had to watch.) They became disciples, but in the end they were always disappointed.

Rajen, the most reflective and articulate of the Rajneeshee therapists I talked to, described the general trajectory of these therapists in talking about his own experience. An Englishman, Swami Anand Rajen had begun his career by working as a schoolteacher. He had moved on to do experimental psychology at Oxford University. But Oxford psychology had frustrated him "because it was not about human beings." Having read a book by Carl Rogers, he went off to a Growth center in La Jolla, California, and found what he was looking for. He returned to London to join a Growth center called "Community," where Michael Barnett, among others, taught. "Like many therapists," he said, "I was into doing my own thing. But all of us were in some sense looking for masters: for people more aware, more loving, and more open than we were. From Carl Rogers what I got was a recognition that I wasn't my personality—that I could slip out of it. In groups I had glimpses of a way of living that was not so constricted by what we want and what we're afraid of. And the therapists seemed to have a greater capacity for living in those spaces than the rest of us. But all therapists have their limitations. There is always a discrepancy between their demonstration of how to be in groups and how they were in their private lives."

As Rajen suggested, the problem was not just that the therapists went home from their "loving spaces of being" and snapped at the dog and the children, but that in the end they were only therapists, only human. And their disciples were not looking for therapists but for personifications of whatever they meant by "authenticity" and "awareness"; they were looking to get high on "peak experience" and stay there.

Even at Esalen the Growth Movement solutions proved inadequate. "A lot of people felt there was something missing," Richard Price, one of the directors of Esalen told me. "Alan Watts introduced us to Buddhism in the mid-sixties, and it seemed to put what we were doing into a more inclusive framework. After that Esalen was a mix of therapy and interest in Buddhism."

In fact it was Alan Watts who constructed the intellectual bridge between the therapists and Bhagwan Shree Rajneesh. In his *Psychotherapy East and West*, published in 1961, Watts proposed common ground between the therapists and the *Sangha*. His opening paragraph read: "If we look deeply into such ways of life as Buddhism, Taoism, Vedanta, and Yoga, we do not find either philosophy or religion, as these are understood in the West. We find something more nearly resembling psychotherapy." On this extraordinary reduction the therapists proceeded: they traveled to India and went from ashram to monastery in the hopes of finding what Watts had seen. But again, they were almost always disappointed, for in addition to meditation, the ashrams and monasteries taught religion and philosophy, much as it was understood in the West, and on top of that, exotic systems of rites and rituals and a social morality: in fact a whole civilization that did not suit the therapists a bit. What was more, many groups put a very high threshold in front of the higher consciousness. The Tibetan Buddhists, for example, required Sanskrit and a memorization of the five thises, the thirty-four thats, and the ninety-six qualities of something else. The priests of the Vedanta were equally demanding; plus they were, in the eyes of the therapists, male chauvinists, and they believed that celibacy helped. Bhagwan Shree Rajneesh turned out to be the exception. He spoke perfect English; he demanded nothing except surrender and trust in him. Like Krishnamurti, he was a modernizer and an iconoclast, and yet he was, so he said, an Enlightened Master willing to take responsibility for the surrender of his disciples. In India he was something of a paradox. He was, as one Anglo-Indian writer later christened him, "the Progressive Guru."

In 1972, when Teertha and Veena first met the guru, Rajneesh was living in an apartment in Bombay and conducting meditation camps outside the city. According to his biographer, a disciple named Vasant Joshi, he was just beginning to move into the third stage of his career. Born in 1931 in a small town in Madhya Pradesh, he came from a family of cloth merchants of the Jain religion. His full name was Chandra Mohan Jain, but his family called him Raj or Rajneesh for short. As a child he was bright, rebellious, and something of a loner; he did well in school, though he often got into trouble for leading his classmates in all kinds of pranks. During the struggle for national independence he joined the youth branch of the Indian National Army and took a stance as a socialist and an atheist. He read a great deal and became a formidable debater. Graduating from high school in 1951, he went to college in Jabalpur, to study philosophy; according to his biography, his propensity for debate so annoyed his professors that they threw him out in midcareer. Admitted to another college, he went through what Westerners would probably call a nervous breakdown. Depressed, full of fears, and suffering from headaches that his family doctor told him were psychosomatic, he ran eight to sixteen miles a day and meditated for hours at a time—sometimes to the point of unconsciousness. At the end of this period—or so he announced twenty years later—he became Enlightened after meditating one night in the public gardens under a maulshree tree.

Rajneesh graduated from college in 1955, took an M.A. in philosophy, and was given a teaching position at the Raipur Sanskrit College; three years later he was appointed assistant professor of philosophy at the University of Jabalpur. In 1960 he began to give public lectures in which he took and defended all kinds of controversial positions: he criticized Gandhi, criticized socialism, and tore into orthodox Hinduism. Many years later he told his biographer that he had no stake in any of these positions, "but when the entire population of a country was absorbed in these tensions . . . there seemed, even if just for fun, a necessity to create controversies." For him it was "just like the acting of an actor." But these polemics brought him attention, and his audiences grew. In 1966 he was able to quit his university job and to support himself by lecturing around the country. The positions he took also marked him, for apparently by force of defending them, he adopted most of them permanently. Gandhi, he argued, was a reactionary and a man who worshiped poverty; he in turn was worshiped because he, like all politicians, followed "the Indian mob" rather than leading it. India, Rajneesh argued, needed capitalism, science, advanced technology, and birth control, for without these it would be doomed to poverty and backwardness. In 1968 he gave a series of lectures on love and sex in which he maintained that the primal energy of sex was divine, and that sexual feelings should not be repressed but gratefully acknowledged. Only by acknowledging his real nature could man be free. In the same vein he attacked religions that preached withdrawal from life; true religion, he said "is an art that shows how to enjoy life to its utmost."

Rajneesh's views shocked and repelled many people, but they attracted others, principally groups of wealthy and progressive-minded businessmen in Bombay. In 1964 he began to hold meditation camps for these men and their families in mountain resort towns. His first real disciple, a woman who took the name Ma Yoga Laxmi, came from one of these families. Her father, a wealthy Jain businessman, had been an important supporter of the Congress party during the struggle for independence and had close ties to many of the leaders: Gandhi, Nehru, and Moraji Desai. Laxmi had gone into social work and politics; in her late twenties and still unmarried, she was the secretary of the Bombay branch of the All-India Women's Congress when she met Rajneesh. After attending two of his meditation camps, she adopted Rajneesh as her Master and began to travel around with him making the practical arrangement for his trips. In 1970 she became his secretary and raised the money that permitted him to stop his travels and settle into a Bombay apartment, where people could come to him. From 1970 to 1981, when Rajneesh left for the United States, Laxmi handled all the practical affairs of the guru, raising money, administering the ashram, and running political interference.

Rajneesh's biography accounts for the move to Bombay and the new phase in Rajneesh's career in spiritual and esoteric terms: the Master had moved from the *rajas guna*, the active and passionate quality in human nature, to the *sattva*, the quality of serenity and wisdom. A Westerner reading his biography might imagine that Rajneesh Chandra Mohan at this point went through a rather abrupt change of career. Until 1970 he had been a professor of philosophy lecturing on politics, sex, and society; now he was a religious man teaching spiritual disciples. But in India such distinctions are not so absolute. Rajneesh had been teaching meditation for some time. He continued to do this, now; instead of lecturing, he gave a regular evening discourse on spiritual and other matters to those who came to his apartment. His approach, however, changed. That summer at a meditation camp he introduced a new technique he called "dynamic meditation." Instead of simply sitting, the participants would begin by jumping about and shouting whatever came into their heads; they would then dance quietly for a few minutes and then hyperventilate by shouting Hoo Hoo Hoo as loud as they could; after that they would relax and watch their thoughts go. In the fall he founded what he called the Neo-Sannyas International Movement and initiated his first six disciples as the first step in creating a spiritual awakening around the world. He gave his disciples new names and, at the request of Laxmi, a wooden necklace or mala with a photograph of him on it. It was Laxmi's inspiration that the disciples should wear the traditional orange robes of holy men. A year later Rajneesh changed his own name as well. Until then his supporters had called him "acharya" or "teacher": Acharya Rajneesh Chandra Mohan. Now he took the title "Bhagwan" from a list drawn up by a disciple, and called himself Bhagwan Shree Rajneesh. A few months later he revealed the fact and the circumstances of his Enlightenment twenty years before.

In Bombay, Rajneesh began to attract some of the Westerners along the spiritual tourist routes. Given his views, it was only likely that he should. Here was a guru unencumbered by tradition, an Enlightened Master who could quote Heidegger and Sartre, and who furthermore believed in technology, capitalism, and sex. Rajneesh was unique along the ashram routes. And he liked Westerners. One of his first six disciples was a young American he had taken on to teach yoga classes and who knew enough Sanskrit to find him the name "Bhagwan." In 1971 he took a young English woman, Christine Woolf, to live with him: this was the woman who drove in the Rolls-Royce with him into Madras, Oregon; her name was now Ma Yoga Vivek. By all accounts Rajneesh gave Westerners special attention, talking to them about their personal problems and aspirations, and encouraging them to take the plunge and become his disciples. He sent them back home—when they really had to go—with instructions to start Rajneeshee centers wherever they lived.

His disciples did not question this attention; they considered it perfectly normal that a guru should surround himself with young Westerners—they considered it only their due. The fact was that many of them did not like India all that much. In Rajneeshpuram not only Veena but almost everyone I talked to told me how happy they were to have left India for this healthy, beautiful place. They had gone for the spiritual country, and in the real country they saw only inefficiency and underdevelopment. Rajneesh encouraged them in this view. When I asked Teertha why it was that Rajneesh had ended up with so many Western disciples, Teertha said, "Bhagwan went all over India lecturing and couldn't find enough people suitable for the Buddhafield. There were some beautiful Indians, of course, but not enough of them. Indians, you know, are still looking for prosperity, while Westerners have it and know that it's not enough. Bhagwan used to tell them, 'If you came face-to-face with God, you'd ask him for a Chevrolet.' "

Rajneesh, though his disciples never knew it, learned a great deal from the Westerners he met in Bombay. Teertha brought him his entire library, and many other sannyasins brought him books. Rajneesh was a voracious reader and quite a good listener as well. His English became colloquial, and he learned how to do the more profound work of translation. When he explained his "dynamic meditation" to Indians, he spoke of waking the goddess Kundalini—the coiled female serpent that lies at the lowest chakra at the base of the spine—and releasing her energies to rise to the highest chakra, the thousand-petaled lotus of the mind. When he explained the "dynamic" to Westerners, he would speak of removing the psychological blocks, lodged in the body as physical blocks, and releasing this body energy to the brain. The conception was still Tantric, but in English it sounded like pure Wilhelm Reich. "I read his *Book of the Secrets*," Price, the Esalen director, told me, referring to one of the guru's early collections of published lectures, "and it fit very well into the Gestalt framework. Rajneesh put Indian philosophy into a digestible form so that it was available to a wide range of people. He reminded me a lot of Alan Watts." That the guru might have read Watts did not occur to Price.

According to Teertha, Rajneesh showed immediate interest in what the therapists were doing and promised to incorporate some of their therapies into his own enterprise. Teertha took that for mere politeness at the time, but three years later, Rajneesh did just that. The Westerners in his ashram first taught Primal Scream and Encounter Group therapies, and later, when there were more of them, branched out into Gestalt, bioenergetics, rolfing, and so on. What the guru made of these therapies is difficult to say even now. On occasions he would relate them to Tantric tradition: "These are not new experiments. They have been tried by seekers of Tantra for centuries. For ages, Sarahapa and Tilopa and Kanahpa tried it. For the first time, I am trying to give these experiments a scientific base. These experiments were conducted in secrecy for so long." On other occasions he would explain them on their own terms, but as the means to meditation: "They will help you unburden the garbage you have repressed within yourself. . . . They will clean you, and only in a clean, clear heart is prayer possible." On still other occasions he would explain them in purely secular terms as cures for Western neuroses. The

Western therapists, for their part, had no interest in the question of how their therapies might fit into any Indian tradition. "I am not on any ancient path," the Master told them, "I am the beginning of a tradition, not the end."

In 1974 Laxmi moved Rajneesh from Bombay to Poona, a city in the hills. The guru's health was bad: he had developed diabetes, asthma, and allergies to almost everything. The climate was better in Poona, and besides, Rajneesh now had enough disciples to warrant an ashram. Establishing a foundation for him—the Rajneesh Foundation—Laxmi bought a villa with six acres of land and several outbuildings in a rich suburb of the city. The guru, who had formerly spent a good deal of time talking with individual disciples, now saw his flock only twice a day. In the morning he would lecture, and in the evening he would hold darshan, answering questions submitted to him, giving sannyas, and talking with those who had just arrived and those who were going away.

One month Rajneesh would lecture in Hindi and the next in English, and his lectures became widely renowned. Sitting on a low platform in a white robe and sandals, he would speak for two hours without notes, his voice soft and sibilant, and he motionless except for an occasional gesture of his long, fine hands. His essential message was the central one of the Hindu-Buddhist tradition: that God was in all things, a living current of energy flowing through the temporary and illusory world of forms, and that the Buddhas were those who saw through the illusion of self and of time to the great Oneness and Suchness of existence. Like Krishnamurti, he admitted Christ, Lao-tzu, and the great mystics of other traditions into his panoply of Enlightened Beings. His early lectures were more or less thematic: he would do a series on the Upanishads or the Tantra or the New Testament. Later he adopted a more personal, eclectic style, telling Zen parables, jokes, stories from the life of Buddha or the Sufi sages, and citing, for example, Gurdjieff, Socrates, and Bob Hope all in a single lecture. When he joked, his expression would turn foxy or puckish and his large liquid eyes would tease.

By 1976 the Shree Rajneesh ashram had become one of the major stopping points along the guru route. In *A Guide to Indian Ashrams*—a kind of *Guide Michelin* to spiritual India, published in 1980—the ashram rated the longest entry and the adjectival equivalent of at least three stars. Thousand of Westerners poured through it—so many, in fact, that the ashram could not house them, and they had to find lodgings elsewhere in the city. Many, of course, came out of sheer curiosity, for Rajneesh's advocacy of sex as a means to transcendence made him the most controversial of Indian masters. But having come thus lightly, many stayed—if not for Bhagwan's lectures, then for all the other activities going on at the ashram. Under Laxmi's direction the permanent workers and residents in the ashram (there were six hundred of these in the end) created an arts and crafts center which turned out clothing, jewelry, ceramics, and organic cosmetics (all for sale at the ashram boutique), and put on performances of music, theater, and mime. The residents offered visitors at least nine types of meditation—dynamic to zazen—and classes in yoga, karate, t'ai chi, acupuncture, Sufi dancing, and shiatsu massage. In 1975 the ashram offered two kinds of Western therapies; by 1979 it offered some sixty of them, including several invented at the ashram. Like an octopus, the ashram reached out and embraced everything that came its way; eventually it included almost every booth in the entire holistic New Age marketplace.

Of those who stayed more than three of four days, many took sannyas, changing their jeans for ocher robes, putting on the guru's mala, and taking the name he gave them. Most of them did so because the guru was quite insistent that they did—and there were no conditions attached. Just try it, Rajneesh told them, just trust me, take the risk and see. He explained that neo-sannyas was different from sannyas in that it meant only the beginning of a search, only the readiness to try and become a new being. He also explained that though he gave sannyas to just about everyone who came to the ashram and just about everyone requesting the mala by mail, he did not give out sannyas indiscriminately. "If you think," he told a disciple,

> that whenever someone comes to me, I just give him sannyas, it is not so. I may say that I will give sannyas to anyone who comes, but this does not mean what it seems to mean. It may look as though I just give sannyas to anyone, but what is really happening is something quite different.

He went on to explain that he could not explain everything in the beginning or all at once:

> Everything is meaningful, but it may not be obvious, and it may not be possible to explain to you. Many things will have to remain unexplained for a much longer time. The more receptive you become, the more I will be able to explain. The deeper your capacities to be sympathetic, the deeper the truth that can be revealed . . . The more rational the discussion, the less truth can be revealed.

Many accounts exist of life in the Poona ashram, for the visitors included a number of writers, filmmakers, and journalists. The ac-

counts of those who took sannyas and those who did not often differ
quite sharply in certain respects, but they are consistent in describing
a madhouse-carnival atmosphere. Each day hundreds, sometimes
thousands of Westerners in ocher robes would flood through the
ashram—and incidentally the city of Poona. The Westerners who had
just changed, or were about to change, their names and their clothes
lived in highly charged emotional states—their emotions enhanced
by a good deal of discomfort and culture shock. Getting to Poona had
been confusing enough. The trains from New Delhi and Bombay left
at odd hours, and the ticketing was unpredictable. At the stations the
crowds were enormous and the heat intense. After you finally pushed
your way through and got on the train, you would sit on a hard bench
for the next four to eight hours with nothing to eat or drink (at least
nothing that was safe), looking out at thatched villages where men
drove bullocks before wooden plows and women did their laundry in
muddy streams. Poona was a modern city, but it, too, was crowded,
hot, and greatly exotic. Getting into the ashram had its difficulties, for
although many of the staff members were Westerners, they did not
work by Western routines, and it was never quite clear who ran what
or how decisions were made. Bhagwan Shree Rajneesh was allergic
to any form of perfume, so a guard at the gate would sniff you for
scented soap or shampoo. If smells clung to you—or if the guard
thought they did—you might not be able to get into his lectures or
darshans for days and days.

Instead a staff member would shunt you off to "dynamic meditation," where hundreds of people would be screaming, singing, or
moaning to themselves as they shook their bodies about; then together they would yell Hoo Hoo Hoo at the top of their voices. "I'm
going to bring your insanity out," Rajneesh said. "Unless you become
consciously insane, you can never become sane. When your insanity
is pulled out, thrown to the wind, then sanity will happen to you."
So there were therapy groups and meditations, though the distinctions between them were not always clear. In one meditation you had
to sit and answer the question "Who am I?" for two days, or until
something happened, and in some therapies people would end up
gazing for hours at a picture of Bhagwan. People were experimenting
a lot with Tantric sex in and out of the therapy groups, either on
general principles or in the hopes of having some experience of the
divine. Just whom anyone was sleeping with seemed to have less
importance than normally, for there were all kinds of love and energy
going around. In some therapy groups people holding hands in a
circle would actually feel an electrical change. Then, too, with a thousand people in ocher robes, who knew who anyone was? You or your

friend might one day wake up Joanie and go to bed Ma Prem Savita. The problem was to lose your mind and be completely spontaneous —to live in the present, not the past or future. Bhagwan thought chaos helped.

The ashram was not, of course, for everyone. It was certainly not for Hindu purists. A German visitor quoted in *A Guide to Ashrams* said:

> I do not see the point of neo-sannyas. Most Hindus wait for the best part of their lives before they feel able to take initiation and accept the holy robe. But here, many kids who don't even know the meaning of sannyas are given the ego-inflating title of Swami This-and-That, and then freak the average Indian by going arm-in-arm with hip chicks while wearing the renunciate's robe.

The ashram was also not for people who worried too much about what disciplehood and surrender might mean—or what the therapies did. Rajneesh said, "The ego has to drop . . . The mind has to disappear for God to be . . . You have to disappear," and so on. An American bioenergetics therapist who had spent three months with the guru in Bombay thought this unhelpful. "Rajneesh encouraged the letting go of one's own responsibility," he said, "and that's where I left. It's one thing to ask people to drop the obstructive chatter that goes on in the head and another to ask them to drop the process of discrimination. Bhagwan made no distinction between the two, and when I asked him why not, he answered cryptically, 'Why do you care? What is it to you?' "

The therapist had taken part in the guru's "dynamic meditation" and was not impressed. "What I saw from the Esalen perspective was a series of cathartic techniques. I had become inured to them by then. So when I saw three or four hundred people doing the 'dynamic,' I saw nothing happening but mass autosuggestion. There were people all around me in states of regression. They had become infantile and were relating to a father figure. . . . People were attached to him as to a God. He himself disavowed it, but it was a simpleminded devotion as to a God. This doesn't happen with just Rajneesh. In my view it's a problem inherent in Hinduism."

The therapist's analysis would have infuriated the Hindu purists, but even more the Rajneeshee. Many of the guru's new disciples experienced this surrender differently. In 1983, on my second visit to Rajneeshpuram I met Ma Satya Bharti, a woman in her early forties who had spent some years working in the Poona ashram and had written two books about her experiences there. In one book she described taking sannyas as "a return to innocence and a liberation."

To surrender to a master isn't to surrender anything that's real. On the contrary, it's to surrender, to give up, all the dreams, all the peripheral accumulations that the ego is made up of. We can't surrender anything that's real, Bhagwan says, because as we are we don't have anything that's real. Everything about us is false, borrowed and inauthentic.

Satya Bharti had taken up "dynamic meditation" in order to get rid of that madness—or that sanity. The first time she really got it, she wrote, she felt as if she were walking for the first time and wanted her mother there to watch her. In subsequent sessions she had what the guru explained were past-life experiences: she became a baby kitten learning how to kill a mouse, and she saw her son—though it wasn't her real son, Billy—hanging with a rope around his neck. In the quiet part of the meditation she would always feel floating and blissful.

After the "dynamic," Bharti wrote, she would go to Bhagwan's lecture:

> I would sit silently on the floor in front of him. I would drink him in. His hands danced their eloquent dance while he spoke, hypnotizing me, mesmerizing me. Sometimes, for no discernible reason, I would feel a flood of tears pouring down my face . . . Bhagwan would glance at me for an instant while he spoke. Suddenly the energy would rise up in me like a violent storm, an earthquake. My body would begin shaking. Violent tremor after violent tremor. It was as if I were a riveting machine . . . My body was doing its own thing, but part of me stood outside the body watching what was happening as if it had nothing to do with me.

Satya Bharti had become a sannyasin in the United States not long after a divorce. She had married a New York stockbroker when just out of college and had three children. Though a math student at college, she had always wanted to be a writer and while married she had written a market newsletter—and later, speeches for Congresswoman Shirley Chisholm. In the sixties she had become "radicalized," she told me; she had gone back to college—to Sarah Lawrence —and had worked in politics and taken up yoga. Finally she had rebelled against the conventional life she and her husband were leading, and against all of his conventional views. She went to the West Coast and started doing meditations at a Rajneeshee center. Having taken sannyas, she decided she had to go to India to live—though it meant leaving her three young children with her ex-husband. In one book she wrote of that decision:

> I had always wanted to save them from their father's world, and he had always wanted to save them from mine . . . To suddenly, willingly, hand

the children over to their father's influence was hard . . . But it seemed inevitable . . . How could I wish for them, as I did most of all, happiness, freedom and continual growth if I didn't allow myself to have it? How can you share with others what you yourself don't have?

The children, she wrote, had finally adjusted to her absence. "Life is like school," her son Billy had said a few years later when he was eleven years old. "I guess being without Mommy is one of the lessons I have to learn." She herself, she wrote, found the attachment more difficult to give up. At the ashram she would rock back and forth crying, "I want my baby back, I want my baby back."

> The pain is incredible, I relive scores of past-life experiences all of them connected with this same feeling of loss; my children dead, dying, killed; taken away from me in one way or another. A loss that's irretrievable, a pain that's unending. In this lifetime no one has killed my children, no one has taken them away from me. I've done it myself; the choice was mine. The pain is no less real because of it.

Finally she went to Bhagwan for help, and he said to her: "Why are you worrying about them? Everything is perfect with them. Everything is happening as it should. They're not your responsibility anymore, I told you that before. They're my responsibility now; I'm taking care of them. They'll come here, don't worry, when the time is right and when they're ready to come." Satya Bharti left the darshan, she said, "feeling as though a weight had dropped from me." Bhagwan, she wrote, "had told me the same thing before, but I hadn't been able to trust him enough to believe it. I suppose trust grows. I trusted him enough now."

In Rajneeshpuram, Satya Bharti brought up the subject of her children, now aged seventeen, twenty, and twenty-one. They had never come to the ashram, and they had not yet come to the ranch to see her. "They love me," she said, "but they feel I'm copping out on life —that I've left the real world. But I'm quite sure that at some point they'll come to see me—just to visit, of course."

A slight, pretty woman, Satya Bharti was sitting in the outdoor café of the ranch when I met her; she was wearing a pink tank-top jersey and pants. She looked younger than her age, and she spoke as rapidly as any New Yorker. She seemed happy.

Between my two visits to the ranch I had asked the American bio-energetics therapist who had left Rajneesh what it was that happened between the disciple and the Master. He said, "For the disciple there's something akin to a transference—on the theory that there's a spark of divinity in everyone and that spark can be projected onto a guru. It's like the transference onto a therapist, only it's far more powerful. If the guru acknowledges responsibility for it, he holds it for a while, as a therapist does, until the disciple moves on. It took me two years to resolve my transference on Bhagwan. I did it in dreams. I became him."

Rajen, whom I spoke with on my second visit, told me much the same thing but in different terms and with a different ending. "There's an analogy between taking sannyas with Bhagwan and the growth groups," he said. "The guru mirrors back facets of our own personality—the series of masks we wear that are culturally acquired and conditioned. Taking sannyas cost me everything—all my possessiveness. In the six and a half years I have been with him, it's been more and more fun to let go. I live in the here and now, and before I never could have accepted this simplicity.

"Once, I left the ashram in Poona. I was scared to stay on, and I ran away to do my own workshops in Europe. There was some residue of wanting to do my own thing. During that time Bhagwan went into silence, and that caused a good deal of inner turmoil for some of us. I thought I had cut the cord, and I lived for a year with that, but it turned out not to be so. I realized that something had happened that wasn't under my control. I *wasn't* estranged from the energy of the Master. I couldn't think myself out of being open and imbibing what Bhagwan was all about."

I asked Rajen whether this would qualify as a transference. "Yes," he said, "it's a transference, but a transference onto a Master. The final attachment, Bhagwan says, is onto a Master."

In Poona, Rajneesh had said that he would go into silence once his disciples had formed that attachment to him. "He said this so many times," Rajen said; " 'I am only entertaining you long enough for something to happen to you just by being in my presence.' Now we can see what he meant." The step was not without precedent. In India it is even customary for holy men to go into silence at some point in their lives. But in an ashram full of Growth Movement therapists, there was some small irony to this. By going silent Rajneesh became the guru equivalent of an orthodox Freudian analyst.

Where Rajneesh differed from most other gurus was in his pragmatic approach to the question of spiritual disciplines and practices. The people of Buddha's time, he said, developed techniques of meditation that worked for them, but these traditional methods did not work for modern man. For twentieth-century people new techniques had to be developed. By this reasoning he turned the Poona ashram into a kind of spiritual garage for anyone with a method, and at the same time into a laboratory for experimentation of all sorts. His test of legitimacy was merely what worked—or what seemed to work. The Western therapists thus came in with the Growth Movement techniques they had learned, and from there on experimented and adapted their techniques to the particular purpose of the ashram. Some of the therapies they invented played a direct role in establishing the master-disciple transference, and in the case of certain individuals, they may have played the deciding role. In one of her books Satya Bharti quoted Karuna (in 1983 the mayor of Antelope) on this point. In the therapies, she said, there was an

> almost tangible sense of Bhagwan's presence. Teertha worked with that a lot in the encounter group. When he felt that someone was open and vulnerable, he would tell them to sit and look at a picture of Bhagwan. It was very powerful. Just by sitting and looking at Bhagwan's picture, I found that I could go beyond the point where I had always gotten stuck before when I was in groups. Bhagwan was there giving me permission to go ahead, to transcend all boundaries."

Satya Bharti had asked Karuna to describe how the ashram therapies differed from the growth therapies practiced in the West, and this was a part of her answer. The other part was this:

> There's a sense of total acceptability in the groups here. Nothing is condemned. There are no limitations, no restrictions; you can take things to the extreme. Group leaders in the West place limits on what happens in their groups because of their own limitations, their own fears. Their self-image is constantly at stake. Here the responsibility is Bhagwan's, so the therapist can allow things to happen; he or she can afford to take risks.

This freedom—or this absolute dependency—was apparently what many of the therapists had been looking for all along. In practice a number of them took tremendous risks—only the risks were not to them but rather to the people in their groups, whose mental health they had not tested and could not vouch for. The film *Ashram* documents some of the risks they took with cathartic techniques, group groping, and so on, for at the time the Rajneeshee thought of these therapies as advertisements for the ashram. (They even went so far as to stage some of them for the film.) Among the other boundaries the therapists "transcended," both on- and offscreen, were the usual strictures against sexual aggression and physical violence. This was only logical. The theory behind "dynamic meditation" was that people should give physical expression to their repressions and frustrations in order to get rid of their "emotional blocks." Teertha and Somendra (the former Michael Barnett) merely extrapolated this notion in their groups; being rather literal people, they encouraged participants to act out all the emotions they felt (however briefly) for each other, including the desire to inflict grievous bodily harm. No one was actually killed in these encounters, but a number of people, naked and weaponless, gave a good deal of time and energy to the attempt. There were several cases of rape in these sessions; there was also a broken leg, several broken arms, and various other injuries. In 1977 Richard Price, the director of Esalen and a Gestalt therapist, visited the ashram, observed one of Teertha's groups, and subsequently wrote a letter of protest to the ashram staff and to Rajneesh himself. In the letter he said:

> My experience in my first two weeks at the ashram in the "meditation camp" was excellent. I felt a deepening, an enrichment, an atunement. During the last two weeks my experience was quite the opposite. I had softened and opened up only to be confronted with Teertha's autocratic, coercive, life-negating style of "leadership"; a style reinforcing violence and sexual acting-out of the most unfeeling kind; a style negating soft emotion and emerging sensitivity, and manipulating group pressure to force conformity. Is *this* what Bhagwan is about?

Price had more than the usual interest in the ashram therapies. Not only had the Esalen Institute given Teertha the only theraputic training he had ever had, but it had sent a great many people to Poona. Price himself had become a mail-order sannyasin two years before he visited the ashram on the strength of his friendships and his reading of Rajneesh's books. He was thus personally and institutionally involved.

> Any decent responsible leader knows how easy it is to protect against most injury—and *not* at the cost of repressing the *genuine* expression of anger, sexuality or aggression—quite the opposite. Teertha actually works to *suppress* that expression while provoking unconnected acting-out of the most vicious kind. It is as if the worst mistakes of some inexperienced Esalen group leaders of many years ago had been systematized and given the stamp of "God."

In 1983 Price told me much the same thing; he also said that he had afterward reluctantly come to the conclusion that "Rajneesh was in the karma of Esalen."

At the time, Rajneesh wrote a reply to Price's letter explaining, among other things, that it was only "objective compassion" to allow those obsessed by violence to get it out of their systems. Laxmi apparently saw these therapies in just this light. In her book *Karma Cola* the Anglo-Indian writer Gita Mehta describes "the matriarch of the progressive ashram" talking with "slight malice" about the visit of "the father of one of California's most advanced touch therapies." She then quotes "the matriarch" as saying:

> "We have a meditation in this ashram where disciples beat each other. Hai Ram, what simple pleasure they get from hitting and thrashing.
> "I tell you only yesterday one boy had his wrist smashed, but he's happy and it's very beautiful. Today, poor chap, he is in massage meditation. He is having oil rubbed over the broken part."

Violence in the ashram therapies ended in January 1979, fourteen months after Price's intervention but only a short while after the Jonestown mass suicide. ("Jones," Price said ironically, "was rather more influential than I was.") A press release from the ashram explained that Bhagwan Shree Rajneesh believed that violence had "fulfilled its function within the overall context of the ashram as an evolving spiritual commune" (a phrase that any American foundation executive might have appreciated). In the same statement Rajneesh said that there would come a point in the development of the commune when therapy groups would be discontinued altogether. According to the press release: "He explained that it was a question of intelligence. Psychotherapies were needed only because the thousands of people coming to his ashram from the West were not yet intelligent enough to heal their own psychological wounds." This was a nasty jab at his disciples—underhanded, one might say. But perhaps it was only fair for Rajneesh to blame his disciples when the therapists were laying all the responsibility on him.

A similar confusion of responsibility was, as it turned out, the main reason for the remarkable dearth of children among the Rajneeshee in Oregon. The guru was a great exponent of birth control for India. According to Laxmi, he had once met Indira Gandhi and taken the opportunity to tell her that she should assume dictatorial powers to enforce a program of sterilization so that no family in India had more than one child. (The advice, as it happened, had fallen on deaf ears since Mrs. Gandhi had just lost the only election she had ever lost in part because of her sterilization program.) At the ashram, Westerners would come to Rajneesh and ask them whether or not they should have a child. The guru would—quite naturally—tell them that they should not if they had any question about it—they should look to their own growth first. What many Westerners heard him say, however, was that they should not have children; possibly this was what they wanted to hear because they had come to Poona precisely to "work on their own growth." In any case Teertha and his colleagues passed this message on unadulterated to their groups. The result was a great many abortions and a good many sterilizations as well. The abortions continued at Rajneeshpuram in part because of this legacy and in part because Sheela and her associates wanted a work crew in the early stages of the commune—and not a lot of pregnant women and babies. There was not a law about babies, but if you had one, it was more difficult to get into, or to stay in, the commune.

By January 1979, the Poona ashram had changed quite decisively in character. In the first two or three years of its existence it had an Indian flavor to it. Westerners would meditate side by side with Indian sannyasins, and on Master's Day the gates of the ashram would open to a procession of men in white robes and women in colorful saris leading white heifers with garlands around their necks. As ashrams in India tend to be for those with the leisure and the maturity to reflect, a lot of these people were middle-aged and eminently respectable people from the business world in Poona. There were many ashrams in the city—Meher Baba's among them—and for the first few years the Shree Rajneesh ashram was not very different from all the rest. As time went on, however, more and more Westerners came to the ashram and fewer and fewer Indians. Finally the balance tipped, and by 1981, when the guru left for the United States, there were four to six thousand Westerners in his audience every day and only a few hundred Indians. The ashram was surrounded by long-haired Westerners walking arm in arm and blissing out or freaking out in the streets.

Rajneesh clearly bore some responsibility for this. Not only did he give Westerners special attention and appoint them to all but the top positions on the ashram staff, but he instituted the therapies and—despise them though he might—gave them exclusive place on the ashram schedule for two weeks out of every month. (For those two weeks there were no meditations except for the morning "dynamic.") And he barred Indians from the therapies. Asked why he did not permit Indians into the groups, Rajneesh explained that Eastern psychology was different from Western psychology: Easterners were "introverts" who needed only to meditate, whereas Westerners were "extroverts" who needed to know how to relate. Rajneesh had remarked that in darshans "a hundred percent of their problems are relationship problems." (He did not, however, say that if Westerners came face-to-face with God, they might ask for a "meaningful relationship.") It was probably true that Indians did not need the therapies. But it was also true that the Westerners did not want Indians in their therapy groups. They did not want Indians unblocking their sexual energies around them, and they told the management that. Rajneesh thus barred Indians from Sufi dancing as well. In addition, the very idea of the therapies shocked the respectable Indians who heard about them.

By 1979 the ashram was having public relations problems in India. The citizens of Poona objected to the crowds of young people holding hands and hugging in the streets. Years later Laxmi berated herself for not having foreseen and forestalled this provocation. But the hugging was probably the least of it. Among the Westerners who came to the ashram there were some borderline psychotics, and since there were no screening procedures for sanity, some of them went over the edge and ended in Poona hospitals on Thorazine. Then, too, some of the young Westerners were financing their sojourns at the ashram in unorthodox ways. A fair number were smuggling drugs—opium, hashish, and marijuana—out of India to Europe, and a few young women were found to be working as free-lance prostitutes in Bombay. While ashram officials claimed ignorance of these activities, the drug smuggling at least was fairly common knowledge in Poona. Then there were the rumors about the therapies. Finally, the guru himself was becoming a public relations problem.

As the ashram's constituency changed, so Rajneesh seemed to change with it. His lecture style altered. His lectures became less and less focused, less and less thought through. By 1979 they were often little more than collections of quotes, jokes, and anecdotes combined with obiter dicta and attacks on political and religious figures. The jokes were now generally ethnic or scatalogical and as vulgar as farmer's daughter or traveling salesmen stories can get. His sannyasins furnished him with these jokes and howled with laughter when he pronounced the vulgarities—like little boys hearing their first dirty joke. His attacks on people were mean-spirited and not at all inventive; in the end they consisted in calling just about everyone a "Polack," beginning with Pope John Paul II. Then, as the quality of his lectures declined, the techniques he employed, or authorized, at the ashram became more and more extreme. After the violent therapies came the "energy darshans" in which Rajneesh, touching the forehead of a young woman, would make her and the person she touched and the next six or eight people jump and twitch like galvanic frogs. The guru, apparently, could not shock his audience enough. His disciples wanted the most extreme forms of experience. Even those women who had been raped in "therapy" said they found the experience valuable.

But while the disciples laughed and applauded, the guru's verbal abuse apparently did not sit very well with a great many people in Poona—and outside of it. The ashram began receiving threatening letters, and several sannyasins were assaulted in the streets. In May 1980, a young Hindu stood up in the middle of one of Rajneesh's discourses and started running toward the guru shouting a protest; before the ashram guards could reach him, he threw a knife in Rajneesh's direction. He was arrested, charged, and tried—but eventually acquitted of attempted murder.

Though most sannyasins remained unconscious of it, the ashram was having not only public relations problems but difficulties with the Indian government. The election of 1977 had brought a surprise defeat to Indira Gandhi and the Congress party and a victory to the Janata party coalition led by Moraji Desai. Laxmi, because of her background, had contacts at all levels of the Congress party. She had introduced Rajneesh to Mrs. Gandhi and, according to *Der Spiegel*, had contributed large sums to her campaign. She had fewer contacts in the new coalition. Her father had been a close friend of Desai's, but the new prime minister was a Hindu conservative, and when she went to see him, he told her that he disapproved of Rajneesh and his ashram. (If there had been any hope of an accommodation, Rajneesh ended it by adding Desai to his list of "Polacks.") The timing was unfortunate since at that point the ashram stood in particular need of government cooperation.

As early as 1976 Rajneesh had talked about founding a "new commune" in the countryside where ten thousand sannyasins could live. As the ashram became more and more crowded and the tensions between it and the city of Poona grew, the procurement of new quarters increasingly became a necessity. Laxmi took to the road. Looking for a large, isolated property, she found a prospect in northwestern Gujarat and two more in the mountains along the northern border of India. But each time she applied for the necessary permissions—in the first case to build on farmland, and in the others to move large numbers of people into military security zones—the government turned her down. She succeeded in finding an arid and barely adequate property just twenty miles from Poona, but then the Desai government removed the officials she knew in the state, and again the permissions did not come through. At around the same time income tax officials ruled that the ashram did not qualify as an educational institution or as a charitable or religious organization, and therefore would have to pay taxes on all donations: back taxes as well as current ones. The Rajneeshee took the case to court and believed they could win it, but they were threatened with a bill of several million dollars if they did not. When Mrs. Gandhi was returned to office in January 1980, Laxmi went to her for help with the security regulations on the border. But by now the reputation of the ashram was such that the prime minister refused to intervene on its behalf.

On May 31, 1981, Bhagwan Shree Rajneesh left abruptly for the United States with twenty of his disciples; of the thousands of other people in and around the ashram at the time only a handful knew of his departure until after he had gone. In late March his lectures had been canceled owing, it was said, to an outbreak of chicken pox in the ashram. Sannyasins had assumed that he would resume lecturing once the outbreak was contained, but in April, Ma Anand Sheela, Laxmi's first assistant, announced that Bhagwan had entered the ultimate stage of his work: he had gone into silence and would lecture no more. For the month of May he sat with his disciples in silence for an hour out of every day, and then on May 31 he left.

Just why the guru came to the United States became a matter of pressing interest to the Portland bureau of the U.S. Immigration and Naturalization Service a year and a half later when he applied for permanent residency. His application for a tourist visa in Bombay stated that he required medical treatment in the United States. Laxmi had written the American consul that he required an operation on his back, and Sheela in conversation with the consul had stressed the emergency nature of the request: the man, she said, was about to croak. In fact Rajneesh had fallen ill in the spring of 1981. His allergies, his persistent asthma, and his diabetes had worsened and sapped his energies; finally his persistent coughing began to affect an old back injury—a prolapsed disc—causing him severe pain. Indian doctors and one of the world's leading orthopedic surgeons brought in from England to treat him testified to his condition. However, on arrival in the United States, Rajneesh did not go to a hospital or seek any outside medical treatment—and at no time was he seen by any but sannyasin doctors. Rajneeshee lawyers later explained this apparent discrepancy by the fact that his doctors had determined that there was a significant risk that he might require surgery—though this would be dangerous—but that in the United States his condition had improved so much that he did not. The INS, however, contended that the guru had a preconceived intent to remain in the United States, and that false statements had been made on his application.

Whether false statements had been made was the legal question at issue, and INS officials never proved their case in court. They had, however, significant evidence that Rajneesh and his followers had a preconceived intent to remain in the United States. In the first place, Sheela had asked the American consul in Bombay about the guru's eligibility for permanent residence. In the second place, Rajneeshee envoys had begun to search for land in the United States in April, and by October, when the guru asked for, and received, an extension of his tourist visa, they had already bought the ranch and sunk a good deal of money into it. In the third place, they had begun to ship ashram property to the United States two weeks before the guru left, and, shortly after he did leave, some thousands of sannyasins left India, many of them bound for the United States. Laxmi, whom I met in Woodstock, New York, living as a sannyasin but apart from the commune, inadvertently added to this evidence when I talked to her by blaming herself for the guru's removal to the United States. She had, she said, failed to find a property in India adequate to his needs, and thus when the medical emergency came, the initiative had passed to Sheela. According to ex-sannyasins, Sheela, who had become Laxmi's assistant in 1975 and director of the business arm of the ashram in 1978, had moved to center stage while Laxmi was away looking for a commune site. Long married to an American and a frequent traveler to the United States, she had proposed that the guru move to America. In April 1981, her Chidvilas center in Montclair, New Jersey, bought the castle that was to serve as the guru's first residence in the United States; around the same time she took over from Laxmi as the guru's secretary.

Rajneeshee doctors and lawyers later testified that the guru had recovered slowly in the salubrious air of America. An ex-sannyasin who had accompanied him, however, told the INS that he had insisted on taking a limousine rather than an ambulance from Kennedy airport and a week after his arrival was walking around the garden at the Chidvilas center and driving his Rolls-Royce. This testimony— combined with the fact that the guru never consulted an outside doctor in the United States—quite understandably caused INS officials to suspect that Rajneesh had never been all that sick and was certainly not at death's door. To read Rajneesh's official biography was, however, to see that there had been similar crises in the guru's life and other visits to death's door.

According to his biographer, Rajneesh thought a great deal about death, and had since he was seven years old. At seven he had watched his beloved grandfather, with whom he lived, die a slow death next to him on a bullock cart as the family drove the thirty-two-mile journey into town. Of that experience he told his biographer:

"When he died I felt that it would be a betrayal to eat. Now I didn't want to live. It was childish, but through it something very deep happened. For three days I remained lying down. I would not come out of bed. I said, 'When he is dead, I do not want to live.' I survived, but these three days became a death experience."

At another time he said:

"His death freed me forever from all relationships. His death became for me the death of all attachments. Thereafter I could not establish a bond of relationship with anyone. Whenever my relationship with anyone became intimate, that death stared at me."

The feelings of the little boy were the classical symptoms of survivor guilt. And these feelings, according to Rajneesh, did not go away. An astrologer had predicted that Rajneesh would face death every seven years and would most probably die at age twenty-one. So at age fourteen he asked his school principal for a seven-day leave from school, saying that he was going to die. He spent seven days alone in the ruins of a temple near his village and had, he later reported, another experience of death and the sense of detachment that comes from contemplating it. But this was not a unique experience for him. He was reckless as a boy; he would jump from a seventy-foot bridge into the river by his village and would dive into whirlpools which would suck him under and expel him just when he had no breath left. According to his biographer, he "used the river to bring himself face to face with death." At age twenty-one he went into a severe depression and felt once again "the bottomless abyss." On March 21, 1953, at the end of a seven-day period of meditation, he had the experience he later called Enlightenment: he felt he was exploding, going mad with bliss. "That night I died and was reborn," he said. "But the one that was reborn has nothing to do with that which died, it is a discontinuous thing. . . . The one who died, died totally; nothing of him has remained."

After that "death" Rajneesh entered into a period of great activity; his depression was gone and his psychosomatic headaches vanished. But exactly twenty-one years later in March 1974 (his biographer reports this but does not seem to notice it), Rajneesh announced that he was withdrawing from all activities "just as the sun withdraws its rays in the evening, as the fisherman withdraws his fishing net." He moved to Poona on March 21 and began to suffer from allergies and acute asthma—illnesses often thought to be psychosomatic in origin. After giving a course of lectures on the Bhagavad Gita in Hindi, he went into almost complete silence and, to everyone's amazement, asked to be returned to Bombay. At the end of April, however, he recovered and began to stroll in the gardens, seeming to like his new surroundings. But he stopped giving meditations in person and thereafter only gave lectures and darshans.

Rajneesh stopped speaking to his Poona audiences on March 24, 1981, precisely seven years after this last event (the coincidence again unremarked by his biographer). According to Laxmi, he had sat quite still in his room for months before that, not reading and paying no attention to her when she fussed around him, emerging only for his public appearances. In March, four specialists pronounced him very ill with allergies, asthma, and a prolapsed disc. On May 31, he left for the United States and a week later he was walking around the gardens of the castle in Montclair, New Jersey. The U.S. Immigration and Naturalization Service either did not notice this pattern of spiritual crisis or thought it went beyond their jurisdiction.

Rajneesh had always said he would never leave India because, although he disliked modern India, the very earth was sacred—so many Buddhas had walked upon it. Not long before leaving, however —in the beginning of March just before he went into silence—he delivered himself of a bilious attack upon his country and his countrymen. India, he said, was "an old, ancient, and rotten country," and "many parts of this rotten goddammed country have to be removed." Of his colleagues he said, "Their hysterical experience has been called *samadhi*. Their madness has been respected . . . Fools have been worshiped, masochists have been thought to be ascetics, sadists have been thought to be great saints. Perversions of all kinds have been given a spiritual connotation. . . . This country is the country of pretenders, and I am hurting them, and I want to hurt them because that is the only way to pull the pus out of their centuries' old wounds." Rajneesh also spoke of the "thousands of people writing against me, shouting against me," and the threats on his life. But I will, he said, continue "to expose this whole lie of a thousand years" because "I have nothing to lose. At the most they can kill me."

Conceivably, Rajneesh was ready to leave India.

Before he went into silence Rajneesh spoke on a number of occasions about "the new commune" he would create. Man, he said, had outgrown the family: it had served its purpose but it had exacted a heavy price in neurosis. The institution of marriage had been founded in a desire for security. Some marriages were spiritual ones, but, as love could not be legalized, most marriages were held together merely by guilt or fear or a sense of dependency. Families stunted children as well as adults, for children grew up obsessed by loving or hating their parents: men spent their lives looking for the image of their mother in women, while women searched endlessly for their fathers. Families demanded obedience from children and thus enforced mediocrity. They taught children to accept religious and political dogmas blindly, and they taught them aggression, competitiveness, and possessiveness. Private property and its attendant ills of jealousy and conflict were the creation of the patriarchal family.

The "new commune" was therefore to be a "liquid family" where men and women stayed together only as long as they loved each other and where children would belong to everyone. Children would have mothers, but they would not know who their fathers were. Women would run this commune because they were more intuitive and down to earth than men—and less involved in their own egos. This commune would have no churches, no orthodoxies, and no rituals. People could discuss all forms of religion and philosophy, and children could learn from all of this accumulated wisdom. This commune would give birth to a "new man" who would not need a high position or a big bank balance but could live joyfully, playfully, knowing how to dance and sing. He would not be a fixed "character" but an "authentic being" with a commitment to "the scripture of nature." He would love others and in consequence be honest and trusting. There would be no ambition and no politics in this commune. "Politics," Rajneesh said, "are neurotic and will disappear."

Rajneesh's proposals for the commune were widely read in central Oregon and widely presumed to describe Rajneeshpuram. For Reverend Mardo Jimenez and others they were proof that the Rajneeshee were "a foreign cult" out to destroy the American family. But the sources of these proposals were hardly Indian. In Buddhist philosophy man must live with institutions just as he must live in the world of appearances: to "transcend" them is not to do without them but rather to see them for what they are. Rajneesh's "new commune" was, in fact, one of those mirrors the guru hung up before his Western disciples, for it reflected quite exclusively the ideals of the American counterculture and the Human Potential Movement. Rajneesh, after all, had learned all he knew about communes from his Western sannyasins. In 1973 he had sent thirty-five Westerners off to a dirt-poor farm in central India without any instructions whatsoever except to learn how to surrender. The South African disciple he had put in charge of the farm had made up the work schedule himself, and introduced the idea of work as meditation—a notion he took from

Gurdjieff. That commune did not last very long, but it was the proto-type for the Poona ashram and the Oregon commune.

In Oregon at the time of my first visit, the Western sannyasins had clearly been struggling with the problem of how to do away with all dogmas and rituals. The struggle was comical, philosophically speak-ing, for the more they talked about "spontaneity," "playfulness," and "authenticity," the more they etched the words into doctrine. In March 1983, the city council had passed an ordinance stating that a joke must be told at the start of every meeting; the ordinance might have been conceived in a spirit of playfulness, but when imple-mented, the joke became a ritual formula and the laughter expected behavior. The command to "spontaneity" could not, logically speak-ing, be obeyed. And the commune, practically speaking, could not do without rules. The only way out of this dilemma was self-deception —a state that many sannyasins seemed to have achieved.

Wadud, among others, had insisted that the Buddhafield would not become institutionalized; yet, as any newspaper reader in Oregon might have pointed out, institutions were growing up like thickets in Rajneeshpuram. There was a school, there were institutes, there were businesses on and off the ranch. There was a financial structure of some complexity; there were also two city governments and a police force with the regulations to go with them. (In theory the businesses and the governments were independent of the Rajneesh Foundation International and the Rajneesh Neo-Sannyas International Com-mune.) And there were a number of commune rules. Some of the rules had to do with fire prevention and safety; others had to do with cleanliness and dress. Sannyasins, for example, could not just wear anything they liked: a color chart drawn up by one of the designers showed them which pinks, reds, and oranges went together and which did not. Then, too, with all the laughing and hugging that went on, the residents worked twelve hours a day by schedule and could not leave the ranch as they pleased. And the number of rules kept growing. In the wake of a nasty incident—a stranger who was possibly deranged, possibly an extortionist, brought a bomb into the Portland hotel and accidentally blew himself up—the commune insti-tuted an elaborate security system. By the time of my second visit to the ranch in September 1983, uniformed guards checked everyone going on and off the ranch; visitors were body-searched and their cars sniffed by police dogs; residents and visitors alike had to wear plastic identification bracelets, and the Twinkies wore uniforms. These se-curity procedures reduced by some important percentage the number of times the guides to the ranch spoke about playfulness and spon-taneity.

That the commune had created certain institutions and adopted certain rules was hardly surprising—though the number and stringency of these rules seemed incompatible with the atmosphere the Rajneeshee wanted. More surprising was the fact that in certain fundamental ways the commune seemed to be evolving in a direction quite contrary to the countercultural model the guru had outlined. A new design was emerging, and at the time of my second visit to the commune, that design was much clearer than it had been before.

In May, Wadud's building plans had seemed wildly ambitious, but by September his "resort and education center" had already begun to take shape. Over the summer the Rajneeshee had paved the streets in the center of town and had built three new restaurants and a boutique shopping-mall. They had added a good many more A-frame housing units, and one complex of them was now a hotel for visitors. The building I had seen going up for the meditation and therapy institutes was now completed with flagstone paths and a flower garden; it now housed the Rajneesh International University. The structure the Rajneeshee had apparently been building for a greenhouse was now a two-acre hall with a sound system and a speaker's platform—much like Rajneesh's hall in Poona. For visitors the Rajneeshee had put swimming and boating platforms on the lake. They had turned part of the lounge into a blackjack parlor and built a discotheque especially for children. Wadud told me that he had abandoned the idea of building on the mountain site for the moment, but that he was now starting construction on thirteen new buildings including a theater, a health spa, a prefab-building-components factory, and a 28-room hotel. According to Savita, the head accountant, the Rajneeshee had now spent a total of about $60 million in Oregon.

In May the idea that the commune might one day pay for itself had seemed wholly fanciful to me. The restaurant-disco in Portland was no hot spot, and few non-Rajneeshee guests stayed at the Portland hotel. As for the ranch, it was a four-hour drive from Portland or Salem, and while tour buses came there, the tourists paid two dollars for a guided tour and went away. But then in July the Oregon press reported that fifteen thousand people came to the ranch for the week of the Second Annual Rajneesh World Celebration. Most of them had come via the Portland airport, where Rajneeshee buses had picked them up and taken them to the ranch or the Portland hotel. Their travel had been arranged by Rajneeshee Travel Corporation, and in addition to their travel costs these fifteen thousand people had paid $500 for the week in Rajneeshpuram. For that sum they had gotten their meals and the space in a tent for a sleeping bag; all else was extra. Some thousands of them had stayed on longer, paying $1100 for three weeks or $3000 for a three months' stay. Many of them had taken courses at the university and paid somewhere between $150 for a three-week program and $3500 for a three-month course of therapy or meditation. In addition the ranch had sold a good deal of beer, wine, and Perrier, a good many pink jumpsuits, and hundreds of books by Bhagwan Shree Rajneesh. The commune had even auctioned off one of the Rajneesh Rolls-Royces at $25 a chance. (The winner had returned the car to the guru.) According to Savita, the commune was now breaking even: it would make the $1 million it needed to cover its running costs for the year.

The great influx of sannyasins surprised Oregonians, even those who now considered themselves expert Rajneeshee watchers, for there were not all that many sannyasins in the United States. There were groups of them scattered across the country, but the major centers had always been in California. These centers had been thinned out in 1982 by recruitment for the Oregon commune, and they had been further thinned this year when Rajneesh in his second public statement since his arrival in Oregon announced that there would be an earthquake along the San Andreas Fault that would devastate much of California—but spare Rancho Rajneesh. The announcement had spread panic among California sannyasins, and a Rajneeshee discotheque in San Francisco had closed. Now the only large and visible center was in Laguna Beach, where a minister had turned his church into a Rajneeshee center and started a hullabaloo among his former parishioners. (An interesting court case over the church building in Laguna was now in the works.) In other countries, however, the movement was much larger; there were sannyasins in Japan, Germany, Australia, Canada, and elsewhere. In Europe—unbeknownst to most Oregonians—the movement had coalesced and flourished since the guru moved to Oregon. In a cover story of February 1984, *Der Spiegel* reported that the Rajneeshee communes across Europe were developing a series of remarkably successful business enterprises. They had started a chain of discotheques and a chain of Zorba the Buddha restaurants, and were now planning a chain of hotels. The disco in Cologne was now turning over 3 million deutsche marks a year, and the businesses in Zurich 4 million Swiss francs per annum. Financially independent from one another, the Rajneeshee communes in each city operated the discos and restaurants on what amounted to a franchise. Most of the communes had meditation and therapy centers, also franchised, and a variety of other businesses as well: natural-food stores, health clubs, cleaning and catering services —even a plate-glass-window manufacturing company. They did whatever their members were good at doing, and generally they had a reputation for giving clean, courteous, and efficient service. (An American journalist in Paris ran into two hookers wearing sunset colors who said they were Rajneeshee and happy with their work.) The starting capital from these enterprises came from their member-ships, and the income they made went into their communal expenses —or into the Oregon commune. The Rajneeshee Services Interna-tional, Ltd., with branches in London and Zurich, sold bonds for the ranch and provided a conduit for gifts and other monies coming from Europe. In addition the communes reserved some of their funds to send their members to Oregon for the festival.

Rajneeshpuram was thus not, as the Rajneeshee had first described it, a commune of some distinct number of people trying to make a go of it on their own. It was the center for a worldwide community of disciples. In that respect it was like the Poona ashram, but in other respects it was something quite new. The emphasis was now on money—on primary accumulation—and the aim, apparently, was to mold the community into a disciplined work force with all disciples in every country working directly for the Oregon commune. Gone was the permissiveness of Poona, and gone, too, were the most radical forms of experimentation with sex and consciousness. The therapies, for example, had changed. Aneesha, a neo-Reichian therapist who had gone to Poona because Esalen was "too intellectual" and "not on the radical fringes of consciousness," told me, "It's different here. Something new is emerging. There's a lightness and a gentleness; it's about love, care, and simplicity—not about all those skeletons in the closet. The energy groups focus on the subtle and delicate spaces of being." Whatever this meant precisely, there did seem to be less em-phasis on cathartic techniques and less group groping. Then, too, among the courses listed in the new univeristy catalog were quit-smoking programs, weight-balancing programs, and courses in stress management: courses that would have fit into any health club pro-gram. In addition there were courses in such things as Buddhafield agriculture, Buddhafield business, and Buddhafield construction. These were three-month apprenticeships quite practically designed to provide the commune with laborors—at some considerable expense to the laborers.

With respect to sex and "relationships" the Rajneeshee had gone through a definite *embourgeoisement* since Poona. According to the Oregon University survey, 74 percent of the commune residents were married and 67 percent had spouses living in Rajneeshpuram. Fur-thermore, some fifteen couples had been married on the ranch in the past year—their announcements and wedding photographs duly published in the *Rajneesh Times*. What these figures signified was not

entirely clear, for most of the new Rajneeshee marriages were between Americans and foreigners, and U.S. Immigration officials believed that 90 percent of them were fraudulent—mere attempts to
gain permanent residency visas for foreigners. But some of these marriages were not just instrumental, and to spend any time on the commune was to observe a pairing-off process going on. Whether they
married or did not, sannyasins were developing long-term attachments (and some of them in spite of instrumental marriages). On my
second visit to the ranch I attended the wedding of a couple who
were perhaps in their early sixties. The bride wore a corsage on her
dress; the groom, whose third marriage it was, wore a red carnation
in the lapel of his white suit. Arup, a former Gestalt therapist, conducted the ceremony in the lounge in front of a small altar with
a picture of the guru on it. She made some remarks about the
couple, led prayers, and read from the guru's work; then she put
garlands around the neck of the bride and bridegroom. After the
ceremony there was a party with drinks and a wedding cake. It
was much like any nondenominational wedding in Santa Barbara or
Asbury Park.

Of course there were still elements of Rajneeshee social life that
would not have found favor with Reverend Mardo Jimenez. There
was still, for example, a good deal of enthusiasm for Tantric practices,
and for visiting sannyasins, Rajneeshpuram was still a great place to
get a date. But the ranch was not the the sex commune that Jimenez
imagined. The resident sannyasins were working twelve or more
hours a day, and the coordinators disapproved of all distractions—
even including blissing out on Bhagwan. Visitors, for their part, had
to wear a special bead on their mala and observe a sexual quarantine
for the first week of their stay. Venereal disease had traveled quite
naturally around the Poona ashram, but here efforts were made to
control it as it threatened the work force.

In May the Rajneeshee told me that they had no religious obser-
vances—that work was their worship. One evening, however, toward the end of my stay, a sannyasin I was talking to over a beer in
the lounge broke off the interview to gather a group of people around
him and kneel down in the direction of the guru's house. The group
then chanted a prayer in Sanskrit—the same that was inscribed on
the gates to the ranch. Not everyone in the room knew the chant—or
even knew they were supposed to do it. The observance, it turned
out, had just been instituted by the commune, and my interlocutor, a
long-term sannyasin, was teaching it by example. When I returned in
September, everyone in the commune was chanting this prayer at
sunrise and sunset every day. By then the commune had also insti-

tuted a regular Sunday afternoon darshan where visitors and others could go and meditate or listen to Teertha reading from the Master's works.

But that was not all. The Rajneeshee were, I discovered, developing all the institutions of a church. For some months the editors in the publishing department had been codifying the guru's works: that is, making a subject index for all the lectures and darshan talks so that Rajneesh's dicta on any given topic could be retrieved at will. In May I learned that some people had been given the title "acharya," or "teacher," by the guru. Ma Prem Isabel told me that she was an acharya, but that she had never officiated at anything and had no precise idea what it meant. Teertha was one, and so was Arup, the brooding Dutchwoman who coordinated the Rajneeshee therapy and meditation centers around the world. Sheela was also one. Earlier in the year Sheela had given an invocation at the Oregon state legislature on behalf of the new religion, but when I asked her about it, she told me that she was "not really a religious person" and that she had decided on the invocation just moments before giving it. In May even Sheela was insisting on the informality of it all. But then in August the commune published a booklet called *Rajneeshism,* which explained the religion in some detail.

According to the booklet Rajneeshee worship was meditation and the meditative attitude in work and play; the message of Rajneeshism was contained in the lectures of the guru; and Rajneeshee education was a lifelong process of learning self-awareness. The booklet gave the whole text of the Sanskrit chant, the *gottchamis,* and explained the ceremonies of *satsang* (or being with the Master) and darshan. It named four religious holidays in the year and described ceremonies to be used on the occasions of birth, death, marriage, and caring for the sick. The birth ceremony, interestingly enough, involved natural childbirth at home with the husband, as well as an acharya in attendence. Thus was the patriarchal family established in Rajneeshism. As to funerals, the booklet prescribed cremation, with the whole community gathered to celebrate with dance and song. On the organization of the church the booklet was quite specific:

> The ecclesiastical organization of the religion is overseen by the Academy of Rajneeshism.
> There are three categories of ministers: *acharyas, arihantas* and *siddhas.* The category into which a candidate is placed depends on the particular type of energy he or she possesses: introverted, extroverted or a synthesis of the two. . . .

*   *   *

To be eligible for the ministry, a person must have the following experience and training: a minimum of
—two years as a neo-sannyasin
—two years of participation and practice in meditation
—two years of participation in religious discourses and teaching with guidance
—one year of worship-meditation or apprenticeship in Rajneeshism
—specific orientation for the ministerial duties.

In explanation for the creation of a religious organization at this juncture the booklet said that the formation of a doctrine and an organization around Rajneesh was inevitable, and since that was the case, it was far better that it should be done while the Master was alive and could give spiritual direction to his disciples, for the alternative was to have it done by "well-meaning but unenlightened followers" after his death. It did not point out that Rajneesh had often said this could not and should not happen. "It will not be possible to make a dogma out of my words. . . . Every institution is bound to be dead. . . . I am destroying your ideologies, creeds, cults, dogmas and I am not replacing them with anything else."

The appearance of the booklet—and the final codification of "Rajneeshism"—might have been a cause for celebration at Rajneeshpuram. It was not. The long-term sannyasins I talked with about it seemed to have no very positive feelings about it. Ma Satya Bharti, one of the first Westerners around Rajneesh, told me that she had always thought a religion would form around Bhagwan but "it's not anything I can connect with." She and others admitted that there was something contradictory about it. "Bhagwan is like Gurdjieff," Rajen said. "His function is blowing preconceptions. The idea of religion is disturbing to me. Those of us who came from religious backgrounds were disillusioned with religion and found freedom in a situation defined only by being with a religious Master. Bhagwan talked about religiousness, not about religion. Of course, he did also talk about the development of a religion while he lived, but it was like his talk of 'the new commune'—it seemed to us to be a kind of myth."

Yet Rajen and the other long-term sannyasins on the ranch accepted "Rajneeshism" just as they accepted every other contradiction the guru had presented them with. "I would have been indignant about the creation of rituals before," Rajen added. "But not now. We have to accept the paradox of it. We have to give up trying to get at it intellectually. The fact is that this is a religion. It's probably true that it would have evolved into one anyway after the Master is gone."

Many Oregonians, of course, suspected that the Rajneeshee had created a formal religious structure purely and simply as a legal ploy to claim all the rights and privileges accorded to religions in the United States. It was not inconceivable that the Rajneeshee had considered the legal advantages; all the same, "Rajneeshism" was a far more elaborate construction than was necessary for external purposes. The booklet was most obviously a plan for the perpetuation of the community of believers after the guru's death. In May, before it was issued, I had asked a number of resident sannyasins what they would do if the guru died. To a man and a woman they said they would leave the commune and start new lives elsewhere. When I asked them whether they were building a ghost town, they replied in Zen terms: they were living in the present—the moment that was all moments—and not thinking of the future. But clearly someone was thinking about the future. Reading the booklet I wondered if any of the Rajneeshee leaders had ever read Max Weber, for here was a textbook attempt to "routinize charisma."

"Rajneeshism" in fact seemed merely part and parcel of the whole enterprise taking shape at Rajneeshpuram. In Poona the Buddhafield had been a realm of free play—a kind of psychic sandbox—but here it was becoming more and more formalized, businesslike, and institutional. In discussing a possible church-state suit against the city, K.D. in May had compared the Rajneeshee to the Puritans; Isabel had mentioned a parallel between the commune and the Oneida Community. Now in attempting to locate themselves in the American tradition the Rajneeshee talked about the Mormons instead. Just why this transformation was taking place was not entirely clear: no one could or would explain it to me, and many Rajneeshee did not seem to grasp precisely what was happening. Possibly it was a natural, organic process. Such transformations, from the ecstatic to the routine, were not unknown in the history of religions; also it accorded very well with the changed temper of the times and the fact that the Rajneeshee, now in their mid-thirties, were of an age to harness the chakra energies and put them to work for profit. If this were the case, then the chances for success were good, for the Rajneeshee had all the talents necessary to make their enterprise work.

To watch the guru—a white-robed figure with a long gray beard—issue forth from his compound every afternoon in a Rolls-Royce with a beautiful young woman beside him, it was not hard to imagine that Rajneesh had simply retreated into passive Buddhahood, content now to live in some comfort and watch these odd creatures, his disciples, work their will on the world. Similarly, to watch the Rajneeshee at work building their city it was equally possible to imagine that the guru had become for them nothing more than an emblem—the modern equivalent of a totem pole or a sacred rock—around which they now organized their considerable energies. The difficulty of drawing a conclusion of this sort was that although the Rajneeshee had all kinds of institutions, they did not seem to have an institution of government—or at least not one they were willing to describe.

Isabel and others had told me that the major policy decisions for the commune were taken at the weekly coordinators' meetings or at general meetings of the commune members. On my second visit Isabel invited me to attend a coordinators' meeting at Sheela's house one Sunday morning. At the meeting Sheela, in a velour warm-up suit, sat curled up on a couch with twenty or thirty sannyasin crowded around her. Most of them were women, and I recognized some of them: Savita; Vidya; Prabodhi, the treasurer of the commune; Kavido, K.D.'s sister and a member of the Antelope city council; also K.D.; Neehar; and Devaprem, the construction coordinator. Some of them sat on sofas and chairs, but as there were not enough of these, most sat on the floor. Sheela talked a good deal of the time. She talked first about an Indian some of them had once known—a very boring man, according to her, who, having taken coures in Yoga, *est*, and Silva Mind Control, was now publishing books on "experiencing the self." Everyone laughed. She then talked about taking one or two of the therapy group leaders with her on her next shopping trip to Portland just to get them off the ranch for a bit; she also described what had happened on her last shopping trip when one of her companions— one of their number—had tried to eat all the french fries in the restaurant. She talked about how much she liked to play blackjack and how it might be possible to keep the lounge with its new blackjack tables open until midnight so that she could play for an extra hour. Savita, always the practical one, objected that a late closing would mean that many people would have to change their work and sleeping schedules, but Sheela persisted. She talked for about fifteen minutes about her great love for blackjack—until finally Savita gave in. That accomplished, she launched into a long story about her appearance on a locally produced television serial, then another long story about herself and the mayor of Portland.

Some of the people in the room fidgeted a bit during these long narrations, but no one tried to stop her and many people urged her to go into more detail. When she told a joke, everyone in front of her would laugh and laugh hilariously. They laughed particularly hard when she mocked local Oregonians for their lack of style or their fantasy that the Rajneeshee wanted to take over a town called Dufur. Dufur! Oddly enough, the humor did not always seem to reach those people sitting around me at the back of the long leg of the L-shaped room.

Occasionally Sheela did bring up some commune business: people were talking on the telephone too much, everyone had to have flu shots, people left their bags around, and some people looked so raggedy and badly dressed that she was thinking of issuing everyone uniforms. She spoke like the housemother of a boarding school dormitory, and the sannyasins, packed together on the floor in their jumpsuits and sweatshirts, giggling and interrupting each other to urge her on, responded in kind. They did not seem like people in their thirties with graduate degrees. At one point Sheela asked them to consider the need for more showers at the worksites and launched a half hour of brainstorming on the ways of getting people dry without using more towels. Suggestions of human car washes and body blow-dryers brought general hilarity. The only solemn moments in the meeting were those in which Sheela criticized two of the coordinators in the room. One of them was her husband, Jayananda, who had apparently blamed someone unfairly for something; the other was an unnamed person who had—she found out—listened to another person's telephone conversation. To this second person she said, "Why do you feel so insecure here? This is your home, so you have no need to feel insecure. The point is not to repeat mistakes, but you have. So, big deal, we've made a mistake, and we'll correct it. We'll find an appropriate place for you."

The meeting lasted for four hours. After it Isabel assured me that coordinators' meetings were not always like that—that sometimes, as just after the bombing of the Portland hotel, important matters were discussed. But these semipublic coordinators' meetings were clearly not the place where important policy decisions were made. Sheela, presumably, had her own way of doing things. The meeting was nonetheless revealing, for it showed that Sheela—with the guru somewhere behind her—was as much in charge of the commune as Laxmi had been of the Poona ashram; it also showed the quality of the relationship between her and the Western sannyasins.

At the time I knew there had been some defections from the commune: a number of sannyasins had left the ranch in anger over policy decisions and over how these decisions were made. One group of them had written an open letter to all Rajneeshee denouncing "the so-called leaders of the Rajneesh Foundation International . . . Sheela and her ruling oligarchy" and signing themselves "The Wild Geese." An editorial in the *Rajneesh Times* denouncing the letter and some of the probable signers confirmed the existence of this group. After my second visit to the ranch I met some of the sannyasins who had left the ranch and who—unlike the residents—were willing to talk about how it was run.

A woman I'll call Jocelyn Roberts was by profession a psychiatric social worker. Now forty-one years old, she had spent eight months in the Poona ashram in 1980 and 1981 and three months in the Oregon commune, June through August 1982. She had contracted amebic dysentery on the ranch (along with a number of other sannyasins) and, as it was of an exotic sort, she had ended up at the San Francisco Tropical Disease Center. She did not return to the ranch because by the time she recovered she had decided that there were a lot of things she didn't like about the place. She had worked on the farm with many people who, in her view, knew a great deal about ecology and farming techniques. She had expected "interesting discussions where people would exchange ideas, sort things through, and come to decisions"; she had expected "participatory democracy." But that was not what she had found.

"I never went to a meeting," Roberts said, "where there was any discussion or helpful criticism or evaluation on the part of any sannyasin. There's no vote on any decisions. What happens at meetings is you're told what to do. Instead of discussion what you get are directives and scoldings—scoldings with the implication that you're not working hard enough."

According to Roberts, all decisions came from the top down. "There's an appearance of collegiality. But the department heads and coordinators have an absolute say in how things are handled. It's a very hierarchical system, and the ultimate authority is Sheela." The department heads, she said, often knew much less about what they were doing than their subordinates because there was no system of promotion by merit. "It's all politics. It's for political reasons that they've got the position, and they can make gross errors." The other side of the coin was that, "You could get stuck with maid work for the whole time you were there and never get a chance to do upper-echelon work."

Roberts had had a great many friends on the ranch and thought highly of some of the coordinators she had run across. She liked Isabel, as most people did. But some of the coordinators she had worked with, she said, had very authoritarian personalities. They would order their subordinates around harshly—and then flatter their superiors. In her view there were a lot of people who were unhappy with the way things were done on the ranch. "I heard a lot of criticism of Sheela while I was there. She's strongly disliked by many, many people, only they'd never say it publicly. . . . The appearance when you go there is that people are so happy . . . but there's an invisible stick held over everyone's head, and that's the threat of expulsion: if you don't like it, leave. I've heard Sheela say that over and over again in public meetings: 'I want to remind you you don't have to be here.' So people are very afraid to speak out about any of the differences of opinion that they have. They're very afraid to challenge or to question or suggest improvements. So there's a lot of role-playing and pretentiousness."

Not only did people criticize Sheela, Roberts continued, but they questioned whether she truly represented Bhagwan. When she quoted from her private conversations with him, they wondered whether he had really said what she said he did. Roberts herself doubted that he had.

There was, of course, no way that lower-echelon sannyasins could have determined what the guru said or didn't say. For the first two years in Oregon Rajneesh had spoken only with a few high-level sannyasins, and in the fall of 1983 he announced—or rather Sheela announced—that he would speak only with Sheela. What was certain, however, was that Rajneesh had created the system they so disliked. His responsibility was obvious—only he had hidden it from them in plain sight.

In Poona the ashram had been run by Laxmi and her assistants with the ultimate authority resting with Rajneesh. It was not a democracy. Rajneesh had once said so in so many words in answer to a woman sannyasin who had questioned him about what she saw as an arbitrary and unfair decision of a guard in turning an Indian sannyasin away at the gates. The question had prompted him to give a lecture on the necessity to surrender to his authority. "This place is to change you; it is not to be according to you . . . Your votes will never be taken," he said. This was hardly surprising since Indian ashrams are not by their nature democracies. But then he went on to warn his disciples never to interfere, never to complain, and never to mention anything that appeared to them to be injustices. "Not a single thing happens here which is not known to me," he explained. "Whatsoever happens here is happening with my knowledge . . . whatsoever happens is happening according to a plan, a device. There is some hidden pattern in it. And nobody except me knows what this hidden pattern is." In other words, to be a disciple you had to believe that everything that happened was literally or mystically the guru's doing. If something appeared to be wrong or unjust or foolish, that was your myopia; it was otherwise in the guru's encompassing vision.

In Poona, Rajneesh put women in charge of practical matters—

women who adored him and who therefore quite naturally fought with each other. This did not make for the most efficient sort of organization, but it did ensure that his authority would remain unchallenged. As he himself told his disciples, "The open secret is that you can be free only if you have put too many women around you. Then they are so concerned with each other, they leave you absolutely alone . . . Their jealousies, their envies are enough to keep them occupied." The creation of jealousy and envy might not seem to be the proper works for an Enlightened Master, but Rajneesh explained that he was teaching these women—through their constant confrontations—to recognize their ugly emotions and drop them. He gave the same rationale for anything that went wrong in the ashram, whether it was the result of sheer disorganization or deliberate policy. Whatever it was, it was for the good of his disciples—to teach them detachment and the surrender of the ego. Many sannyasins believed this. In one of her books Ma Satya Bharti wrote: "Ashram life continually forces us to live in a state of insecurity. . . . All sorts of crisis situations are created, until finally there's an explosion. And in its wake, a transformation." The strategy was brilliant. While maintaining his control over the ashram and shielding his assistants from any blame, Rajneesh also maintained a reputation for infallibility. Now you see it, now you don't.

In Poona, Rajneesh had gone so far as to tell his sannyasins what he would do when he eventually retired from the system. "When the new commune happens," he said, "you will see, I will put so many women in charge that even if I die it will take you years to discover that the man is no longer there! They will make so much fuss and dance and love and all kinds of foolish things that you will not even come to know whether I am still here or gone." In 1983 this was precisely the situation that obtained, for only a handful of sannyasins knew for certain whether he was directing the commune or not. To an outsider it was unimaginable that Sheela had made up all her conversations with him and was running the commune single-handedly. But to dissident sannyasins this could be the only explanation for what was going wrong.

In fact, of course, given the nature of the system, things were bound to go wrong no matter who was running it, for the trouble, as Jocelyn Roberts had observed, was systemic. Rajneesh had created a traditional Oriental despotism, and this form of government—as he said—quite inevitably gave rise to resentments, rivalries, cliques, and factions: the very things that the Rajneeshee (being somewhere conscious of this problem) had said they were learning to do without. In Poona this had not mattered very much as the ashram was merely a stopping-off place for Westerners. In Oregon, however, it mattered a great deal, for the commune was an enormous enterprise involving millions of dollars and the livelihoods of thousands of people on and off the ranch. Also, it was not in India but in the United States, where sannyasins' ordinary reflexes about their rights and freedoms might be expected to reassert themselves. Were Sheela the most brilliant of administrators, she would have to make some mistakes and, as the guru was silent, there would have to be some disagreements over policy. When these occurred, sannyasins would quite naturally blame her and question her legitimacy—since the only alternative was to blame Bhagwan himself. As a corrective the Western sannyasins (psychologists all) had introduced a system of "coordinators"—Maslovian managers—to reduce interpersonal frictions on a day-to-day basis and to suppress dissent. Watching for "negativity," the coordinators might have become an efficient thought police except that they, too, were a part of the system—a system that taught its members the habits and attitudes of Persian courtiers: obsequiousness to superiors, imperiousness to subordinates, and suspicion of everyone. Given their own insecurities, they could see only the most obvious signs of discontent beneath the pervasive "role-playing." The real irony was that they could not see how they themselves were being "programmed" and "conditioned" by the guru's style of governance— even though the guru had explained it to them. This was surely one of the best of Rajneesh's jokes.

According to those who had left the ranch, the resident sannyasins put up with a great deal of hardship during the first two years—more of it than any visitor knew. There were always more people on the ranch than the Rajneeshee spokespeople told the press or the state authorities, and there were always more people than the trailers and A-frames could comfortably accommodate. For the first year or so most lower-echelon sannyasins slept six or eight to a room, and the children lived in a separate dormitory without much supervision. There were not enough toilets or showers, and the medical care was inadequate. There were doctors but not enough beds or equipment in the infirmary to accommodate the sick. The Rajneeshee leaders were in a tremendous hurry. The rule was that those who could not work had to leave; thus many people continued to work twelve hours a day with more or less serious ailments: bronchitis, dysentery, and so on. Then, when the managers made errors, as they sometimes did, the ordinary sannyasins ended up paying for them. Satya Bharti told me that one day she and another woman had to do the wash for the entire commune—a job that normally took ten people. Satya Bharti, of course, found the experience valuable to her; it was yet another spiritual lesson emanating mystically from Bhagwan.

Life was not all hardship, of course, and people did have fun, certainly a good deal more fun than most Marines have in boot camp. The extraordinary part was not that they weathered its ardures but that they did not notice the most obvious warning signals flashing up around them, for while the pressure to work was intense, the pressure to give money was even stronger.

In Poona there had always been enough money. Over the years the Rajneeshee had developed some extremely effective fund-raising techniques. The usual tactic was to argue that surrender to Bhagwan meant the surrender of everything—including all wordly goods. You had to take the risk, you had to give it up, they said, or no transformation would occur. At some point a group leader or ashram staff member would find out about the new disciple's assets in some detail, and if the disciple did not immediately rid himself or herself of these obstacles, the staff member would pass the information on so that in future others could request the specific assets that he or she was holding back. Sheela had managed to take a good deal of money out of India one way or another, but the ranch was an expensive proposition, and now there never seemed to be enough. Sheela and her main fund-raiser, Sushila, visited rich sannyasins in Europe and the United States and asked them for stocks, bonds, jewelry, or paintings —whatever they had to build the Buddhafield. They also raised money from their worker-sannyasins. They told those with wealthy parents to go home, make up with their parents, and ask for money —money to have an operation, perhaps. They asked the parents who came to the ranch to make over money to them. And they told sannyasins with little money to give what they could. Not all those who worked on the ranch gave money, but many of those who came sold their houses, sold their cars, and emptied their bank accounts into the Rajneeshee treasury. Still the fund-raising did not stop. Several former sannyasins remembered a meeting at which Sushila, her arms jangling with bracelets, asking the working disciples to contribute the cash in their pockets, the watches on their wrists, and the rings on their fingers. In the end many sannyasins had all their savings tied up in Rajneeshpuram. And the leaders, needless to say, made no accounting to them. They bought more Rolls Royces—that was all people knew. It was, as the Rajneeshee said, a gamble.

In Poona, sannyasins—even ashram workers—had been free to come and go. But in Oregon "the organization," as it came to be known, demanded total commitment to the building of the commune.

Sheela, K.D., Niren, Isabel, and others traveled a good deal on business, but most sannyasins never left the ranch: they were told they could not leave temporarily except as a matter of dire necessity. Their families could visit them, but there was never much time to spare; and as there were only a few telephones available for private calls (and all of them in public places), people did not generally call family or friends outside just for a chat. The work schedule gave sannyasins little time for objective reflection and little time to themselves. Then, too, the ranch was so isolated in its bowl of hills and so different from it surroundings that it seemed a foreign country. The tourists went through in their buses; other sannyasins came in for the festivals. But most residents had little contact with outsiders—least of all with their neighbors in central Oregon. And by the fall of 1983 the tension between the Rajneeshee and their neighbors had gone up a notch.

Just who was responsible for the state of hostilities between the Rajneeshee and their neighbors was for me an open question when I first visited the ranch. The division of opinion in Oregon about the Rajneeshee was so wide that any given opinion seemed to say more about the observer than the observed. Clearly the breakdown had begun during the battle over Antelope, but that story was a complicated one—more complicated than most outsiders knew. By October 1981, the Rajneeshee had bought several properties in Antelope to use for extra housing and had asked the town council for a permit to build a printing plant and office complex large enough for a hundred workers. In November they asked, and received, permission from the Wasco County Court in The Dalles to hold an election to incorporate a town or "city" on their ranch. Immediately they did so, 1000 Friends of Oregon, which had warned them against "urban-use" building on the ranch, challenged Wasco County's decision on behalf of four local ranchers on the grounds that Oregon's land-use laws forbid the creation of a new "city" in the midst of agricultural land without state approval. In a brief before the Land Use Board of Appeals, 1000 Friends proposed that the Rajneeshee locate all structures not intended for farm use in Antelope and said that the Rajneeshee "may not rely on the hostility of Antelope residents" to excuse their failure to do this. They made this argument to show that all avenues to development were not cut off, but they were in effect suggesting that the Rajneeshee push into Antelope over the residents' objections. And the residents did object; they objected specifically to the printing plant and office complex. The Antelope town council refused to issue a permit for it on the grounds that there was not enough water for a hundred new people. In fact there was not enough water. The Antelope city plan prohibited further development until the water supply could be enlarged. However, because the the town council had neglected to pass an ordinance implementing the plan (the town with its forty people did not always observe such legal niceties), they had no legal grounds for refusing the permit. And the Rajneeshee sued.

By mid-March 1982, the Antelope residents had decided that the only way to save their town from Rajneeshee building projects was to disincorporate it—thus barring urban-use development. An election was scheduled for April 15. On the day there were hundreds of people in town, many of them reporters, but many of them people who had come in to vote in the election. By Oregon law any state resident (and U.S. citizen) could vote in a town election if he or she had "an intent to reside" there and had spent at least one night in the town. The secretary of state, Norma Paulus, came to oversee the election herself because of the problem the "intent" clause was bound to pose. When the votes were tallied, the Rajneeshee won, 67 to 42. All the outsiders who came to vote with the Antelope residents were disqualified either because they had not spent the night there or they clearly had no intent to reside in the town. The sixty-seven Rajneeshees, however, qualified because they had spent at least one night there in Rajneeshee-owned buildings. "All they needed was a sleeping bag," Paulus said. Later she assured me that all the Rajneeshee votes were legal, unfair as that might have seemed to the long-term residents. The law, she added, was passed during Mark Hatfield's term as governor" at a time when social mores made it less problematic."

By June there were a dozen lawsuits outstanding between the Rajneeshee and the Antelope City Council. Rajneeshpuram had been incorporated by then, but the 1000 Friends suit still held it in jeopardy. A number of mediators—one from the federal govenment—came in to try and resolve the Antelope-Rajneeshee disputes, and finally an agreement was reached permitting the Rajneeshee to develop their existing properties but prohibiting any future development. The agreement, however, soon broke down with both sides accusing the other of bad faith. In the town council election in November the Rajneeshee once again outvoted the older residents and put their own people into the town council—thus resolving the issue for good. They never built the printing plant, but in the months that followed most of the original Antelope residents pulled up their stakes and left town.

A professor from a university in the western part of the state who had sat in on most of the negotiations between the Rajneeshee and

the Antelope residents told me he thought Antelope "a Greek tragedy" in the sense that the outcome was inevitable given the character
of both groups. He added, however, that the disaster might have
been averted had there been any coherent political power in the state:
a governor as popular and as powerful as the late Tom McCall might
have imposed a compromise settlement that in the end would have
seemed fair to all. As it was, Oregon politics were both extremely
clean and extremely fragmented. As it was, every issue went to court,
and in court the Rajneeshee money and legal sophistication gave
them an overwhelming advantage. As it was, the law and people's
sense of justice did not coincide.

To talk to the Rajneeshee and the long-term Antelope residents
was, however, to get a slightly different picture of the struggle—one
in any case colored by the emotions involved. On my first visit to
Rajneeshpuram I talked to K.D. about the Antelope affair—K.D. having been with Sheela a principal actor on the Rajneeshee side. He said
they had tried to cultivate good relations with Antelope, but the town
council would not give them a single building permit until they sued.
They had not wanted to take over Antelope, but the residents, out of
fear that they would, held the disincorporation election and broke the
subsequent agreement, forcing the Rajneeshee to vote themselves
onto the city council. "Now because the new council is there," he
continued, "people feel helpless, and because they feel helpless, they
assume we're unreasonable. Some have threatened violence—but
that's just the usual redneck talk." When I asked K.D. why he, as a
psychologist, could not have foreseen and forestalled such a reaction,
he said there wasn't anything he could do about it: it was just bigotry
stemming from fear and ignorance.

K.D. had sounded defensive when he talked about the Rajneeshee
behavior. All the same, it seemed quite plausible to me that the Antelope residents might have exaggerated the threat from the Rajneeshee and thus precipitated exactly what they feared. And there was
some religious bigotry floating around the area. On television a former Antelope resident, Donna Quick Smith, had quoted an Indian
correspondent of hers as saying that the Rajneeshee were criminals
and ought to be slaughtered. The Rajneeshee had sued her for libel,
and they had sued Rosemary McGreer, the wife of a local rancher, for
making some unpleasant (though not, as it turned out, libelous) remarks about them on the air. The result was that people in the area
were now being very careful what they said to reporters and were
keeping their feelings to themselves.

Still, most of the older Antelope residents and local ranchers I met
were solid people who did not have K.D.'s quality of defensiveness.

Margaret Hill, a retired schoolteacher, and Don Smith, a retired U.S. Marine colonel, and a number of others told me their side of the story in impressively precise detail. Mrs. Hill, the former mayor of Antelope and an intelligent, even-keeled woman, told me that they and the Rajneeshee had gotten along quite well in the beginning. The Rajneeshee had thrown a party for everyone in the area with lots of drinks and live music. She began, she said, to wonder about them only when in the course of a conversation about a routine permit, Sheela had talked of recourse to legal action if the council did not issue it. People did not often threaten legal action in that part of Oregon. Then, when the council refused the permit for the printing plant, the Rajneeshee sued. Mrs. Hill had discussed the issue with them on a local television program. The Rajneeshee, she said, had broken into gales of laughter every time she made a point and called her "ignorant and stupid." After that, Sheela, K.D., and others took to calling her and her neighbors all manner of names—"rednecks," "bigots," and so on. In an open letter to the governor of Oregon, reprinted in the Madras newspaper, Sheela wrote, "Oregon can hardly prosper if it is filled with stagnant, dilapidated little towns like Antelope—places where indolent old people go to mark time until they die." K.D. had once come to Margaret Hill's house and called her a "liar and a hypocrite" to her face. "I tried to keep the lines of communication open," Mrs. Hill said, "but it was no good." During the period surrounding the two elections, the Rajneeshee had gone about Antelope noting down car registrations, photographing people, and videotaping every town council meeting. "They didn't do anything," she said, "but they were always at you. It was harassment. A lot of people got very nervous, and being elderly people, they just couldn't take it." When Mrs. Hill refused to go to the ranch lest she incur some obligation to the Rajneeshee, Sheela sent her letters by courier every day, then came to see her personally, and threw a fit. Mrs. Hill finally lost her temper. "They could have done eighty or ninety percent of what they did without all the rancor and ill feelings," she said.

The Rajneeshee's nearest neighbor was Jon Bowerman, a rancher whose fields sloped down to the John Day River just opposite the Rajneeshee truck farm. The evening I went to see him, he and his wife—she pregnant with their first child—were walking around the pastures looking at the Brahma bulls and the bucking horses he raised for the rodeos. Narrow-hipped, wearing faded jeans, a sweat-stained Stetson, and scuffed boots, Bowerman looked the quintessential cowboy: the genuine article. He was in fact the son of Bill Bowerman, the great track coach and the inventor of the Nike track shoe; he himself had coached the U.S. ski team for three years. As we walked toward his house—it looked like a nineteenth-century ranch house, though he had just built it—he told me he was the fourth generation in his family to farm that land. "It gets me hot," he said, "to hear the Rajneeshee talk as if religion was the issue. Ninety-nine percent of the people around here could care less about their religion—though unfortunately there are a few very vocal people who do. One of the serious issues is water. It's a semiarid country, and deep wells sucking groundwater could put alot of their neighbors out of business in a dry year. Then, a lot of people are concerned about land use. We don't want a city in our backyards."

The Bowermans' living room had bare floors and not much furniture: an old couch, some straight chairs, and a table with an ancient typewriter on it. "I took a very casual attitude toward them until Antelope," he continued. "I used to go and visit. There are some fine people over there. But they turn out to be bad neighbors, and I don't like the attitude they have: 'If I want it, I'll buy it.' They're like the worst kind of American tourist—loud, boisterous, demanding, waving fistfuls of dollars. I remember sitting in a café in Chamonix when a group of Americans came in and started shouting at the waitress in English, demanding service. That's what they're like."

Bowerman was now upset about the Episcopal church in Antelope —the church his family had attended for as long as he could remember. Because the church had no resident minister, the town of Antelope had owned the building; just before the Rajneeshee took over the town council, the old council had given it to the Episcopal diocese. And now the Rajneeshee were suing to get it back. Bowerman had written many letters to the local papers about the issue.

In September—the time of my second visit to the ranch—the Rajneeshee took over the school in Antelope. The move was abrupt; it came just a few days before the school year began, and it surprised everyone including the state education officials. In December of the previous year the Rajneeshee had told officials in Wasco County that they wanted a public school for their children in Rajneeshpuram. The officials agreed but warned them that the creation of a new school district took two years. Sheela pointed out that Rajneeshee voters already controlled the Antelope school district in the sense that they could outvote the ranchers whose property lay within it and could, if they wished, slap a half-million-dollar tax levy on the district. The Rajneeshee proposed to redraw the district so that it included only the town of Antelope and Rancho Rajneesh; all the other ranches would be put into the neighboring districts of Madras and Maupin. Because Antelope had a primary school, this redistricting would force the ranchers to send their primary-school children along with their older kids to school thirty to fifty miles from their houses. But it would get them out of a Rajneeshee-controlled district—and it would take only a year. The ranchers therefore agreed to the plan, as did the Rajneeshee.

A few months later, however, the Rajneeshee decided they did not want to wait a year for their public school. In the summer they voted down three school tax levies for the transition year: they would not, Sheela said, pay for the ranchers' children when their children were being kept out of public school. In August the ranchers decided to close down the Antelope school and to use the $50,000 they had in leftover funds to help tuition all of their children to Madras that year. At this point Wadud, the one Rajneeshee member of the school board, proposed a deal: the Rajneeshee would vote a tax levy and tuition the ranchers' kids on condition that they be allowed to reopen the school for their own children, employing volunteer teachers. Wadud wanted an immediate answer, but there was none forthcoming. The other members of the board said they wanted to think about the plan; meanwhile county officials raised problems having to do with teacher certification and drew up conditions that the Rajneeshee would have to fulfill if the school were to be certified as a public— rather than a religious—school. While some education officials felt that the only solution was to give the Rajneeshee the school, the other school board members were in a bind. On one hand, they were terri- fied that the Rajneeshee would play their trump card and tax them out of existence; on the other hand, they were furious and they were under pressure from people in five counties not to give an inch to the Rajneeshee. Over the next two weeks they offered a number of alternate proposals, including one that the school be reopened for all primary-school children in the district, Rajneeshee and non- Rajneeshee alike, and that all secondary-school children be bused to Madras. Wadud turned these proposals down.

In the event, the issue was resolved by a legal technicality. It was discovered that by law those petitioning to get out of a school district —as the ranchers were—could not vote or pay taxes in that district. This suited the ranchers, but then the Rajneeshee lawyers found out that they could not legally sit on a school board either. The Rajnee- shee demanded the resignation of the old school board. They then got authorization from the county to appoint their own board and a week later reopened the school with Rajneeshee children and Rajnee- shee teachers, all of them wearing red, but as a concession to reli- gious-establishment clause, the teachers wore their malas tucked inside their shirts.

There was one further piece of business. Now that the Rajneeshee had set up a school, kindergarten through twelfth grade, they refused to pay the $62,000 it cost to send the ranchers' children to school in Madras and Maupin. When I asked Wadud about this, he said, "They backed us into a corner. We have only fifty thousand dollars for fifty of our kids and twenty of theirs. So the board decided not to pay their tuition. We say, come to the Antelope school—or perhaps Madras will pay the tuition." What he neglected to say was that the $50,000 in carryover funds did not come from Rajneeshee pockets but from the state and the other district taxpayers. But Wadud was angry. "We pay all kinds of levies to the county for sheriffs and roads and so on, and we get no services. More and more they try to stop us, to screw us. So we don't give a damn anymore. We're about to launch a lot of lawsuits. The former board was incompetent. We could have passed a bond issue of a million dollars, but we had no intention of doing that. They lost fifty thousand dollars out of this. They would have gotten more if they had cooperated with us."

Wadud thought the Madras school board would pay the tuition charges. But if it did not, he said, "Their children can come to our school. It will be good for them. They have no idea what a really good school is like."

The Rajneeshee behavior over the school issue brought the entire struggle over Antelope into sharper focus. Here was no "Greek tragedy." The Rajneeshee had reneged on an agreement and had taken over the school in a bare-knuckle power play, causing maximum hardship for their neighbors. They had taken the $50,000 in carryover funds; they now assumed the state subsidy for the coming year— about $30,000—and they refused to pay anything toward the schooling of the ranchers' children. Wadud said they were "backed into a corner," but, as he well knew, the ranchers had not the power to do this, and the county educational officials had raised only appropriate legal and bureaucratic considerations and then bowed to Rajneeshee demands. Explaining Rajneeshee tactics in previous battles, Subhuti, the editor of the Rajneeshee paper, had told me, "We're ruthless where our real interests are concerned. We have to be." I had understood him to mean that the Rajneeshee would be ruthless when it came to life-or-death issues for the commune. But the school was hardly a life-or-death issue for them: they would have had it anyway a year later, and their own school at Rajneeshpuram did not cost them very much. Jon Bowerman's assessment of them now seemed accurate to me.

Wadud's antagonism to the ranchers surprised me, but more surprising was his lack of concern for the political consequences of this new battle with the neighbors. The Rajneeshee now faced two separate legal and administrative challenges to the very existence of Rajneeshpuram: the INS case against the guru, and the land-use lawsuit. Not only that but they needed the cooperation of county and state officials to continue building their city, educating their children, and so on. The first Antelope battle had had serious political consequences for them in the state and had affected the administrative services.

In late May of 1982, six weeks after the disincorporation election, the INS in Portland received a call from an aide to Senator Mark Hatfield. An INS memo of the conversation reported the aide as saying, "Mr. Hatfield is very concerned about the operation of this religious cult, which the Senator believes is endangering the way of life for a small agriculture [sic] town in Oregon, as well as constituting a threat to public safety." In December 1982, the Portland bureau of the INS issued two orders, one denying the guru permanent resident status and the other denying him classification as a religious worker. The Hatfield call may have had nothing to do with this, but congressional delegations often do have influence in immigration decisions, and some of the statements made in the two orders suggested that INS officials were not without feeling about the guru. "It could be argued," the second document read, "that the beneficiary does not teach religion, but rather the antipathy of religion, and thusly not the kind of religion intended by this regulation. However, there is no need to address this issue."

The INS had not only no need to address the issue but no right to under the religious-establishment clause. The two documents were also almost mutually contradictory in that one contended that the Rajneeshee had lied about the guru's ill health and suggested that he had not been sick enough to require treatment in the United States, while the other contended that his ill health—and his self-imposed silence—rendered him incapable of performing his job as a religious worker. The two documents were flawed in a number of ways, but operatively by the fact that the INS did not give the Rajneeshee the derogatory evidence on which the decisions had been made. Recognizing this, the legal counsel for the INS had told INS officials to withdraw the orders, hand over the evidence, and give the Rajneeshee time to rebut it. Nearly a year later the INS gave the guru the priority classification he had asked for—but not the green card.

The land-use case also had a political dimension, though it had been brought before the Antelope battle and was in its essence a straightforward question of legal interpretation. Since the adoption of the Oregon land laws in 1973, no county had ever incorporated a "city" in the midst of agricultural land. Could a county do this, as Wasco County had, without submitting the incorporation to state land-use goals? The wording of the law was somewhat vague on this point since the framers had been principally concerned with the encroachment of existing cities onto agricultural land, but 1000 Friends maintained that a proper reading of the law would show that the land-use goals applied to new cities as well. By the spring of 1983, the case had made its way through several courts and was proceeding more or less as 1000 Friends had hoped. At this point K.D. and Isabel went to the state legislature to propose a deal: the Rajneeshee would get out of Antelope if the legislature would pass a bill legalizing the incorporation of Rajneeshpuram. But the reaction was negative. Legislators who were in no way "bigots" told me that they didn't feel like doing the Rajneeshee any favors after what they did to Antelope.

In July the Oregon Land Conservation and Development Commission adopted a set of temporary rules clarifying the land-use laws to read that a county had to come to it before incorporating a "city." That the commission made these rules retroactive to August 1981 suggested that the commissioners wished not merely to stop the loophole but to stop Rajneeshpuram. In September the 1000 Friends suit, having made its way through another court, arrived at the Land Use Board of Appeals. This administrative appeals court in its turn ordered the Wasco County Commission to hold new hearings and justify the incorporation by making a compelling case that a city was needed on Rancho Rajneesh. The likelihood that the three Wasco County commissioners would make such a case had by then, however, radically diminished.

Central Oregonians generally disliked the land-use laws, since these laws treated the wide-open spaces of the rangeland much as they treated the remaining green fields and the delicate ecological system of the Willamette Valley. The ranchers usually complained they couldn't build a lean-to without permission from the bureaucrats in Salem. That was not quite the case but in their view, it was near enough. Because of Antelope, however, many central Oregonians began to think that their county commissioners had not represented their interests by finding for the incorporation of Rajneeshpuram. At the Land Use Board of Appeals hearings the lawyers for 1000 Friends had charged that one of the commissioners, Richard C. Cantrell, had sold the Rajneeshee $17,546 worth of cattle at the time of the vote. He had not disclosed the sale or excused himself from the decision. A subsequent investigation by the Oregon Government Ethics Commission had shown not only that the charge was accurate but that Cantrell had been under some pressure to pay off a bank note just at that time. But the commission decided that conflict of interest would be too difficult to prove under Oregon law. So the citizens of Wasco County took matters into their own hands. Cantrell was, as it happened, a Mormon, and not long after the commission announced its findings, Mormon church officials in Salt Lake City gave notice that Cantrell was wanted immediately in their mission in Nigeria. Cantrell, then aged sixty-one, had planned to serve out his term as county judge before doing his missionary service, and his wife had a good job at a bank. But the church gave him little alternative, so the couple quit their jobs and left for a place which many central Oregonians would have conceived of as hell. At around the same time the second judge who had voted for the incorporation changed his mind about the virtues of supporting the Rajneeshee. This was no coincidence, since the same group of Wasco Country citizens who contacted the Mormon church put some forceful, and finally persuasive, arguments to him.

In the wake of the Antelope school takeover, a number of new legal problems cropped up for the Rajneeshee. In October the state attorney general, David Frohnmayer, issued an opinion that the municipal status of Rajneeshpuram violated the religious-establishment clause in the state and federal constitutions. The issue in Frohnmayer's view was not that religious people ran the city government but that the city was actually owned and controlled by a church—that is, the Commune and the Rajneesh Foundation International. The church could decide who might visit the ranch and who might visit its private property—yet it collected state funds and exercised police and other government powers. The Rajneeshee had anticipated such a ruling months before it came down and had already prepared much of their defense. What surprised them were the two new rulings by the Wasco County Circuit Court judge (a different judge from those on the commission): the first held up $30,000 the state and county educational authorities had approved for the Rajneeshee school; the second enjoined any further construction at Rajneeshpuram until the settlement of the incorporation case. This last ruling was a serious blow to the Rajneeshee. Until then they had been able to continue building their city—and digging themselves into the Oregon landscape—even while they batted lawsuits around from court to court. But now they were effectively stalled, able only to complete the work they had already started.

Wadud, for one, understood perfectly well the kind of opposition the Rajneeshee faced in Wasco County. At the same time he was forcing the school issue, he told me that the Rajneeshee lawyers were building a case against the county, and in particular against the circuit

334 C I T I E S   O N   A   H I L L

court judge, for bigotry. "We used to try and accommodate," he said, "but more and more, it's just war." Now, instead, they would go to Jefferson County and ask for the incorporation of a new city. True, Jefferson County had turned them down before, but that was "just politics." They would go ahead anyway. "People here said screw it, we'll incorporate another city. We'll just push them a little bit, and if it can be shown that the decisions are obviously prejudiced, we'll sue for our rights. Eventually we'll get a city in Jefferson County because that's what's right. Remembering the Jefferson County judge who had walked out of the propane-gas-tank explosion, I felt that Wadud had become quite seriously detached from reality.

In fact from the very beginning the Rajneeshee had quite often seemed to act against their own self-interest. Not long after their arrival in Oregon they had hired Robert Davis, a former aide to Governor Tom McCall and the most respected and influential lobbyist in the state, to act as their political consultant. Davis had advised them to conciliate their neighbors, but instead of taking his advice they had used him—and his considerable reputation—to make promises about getting out of Antelope that they would never keep. Davis had finally quit, leaving them without a champion in Salem. This kind of behavior was puzzling because in many ways the Rajneeshee managers promoted the interest of their organization extremely well. Isabel and her colleagues put a great deal of effort into charming visitors and cultivating journalists. Always reasonable and diplomatic, they were patient with people they felt were hostile, warm and jokey with everyone else. As a result, the Rajneeshee enjoyed generally good relations with the Oregon press. The major newspaper in the state, *The Oregonian*, championed their rights in editorials and ran nice feature pieces about them. (In mid-1984 it began an investigative series on them, but the series did not run until July 1985.) For every attack on them in the central Oregon press there was a favorable story about them elsewhere. Niren, for his part, did an excellent, professional job of representing Rajneeshee interests, and Wadud and Neehar often impressed the professionals in their fields. Sheela gave cocktail parties for "friends and associates" in Portland and exuded charm. The Rajneeshee sometimes said they were "integrating themselves into society," and sometimes this seemed to be true.

But now a more consistent pattern of behavior seemed to be emerging. While Isabel remained diplomatic as ever, all the other Rajneeshee spokespersons now seemed to be going out of their way to alienate everyone in the state whose support might be helpful to them. They called Senator Hatfield a bigot and they spoke insultingly of the governor, the secretary of state, the attorney general, and local

representatives to the state legislature. When the church-state opinion
came down against them, Sheela and K.D., acting as spokespersons
for the commune, behaved as if they had never heard of the issue
before. "I'm outraged beyond words," Sheela said in a prepared statement. "The attorney general's statement is in the long tradition of
bigotry which this state has exhibited since birth." She added that
Frohnmayer needed psychiatric help and should report to a Rajneeshee clinic.

Such remarks directed at Oregon state officials seemed merely
childish—a reflection of the boarding school atmosphere of the coordinators' meetings. But the Rajneeshee attacked their neighbors and
others they had some power over in much the same way, and if this
was childish, it was something else as well. In particular one incident
that occurred during the summer showed there was a dark side to
them. In June, Paul Gerhardt, Jr., a land-use planner, and Mark J.
Greenfield, the lead attorney for 1000 Friends in the Rajneeshpuram
case, visited the ranch to inspect the building and land-use permits
issued by the city. According to Gerhardt's memo of the event, the
two went to the city offices and were sitting with Wadud looking over
the permits when three Rajneeshee came over and began asking them
hostile questions. When Wadud did nothing to stop them, the three
came closer and fired questions in such a way that Gerhardt and
Greenfield could no longer do their work. One of them—he had a
German accent—made a series of anti-Semitic remarks, including a
remark about "Jews in toasters." At twelve-fifteen Wadud told them
the building was closed until two-thirty, and they would have to
leave. Gerhardt and Greenfield drove out along the country road and
were followed by a parade of Rajneeshee cars (one with Sheela and
her husband in it); when they got out to take a photograph of a
construction site, they were harassed by people and photographed by
the video team. Returning to the city offices, they were greeted by a
crowd of Rajneeshee chanting slogans and yelling, "Get the hell out
of here, we don't like you." They resumed their work, but the demonstrators closed in on them, shouting so loudly they could not continue. Wadud and the city attorney, Sangeet, just laughed. Gerhardt
and Greenfield drove away quite shaken by the experience.

When I asked Wadud about the incident, he denied that there had
been any "negative harassment"—or any anti-Semitic remarks made.
"There was just singing and joking. To us such things aren't serious
—it's all play. Greenfield's asleep—he's off on his own ego trip. People were just letting him know what they thought of him. Whoever
comes into contact with us has to wake up a bit. It's like an encounter
group." Both Gerhardt and Greenfield, however, had heard the anti-

336   CITIES ON A HILL

Semitic remarks; Gerhardt had written his memo about the incident
the day after it occurred.

Wadud's explanation was nonetheless interesting, for he had made
a clear connection between what the Rajneeshee thought they were
doing inside the community and their hostile behavior toward outsiders. Later, in talking with other sannyasins, I found that there was
a well-developed rationale for this kind of hostility. Subhuti, for example, put it this way: "Being here, you see the phoniness of all
politics. Everyone, consciously or unconsciously, is trying to manip-
ulate everyone else—and necessarily so as everyone is imprisoned in
his own ego. Only we are not into that. So it's better to offend people
to the point where they say what they mean. I feel more comfortable
when people don't like us because when they're for us, they're for us
for all the wrong reasons." Subhuti was a gentle person who would
not offend anyone if he thought it would hurt. Much the same was
true of Videh, the water manager, but speaking of his own experience
of state water boards and commissions, Videh said: "No one really
wants to change things. Agencies would rather regulate than solve
problems. Citizens blame each other for problems—so there are lots
of intellectual discussions and lots of emotions, but no one jumps out
of his own focus for long enough to get it. Then we do something
really outrageous—which comes right from our guts—and it gets
people into a different level of functioning." When I asked if politics
in general were hopeless, Videh said, "This country is a kind of anarchy. It tries to deal with ongoing problems and pretends to be a
democracy, but nothing works. I realize this is a delicate conversation,
as what I said might be used to justify fascism. But I'm not talking
about democracy as an ideal—I'm talking about what's going on now
here and in most countries." What were the Rajneeshee doing about
this? "Well," Videh answered, "we're playing this game on a pretty
large scale, and we've had a good deal of impact on the state—forcing
the hands of government agencies that should know better. But our
focus is really on our own transformation. We're trying to free ourselves up from social patterns and social conditioning. And we can
free ourselves more easily when people aren't telling us we're good
guys all the time."

On page 56 of the booklet *Rajneeshism*, there was a quotation attributed to the guru which began: "Man is now living in his most critical
moment and it is a crisis of immense dimensions. Either he will die or
a new man will be born. Rajneeshism accepts this challenge and is
making the only worldwide effort to transform human consciousness
so that man can die and a superman can be born out of his ashes."
The quotation went on to predict floods, volcanic eruptions, and nu-

clear war in the next decade. When I asked Ma Mary Catherine about this passage, she more or less dismissed it as hyperbole: Bhagwan said all kinds of things he did not mean to be taken literally. But clearly the Rajneeshee did believe in the New Man. What was more, they believed that no one but themselves had a legitimate point of view. Provocation, they believed, was the only way to deal with outsiders, and if they made themselves disliked, even detested, that would only help their development.

This doctrine was, of course, chilling. It was all the more so in relation to another theme the Rajneeshee were now playing heavily upon. The theme had first been sounded by Sheela in April. In a letter to the *Rajneesh Times* she wrote:

> . . . a small number of people who are themselves no better than thugs have been trying to scare us out of the state by threatening the lives of Rajneeshee, or those of our friends, or trying to destroy our property. . . We are tired of this uncivilized, barbaric, unsophisticated and violent way of trying to intimidate a religious minority. Once and for all, we wish to make it clear that we are here in Oregon to stay at whatever the cost. If that means that some of our blood is spilled, or some of our property is vandalized, then this is the price we are prepared to pay.

At the time this sounded like pure melodrama—the very diction of the letter asked that it not be taken seriously. But since then the Rajneeshee had reiterated this theme of violence over and over again. Wadud had mentioned it to me in connection with Gerhardt and Greenfield. "A Thousand Friends," he said, "gives people hope that they can get rid of us legally, but once people find that we're here to stay, the other shoe will drop and there will be violence. We've gotten a lot of threats already as people get tired of waiting for the law to act for them." Subhuti told me that he had butterflies in his stomach every time he went into Antelope. And many sannaysins talked about the bullet holes in the signs and the shot that wounded a horse belonging to Harry Hawkins, the county sheriff who trained the Rajneeshee Peace Force. On ABC's "Nightline" in July, Sheela accused the Antelope old-timers of "persecuting" the Rajneeshee. Don Smith, she said, had threatened to run them out of the country, and there had been anonymous threats to burn Rajneeshpuram down.

In fact the Rajneeshee had received a good many threats in the previous months. According to a journalist hostile to the Rajneeshee, a local man had approached K.D. and said, "Dave, you're a psychologist. Just how much more of this crap do you think I can take before I crack and start pulling the trigger?" But whether most of these threats deserved to be treated any more seriously than bar talk was questionable. Don Smith, who was on the same "Nightline" program, said that he believed that the guru was in the country illegally—and that's what he had said. To anyone watching the program, the idea that this man in his seventies could have threatened the Rajneeshee, whatever he had said, must have seemed patently absurd. Then, too, there had been no violence in Antelope or Rajneeshpuram. (The Portland hotel bombing had been the work of a deranged California man.) True, the commune was the object of enormous hostility in the two counties surrounding it, and on occasion men would show up in pickup trucks with guns. But if the Rajneeshee were really worried about violence, they might have taken some steps to allay it—as they had when the demonstrations in Madras turned ugly. As it was, they continued to provoke hostility against themselves—and often in a very deliberate manner.

A few non-Rajneeshee still attended the meetings of the Antelope City Council, and a few of the ranchers' wives still went to the school board meetings, though these were now held in Rajneeshpuram. The Rajneeshee often used these meetings for theater. In one city council meeting, for example, Ma Prem Karuna, the mayor, announced that she had been thinking long and hard about creating a park for nudists in Antelope. There were costs, she said: the park would offend those people who did not live in the twentieth century, and building it would be an expense to all taxpayers. But the benefits of having a place where people could feel at one with nature finally outweighed these costs, so she was now proposing an ordinance for it. The ordinance was passed, but the park was never built—perhaps because the Rajneeshee already had such a park in Rajneeshpuram. A few months later the same city council changed the names of all the streets in Antelope. Main Street became Mevlana Bhagwan Street, College Street became Mansour, and so on. In reporting this story, one Oregon journalist recalled the colonization of Indian country by white settlers.

Sometimes these provocations were initiated by K.D., Karuna, or Wadud, but most often it was Sheela who took the offensive. At a school board meeting in front of television cameras from a Portland station, Sheela declared that the children of the ranchers looked retarded, and Margaret Hill, the former schoolteacher, looked retarded too. Staring straight at a young woman whose husband had just been killed in a hunting accident, she said that such was the state of affairs in Antelope that a man had just committed suicide because his wife was "screwing around" with another man. The young woman left in helpless tears. On "Nightline" Sheela told Margaret Hill that she "should have shut up a long time ago," and in response to Don Smith's charge that the guru was here illegally, she screeched "Bullshit" and then "Bullshit" again. (A local court finally awarded libel damages to Rosemary McGreer, the very woman the Rajneeshee were suing for libel, because Sheela had called McGreer a "racist" and a "bigot" among other things.)

Wondering if this could not be simply Sheela's way, I went one day to ask her why she so often made such a spectacle of herself. Sheela was receiving in bed that day—she suffered occasionally from phlebitis—and a number of her women coordinators were sitting on the floor around her bed. K.D. hovered about in the doorway. In answer to my question she said in a loud voice, "I'm here to say the words of the Master. He calls a spade a spade, and I can't do anything else. Truth can be harsh and sharp. That's the nature of the truth."

"It wakes people up," K.D. interjected. "If a person's not intelligent, they can't understand it any other way."

Sheela went on to say that the reactions she had gotten to her performance on "Nightline" had been entirely favorable, and besides, Ted Koppel had decided to put Niren on the show the next night to debate the INS case because she acted as she did. "All publicity is good publicity," she said, "and I can get it for free. Not even the governor can do that!" She paused and then added in a harsh tone of voice, "Donkeys can only understand a kick. The Antelopians are your average day-to-day bigots. Their brains are in the fifteenth century."

The insults were not, then, spontaneous—or authentic expressions of Sheela's personality. They were calculated. But what was the calculation? To know Sheela at all was to know that she could not be operating out of some fuzzy Western-style philosophy about the death of politics and the birth of the New Man. (This was K.D.'s Maslovian province.) Sheela said she wanted to attract publicity, and clearly she succeeded a good bit of the time, for better or worse. But the harassment of Gerhardt and Greenfield was no publicity stunt, and many of Sheela's outbursts were heard only in Wasco and Jefferson counties. The explanation now current among county officials and ranchers was that the Rajneeshee were quite deliberately making enemies for the sake of their own internal cohesion.

The explanation was a plausible one. There were antagonisms within the commune, and by stifling dissent the Rajneeshee leaders were causing them to build up in silence. They needed an enemy, and the neighboring ranchers and the people of Antelope could not do serious physical damage to the commune even if they wanted to. Yet, isolated as they were, it was easy to persuade sannyasins to believe they lived in the midst of a wilderness populated only by rednecks with guns. (Some sannyasins told me this; others said they felt like blacks in the South—apparently meaning it.) Possibly all the New Man notions they had developed were merely rationalizations for this requirement. Still the whole world of illusion the Western leaders lived in seemed more complicated than that.

Sheela had told me that her outrageousness made for good publicity. She also told me that she was doing the bidding of Bhagwan himself. And there was some evidence that this was the case. Circulating around opposition circles in Oregon at the time were two documents purporting to be the minutes of two coordinators' meetings, one dated November 1982, and one January 1983. The documents sounded authentic and were later authenticated by two sannyasins present at the meetings. One ended with the directive, "Please shred these notes immediately after use," and both contained reports of discussions a good deal more sensitive than the one I had listened to, and apparently among a far smaller group of people. Both memos indicated that there was dissension with the commune, and both reported the gist of conversations Sheela and others had had with the guru. One entry in the November minutes, for example, read:

> Bhagwan said not to worry about why people left, focus attention on work here. He doesn't want to speak again but if money becomes too difficult, He would do. He wants to attract people who can sit silently and also enjoy the work.

An entry in the January minutes read: "Sheela was on CBS Eyewitness News. Bhagwan was very pleased she is so feisty. 'It's all bullshit.' "

The guru had apparently liked that word. Then, in the first set of minutes there was a report of the commune's dealings with Bob Davis. In a meeting with Sheela, Isabel, K.D., and Niren, Davis had complained that the Rajneeshee were not taking his advice—that the guru's teachings always took precedence over political or legal counsel. Niren had taken Davis's side, Isabel had remained silent, and K.D. had supported Sheela against Davis. Later Davis had told Jayananda (Sheela's current American husband) that he would like to meet him privately but that he would not deal with Sheela or K.D. The meeting apparently did not take place. According to the minutes, "Sheela and Bhagwan explained the trap involved . . . Bhagwan called Jay and Isabel to tell them that we have to be 100% supportive and because we are a minority we have to be very assertive and very together to survive." The guru, in other words, had been responsible for undercutting Davis's excellent political advice against the better judgment of Jay and Niren.

That the guru himself was directly responsible for the policy of provocation made a great deal of sense. Rajneesh, after all, had made a career out of outrageousness. As an assistant professor at an obscure university, he had drawn crowds in cities across India by attacking Gandhi, socialism, and orthodox Hinduism—just to provoke. Later he became the outrageous guru who attacked Pope John Paul II, Mother Theresa, and Moraji Desai. It had been a great success. Westerners had poured in and laughed at his anti-Catholic jokes, his anti-Semitic jokes, his anti-Hindu jokes, and his dirty jokes. He made his listeners feel that they belonged to an elite of truly freethinkers who saw beyond the superstitions and pathetic social props of everyone else's existence. Instinctively, perhaps, Rajneesh understood the sociology of in-groups and out-groups: He had talked about the provocation that people wearing red clothes and malas were to everyone else. At the same time there seemed to be another purpose to his provocations.

In the set of minutes wherein it was reported that the guru congratulated Sheela for her "feistiness," there was an entry a little farther down which read:

> He said we are not politicians so we don't need to please people for their votes. If we are silent, e.g. on TV when negative people are speaking against us, it gives false impression, we should show them where they are coming from but not be angry only assertive. He spoke about Pontius Pilate's wife persuading Pontius to listen to Jesus and he tried to advise Jesus how to be tactful, but Jesus would not compromise. We should not compromise but remain authentic to ourselves. We have nothing to lose, we have lost it anyway. "Life is such a little thing, so short anyway . . ."

The story was not reassuring considering what happened to Jesus when he refused to compromise. But it was vintage Rajneesh. In Poona, Rajneesh had lectured on so many occasions on the martyrdom of Jesus and Socrates and had added more than once that his disciples would surely serve him better than Jesus' disciples had served their master. Martyrdom and persecution were constant themes with him. When he settled in Bombay and revealed that he had been Enlightened twenty years before, he told a disciple that the reason he had not revealed this up until now was that in all his years of traveling he could very easily have been killed by "the stupid mob." At the same time he revealed that his last incarnation had been as a great sage seven hundred years ago; the reason that he had not at that time escaped the great chain of being into Buddhahood was that he had ordered a disciple to kill him just three days before his appointed death in order to be able to return in the twentieth century. In Poona, just before leaving for the United States, Rajneesh told an audience that he would take the risk of exposing orthodox Hinduism (hardly an original risk with him) because "the most they can do is kill me." The year before a Hindu had made a run at him with a knife in the middle of a lecture, but the guards had tackled and disarmed the man before he got to the front of the lecture hall. The ashram press release on the incident had read in part:

> Today in Buddha Hall the history of assassination, abuse and hostility which has been India's reaction to all its great mystics and seers repeated itself. These are the people who stoned Buddha, tortured Mahivira and who now wish to silence Bhagwan . . .

This reading of Indian history, a history in which thousands of great mystics, including the Buddha, had died quite peacefully of old age, recalled Sheela's reading of Oregon history.

In the last few weeks before Rajneesh left Poona for the United States, there was, according to his biographer, an alarming increase in the number of threatening letters and phone calls to the ashram. Most of the threats were apparently anonymous, but, according to an ashram press release, one was signed "The Roman Catholics of Bombay and Poona." Three days before Sheela put the guru on the plane, a fire broke out in the castle that Laxmi had leased for the "new commune" outside of town. The next day arson destroyed a Rajneeshee book storage warehouse, and at the same time an explosive device was detonated at the ashram's medical center. No one was hurt in these incidents. The Indian police never discovered who or what caused the fires. The company that insured the warehouse later sued the Rajneeshee for insurance fraud and in the end paid only a minimal sum.

The guru had predicted acts of violence against himself and his disciples. This took no great prescience since he himself had done his best to provoke them. To be noted, however, was that the acts of violence (including the ineffectual assassination attempt) did little damage to the ashram or any of its inhabitants. Possibly the Rajneeshee had set the fires themselves to collect insurance. In any event, what caused far more trouble than any violence was the alienation of the Poona citizenry and the Indian government—resulting, as it did, in a denial of the tax-exempt status for the ashram and the government's refusal to give the necessary permissions for the building of the "new commune." In the fall of 1983 this pattern seemed to be repeating itself in Oregon. Sheela, K.D., and others were doing what they could to provoke violence from their neighbors, and it was not altogether out of the question that some hothead would start a fire on Rajneeshee property or take a potshot at someone. But the real damage they were doing was political. The constant prodding and poking of the Antelope people were creating ripples of hostility across the state; it was turning the politicians and bureaucrats against them and slowly strangling the commune in litigation. With all the great ambitions the Rajneeshee had for their commune, they seemed quite unconscious of this banal form of danger: what they saw was merely the mythopoetic world the guru had created around them.

By the winter of 1983–84 many Rajneeshee watchers in Oregon believed that some form of denouement was now inevitable. The Rajneeshee lawyers were still quite masterfully holding back all the legal challenges to the commune's existence, but there were a great many forces arrayed against them, and the Rajneeshee leaders seemed bent on a course of conflict. Considering the guru's interest in martyrdom, a number of Rajneeshee watchers, including some Madras residents and former sannyasins, now feared the worst: when the Rajneeshee leaders found themselves wholly frustrated, they would create a violent confrontation and ask their disciples to give up their lives for the commune. To other people, including myself, a Jonestown-style denouement seemed quite unlikely. It would, I thought, be out of character for the Rajneeshee. In the first place, the guru was a survivor—that was his life story, his drama; while he continued to flirt rhetorically with martyrdom, he also continued to accumulate Rolls-Royces (there were now sixty or seventy in the garages around his house), diamond watches, and other consolation prizes for remaining on earth. Sheela, for her part, spent a great deal of time raising money for these and other extravagances; no one knew where the money went or even how much of it there was, but Sheela, like Madame Nhu and the other great iron butterflies of Asia, seemed to me a practical person when it came to money and personal survival. Also she had a non-Rajneeshee brother in the United States—a financier of some undefined sort, whose very existence she kept a secret. Finally the Rajneeshee sannyasins as a group did not seem to me the best candidates for self-immolation. They did not, after all, suffer from guilt or the lack of a sense of self-worth; their affliction was rather a sense of superiority, and, certainly, they overestimated their importance to the world. (Even those who disliked Sheela imagined that her television performances left a strong impression on the whole American public.) If a crisis came, some might be capable of conceiving that they had to fight for the commune, but others, I felt quite strongly, would see a clear alternative in the hot tubs of Mill Valley. On the whole it seemed to me more likely that the denouement would come via the slow, banal processes of politics and the law.

Eight months later, however, I could no longer be confident of this, for the Rajneeshee had made all the preparations for war. Beginning in the spring of 1984, disciples, using their sannyasin or their given names, had gone to arms dealers in cities across the country; by the fall they had, according to *The Oregonian*, amassed an arsenal that included at least twenty-eight semiautomatic weapons—thirteen Uzi carbines and fifteen Galil assault rifles—in addition to rifles and handguns. They had tried to buy automatic weapons on a number of occasions, but the U.S. Bureau of Alcohol, Tobacco and Firearms had prevented the sales from going through—at least when they had tried to buy them legally. Sannyasins also bought hundreds of human silhouette targets for weapons' training and spent $25,000 for ammunition (or more than half what the city of Portland spent in that year). In addition to the Peace Force there were now 150 sannyasin security guards patrolling the ranch—plus two helicopter reconnaissance teams.

There were other ominous signals from the commune. In March the guru announced, via Sheela, that AIDS was the scourge predicted by Nostradamus: the disease would cover the earth, and billions of people would die from it in the next ten years. Only the Rajneeshee commune would be safe from it, for protective measures would be taken. Sannyasins, the guru said, should stop sex altogether, or stay with one partner or take extraordinary precautions. (The following day the commune bought all the prophylactics and rubber gloves immediately available from suppliers in the state of Oregon.) The guru's message was shocking, particularly as it was only the third public statement he had made since coming to Oregon. The first was his prediction of nuclear war; the second was his earthquake alert, which, among other things, brought a number of gay sannyasins from San Francisco to the commune. Rajneeshee spokesmen denied having anyone with AIDS on the commune, but, given the fact that they never admitted to having any serious diseases, it seemed probable that they did. Then, some months later they built a rather elaborate gas-fired crematorium.

Around this time extraordinary stories began to travel around the network of ex-sannyasins in the country. Former sannyasins told me that the Rajneeshee, believing in an imminent holocaust, were stocking caves in the mountains with all the necessities for survival including microchips or computer tapes containing the information required to begin civilization all over again. One woman, who described herself as a former aide to Sheela, told me with some certainty that the commune was involved in a triangle trade of gold, drugs, and arms across the world: the guns and the drugs were hidden in caves, and the whole operation was (she suspected) run from a giant computer installed in Bhagwan's house. Another told me (though not for attribution) that the Rajneeshee had infiltrated the highest levels of the Oregon state government and had blackmailed Oregon politicians with photographs of themselves in compromising positions with Rajneeshee women. Yet another former sannyasin—now one of the group's most outspoken opponents—told me there might be an esoteric death cult in the commune: a sannyasin who had just left the ranch had told him there were rumors of an inner sanctum where the goddess Kali was worshiped and where there had been a human sacrifice.

There was, of course, no evidence for any of this, but with the AIDS alarm, the weapons purchases, and the building of the crematorium, it was now impossible to dismiss any mythopoetic scenario out of hand.

In June the word went out informally along sannyasin networks that the guru might "drop his body"—that is, die—during the Master's Day festival in July. Many outsiders, however, suspected a banal purpose to this, and a year later when *The Oregonian* published its investigative series, they found their suspicions confirmed.

According to *Oregonian* reporters, the European movement had flourished in the first two years after the exodus from Poona. Sannyasins had opened dozens of new centers and started small businesses —restaurants, bookstores, meditation classes, and so on. But beginning in 1982 Sheela and her minions—Arup, Sushila, and others— made a concerted effort to rationalize these centers and bring them under the control of the ranch. They ordered the small centers closed and insisted that all sannyasins live together in large communes in the major cities. They then required these large communes to start ambitious new businesses with their own capital—the Rajneeshee financial organizations accepting their profits but not the losses or the debts. While denying that the ranch had any control over the communes, they insisted on the standardization of logos, restaurant food, therapies, and so on. "All the communes are patterned alike," Rajhneesh said at one point, " . . . exactly patterned like the commune here." Finally, of course, the communes were required to contribute heavily to the ranch in Oregon. These measures, combined with the high-handed manner of "the duchesses" (as Sheela and the others were now called), did not sit well with the Europeans. A number of the therapists had become quite successful in their own right, and they assumed they had a direct, personal relationship with the guru. Most ordinary sannyasins could not or would not move to the large communes. And a good deal of the business advice turned out to be bad. The result was turmoil in the movement. Some of the therapists refused to close their centers and were "excommunicated" by Sheela; others obeyed orders but then lost their own followings. A number of the large communes had business failures. Indeed, the very month *Der Spiegel* did its story on the Rajneeshee, some of the discos failed; as for the "chain of hotels," it never materialized. Then, with the small centers closed, the Rajneeshee had lost their most effective recruitment centers, and the numbers of new people dropped off. The leaders had, in other words, managed in an excess of tidiness to cut off the roots and branches of the movement.

Rajneeshee financial statements for 1981–83 showed a total of $20 million in gifts to the foundation and the commune, but in sharply decreasing amounts. The foundation, for example, received $5.1 million in 1981 and only $1.3 million in 1983. (What these sums represented in terms of the total of Rajneeshee funds was not at all clear, but the relative decline was nonetheless significant.) The decrease in contributions would not, of course, have mattered if the ranch businesses had grown increasingly successful, but this was not the case. In the spring of 1984 the leaders seemed to have anticipated that the Master's Day festival would bring fewer people than it had the year before. It was at the point that word went out that the guru might "drop his body."

In the event, however, the guru made no move to shed his earthly coil, and the festival went off without incident—except that Sheela, packing a Smith and Wesson revolver, managed to terrify a number of reporters. Then, too, in spite of the fact that no good sannyasin would have wished to miss the guru's moment of passage, there were noticeably fewer people at the festival than there had been the year before. In the weeks following, ranch personnel wrote or telephoned every American sannyasin and every American who had ever stayed at the ranch to offer a six weeks' to three months' stay at Rajneeshpuram at very reduced rates—indeed, virtually free of charge. But very few people came. "We opened the ranch to all in the United States, and nobody came," Satya Bharti told me later. "Bhagwan does not seem to attract so many Americans these days." At the time, however, the very small number of American arrivals must have surprised the ranch managers, for they had, as it turned out, big plans.

At the end of August the Rajneeshee announced that they were collecting homeless people from the big cities across the United States —New York, Los Angeles, Houston, Miami, Chicago, and so on— busing them to the ranch to live there with them. In this their "Share-A-Home program" the homeless would be given free room and board; they would be free to work on the commune if they wanted to and free to leave when they liked; if they left, they would be given bus tickets to the city of their choice. It was, the Rajneeshee said, an experiment in communal living: "We have such abundance here, we want to share it." When journalists remarked that altruism ran counter to the usual philosophy of the commune, Isabel said, "We don't have at all the traditional approach to charity. We are sharing something we have—a beautiful life-style, a beautiful environment." By September 6 there were, according to the Rajneeshee, six hundred homeless people on the ranch; by October 1 there were two thousand by their count, and by this time many Oregonians were quite beside themselves.

According to reporters—now flocking into the ranch from all over the country—the "homeless" included derelicts, people down on their luck, curiosity seekers, hitchhikers who had run out of money, drunks, bums, petty criminals (or former petty criminals), and street hustlers. Many of them were black and all of them were over eighteen (Rajneeshee charity apparently did not extend to homeless families). Out-of-state reporters could not but see some comedy in the spectacle of hundreds of street people suddenly and mysteriously delivered into cowboy country to join a lot of Human Potential Movement therapists and an Indian with seventy-odd Rolls-Royces. Central Oregonians were, however, not amused. They were not, to begin with, keen on having such new neighbors, and after that came the question of what the Rajneeshee intended to do with them. The commune had an arsenal of weapons, and many of the "homeless" were tough-looking young men. Would they be given terrorist training? Drugged into zombies? Or simply let loose on the streets of Madras with knives? The darkest suspicions abounded. On September 26 the state attorney general's office called a meeting of some forty top-ranking police, military, and civilian officials in the state. Officials refused even to say what agencies were represented at the meeting—much less what was discussed. They did, however, set up an information hot line for rumor control.

In fact the dominant view in Oregon was that the Rajneeshee were importing the street people as voters and planning to take over Wasco County in the November election. The theory was not so farfetched, as two of the three seats on the Wasco County Commission would be on the ballot November 6, and the relationship between the Rajneeshee and Wasco County had turned ugly. In recent months the commissioners had, among other things, voted to repeal Rajneesh-puram's comprehensive plan, delayed the festival permit, and denied tax-exempt status to Rajneesh Mandir—the greenhouse-turned-reli-gious-meeting hall. The Rajneeshee, for their part, had changed the name of their second "city" from Antelope to Rajneesh. The county planner, Dan Durow, had tried to visit Rajneeshpuram twice, but both times had found Rajneeshee vehicles blocking the roads. Then in the first week of September three county commissioners had visited the city and two of them had become ill. The chairman of the commis-sion, Judge William Hulse, later testified that the three of them had toured the ranch in a Rajneeshee car and returned to the visitors' center to find his car with a flat tire. During a long wait while the tire was changed, Sheela had offered the three men glasses of water; the glasses had been brought out by the woman who was the head of the Rajneeshee medical services. They had drunk the water, and later Hulse (who had taken the strongest line against the Rajneeshee) went to the hospital and nearly died of toxic poisoning; the second commis-sioner was slightly ill and the third unaffected. A week later there was a large and mysterious outbreak of salmonella poisoning in The Dalles, the main population center and seat of Wasco County. The infection, it was discovered, came from the salad bars of eight sepa-rate restaurants, but it could not, as is normal in such cases, be traced to a single food source or a single group of food handlers. About seven hundred people were taken ill with the salmonella, and because of Hulse's experience, many people believed the Rajneeshee had poi-soned them.

The Rajneeshee indignantly denied that they had imported the street people for the election and, of course, the suggestion about the poisoning: their only desire, they said, was to share their wealth and "inspire a life of dignity with love and respect." They added, how-ever, that the people in their Share-A-Home program might vote in the election, as was their constitutional right. The announcement had a marvelous effect on citizenship in Wasco County: it inspired 2000 non-Rajneeshee to get out and register, bringing the voting rolls from 12,000 to 14,000 (of which about 900 were previously registered Rajneeshee). It also inspired a fundamentalist group from Albany, Oregon, to threaten to bring 1000 people from around the state to vote in the Wasco County election. On October 5 Sheela announced that the Rajneeshee were putting up two write-in candidates for the Wasco County Commission; two days later a ranch spokesman said that there were now 7000 people in Rajneeshpuram, including 1500 residents, 1500 paying guests, and 4000 in the Share-A-Home program. Apparently it was Antelope all over again but on a much larger scale. This time, however, Norma Paulus, the Oregon secretary of state, was prepared. On October 10 she brought voter registration in Wasco County to a halt and later set up a special hearing process for all prospective voters: fifty lawyers would interview all those wishing to register at mass hearings in The Dalles and would make their own subjective judgment about each applicant's intent to reside in Wasco County. The Rajneeshee protested the order and took it to court, but there the order was upheld.

On October 17, the last day newcomers to the county could sign up to vote in the county elections, the Rajneeshee were dispatching aircraft—three DC3s and two Convairs—to nearby states to bring in sannyasins. The next day Isabel announced that the Share-A-Home program had reached capacity and that the recruitment of street people had stopped. By October 21, Sue Proffitt, the Wasco County clerk, had received 3000 voter registration cards from Rajneeshpuram—all of them since October 10—and more of them were coming in daily. She was also, she said, receiving fraudulent voting cards in the names of non-Rajneeshee citizens. She knew they were fraudulent, she said, because she knew some of the names, and they belonged to people who had already registered with different addresses, or they belonged to people who had died. Around the same time Wayne Fawbush, the county representative to the state legislature, and another Rajneeshee opponent up for election discovered that fraudulent letters were going out under their signatures.

But then on October 26, a Rajneeshee city official announced that she was going to urge all Rajneeshee to boycott the county election. Rajneeshee spokespeople had been complaining ever since the Paullus order came down that it was unjust for their prospective voters to have to go all the way to The Dalles; now the mayor, Krishna Deva, said that the city lacked the transport to bring all of their people to the hearings. On November 1 and 2, the dates of the scheduled hearings, fifty volunteer lawyers sat idly in The Dalles armory: the street people never showed up. The Rajneeshee entered poll book challenges against the 2000 new Wasco County voters and warned that a contested election might result. Later, however, they called off the challenges, and on November 6 most of their registered voters voted only for their own municipal offices. Ten days later a spokesman said that about half of the street people had left Rajneeshpuram and only 2000 remained.

The Rajneeshee, it appeared, had made an extraordinary series of miscalculations. In the first place, they never came close to having enough voters to win. Even if the non-Rajneeshee had split their votes evenly between the two non-Rajneeshee candidates for each job (an extremely unlikely event if a Rajneeshee were in the race), they would have to have had over 7000 votes in order to win. On October 10 they claimed to have 7000 people on the ranch, but, according to observers, they had nowhere near that many. They had, after all, very few paying guests, and though they had bused a total of 4200 street people to the ranch, some of the homeless left just a week after the first bus pulled in, and after that there was a steady exodus of them. Only 3000 people signed voting cards—and some of these people had left by the end of October. In fact the Rajneeshee could have only hoped to win by fraud: by overwhelming the Wasco County system with a mass of new registrations just before the election, by casting votes in the name of street people who had already left (or who did not exist), and by putting enough fradulent voter cards in the system so as to contest all the new Wasco County voters successfully. Norma Paulus had most efficiently prevented any of this from happening. But had she not taken action, Wasco County officials surely would have. That the Rajneeshee leaders had somehow imagined that the county and the state would let them get away with rigging an election showed just how far they had gone into their own world of illusion.

What happened to all of the street people no outsider precisely knew. Some of those who talked to reporters said they had had a good time in Rajneeshpuram: they had free room and board, people were nice, it was a change of scene. Others—clearly—couldn't stand the wide-open spaces. Still others objected to the regimentation: they had been searched, given medical tests, and there were guards everywhere with guns. Some thought they had landed up in some kind of Jonestown and that the Rajneeshee were putting drugs in their food. The last was quite probably true. In the first place, the Rajneeshee had in their charge a number of alcoholics, some people who were not right in the head, and some who might well have become violent. In the second place, the Oregon Board of Medical Examiners discovered that the Rajneeshee had bought large quantities of Haldol—a colorless, odorless, and tasteless tranquilizer. In the third place, there was one known casualty of the experience: a man found dead in front of a tavern in a central Oregon town with a good deal of alcohol in his blood and an antidepressant the Rajneeshee admitted he had received in Rajneeshpuram. Whether this was the only casualty it was impossible to say for certain, as only the Rajneeshee knew the names of all the street people and how many there were. In the beginning they had offered round-trip tickets to the ranch, but so many people left after a week or so that, after September 23 they offered only a one-way ticket. Thus, when the newer recruits insisted on leaving, they simply bused them off the ranch and dumped them in some Oregon town. Oregonians protested mightily, and Curtis Sliwa, the head of the Guardian Angels, came all the way from New York to demonstrate against the Rajneeshee—but to no avail. Street people—the very people many Oregonians lived in Oregon to avoid—kept turning up in Madras, Portland, and The Dalles, often without money or winter clothes. Churches helped them, and the Salvation Army spent a hundred thousand dollars to feed them and give them bus tickets back home. In February, Siddha, the therapist, said that eight to nine hundred remained on the ranch, but outsiders estimated that there were two hundred or fewer.

For the Rajneeshee this whole extraordinary enterprise was very expensive. According to their spokespeople, it cost a million dollars. Whether the figure was accurate or not, it cost a great deal of money they could ill afford to lose at this juncture, and it spurred a great many people to take action against them. The two major cases against them—the land-use case and the church-state case—were still in litigation; the INS ruling was still pending; and a number of old grievance cases were still in the works. But now there were a number of new suits against them. Margaret Hill, her son, and the woman whose husband had died in a hunting accident had brought suit against Sheela for her behavior in the school board meeting. A lawyer representing seven street people sued the Rajneeshee, claiming fraud, coercion, physcial abuse, and theft. A former Rajneeshee had brought suit claiming that she was deceived into giving the group $310,000 in Poona—and a local judge had awarded her $1.7 million in damages. The list went on. And the legal problems for the Rajneeshee were now compounded by the fact that it was hard to find twelve jurors unbiased against them anywhere in the state. A study their legal services had commissioned from a Portland research group showed that over two-thirds of the people in four counties believed that the Rajneeshee were using the legal system unfairly and would lie to further their own interests; only 30 percent of those surveyed believed the Rajneeshee "were not hurting anyone and should be left alone."

Oregon politicians and officials were now under heavy pressure to do something about the Rajneeshee, and the politicians who represented central Oregon had strong feelings of their own. U.S. Congressman Jim Weaver and two of his colleagues held hearings on the Rajneeshee use of the federal land in and around the ranch and made as much trouble as they could on this score. Wayne Fawbush and Bill Bellamy, the local representatives to the state legislature, introduced three separate bills aimed at the Rajneeshee, and Fawbush started a petition drive to put a measure on the ballot that would repeal the charter of Rajneesh City on the grounds that it violated the separation of church and state. Around the same time the state superintendent of schools, Verne Duncan, noted (for the first time) that the work-study program in the Rajneeshee school put public-school children to work in religious organizations, and he threatened to cut off state aid to the school. The Rajneeshee protested but finally dismantled the program. Then the county planner, Dan Durow, finally gaining access to Rajneeshpuram, took a look at the 640 structures the Rajneeshee called "winterized tents" and decided they were permanent structures built without permits. The state then issued fines totaling $1.4 million for violations of the electrical code, and while the fines were eventually reduced in court, the Rajneeshee had to dismantle the structures. Meanwhile a fire broke out in the offices of the county planning department, destroying a third to a half of the county records; The Dalles police believed it was arson, as file drawers were open and records had been vandalized before the fire broke out.

On June 21, 1985, the Rajneeshee filed a suit alleging that state and county officials had conspired in an attempt to drive them out of Oregon; they named the governor, the attorney general, a number of Wasco County officials, Henry R. Richmond, executive director of 1000 Friends, and others as defendants. This suit was, however, eclipsed by another they brought against the U.S. attorney general, Edwin Meese, Secretary of State George Schultz, and the State Department, the U.S. Immigration and Naturalization Service, its commissioner Alan C. Nelson, and eight other INS officials, accusing them of engaging in a "program of unlawful and intrusive monitoring" and surveillance which violated their constitutional rights. This second suit—which the Rajneeshee nicknamed "God versus the Universe"—was clearly a preemptive strike against the INS proceedings against them. Sheela claimed to have information that a grand jury indictment was coming down and she and the guru would be arrested. But no ruling came down and no arrests were made.

"God" was by this time speaking in public again—just as he had promised he would "if the money were needed." He had begun giving lectures to small groups of sannyasins the previous fall (lectures that were videotaped and shown to the ranch population the day after). His first lecture was on October 30—just days after the Rajneeshee decided to boycott the election and give up on the Share-A-Home program. The guru lectured to small groups for the next eight months, and then, on June 30, just before the Master's Day festival, he began giving public lectures in the two-acre meeting hall. Asked why he had resumed lecturing, he said that he had stopped in order to create a hiatus in his own work and to get rid of a lot of people who had been hanging around him just for his words. But if that had been his purpose, he had apparently succeeded all too well, for the festival that year drew far fewer people than had come the year before. By all accounts, the European movement was now in disastrous decline: the two large communes in England had closed, so had the centers in France, Italy, and Scandinavia, and now there were only nine communes left—one in Amsterdam, one in Zurich, and the rest in West Germany. When the festival was over, Rajneesh held a press conference—the first of his career—and thereafter granted an interview to virtually any journalist who put in a request.

By the end of August 1985, when I visited the ranch once again, the decline in the fortunes of the Rajneeshee had become visible, obvious. A huge and extremely ugly prefab man camp the Rajneeshee had bought from a defunct mining company now dominated Antelope— or Rajneesh city. But the complex had not been finished, and a row of bulldozers lay idle, and apparently abandoned, in a gash of red earth in front of it. In Rajneeshpuram there were many more buildings than there had been two years before—a hotel, a visitors' center, a two-story mall—but most of these had been under construction or in the advanced planning stages at the time. No new building was going on and there was no new acreage under cultivation. The creek beds and farmlands looked lush and green, but the landscaping around the town remained minimal (rows of trees that had been planted that year just in time for the summer festival had predictably died of the heat) and the horses had gone. The town itself looked empty and motionless by comparison to two years before. The hotel was almost empty, the lake deserted, and the visitors' center had very few visitors: a few family members and a few journalists come to interview the guru. For most of the day the town was as quiet as any other small Oregon town. Isabel told me that there were about forty-five hundred people on the ranch, but this simply could not have been true. Counting heads in the cafeteria and at the guru's lectures (which most people on the ranch attended every other day), I estimated that the population could not be over two thousand.

The atmosphere in this half-ghost town had become decidedly spooky. In the first place, there were security guards all over the place, and the restrictions on visitors were like those of a federal prison. From the entrance of the ranch to the reception center, there were five guard posts, each staffed by two Rajneeshee in uniform. At the reception center there were more uniformed guards with guard dogs to search all comers. Visitors were now asked to sign three separate regulations forms before being given an identification bracelet. Visitors, I discovered, could drive on the county roads, go to their lodgings, and walk around the mall at the center of town unaccompanied, but virtually everything else on the ranch was off limits to them. Security guards posted by the roads and in front of buildings would stop you if you went off course. The only hiking trail open was a short one that led around the lake and past the crematorium; visitors had to check in at the reception center before and after taking this walk. Then, too, there seemed to be places that even resident sannyasins were forbidden to go. Beyond the farm—which I visited with Isabel—there was a NO HIKING sign on the path where I had once walked along the John Day River. All of this created a sense of constriction and threat—a feeling mightily strengthened by the fact that the guards and ranch managers could not, or would not, explain the reasons for the particular barriers and roadblocks. Taking a stroll one evening, I was stopped a few hundred yards from the hotel by a guard who told me I could not go into an area where sannyasins were planting shrubs since that was a "worship site"; she said she really didn't know the reason for the regulation but perhaps it was to prevent visitors from disturbing sannyasins. Isabel pleaded ignorance about the NO HIKING sign, and Wadud told me he had no idea of the reasons for particular regulations. Wadud, however, said that security at the ranch was very important—far more important than the convenience of visitors. He said that his life had been threatened in The Dalles and that the security measures were alone responsible for the fact that Bhagwan was still alive today and the commune intact. The paranoia in the air persuaded me not to say very much over the telephone and to interview lower-level sannyasins only outside the hotel. What I could not decide was whether the Rajneeshee leaders had something to hide or whether they had created this atmosphere for mythopoetic purposes alone.

Along with the security restrictions a miasma of secrecy and prevarication had risen up thick through the commune. Ranch managers would tell me that their production had doubled in two years—and then give me the same figures they had given me two years before. Their estimates of net worth in Oregon had always been inflated, but now they were four times the figure that appeared on their last financial statement to the Internal Revenue Service. One of the Twinkies told me that over four hundred street people remained on the ranch; two ordinary sannyasins told me there might be a hundred; I saw only a handful I could recognize as such. (On the farm Neehar pointed out three young black men working on the farm machinery —apparently with enthusiasm.) So it went with most matters of fact on the commune. In some cases there were three or four different answers to the same question, and in some cases none. Wadud lied to me about a matter of public record—a lawsuit he was being deposed for—when he thought I knew nothing about the issue. The Twinkies would evade factual questions or contradict the evidence before one's eyes. It was disconcerting, particularly as in many cases it was difficult to figure out why they went to the trouble. Ordinary sannyasins sometimes gave me more plausible answers to questions of fact than the Twinkies or ranch managers did. But often they would plead ignorance or recite the general line the Twinkies gave me with great earnestness and all the appearance of sincerity. About half of those I had seen before, including Siddha and another therapist, had left the commune.

Another strange thing about the commune was the series of measures it had adopted to prevent the spread of AIDS. Since the guru's announcement about it the year before, the commune had been supplying condoms and rubber gloves along with the toothpaste. More recently, however, Ma Anand Puja, the former medical coordinator, now the secretary-treasurer of the Rajneesh Medical Corporation, had drawn up a long list of rules for AIDS prevention covering not just sex but eating, drinking, swimming, and other activities. All sannyasins, for example, now had to wash their hands with alcohol before going into the food line; they were not to share food, drink, or cigarettes, and if they were sharing a candy bar, they had to break it with the wrapper on. If they used a public restroom, they were to take a small bottle of alcohol and wash the faucets, the toilet seat, and the doorknobs. They were to clean telephone mouthpieces with alcohol and to shower before swimming in the lake. They were not to lick envelopes, lick their fingers to turn the pages of books or newspapers, or lick threads when threading a needle. Dentists on the ranch had to wear gowns, masks, gloves, and "protective eyewear," and large electric bug killers had been put outside the residential buildings in case mosquitoes could transmit the AIDS virus. Now each bathroom had a regular wastebasket and plastic-lined basket marked CONTAMI-NATED WASTES into which residents were to put everything touched by their bodily fluids, including cigarettes and gum.

The Rajneeshee were, of course, quite right to take precautions against AIDS. In a small, sexually active community such as theirs, the disease, once introduced, could actually wipe out the population. They would have been right to follow the recommendations of AIDS experts—and then take some further precautions for good measure, as there were still a few medical uncertainties about the transmission of the disease. But the regulations Puja had drawn up—and which they were now observing—were clearly excessive. Not only did they go far beyond anything recommended by public health authorities, but some of them, such as the injunction not to lick thread, did not involve the exchange of bodily fluids at all. This was not for lack of expertise or information. The Rajneeshee doctors had clearly read all the AIDS literature available, for they published the most current information week by week in the *Rajneesh Times*.

Wondering about the reasons for these measures, I remembered that the commune had always been fairly compulsive about cleanliness—or, alternately, about the disposal of its wastes. From the beginning it had sorted its garbage into five categories—compost, recyclable paper, recyclable cans, glass and trash. That had seemed sound environmentalism, and it still did. But now there were new measures. Videh, who had been worrying about the pollutant effect of detergents when I was last here, was now worrying about the minute amount of chemicals (bleach, photographers' development solution, and so on) that the commune had accumulated. Taking me on a tour of his impeccably clean farm buildings, Neehar told me that sannyasins now cleaned up the manure in the cow barns every few hours. Neither Videh's concerns nor Neehar's measures seemed wholly irrational in themselves, but when seen in the light of the AIDS prevention measures, they suggested that the commune had become obsessed by pollution—obsessed by what happened to its bodily fluids and wastes. Then, too, this concern about pollution had a metaphorical analogue in the (clearly excessive) security measures and restrictions—and in the attempt by Sheela and others to consolidate and regulate the European communes. The impulse in each case was to control, and the concern in each case was for purity. What seemed most extraordinary about all of this was that in Poona the commune had been just the opposite. There the Rajneeshee had celebrated spontaneity, sexual abandon, "openness," nakedness, chaos, and a "dissolving" or "melting" of the individual into the group. But in Oregon the commune had clenched up like a muscle, to become rigid, controlling, and compulsive. Possibly, I thought, its concern for purity was a reaction to the disorder and impurity of its past in India. But possibly it was a clenching up in fear of losing its own membership, its own substance.

Then, too, another tendency in the commune had developed mightily in two years: in ceremony, costume, and hierarchy, the religious organization had become elaborate, baroque. The degrees and titles awarded to the leaders had, for example, multiplied four times over. Sheela was now formally known as Bodhisattva Ma Anand Sheela, M.M., D.Phil.M., D.Litt, M. (RIMU), Acharya. One of the editors of the guru's lectures was called Sambodhi Ma Prem Maneesha, S.R.N., S.R.M., R.M.N., M.M., D.Phil.M. (RIMU), Acharya. Just as before, Rajen told me that the titles and the degrees from Rajneesh International University meant nothing to him—they were for newcomers. But now there were no newcomers; the university, the meditation and therapy center, was almost empty the day I went to see him. As before, Rajen could not, or would not, tell me who had invented all these titles. But Sheela seemed to me a likely candidate. For a year or so now Sheela had been dressing for special occasions— such as press conferences—in long red robes with the Rajneeshee symbol embroidered on the front, a mala with pearl or diamond beads, and an embroidered scarf on her head. It was papal raiment. But then for a year or more the guru himself had been dressed up like a Christmas tree. In Poona he had worn plain white. Here he wore woolen caps shaped like crowns, diamond watches, and glittering, floor-length robes. He had always liked a little theater, but now he went in for pageantry. When he drove the few hundred yards from his house to the lecture hall or the half mile to Sheela's compound for a press interview, his Rolls-Royce (now a stretch limousine, chauffer-driven) would be accompanied not only by guard cars but by two helicopters—the racket of them quite enormous in the narrow canyons. In the lecture hall he sat flanked by four guards, two of them with Uzis at the ready, with four more guards on a catwalk overhead raking the audience with their binoculars. When he went to a press interview a small crowd of sannyasins would be standing in front of Sheela's compound clapping, singing, and waiting to throw rose petals in his path. Two and a half hours later the crowd would still be there to applaud the conclusion of the interview and to throw more rose petals. The performance was a cross between Oscar night and the evening out of a Latin American dictator.

To listen to Rajneesh lecture, however, was to understand some of his attraction for his disciples. He was—in a way that could not be appreciated on videotape—a brilliant lecturer. He spoke slowly—the right pace for a lecture hall—and every sentence was well-formed. His large eyes were expressive, but as he moved hardly at all, the words seemed to come from the interior, from somewhere beneath the long gray beard that descended his chest. The gist of his lectures was familiar to me from his books, but what I had not gathered from reading the lectures was his talent as a comedian. The jokes sounded better than they read, for his timing was perfect, but far better were the comic riffs he would go off into once or twice in a lecture—the little experiments in the language and the play of associations. Also Rajneesh was a world-class hypnotist. One of his lectures ended with a description of a dewdrop sliding off a lotus leaf and being carried down a stream to the ocean. It put virtually everyone in his audience into an alpha-wave state at ten in the morning. But Rajneesh's talents as a speaker did not come across in his television interviews. He needed the long form to draw the audience into his world, and on television his eyes seemed large and protuberant as the eyes of fish from hundreds of feet down. What was more he seemed to be trying too hard in the interviews. He would speak ill of Jesus, talk about his own past sex life, make funny faces—anything to entertain or to shock. It was, in fact, buffoonery, and it made some reporters feel they were being used. Isabel, of course, thought the interviews wonderful; she thought Rajneesh was attracting favorable attention—which in turn would attract people to the ranch. But if this was the purpose of his giving interviews, then the results were not appreciable two months after he had begun.

Possibly the day for gurus—or gurus of this sort—had passed. Wadud said as much. He said that people were not now drawn to the Buddhafield for spiritual reasons as they did not understand the master-disciple relationship. His plan was therefore to create programs for alcoholics, drug abusers, and others in need of healing to attract people to the religion. This seemed to me something of a last resort. According to a new survey done by the psychology professors from the University of Oregon, the average age of sannyasins at the ranch was now thirty-seven. The Rajneeshee had thus simply grown older —and they had lost a good many of their number.

In two years the commune leaders had done many things which ordinary sannyasins might have construed as contradictory, stupid, vicious, or nuts. Those who had left had doubtless construed them as such. But those who remained denied the existence of what could be denied (as the attempt to rig the Wasco County election), and for the rest they used the magic formula the guru had given them—the formula that would turn wrong into right and evil into good. In the past I had suspected that this formula was simply a trick that would not work when put to any real test. But now it was clear that for many it had worked. On the subject of the security measures, for example, the ordinary sannyasins I spoke with told me that they actually liked having the guards around as they helped them come to terms with their own true feelings about policemen, guns, and violence. It was, one said, the kind of device Gurdjieff might use: that is, one that was particularly appropriate to a place where there were no police and no acts of violence. Ma Prem Nura, who had been a schoolteacher in Salem, told me that her husband was a security guard and happy to be one since it taught him to become aware of things. When I asked her why he did not become a policeman in the outside world if he liked that kind of thing, she said that this was different from becoming a policeman: it was becoming a policeman on another level of consciousness.

Sannyasins used a similar variety of reasoning to explain the virtues of the Share-A-Home program. The former Marxist historian from New York I had met on my first trip said, "At first I didn't know what the idea was. The mall at the center of town looked like Forty-second Street—everyone hanging about with ghetto blasters. But then I thought it was really beautiful: it was pushing a lot of buttons, shaking us up. A lot of liberal shit came out . . . you know, people thinking that because someone was black he or she could do no wrong. It was a wonderful way for us to look at ourselves." As a postscript, the former Marxist added that some of the Share-A-Home people had stayed on (though he didn't know how many) and they were beautiful people.

Rajen, the therapist, had a slightly different version of the same event. He told me that he and a number of the other therapists had led dance and rap groups for some of the street people in the meditation hall. "We tried to help them express themselves. The idea was for them to say what they wanted and to get rid of their defenses and the rest of the garbage they had brought with them."

Garbage! The word leaped out at me. I had forgotten that "getting rid of garbage" or "shit," as the historian put it, was a central concept in the Human Potential Movement. Now everything had been transmuted into it, including the most useful kind of suspicion.

"It was wonderful for me," Rajen went on. "It changed my work— it fine-tuned it. These people were so defensive they would react to the slightest hint of tension in your voice and interpret the slightest flippancy as a put-down. So I had to let go of something in myself. I had to become more loving. The media focused entirely on what happened to *them*. But we focused on what happened to us—and, of course, on those who stayed. The whole experience left us more relaxed, more able to be happy and in love."

Not one sannyasin I spoke with expressed any concern for the street people who had left, or who had been ejected by the commune. A number of people, however, told me how much more relaxed and happy and in love they now were. Niren told me this when I met him for dinner in the restaurant. He had been talking with Krishna Deva in the bar and he seemed very tense; he snapped at me and did not relax until Isabel came and sat down.

While I was there Puja put out a press release saying that the

Rajneeshee medical service was in the process of giving the AIDS test to everyone in the commune, and that so far two people had tested positive for the AIDS virus; the two people, so the release said, had been given separate living quarters on the ranch. This sounded odd to me. I had assumed that if there were any AIDS victims on the ranch, or any HTLV-III carriers, they would have been sent away; the Rajneeshee, after all, never admitted the existence of any serious illness on the ranch—they merely sent the very sick to hospitals elsewhere. Why now were they advertising the AIDS virus? The rumor going around was that the commune would soon announce it was creating an AIDS-care facility for the general public. I asked to see Puja, and a woman appeared at the hotel wearing a sequined cocktail dress in the middle of the afternoon. She was a Filipino by birth, and she had, she told me, a nursing degree. She said the commune had never had an AIDS case, but that two people, a man and a woman, had tested positive for the virus. She said that the two were now totally isolated, visited only by doctors and nurses, and that everything they touched was sterilized. I asked why people who had simply tested positive and might never get the disease would put up with total isolation. She said that the two people were grateful to be taken care of by the commune. When I asked about the rumored announcement, she told me there would be an announcement having something to do with AIDS on September 15, and that it would be an important one.

On Monday, September 16, Rajneesh called a press conference to make an announcement rather different from the one anticipated. He said that Sheela and a dozen other commune leaders, including Puja, had left the commune over the weekend and gone to Europe. Calling them a "gang of fascists," he charged them with attempting to poison his doctor, his dentist, his female companion as well as the Jefferson County district attorney and the water system in The Dalles. He also said that Sheela had mismanaged the commune finances, stolen money, and left the commune $55 million in debt. The next day and then later on in the week, he added a number of new charges to the list: Sheela and her gang had robbed and set fire to the Wasco County planning office and had planned to crash an explosives-laden plane into The Dalles courthouse; they had engineered the bombing of the hotel in Portland; they had poisoned the county commissioner, Judge William Hulse, and quite possibly they had been responsible for the salmonella outbreak in The Dalles. They had harassed the people of Antelope and created a Stalinist regime on the ranch, bugging rooms and telephones and communicating with each other in secret codes. Finally, and most treacherously, they had bugged his own bedroom and tried to kill or incapacitate him by poisoning him with substances they prepared in a secret tunnel behind Sheela's house.

At his press conferences Rajneesh said that he had known nothing about any of these crimes until Sheela and her gang left and other sannyasins came and informed him. He also insisted that things would be different on the ranch now that the fascists had left and their crimes had been exposed. Sannyasins would dance and sing, they would talk to their families and outside friends again; they would make peace with their neighbors and give Antelope back to its rightful owners. He added that Sheela had wanted to put an AIDS treatment center in Antelope, but that he had thought it unsafe and had put a stop to the plan.

The guru's revelations produced, as might be expected, an electrical effect on Oregon. Journalists poured into the ranch, closely followed by the representatives of six law enforcement agencies. Congressman Jim Weaver said the FBI had promised an investigation, adding that for a year, law enforcement officials had been looking for "a stool pigeon." Now, he said, "We've got the biggest one of all. The Bhagwan himself. That's going to break it." County, state, and federal officers set up an interagency task force on the ranch and gave press briefings twice a day. During the first crucial week, however, they turned up very little in the way of tangible evidence to support the guru's most serious charges. The Rajneeshee showed them an enormous number of sophisticated wiretapping devices installed in the phone system, in the hotel rooms, and in other places around the ranch. They also showed them a secret tunnel that could be entered through a closet in Sheela's house and ran underground, coming out in an irrigation ditch some distance away. But the main thing in the tunnel was a large lavender hot tub.

According to the Twinkies, sannyasins greeted the revelations with a mixture of horror and relief: horror at the heinous crimes committed by Sheela and her henchmen, relief that the reign of terror was over now and the commune could become the beautiful place it always should have been. The Twinkies' account was, of course, difficult to believe, but one worried mother of a sannyasin called her daughter and found that it was essentially correct. Her daughter, who had stoutly defended Sheela at her most obnoxious, now confessed that she had never liked the woman at all: she had defended her merely because she thought she was Bhagwan's choice for the commune. Now all would be well. After Bhagwan had told them they should not be so isolated, she had gone to Madras for the first time in a year and a half and had wandered around the streets feeling full of love for everyone.

Asked why Sheela had left and how the guru had come to know what he told the press, the Twinkies told the following story. In the past year Sheela had been spending a great deal of time in Europe and Australia. On September 13, a Friday, Bhagwan had received a letter from her saying that she was "more excited" in Europe than in Rajneeshpuram. He called her in and told her that this was only natural: she had been the supreme power and center of attention in the commune when he was silent; she preferred it that way: she was on a power trip. Sheela had been very upset by this rebuke, and on Saturday she had left by plane with Vidya, the president of the commune, Puja, and her own personal assistant and hairdresser. Thirty or forty sannyasins gathered to say good-bye to her at the airport— little knowing what she had done. The next day a dozen other sannyasins had left by plane including Savita, the chief accountant, Ma Anand Su, the president of the Rajneesh Investment Corporation, Shanti Bhadra, the treasurer of the Rajneesh Foundation International, K.D., the mayor, and two municipal officers (one of which was K.D.'s girlfriend, Sagun). Only after they had left did sannyasins dare to go to Bhagwan and tell him about the crimes these people had committed; he had not known anything about them before as Sheela had deliberately kept him uninformed.

The story was, of course, not remotely plausible. To believe it you would have to believe that the entire top echelon of the organization had carried out a coup against itself and then driven itself into exile for no reason, and then that the guru and all his sannyasins had not noticed that all of the leaders, including all of the chief finance officers, had gone. The story became even less plausible as time went on. Within a week it came out that Rajneesh had replaced all of the departing officers even before their departure and had installed at the center of power a group of wealthy American sannyasins whom Sheela had called "the Hollywood gang." The new secretary to the guru and president of the Rajneesh Foundation International was Ma Prem Hasya, formerly Françoise Ruddy, a Hollywood movie producer (she and her former husband, Albert S. Ruddy, had produced *The Godfather*) who had come to the ranch for the first time in 1982, with three friends also from "the Coast." The four, having contributed a good deal of money, had lived a privileged existence on the ranch in private accommodations apart from the commune. In March 1984, Hasya had married the guru's personal physician, Deveraj, and a member of her group, Dhyan John, had been made head of the Modern Car Trust, the organization that owned the guru's Rolls-Royces. The group thus had direct access to the guru, and though Hasya was not known to be ambitious, Sheela had for some time quite naturally regarded her as her rival. Dhyan John was now head of the Rajneesh Investment Corporation and a third member of the group, Swami David, the vice president of the commune. The new leaders quickly reassured commune members that in spite of what the guru had said (Bhagwan often used figures loosely), Sheela had not taken money from the ranch accounts, and the Rajneeshee organizations were in good financial shape. In other words Sheela, Savita, and the others had not taken with them all the keys to the safes.

The commune police chief, Deva Barka, had promised that the Rajneeshee would cooperate with the law enforcement agencies in investigating the alleged crimes. But while many ordinary sannyasins gave testimony to the police, the Rajneeshee officials and lawyers gave rather limited cooperation. They allowed police divers to make a completely fruitless search of the bottom of the lake, but they refused to let the various agencies examine their files or search all of their buildings. Every time an investigator found something he thought might be a piece of evidence, the Twinkies would arrive trailing dozens of TV camera crews behind them. As for the guru, he would speak to law officers only in front of television cameras (the FBI men had to remove their shoes), and while he described in extraordinary detail Sheela's vile plots againts himself and his physician, he remained quite vague about the other charges he had made. After a while he began to complain that instead of arresting Sheela et al., the investigators were trying to find evidence to destroy his commune.

Toward the end of September, Rajneesh announced that "Rajneeshism" had been entirely Sheela's invention: he himself had never claimed to be a religious leader—indeed he was nothing more than a friend to his sannyasins. He urged the commune members to destroy all traces of the religion and said there was no necessity for them to wear malas and sunset-colored clothes. Obligingly his disciples made a bonfire of Sheela's red robes and all extant copies of the booklet *Rajneeshism* and sang and danced around the flames. The guru expressed pleasure at this: what had burned, he said, was poor Frohnmayer, for as there was no religion, so there could be no church-state suit. (But when sannyasins appeared without their malas and in green or blue, he chided them for so easily giving up the symbols of their attachment to him. The malas and red clothes went back on again.) At around the same time he announced that the commune lawyers would drop their suit against state and county officials and change the name of Rajneesh city back to Antelope. Oregonians, he suggested, might now want to drop some of their lawsuits against the commune.

The guru's strategy now seemed to be quite clear. He and the other commune leaders apparently believed they could limit the investigation as they wished, pin the blame for everything on Sheela and the others who had fled, extricate themselves from a number of expensive lawsuits, mend their political fences, and get a great deal of free airtime to boot. Sheela, for her part, seemed no less sanguine. Now ensconced with her "duchesses" in a resort near the Black Forest, she was selling interviews to the German press in which she blamed Rajneesh for ruining the commune with his incessant demands for more diamond watches and more Rolls-Royces—and his absurd idea they should build an AIDS treatment center in Antelope.

In fact the investigators were not quite as helpless as the guru and Sheela seemed to suppose. For two weeks they had proceeded with great caution as they feared the heavily armed Rajneeshee guards might start shooting and precipitate a violent confrontation—if not, a Jonestown-style denouement. Finally on October 2 they issued search warrants for the commune buildings and served subpoenas on a hundred sannyasins. Three National Guard troop-carrying helicopters were standing at the ready in case the officers serving the warrants needed help—but these proved unnecessary. The Rajneeshee allowed the search to go ahead. The investigators found some tapes, but much in the way of documentary evidence, and they supposed that Sheela and/or her successors had destroyed a good many files. Still, they were accumulating testimony, for many ordinary sannyasins told the investigators what they knew, and then three of the people who had left the ranch with Sheela returned to give state's evidence. By mid-October the commune leaders had put the Portland hotel and two airplanes up for sale and were trying to buy a jet. The guru, conceivably, had begun to feel threatened.

Then on October 23 a federal grand jury convened by the local U.S. attorney, Charles H. Turner, on behalf of the INS issued a thirty-five-count indictment charging the guru, Sheela, and six other disciples with a conspiracy to evade the immigration laws. This was the indictment that the Portland branch of the INS had been working on since 1982; it charged that the guru had lied on his visa application and that he and the others had arranged sham marriages so that foreign disciples could remain in the United States. The indictment was returned in camera, but word of it was leaked via a media source to Isabel and Niren. The following day, a Friday, lawyers for the Rajneeshee went to Turner to ask that the guru be allowed to surrender in Portland when the indictment came down; they called Turner again the next day, but no deal was struck. On Sunday night two chartered Lear jets left the ranch, filing flight plans for Salt Lake City and Pueblo, Colorado, then on to Charlotte, North Carolina. Two female sannyasins were at the Charlotte airport when the planes arrived, having made arrangements for another chartered jet to fly to Bermuda with eight people and their luggage. But federal customs agents were there, too, and, ordering the passengers out of the Lear jets, they found the guru with six of his disciples—also a gun, $58,522 in cash, and a box containing thirty-eight jewel-encrusted watches and bracelets.

There followed an extraordinary sequence of events—much of it recorded on national television. The guru went to jail; he was stripped of his robes and hat, issued green prison pajamas, and put in chains for court appearances. The Rajneeshee lawyers desperately tried to get him out on bail, citing his delicate health ("It's almost a bubble boy situation," Niren said), but the local judge refused to release him on the grounds that he had been fleeing arrest and might leave the country. Hasya and others protested that he had just been going on a vacation—but in vain. The guru spent a week in a medical cell of the Mecklenburg County jail. At first he seemed quite happy with the situation—he smiled his foxy smile a lot and said outrageous things to the press. He seemed less pleased as the days went by, but he never complained to the prison nurses looking after him: he ate the prison food (all but the hominy grits), did what they told him to do, and apparently suffered no ill effects. On November 4 a U.S. marshal's flight took him to a federal prison in El Reno, Oklahoma, and three days later another flight took him back to Portland.

On arrival he pleaded innocent to all charges and was released on a $500,000 cash bail to go back to the ranch. His lawyers were, however, already cutting a deal with the U.S. attorney's office, and on November 14 he returned to Portland and pleaded guilty to two felonies: making false statements to the authorities in 1980 and concealing his intent to reside in the United States. He received a ten-year suspended prison sentence, agreed to pay $400,000 in fines and prosecution costs, and to leave the country within five days, and not to come back for at least five years without the explicit permission of the U.S. attorney general. A year or two before the Rajneeshee lawyers would no doubt have succeeded in dragging the case out for months or years—if not actually winning it in the end. But now the commune was in disarray, and the guru was ready to leave the country. The same day he boarded the plane for New Delhi with Vivek, Deveraj, and his seventy-two-year-old mother and declared that he never wanted to see the United States again.

On October 28, the same day the guru was arrested in North Carolina, the West German police arrested Sheela, Puja, and Shanti Bhadra in their Black Forest resort hotel. The U.S. attorney in Portland, Charles H. Turner, and the state attorney general, David Frohnmayer, had wanted to have the German police pick up Sheela on the immigration charges before federal officials arrested the guru on the ranch, but they had discovered that the extradition treaty between the two countries did not cover immigration fraud and might not be enough to keep her in prison in Germany. Thus on October 25 the lawyers from Frohnmayer's office convened the Wasco County grand jury that had been hearing testimony from the Rajneeshee, and that afternoon the three women were indicted for attempted murder, conspiracy to commit murder, and first-degree assault on Deveraj. Officials then took these charges to the German police and, shortly after the arrests were made, began extradition proceedings. The women were returned to the United States in February but before that the same grand jury indicted Sheela and Puja for the poisoning of County Commissioner William Hulse and his colleague and for the burglary and arson at the Wasco County planning office. Also in December federal authorities indicted Sheela and twenty other sannyasins, including Puja and Shanti Bhadra, on wiretapping charges. Three months later Sheela and Puja were charged with causing the salmonella outbreak in The Dalles.

After the final departure of the guru from the ranch, Dhyan John assured sannyasins that the commune would continue to exist and spoke of various ways in which the ranch might be made profitable. But exactly a week later Niren announced that the commune was closing down and that sannyasins should make arrangements to leave. He did so just hours after K.D.—who had returned to the ranch early in October and then disappeared from sight—turned up at the Wasco County Courthouse in the company of officials. K.D. had gone to the authorities and agreed to plead guilty to charges of racketeering and immigration fraud and promised to tell prosecutors everything he knew in return for immunity from further prosecution. Shortly after he made his plea, Frohnmayer went to the U.S. District Court with an affidavit from him supporting the state's contention that the incorporation of Rajneeshpuram violated the religious-establishment clause. By K.D.'s testimony, the religious entities on the ranch had directly controlled the city government; among other things, the guru himself had chosen city officials and selected the design for the city's stationery. Two and a half weeks later the District Court judge ruled Rajneeshpuram unconstitutional by summary judgment. The Rajneeshee appealed the ruling, though by that point the judgment was more or less moot, for the commune was closing down.

By now a great number of sannyasins had talked to investigators and grand juries. A dozen of them had pled guilty to charges of arranging fraudulent marriages or to implication in the electronic eavesdropping scheme and had been let off with light sentences (five years probation in most cases). Then, too, a few key figures, including K.D., his girlfriend, Sagun, and Ava, Sheela's personal secretary, had turned state's evidence. The investigators thus had a great deal of information about what had transpired in the commune. While some of it remained confidential, some of it had come out in court affidavits and a good deal more had been leaked to the press (notably during the period the authorities held the guru in jail). *Oregonian* reporters had collected all of this information and done some more investigative work on their own. According to *The Oregonian*, most of the guru's charges had solid basis in fact; in addition to that, Sheela and her minions had committed a number of crimes that the guru had not even mentioned—and had planned crimes that surpassed the imagination of even the most fervid opponents of the commune. The sannyasins I spoke with later confirmed all of these stories and added a few of their own; from what they said it was possible to sketch out a picture of what had happened in Sheela's inner circle at the center of the commune.

When Sheela took over as the guru's secretary in 1981, she seemed, initially at least, more open and available than her predecessor. Laxmi had given orders; Sheela laughed and joked with ordinary sannyasins. But this collegiality was largely a facade. Sheela had had to scheme in order to get her position, and she felt she had to scheme in order to keep it. She was jealous of long-term disciples who had personal relationships with the guru. She sent some of them (including the guru's former bodyguard) away; she co-opted a few of them and she "blacklisted" the rest, giving them only menial jobs, restricting their access to the outside world, and setting other sannyasins to spy on them for "negativity." At the same time she created a coterie of sannyasins loyal to herself. The membership in this coterie changed over the years (Sushilla, for example, was her main fund-raiser until 1984, when Sheela read her out of the movement), and it had various circles within it: Isabel, for example, remained on an outer circle while on the inmost circle were people like Savita, who knew everything about the movement's finances, and people like Su and Shanti Bhadra, who worked closely with Sheela. Puja was perhaps the nearest to the center, for Puja supplied Sheela with Percodan, Valium, and Demerol—the drugs she increasingly needed to keep going; Puja ran the medical clinic dictatorially, and she had ways of dealing with Sheela's enemies.

Unlike Laxmi, Sheela—and the commune she created—always had something to hide from the authorities. In the beginning there were always more people on the ranch than the land-use laws allowed, and there were foreigners on the ranch without visas; later, of course, there were foreigners who had married Americans to get around the immigration laws. Sheela told sannyasins to be very careful what they said in their telephone conversations, as the federal authorities were very probably bugging the ranch. Perhaps she believed they were. In any case, she worried a good deal about information leaks. In November 1983, a few months after she had installed the first security system of guards and guard dogs at the entrance to the ranch, she ordered a series of bugging devices installed in the Alan Watts cabins, where at the time journalists and other visitors stayed. A few months later the eavesdropping system was expanded to cover four rooms in the newly built Hotel Rajneesh, the cabin where Laxmi lived when she returned to the ranch in 1985, the six public pay phones on the ranch, and the entire ranch telephone system. An English electronics expert, Swami Anand Julian, set up the system, and sannyasins—a goodly number of them—took turns monitoring the calls at a listening post in the administration building. Now the ranch had something else to hide.

Most sannyasins who knew about the wiretapping justified it to themselves on the grounds that it was necessary for the protection of the guru and his commune. Sheela, however, had other purposes in mind for it. In the first place she was more vulnerable to charges of immigration fraud than the guru. (Since they had come to the ranch Rajneesh had been quite effectively insulated from all legal proceedings.) In the second place she worried a good deal about dissidence within the commune. There was, of course, no open dissent, and as a result, she had increasingly to worry about secret dissenters. She was not concerned about ordinary sannyasins but about the people who knew in detail about the illegalities. The ordinary sannyasins could leave or stay as they wished, but those who knew things or who were in positions of power and objected to her management could not be allowed to pass their "negativity" on to others. Puja, however, had a solution to this problem.

Many sannyasins now thought that Puja had been using drugs and other poisons on recalcitrant sannyasins for years. Satya Bharti, who left the ranch a week before Sheela's departure, later told me that—in light of hindsight—she believed she had been a victim in Poona. There a medical administrator had persuaded her to go into the clinic to get a slight neck ailment treated. Satya had thought treatment unnecessary, but she had gone to the clinic and was given a series of powerful drugs—Quaaludes among others; she became drug-dependent, and her weight went down dangerously. When she questioned her treatment, Sheela and Puja told the doctors that she was just crazy. Finally, when her weight went down to seventy-nine pounds, Sheela had told her she should go home to America—but without seeing the guru. Satya left, certain she was going home to die, but once home, her father, a doctor, told her that there was not much medically wrong with her except for her drug addiction, and he asked her who at the ashram wanted to get rid of her. Satya could not believe that anyone did, but when she went to the Oregon commune, she was blacklisted. Then, too, she noticed that when people who worked at the medical center wanted to leave, they left secretly in the middle of the night. But she drew no conclusions until afterwards.

After Sheela left, a number of sannyasins reported that they had been drugged, poisoned, or otherwise medically ill-treated on the ranch. Devaprem, the chief of construction, told *Oregonian* reporters that he was drugged just after he told Sheela that he wanted to leave the ranch. Puja gave him a tranquilizer, telling him what he needed was rest, and then put him under heavy sedation in Sheela's house. When Arup asked about him, she was told that he was overworked and overwrought: that if he was in his right mind, he would not want to leave. After three days of this "rest cure," Devaprem said he had changed his mind about leaving and struggled back to work. Two weeks later he left the ranch in secret and went to live incognito in another state.

By all reports at least three other sannyasins were given this kind of "rest cure," and one of them, Hasya, was isolated at the medical clinic for thirteen days. Others had worse things done to them. One woman developed a serious neurological condition while working in the legal department; the ranch managers then began to suspect her of "negativity" and would not allow her out to go to a specialist: her condition remained dangerously untreated for a year and a half. Another woman, Samya, the publisher of the *Rajneesh Times*, fell ill after Sheela intercepted a letter she sent the guru warning him about Sheela's group. A hysterectomy was performed on her, and afterward Puja gave her medicine which, she said, made her "emotionally unstable" for a very long time. Worst of all in some ways was what happened to Zeno, the former arts editor of *Ramparts* magazine, whom I had met in 1983. Zeno worked for Julian in the audiovisual department; she suspected he had set up wiretaps and she did not like it; also she associated with a few of the blacklisted people on the ranch. In December 1984, Puja gave the AIDS test to a number of sannyasins and subsequently told eleven people they had tested positive for the

HTLV-III antibody. One of them was Zeno. Puja asked the eleven people whether they would prefer to leave or to stay, and all said they wanted to stay even though their contact with other sannyasins would be severely restricted. The following July, Puja moved them to an "AIDS village," a nest of cabins in a remote area of the ranch. Over the summer Zeno developed headaches and cramps and thought she must be coming down with AIDS. But the symptoms disappeared when Puja left in September. Later Hasya had all eleven people re-tested, and two of them tested negative: Zeno and a man who was suspected of supplying Puja with drugs from Europe. (Thus when Puja told me in August that a man and a woman had tested positive, she was apparently referring to the two who did not—since all the rest were men. She had denied that there were any AIDS victims on the ranch, but in late September one sannyasin, a gay man, died of AIDS. He was apparently the only one who had the disease.)

Whenever Sheela and Puja had begun to use medical terrorism on their fellow sannyasins, there was clearly a progression to their activ-ities—a progression that followed their spiral into desperation and craziness. According to Ava, Sheela's twenty-five-year-old secretary, the spiral began in the spring of 1984. By then the movement was quite obviously faring badly under Sheela's management: the Euro-pean communes were in chaos, the flow of money to the ranch was uncertain, and the moratorium on building had left the commune with nowhere to go. When Deveraj—whom Sheela hated—married the golden girl of the Hollywood group (the only group to bring a new infusion of money to the ranch), Sheela began to worry seriously about maintaining her own position. During the summer festival that year Deveraj came down with extremely bad diarrhea, which made him stagger about as if drunk. He went to the clinic, and Dr. Shunyo, a colleague, was there when Puja gave him an IV—very much against his wishes. Within twenty-four hours he was in septic shock with a very high fever and dropping blood pressure; Shunyo resuscitated him and later found an unusual sort of bacteria in his blood culture. Around the same time—or so it was later reconstructed—Puja began asking the pharmacists and herbalists on the ranch if there was a way to poison someone without actually killing the person. People thought she was worried about outsiders trying to poison sannyasins; but as it turned out, she had created a secret laboratory on the ranch and was experimenting with poisons on mice. Apparently she found what she wanted, for in September William Hulse and his colleague were poisoned after drinking glasses of water she gave them.

Sometime during the summer Sheela decided that the only way out of the political impasse in Oregon was to try to take over Wasco

County in the election. An American sannyasin suggested importing homeless people. It was a crazy idea. Among other things, the Rajneeshee would have had to collect and house two or three times their own number to win the election—or even to rig it plausibly. At the time the outbreak of salmonella poisoning occurred, even those people who suspected the Rajneeshee of poisoning the salad bars could not imagine what their motive might be—apart from sheer spite. But the poisoning—according to informants—was merely a test run for Election Day, when Sheela's minions would poison the entire water system in The Dalles. In December, according to sannyasins, members of Sheela's inner circle vandalized and set fire to the Wasco County planning offices.

The commune leaders had for some time seen themselves engaged —as Wadud once said—in "a war" with Oregon politicians and administrators. But after the failure of the election attempt, they began to see themselves as engaged in a war they might lose. The Share-A-Home program was enormously expensive: it cost well over a million dollars—the medical bills were huge; it turned most of Oregon against them, and it put doubts in the minds of a number of resident sannyasins. Sheela, now increasingly desperate, took a series of trips abroad to try and raise money and to try and find a place where the guru might take refuge—if that became necessary. Laxmi was also involved in trying to find a place for him abroad. On her trip to Australia, Sheela virtually destroyed the Australian movement by behaving in exactly the same way she behaved in Oregon. Her long absences, and her lack of success, made her feel all the more vulnerable. On one trip she married Dhyan Dipo, a Swiss sannyasin who ran the Rajneesh Investment Services International, presumably as an insurance policy for herself. She, however, neglected to get a divorce from Jayananda until after she was married, and months later Jayananda investigated and found an illegal, backdated divorce in Nepal. When she returned to the ranch, she had bugging devices installed in twenty-four rooms of the hotel, in the Hollywood people's quarters and the table they used at the restaurant, and in the bedrooms of everyone who might betray her, including Shunyo, Isabel, and Niren, and the guru himself. She trusted no one now, and it was around this time that she sent Hasya to the clinic for a "rest cure."

Two weeks before the summer festival that year, Deveraj fell ill with the same mysterious form of diarrhea he had had the year before. He told Shunyo that he had fallen ill just after having tea with Sheela and that he suspected her of poisoning him. Shunyo ran a toxic screen on him that would pick up traces of ordinary drugs and poisons, but the screen showed nothing. As Shunyo knew of the hostility that existed between Deveraj and Sheela, he put Deveraj's suspicions down to paranoia and his condition down to stress before the festival. On Master's Day, however, Deveraj fell deathly ill in the crowded assembly hall. When Shunyo arrived, Deveraj, thinking he was dying, told his colleague that Shanti Bhadra had come up from behind him and stuck him with a needle—and within minutes he had felt woozy. He wanted to show Shunyo the mark of the needle, but he went into shock and couldn't breathe. Shunyo performed a major resuscitation and flew him to an intensive-care unit in the major hospital of the region in Bend, Oregon. Deveraj revived, but only because of these measures; he had a puncture in one of his buttocks and clearly the shock was noncardiac: it came from a capillary leak.

When the crisis was over, Shunyo called Vivek and told her Deveraj's suspicions, adding that he himself found it impossible to believe that Shanti Bhadra had poisoned his colleague. A few minutes later Sheela called him to say that there were stories about people being poisoned, that she was horrified, that she would mount an investigation, and how could he, Shunyo, suspect Shanti Bhadra? Not long after that Durga, one of Puja's nurses at the clinic, showed Shunyo an open safety pin she said she had found in Deveraj's trousers— thus accounting for the puncture Shunyo had found. It was only after Sheela had left and Rajneesh made his accusations that Shunyo could bring himself to believe that Deveraj had been poisoned. At that point he remembered that Mike Sullivan, the Jefferson County district attorney, had gone into the same kind of severe capillary leak shock—for which there was no apparent cause—in the Madras hospital in February 1983. It was a freak condition that a doctor generally wouldn't see more than once in a lifetime. Shunyo, who was working at the Madras hospital at the time, had been called into the emergency room by Sullivan's doctors to help out. Later Sheela had telephoned him to suggest that Sullivan might have been poisoned. Shunyo had not thought of this as a possibility, but he brought it up to the state medical examiner, who told him that very little was known about poisons: there were, after all, very few cases of deliberate poisoning. Sullivan's doctors, for their part, conjectured that the shock might have been brought on by a trace of pneumonia—a trace so small that the bacteria did not show up in his blood culture. After leaving the ranch Shunyo asked a number of specialists what kind of poison might have created such a condition—but thus far he had no answer. Also, in the case of Mike Sullivan, there was no obvious answer to the question of motive. Sheela and Jay had gone to Sullivan for help, and Sullivan negotiated an end to the demonstrations in Madras. But perhaps Sheela or Puja had not really wanted a compromise solution.

By June, Sheela had come to believe that the authorities would soon be coming to arrest her and Rajneesh. She said this when she launched the suit against INS and other federal officials they called "God versus the Universe." She had other worries as well. The U.S. Internal Revenue Service had given her notice that its criminal division would be investigating her personal income taxes; and she knew that *The Oregonian* was about to publish its long investigative series on the Rajneeshee. A former sannyasin, Helen C. Byron, had just won a huge judgment against Sheela, and financial pressures were on again. The previous year Sheela had created a "dirty tricks" unit to carry out her attacks on The Dalles. Now, according to testimony, she and her group planned to sabotage the microcomputer system used by *The Oregonian* reporters. K.D. was dispatched to reconnoiter the building; so were a few Rajneeshee women posing as employees of a maintenance company, but the women were discovered and ejected from the building, and the plan broke down. Now the unit drew up a hit list of Rajneeshee enemies, a list that included Charles H. Turner, David Frohnmayer, Daniel C. Durow, Leslie Zaitz, the chief *Oregonian* investigative reporter, Helen C. Byron and her daughter, Laxmi, and Vivek. Sheela and three others obtained false identification papers and bought handguns in Texas; a team of women then staked out Charles Turner's house in Portland and elaborated a plan to ambush his car and shoot him. The plan, however, came to naught.

When Sheela and fifteen other sannyasins left the ranch in mid-September, their main motive, according to sannyasins, was to escape indictment for immigration fraud—an indictment they supposed was coming down from the federal grand jury on October 3. (In fact they had the date wrong; it was planned for November 1.) On the face of it their fear of the immigration charges seemed unjustified: the Rajneeshee lawyers who had fought off the INS since 1982 were confident they could continue to fight the charges. (The U.S. commissioner for the INS, Alan C. Nelson, later suggested that the Rajneeshee suit filed in June had delayed the indictment and acknowledged that Sheela's departure and all that followed from it "enhanced the final resolution of the matter.") But Sheela and her intimates were not up to a battle in court. According to Ava, they had long ago passed the point of rationality. They were exhausted, crazy with tension, and in a state of acute paranoia; Vidya had fallen ill under the pressure, and all the drugs that Sheela was taking did not help her sanity. Sheela trusted no one outside her inner circle—and she could only expect the worst if Vivek or Deveraj were to take the witness stand. She did not trust the guru himself (she had been bugging his bedroom for several months), and he had clearly run out of patience with her. He meant—it was rumored—to displace her and make Hasya his new secretary. Quite conceivably Sheela and her companions suspected that when the indictments came down, Rajneesh would make them take all the responsibility. On departing, Vidya was heard to say, "I don't trust Bhagwan enough to go to jail." Still, according to all sources, Sheela and her companions never suspected that the guru would come out and charge them with crimes the authorities did not know about or had no evidence of. Why would he, after all? It would mean a police investigation, and besides, Sheela could give all kinds of testimony about her past conversations with him. Perhaps they thought he had some affection for them, or some gratitude for their long and faithful service. In any case, they seriously underestimated him. Rajneesh loved a public drama and he loved taking dangerous risks: he, after all, had always survived them.

The following summer Sheela, Puja, and Shanti Bhadra pled guilty to having attempted to murder Deveraj with an injection of adrenaline; Sheela and Puja pled guilty to wiretapping charges, the poisoning of William Hulse and his colleague, and to causing the outbreak of salmonella poisoning of The Dalles; Sheela, in addition, pled guilty to immigration fraud and to setting fire to the Wasco County planning offices. Sheela and Puja were given maximum twenty-year sentences in the assault cases, and Sheela was fined nearly half a million dollars; officials estimated the two women would spend an additional three and a half years in jail.

By the end of December 1985, most of the sannyasins had departed the ranch, leaving behind them only a caretaking crew and a legal administrative staff. The Rolls-Royces were sold (there were now ninety-three of them) and the ranch itself was put up for sale to pay off the Rajneeshee debts. The ranch equipment was sold separately, and in December an *Oregonian* reporter found that, among other things up for immediate sale, there was a flight simulator, a $15,000 Weertman cello, two baby grand pianos, two samadhi floatation tanks, and twenty-one Israeli-made Galil assault rifles. Interestingly, the ranch accounts appeared to be in fairly good order. If Sheela and her confidantes had stolen money (and they appeared not to lack for it), then they had skimmed it off the donations before these went into the organizational accounts. The ranch had paid its bills, and its only large outstanding debt—estimated at $35 million—was to sannyasins who had made loans to the foundation or to other entities. Only one creditor complained of irregularities: a German woman claimed that the Rajneeshee Services International had moved $800,000 from her bank in Switzerland to the commune account without her permission. The woman had, it appeared, given Dhyan Dipo, Sheela's putative husband, her power of attorney—but not the power to transfer money without her permission. She sued and won a huge settlement.

The new administrators clearly aimed to pay back the loans from sannyasins, but whether they would succeed was now uncertain, for a good many Oregonians had gone into competition for what was left of Rajneeshpuram. In December the state of Oregon filed a civil racketeering suit against twenty-six Rajneeshee corporations seeking $6.5 million in costs and penalties. The state also asked over $100,000 in civil penalties for violation of the electrical safety laws (this was the old case of the "winterized tents"). Four restaurants in The Dalles filed multimillion-dollar damage claims against several Rajneeshee corporations for the outbreak of salmonella poisoning. Around the same time two of the older civil suits came up for settlement, and juries awarded hundreds of thousands of dollars in damages to the plaintiffs. One of these cases suggested that future juries might well consider the Rajneeshee corporations liable for what Sheela and her friends had done. Then, too, what claims the Rajneeshee could pay depended on the outcome of the land-use case—which was still going through the courts. If 1000 Friends won, then the ranch would be worth little more than what Sheela had paid for it.

By February only a hundred people remained on the ranch; the rest were taking up their lives in "the world" again, and only a few—a very few—were holding themselves in the ready to go to the guru if he called them again. (Since his departure Rajneesh had moved from India to Nepal to Crete, where, in February, he was staying with a Greek producer of X-rated films. According to sannyasins, he had proved physically quite tough. Indeed, it was said that on his first stop when he had found that Laxmi had rented, not bought, the Himalayan hotel he stayed at and had obtained only three-week visas for his non-Indian sannyasins, he took a bus by himself to New Delhi and left Laxmi with the hotel bills.) Most of his sannyasins—former sannyasins—were now engaged in the practical problems of finding jobs, getting credit, finding a place to live. Some of them, such as Videh, the former water manager, were doing these things for the first time; others were doing them for the first time in eight or ten years. They were like Rip van Winkles come down from the mountain —the more so because they could not tell prospective employers, credit managers, and so on where they had been. Of course, a number of them had resources, and some of them, like Isabel and Niren, had simply sailed off to Europe or South America for vacations. Others, however, were working just as hard as they had on the ranch—working as waitresses or housecleaners and going to school at night—and facing the fact that at the age of thirty-five or forty they had to start all over again from scratch. Yet with one or two exceptions none of them I talked to were angry, bitter, or depressed about what had happened. On the contrary, they seemed just as cheerful and energetic as before. Over lunch in San Diego, Videh, who was looking for a job as a salesman, said, "I can't seem to make my parents understand that I was fine when I was on the ranch, and I'm fine here, too." Most of them, including Videh, told me how grateful they were for having had such an experience.

In the past I had always wondered how much of what ordinary sannyasins said they said because they had to (or felt they had to) and how much they actually believed. Now most of those people I had met before told me that they had had—and concealed—many objections to the way the commune was run. "I hated this Us-Them syndrome that Sheela created," one ex-Twinkie said. "I never felt that all outsiders were hostile, and I felt that we were just driving people away." Two of the other ex-Twinkies I met said the same thing, and all of them said they did not like having to lie to journalists—two of them had resigned their press jobs to avoid it. Most of the people I talked to had seen the power struggles going on around Sheela and had noticed the way they had turned those involved into petty tyrants. Many, too, had noticed the growing paranoia on the ranch and had thought the guards and the guns unnecessary and perhaps even dangerous. A few had left the ranch because of these things, and a great many—indeed most of those people I talked to outside the leadership circles—had gone into a kind of internal emigration. "My friends and I just gave up on trying to make the commune the way we wanted it," Subhuti, the former *Rajneeh Times* editor said. "We went low-profile and had a good time. If we had known people were being poisoned . . ." Videh told me he had made an effort to stay out of policy-making circles as he had watched people within them doing and saying things they had in some part of their being to feel were wrong. He had decided just to do his job as well as he could. Anuradha, an Englishwoman and the president of the commune since September, said that she had remained coordinator of the garage for years, turning down other jobs in order to maintain her distance from the direction the commune was taking. "I was in a double bind," she said. "I had no idea whether Sheela had some personal need to run the commune as she did—or whether it was Bhagwan. In Poona, Bhagwan's line had always been, if you don't like it, leave. I agreed with that in principle—and I didn't want to leave."

None of the ordinary sannyasins had, of course, known that Sheela was drugging and poisoning people—and not very many had known about the wiretapping. The astonishing thing was that most did not even suspect that something terrible was happening—given all the clues that lay around there. But most did not. Like Shunyo, they could not believe it—and some of them, like Zeno, had suffered mentally or physically because they did not. Sampati, a former Twinkie who had left the ranch the previous spring because she had doubts, explained it this way: "When you're around a Master, you have to trust. You have to suspend judgment in order to open yourself up to new experiences. You have to see how things feel before making judgments. Otherwise how can you get out of your old patterns, your social conditioning? There was an innocence about sannyasins." The new vice president of the commune, a bearded, long-term sannyasin called C.C., went into more detail on this point. "Sannyasins have an inclination to surrender. That's the Eastern quality to our work. Each one of us mirrors what is going on inside everyone else. That's the basis of living in the Buddhafield. I never cared for the Us-Them dichotomy, and the commune wasn't the way I would have wanted it. But we trusted him—or her, or whoever he was. There are many levels around Bhagwan's work—those you can see and those you can't."

The guru had often told his disciples that they were asleep, and that was certainly the way it looked now. They had all done their jobs and not asked questions and gone along. Now, looking at this experience in retrospect, Sampati, C.C., and all the other sannyasins I talked to said that they had been wrong to trust in this way and that they bore some responsibility for what had occurred. But then they said something else. "When Bhagwan started speaking again," Sampati said, "he talked about the importance of having doubts, trusting our own feelings, and taking responsibility for ourselves. That's what I heard, anyway, and that's why I left. I could not say yes enthusiastically enough. But not everyone seemed to hear this." C.C., who had stayed at the ranch and who still wore red clothes and a mala, surprisingly seemed to agree. "In Poona, Bhagwan emphasized surrender. But here, where we had to build a large organization, that kind of trust was not appropriate. He said as much but most of us did not listen."

Not everyone I spoke with seemed to think that the only error lay

378   C I T I E S   O N   A   H I L L

in not listening to the guru closely enough. Some acknowledged that
Rajneesh often said contradictory things. But all said that they had
learned a lesson. Subhuti, who was struggling with the facts of the
matter in order to write a book, said in answer to a question, "Yes, I
suspected that Hulse's illness and the fire in the planning office were
caused by us. But it wasn't a big thing for me. I went unconscious on
it. It's all in Bhagwan's hands, I thought to myself. That was the
reasoning. We saw Bhagwan as this big Daddy who could take care
of everything. But we've learned that you can't avoid taking responsibility for yourself."

The lesson did not seem to be a very remarkable one. Many sannyasins doubtless knew it before they joined Rajneesh. But Subhuti,
Videh, Sampati, and others told me over and over again how grateful
they were to Bhagwan for it and how good they felt about it. They
then went on to suggest that they had not learned it at all. "Every
phase of Bhagwan's work is different," C.C. said. "Here it was an
experiment in the collective unconscious. Bhagwan made us look at
our will to power and that of people on the outside. You see, outsiders came into his Buddhafield, too, and all of us had to struggle
with the same fears and insecurities." Videh, for his part, said, "I
wouldn't have missed the experience for anything. Bhagwan showed
us at firsthand how power corrupts. He showed us how fascism
comes into being. Where else could you learn something like that?"
Even Ava—Ava who had been a member of Sheela's "dirty tricks"
squad—was grateful for the same lesson. "Bhagwan's outrageous!"
she said when I first talked to her. "There's no one like him! If I put
up with horror to be near him, it was all worth it. I got to see the
horrible, sinister side of myself and to accept it. I don't have any
regrets."

This, then, was the reason for the extraordinary cheerfulness of
sannyasins and former sannyasins. They had "taken responsibility,"
as the therapists liked to say, without taking any responsibility at all.
They had nothing on their consciences, for the guru "on some level"
was responsible for everything that occurred. Almost all of them believed that Sheela was in practice responsible for the criminality and
that the guru knew nothing about it—but that did not change their
view. They also believed that they themselves would never have done
violence to anyone on Sheela's orders. The open question was how
many of them would have committed crimes if they thought the guru
wanted them to. For most of them this was a nonquestion, as they
believed Rajneesh incapable of doing, or willing, violence against another person. For one woman, however, it was not. "Masters," she

said, "throw you into the moment. They create crises and make you live on the edge. They create the fever-pitched moment in order to throw you back into yourself. Bhagwan was doing that for us. If humanity would be saved in this way, well, it might be at the expense of other people, and criminal acts could be justified." What this woman (she was one who had physically suffered on the ranch) was saying was that a master-disciple relationship of this imperial, world-conquering sort, might well lead to criminality. That was the logic of it, and in practice that was where it had led. Yet this woman did not blame herself for having accepted the logic. "I have no respect for Bhagwan anymore," she continued. "He's an intelligent man, and he influenced everything we did. I think he told Sheela to do a lot of the things she did—like the burning of Durow's office and the salmonella poisonings in The Dalles. I can't prove it, but at a meeting I went to after the Share-A-Home program, he said that he told Sheela exactly what to say. So in the end when he blamed Sheela for everything, there were a lot of people who knew this was not true. By the end the ranch was set up so that no one trusted themselves. I can't trash the whole experience. I had so many friends there I really liked a lot. It was just the people who were running the place . . ."

A number of sannyasins and former sannyasins used the word "innocence" about themselves. But they were not really innocent, for many had doubts and reservations, and many, like Subhuti, had suspicions. They merely acted as if they had none, concealing their suspicions not just from outsiders but from themselves and from each other—the very people they claimed to "mirror" and trust. In fact the ranch was something like a hall of mirrors without windows. The outside world did not exist. Then, while sannyasins thought the guru was "mirroring" them, they had lost him—the man himself—among the reflections of themselves. On the other hand, because they thought they existed only in the reflection he gave them, so they had lost themselves in an endlessly receding series of images, each one a step further removed from reality. While all now thought they knew what they had done, they were still looking past themselves into reflections and imagining that the hall of mirrors encompassed the world.

While talking at length with Subhuti (who was still living on the ranch), I, and then he, realized that he had forgotten certain things. He had forgotten, for example, what he had said to me six months before about the New Man taking shape in the commune. He could in fact no longer remember that he had thought anything like that. He asked me to tell him exactly what he had said so that he could use it in his book. Then, later, when he was talking about the way they had seen how power corrupts, he said how amazing it was to watch Oregon politicians ganging up against the commune, passing laws against it any way they could. When I reminded him that this had happened after the commune's attempt to rig the Wasco County election, the salmonella outbreak, and so on, he laughed in surprise. "I guess they had some reason to think we were dangerous," he said. "And you're right, the means they used were perfectly legal—unlike ours."

Videh, I discovered, had forgotten things, too. He no longer remembered making a theoretical justification for the hostile, provocative behavior of the group. And he could not remember having ever made a provocative gesture himself—though six months before he had told me about one. "I never liked the Us-Them thing," he said, "and I always did my best to keep friendly relations with those people I worked with on the outside." Looking at Videh, I knew he believed what he was now saying just as sincerely as he had believed what he said six months ago. I had never thought Subhuti or Videh capable of hurting anyone—and the record showed they had not. But there were people in the commune who had.

"Sheela flipped out . . . she went crazy" was the verdict of most sannyasins and ex-sannyasins these days. Two people who had gone to see her in a Portland jail after her extradition to the United States reported that she had promised she would always be the "ma" to her sannyasins. "She's really crazy," people said who heard that. People thought Vidya crazy, too, for Vidya was not hiding out in Europe, she was calling a number of them, saying where she was and offering to produce character witnesses for Sheela. Ava thought both of them had gone right around the bend. She could not imagine what had come over them. But then without realizing it she provided an explanation. "You know, it's curious," she said, the second time I spoke with her. "After I spent two weeks being debriefed by the FBI and everyone else, I went back to the ranch and everyone was talking about how wonderful things would be now Sheela was gone, how they were going to make a new start and so on. I thought everyone was nuts. I knew this couldn't be. But then—this is strange—I started forgetting things. I conveniently forgot things because they seemed impossible to remember. I forgot . . . well, I forgot the tape Sheela had of a conversation with Bhagwan which showed that he was involved, well, in things he said he wasn't. Things like that. I stuffed these things away, and I remembered them just a few days ago. I remembered them because I went to Portland to testify again, and I talked with K.D. and Sagun for the first time since we left the ranch, and they reminded me. For three days I was just so *angry* at Bhagwan. But I'm over that now."

Ava called in a third time to say that she hoped she had not sounded too negative before. She had been in a bad space but now she had accepted everything and Bhagwan was still her Master.

Starting Over

In the fifties and early sixties a distinguished group of American historians and sociologists, including Richard Hofstadter, Daniel Bell, David Riesman, and others, made a study of the radical Right of the period. The task they set themselves was to explain why a fairly substantial number of people in the United States—McCarthyites, Birchers, and others—believed, or seemed to believe, that a Communist control mechanism had taken over the United States government, and that Wall Street and the major American universities were filled with Communist sympathizers and dupes. The radical Right included all kinds of people: Catholics and fundamentalist Protestants, retired military officers and entrepreneurs on the make, members of the

DAR, second- or third-generation immigrants, and a few "soured patricians" such as Archibald Roosevelt. Yet all these people, puzzlingly, insisted on their own "Americanness"—as opposed to the "un-Americanness" of others. The phenomenon was startling. It clearly had no counterpart in Europe, but what was more, it went so much against the grain of conventional wisdom about American politics that it posed large questions about the nature of American society and political behavior in general.

Taking a closer look at the members of the radical right-wing groups, Bell, Hofstadter, and others discovered that most of them would fit into one or another of two general patterns: either they were people on the way down who had belonged to a previously dominant group and were thus eager to assert their own particular claim to the American tradition, or they were people on the way up who came from one of the new immigrant groups and were desperately anxious about their own standing as Americans. The real enemy of the radical Right was clearly not "the Communist menace" as such, for McCarthyites and Birchers had little interest in the external threat the Soviet Union might pose to American security and American interests abroad. The real enemy—so Bell proposed—was the American technical and professional intelligentsia now running the increasingly complex institutions of mid-twentieth-century America. Right-wingers were, after all, far happier attacking "Eastern Ivy Leaguers" or Roosevelt and Acheson than they were denouncing people like the Rosenbergs. It was the people at the top that they saw as responsible for their declining status—or as the roadblocks to their advancement. And it was in contrast to these people that perfectly well-off Americans felt themselves to be dispossessed.

Over the years the scholars wrote a number of essays on the radical Right, and a collection of them was published in 1963.* The theme that drew these essays together was Hofstadter's conception of "status politics." There were, Hofstadter wrote in a 1955 essay, at all times two different kinds of political processes going on in the country: *interest politics*, or the clash of material aims and needs among various groups, and *status politics*, or the attempt of groups to enhance their social status or to win reassurance that their values were respected by the community-at-large. Ordinarily the two processes were inextricably connected, but times of depression or economic hardship tended to bring interest politics to the fore, whereas times of prosperity liberated people to express their moral concerns or to give vent to their

* Daniel Bell, ed. *The Radical Right: The New American Right* (New York: Doubleday, 1963).

"more luxurious hostilities." The phenomenon of the radical Right—
or what he called "pseudo-conservatism"—was, he wrote, "in good
part a product of the rootlessness and heterogeneity of American life,
and, above all, of its peculiar scrabble for status and its peculiar search
for a stable identity."

By 1963, however, Hofstadter had changed his mind about the very
notion of "status politics." In a postscript to the original essay, he
wrote,

> That there is need for some such concept I have little doubt. . . . How-
> ever, it now seems doubtful that the term "status politics" . . . is an ade-
> quate term for what I had in mind. No doubt, social status is one of the
> things that is at stake in most political behavior, and here the right-wing is
> no exception. But there are other matters involved . . . If we were to speak
> of "cultural politics" we might supply a part of what is missing. In our
> political life there have always been certain types of cultural issues, ques-
> tions of faith and morals, tone and style, freedom and coercion, which
> become fighting issues . . . There are always such issues at work in any
> body politic, but perhaps they are particularly acute and important in the
> United States because of our ethnic and religious heterogeneity.

What had happened was that for Hofstadter the study of the radical
Right had proved the beginning of an intellectual Ariadne's thread.
As fundamentalists played a large role in the Birch society and other
right-wing organizations, so it led him to the study of fundamentalism and the evangelical tradition in the United States. An amendment
to the notion of "status politics" thus became necessary. While the
Birchers and the McCarthyites might be discussed narrowly in terms
of status anxieties or even some particular brand of sociopathology
(*The Paranoid Style in American Politics*), there was clearly much more
at stake in, say, the temperance movement, and in all the other fundamentalist and evangelical movements of the nineteenth and twentieth centuries.

I reread this volume of essays while I was writing on Jerry Falwell
and his church. The notion of "status politics" did not really seem to
account for the New Right of the seventies and eighties, as its concerns (for school prayer and so on) were as clearly moral and cultural
as those of the temperance movement. Thus Hofstadter had been
right to drop the term. Still, the book seemed to me to contain important clues to the nature of all the new political movements of the
sixties, seventies, and eighties.

In the first place, of course, Hofstadter's conception of "cultural
politics" served to make the necessary connection between the overtly

political movements of the sixties, such as civil rights, those usually categorized as "social"—feminism, for example—and the various religious and cultural experiments of the day from Beat poetry to New Age communes to the Krishna Consciousness movement. It provided a link between Falwell's church, the Castro, Sun City, and Rajneeshpuram. All of these phenomena appeared in a time of prosperity and all were concerned with questions of culture and identity. The two-party system could not wholly absorb them, for in what seemed to be a characteristically American division of labor, it dealt primarily with questions of the political economy. Still, it was true, as Hofstadter suggested, that all peoples and nations have some variety of "cultural politics" and some concerns that cannot be reduced to, or explained away as a cover for, economic politics. The notion was too vague and did not explain what at least felt so American about the radical Right of the fifties and all the subsequent "cultural politics" movements. But there were other clues.

In studying the evangelical tradition Hofstadter had certainly located one of the main historical threads going through American "cultural politics." Prohibition, the campaign against the Catholic candidate, Al Smith, and most of the other cultural battles of the twenties were in fact only twentieth-century manifestations of a struggle that had been going on since the 1840s: evangelical Protestants pitted against Catholics, newer immigrant groups, and the cosmopolitan mores of the big trading cities on the coasts. Over the years nativist Protestant forces had gathered again and again under different banners ranging from the Know-Nothing party to the Populist movement, the temperance movement, and the Ku Klux Klan. The fundamentalist crusade of the seventies and eighties and the role played by politicians like Senator Jesse Helms showed that this strain in American politics still had a great deal of life in it.

On the other hand, this now-traditional struggle did not dominate contemporary politics as it did the politics of the twenties. For the most part the forces at work in the sixties and seventies were quite new. To begin with, black Americans entered the political arena for the first time in American history, asserting their rights to equality before the law. American Indians and Hispanic-Americans followed suit, joining the political debate in a way they never had before. Then, too, the sixties' youth movements had nothing to do with the old ethnic and religious tensions in white society. The social composition of these movements and those of the backlash showed that these struggles had become largely outdated. This was true even on the extreme Right (short of the Posse Comitatus and other quasi-criminal

Aryan supremacy groups). The anti-Communist crusades of the fifties had brought Protestants and right-wing Catholics together for the very first time. In the seventies Richard Viguerie and other New Right leaders cemented and broadened this alliance, partly by well-camou-flaged appeals to white racism, partly by working out a common program between Catholics and fundamentalists on abortion, aid to religious schools, homosexuality, and other issues. The strategists of the New Right would have liked to have made the movement wholly ecumenical: it was not, but Falwell and others made notable, if not entirely successful, attempts to reduce anti-Semitism among funda-mentalists and to build bridges to conservative Jews. Notable also was the gradual fadeout of the old theme of rural purity versus city corrup-tion in the rhetoric of fundamentalists and right-wing evangelists. Falwell, at least, meant to beat the cosmopolitans at their own game. What was true on the Right, was, of course, even more true on the Left and center. The liberal political movements were wholly ecumen-ical, and for feminists, gay rights advocates, and so on, ethnicity was almost entirely irrelevant. This was not really their doing. It was sim-ply the case that by the mid-sixties the whole deck of white middle-class society had been reshuffled, and the old cards of identity—Italian-American, WASP, Russian Jewish-American—had lost much of their meaning.

Thus, to return to Hofstadter, most of the "cultural politics" of the sixties and seventies had nothing—or at least nothing directly—to do with the (traditional) religious and white ethnic heterogeneity of the United States. In fact, quite surprisingly, the "cultural politics" of Europe in the seventies were much more affected by traditional reli-gions and ethnic groups. In Poland, after forty years of Communist rule, Catholicism reemerged as the strongest force for national cohe-sion; in Spain, the Basques and the Catalans demanded cultural au-tonomy. In Eastern Europe not only the Serbs and the Croats but also the Slovenes and the Hungarians in Rumania, did the same. Scotland and Wales called for devolution, and in Northern Ireland graffiti on the borders of Catholic and Protestant districts sometimes read merely '90 or '98: no more was necessary, for everyone knew that the signs meant 1690 and 1798 and they knew just why they were fighting words. But in the United States the grip of history was not that strong, nor cultural identity so firmly rooted. The American cultural move-ments of the day looked ahead to this transformation of society—beginning with their own membership. It was this transformative quality that linked the Rajneeshee, the gay activists, Sun Citians—but also the new fundamentalists. This and, oddly enough, the evangeli-cal mode.

Ken Maley had remarked that the process of "coming out" resembled the experience of being "born again." Jerry Falwell would have objected to the comparison, but "coming out," after all, entailed an act of faith and an act of will—a leap into the unknown. It entailed an internal transformation, or a change of consciousness, as gay liberationists put it. The Rajneeshee, of course, objected to any analogy between themselves and evangelicals, but they, too, were "born again" in the sense that they took on new names and new clothes and left their personal histories behind them. The specific link between the Rajneeshee and certain gay rights activists in the Castro was the Human Potential Movement with its injunction to "liberation and transformation." In Human Potential Movement philosophy the individual had merely to strip away all the roles, patterns, and neuroses that the society had imposed upon him or her to emerge like a Wordsworthian child—innocent, beautiful, spontaneous, and capable of forming authentic relationships with others. This was the "rebirth" the therapists offered; it was in many ways not different from Falwell's—the principal difference being that the therapists did not believe in sin, original or otherwise. Sun Citians, of course, did not go through a conversion process, and they were different in this respect from the three other groups. All the same, they were starting new lives, and, as Jackie Fenzau, the social director, said, they had to forget their former occupations and the status they enjoyed in order to be happy in Sun City; they had to live in the present—the here and now, as the therapists would have put it.

Sidney Mead, the great authority on the American Protestant tradition, wrote in *The Lively Experiment* that evangelical Protestantism was characterized by an emphasis on direct experience rather than knowledge of doctrine or ritual practice, and, as a consequence, by anti-intellectualism, ahistoricism, and a pragmatic experimentalism. In fact all four groups—Falwell's church and the others—shared these qualities. The Rajneeshee were wholly anti-intellectual in spite of their university training; they were interested in experience—an experience that for them transcended history. The gay leaders in San Francisco were anti-intellectual in regard to their own enterprise; they were pragmatic activists who, like the Rajneeshee, preferred to suspend judgment in favor of simply watching where their experiment would lead. For Sun Citians, it was activity that counted, not reflection: the focus was always on the present and future. Then, too, membership in all four groups was, at least theoretically, membership in a wholly egalitarian society—a brother- and sisterhood, or a society of children who had no past but only a present and a future. Also, it was not just the fundamentalists who engaged in millennial thinking and apocalyptic scenarios: it was the gays and the Rajneeshee, and indeed most of the groups that came out of the counterculture and the New Left.

The evangelical style of these groups was not altogether surprising in that, as Daniel Bell wrote in one of his essays on the radical Right, evangelical Protestantism was historically far more important than "puritanism" or "the New England Mind" in coloring the moral temper of Americans (indeed it was only the error of literary intellectuals to think otherwise). It was certainly one of the reasons that all these groups felt so very American. The evangelical movement had begun in England during the industrial revolution with John Wesley at a time of great social disturbance there. Yet now it seemed to have far more resonance in the United States. Possibly this was because of the "rootlessness and heterogeneity of American life" and its "peculiar search for a stable identity." Certainly American society in the sixties and seventies had a volatile quality to it.

Anyone who watched the demonstrations in Paris in May 1968 and those in Chicago in August that year might have imagined that the youth movements were the same on both sides of the Atlantic and would have the same consequences. There was a great deal of communication and commonality between them—that was obvious. Everything from New Left manifestos to fashions in blue jeans crossed and recrossed the Atlantic. And the initiatives were not all American ones. France had influential feminist and New Left intellectuals, West Germans pioneered some of the ashram routes, and England had the Beatles and the Rolling Stones. Yet neither feminism nor gay rights created the political conflicts in Europe that they did in the United States; they were not organized to do so, and they did not change European societies in the same way. The one organized youth grouping of any size—the Greens in Germany—turned into a political party and pursued coalition politics. During the sixties and seventies much of Western Europe went through the same transition to "post-industrial" technology that the United States did; the structure of its work force changed a great deal; there were political changes, and yet socially, culturally, it changed not very much at all. The English class system survived the Beatles; in Paris a government education plan of the eighties provoked clerical and anticlerical demonstrations with slogans resonating back to the French Revolution. Nowhere in Europe were there any new religious or cultural wars. Europeans had feared homogenization and Americanization, but the sixties and seventies proved to be decades of revival for ethnic and cultural minorities long submerged in nation-states. It was only in the United States that large numbers of people decided to forget the past and start all over again.

On the individual level rootlessness and the search for self-definition were, as Hofstadter suggested, permanent and characteristic features of American life. It was a consequence of occupational and geographic mobility and the loose weave of the society. Then, in many periods of history, Americans created new religions and new social movements as a way of restitching the fabric for themselves. But there were very few periods in American history in which the dominant sector—the white middle class—transformed itself as thoroughly as it did in the sixties and seventies: transformed itself quite deliberately, and from the inside out, changing its costumes, its sexual mores, its family arrangements, and its religious patterns. In fact since the Revolution there was probably only one other such period, and that was the period when the American evangelical tradition was born: the Age of Jackson and the Second Great Awakening. Historians such as William G. McLoughlin* have pointed to extraordinary parallels between the two periods, and indeed the history of the religious revivals of the 1830s and 1840s throws a good deal of light on the events of the 1960s and 1970s.

Jerry Falwell, the Rajneeshee, gay activists, and Sun Citians laid claim to the American tradition—not the tradition of the Founding Fathers but that of the Puritans. What most of them had in mind, of course, was the tradition of radical dissent, separation, and heroic struggle to build a new world on hostile ground. (Falwell and the Rajneeshee also looked to the precedent for religious government.) In this sense the claim was proper, but in another sense the claim, or reference, was wrong, for the Puritans were Calvinists who believed not at all in the ability of humans to liberate and transform themselves. The preamble to John Winthrop's covenant, after all, read: "God Almighty in his most holy and wise providence hath so disposed of the conditions of mankind, as in all times some must be rich and some poor, some high and eminent in power and dignity, others mean and in subjection." This was the Calvinist vision of society as a permanent hierarchy—the destiny of every individual fixed within it from birth. Calvinist theology—which was anathema to Falwell—proposed that God had predestined only a chosen elect for salvation and condemned everyone else to hell. Man could in no way affect his fate, since human nature was totally corrupt and God infinitely distant.

---

* William G. McLoughlin. *Revival, Awakening, and Reform: An Essay on Religion and Social Change in America, 1607 to 1977* (Chicago: University of Chicago Press, 1980).

Man had therefore merely to accept His will. This harsh doctrine, softened only somewhat by Jonathan Edwards and the other preachers of the First Great Awakening, dominated American Protestantism until well after the Revolution. The doctrine of salvation Falwell and all other American evangelicals preached dated from the Second Great Awakening—or, roughly speaking, from the second decade of the nineteenth century. It was at this point that Methodists and Baptists, followed by breakaway Presbyterians and Congregationalists, repudiated Calvinism for Arminian, or free-will, doctrines. In their Arminian New Light theology all men—but also all women—were morally responsible and free to choose their own salvation or damnation; all were capable of attaining salvation—it took no special knowledge and no accumulation of good works but merely the acceptance of Christ as a personal savior. Therefore those who—at any time— chose to take Christ into their hearts would receive sanctification or "the second blessing": they would be as reborn, their sins forgiven, washed away by the blood of the Lamb. The break with Calvinism was radical. Evangelical Arminianism proposed that human nature was not despicable, and that God was not so distant or implacable, for He had sent His only begotten Son to redeem mankind from the sin of Adam. Furthermore, the individual was not helpless but powerful: sin and error, of course, existed, but he or she could be redeemed by God's grace and an act of faith—or will. Then, as the individual could be redeemed, so in the postmillennial version of evangelical theology, the regenerate could reform the society and hasten the millennial reign of Christ on earth.

According to historians, the Second Great Awakening began, chronologically speaking, just after the Revolution, with a series of camp-meeting revivals in the frontier states of Kentucky and Tennessee led by Methodist and Baptist preachers on horseback. The revivals—to trust the accounts of outsiders—were wild, emotional affairs. (The Wesleyans, coming straight from the poor and demoralized districts of the new industrial cities in England had found a method that worked among the rootless and the culturally disoriented.) At the time, however, the American Protestant Establishment condemned these meetings as barbarous and perhaps the work of the devil. It was not until the 1820s that respectable, seminary-educated ministers appropriated elements of the Methodist preaching style along with their New Light doctrines. These preachers had a prolonged and bitter struggle with the Calvinists, but they prevailed and went on to hold mass revival meetings throughout the northern states—in the new territories, in New York, New England, and finally again in New York City, in 1857. The revivals seem to have more than doubled the number of practicing Protestants in the country, but they did a good deal else as well. The changes would be difficult to map except that in a few counties of upstate New York between Lake Ontario and the Adirondacks they happened very quickly and very dramatically. During the Second Great Awakening those counties—including Genesee, Wyoming, and Chautauqua, and the cities of Rochester, Utica, and Rome—were probably the most strenuously evangelized areas of the country. The fires of revival swept across them so hotly and so repeatedly that people took to calling this "the Burned-over District." Religious enthusiasm climaxed in the decade in 1825–37 when Charles Grandison Finney crossed and recrossed the district. By far the greatest evangelist of the day, Finney added to New Light theology the doctrine of perfectionism, or the doctrine that the regenerate might achieve perfect holiness and might by collective effort re-create the purity of primitive Christianity: the society that Christ himself had in mind. This was strong stuff, and in the Burned-over District it set off a chain reaction and a series of secondary explosions that bore extraordinary resemblance to the events of the sixties.

In 1830 Joseph Smith, the son of a poor farming family that had settled near Palmyra, New York, declared that some years before (perhaps in 1823—the moment has still to be pinned down) he had seen an angel and found the gold plates of a book written by a fifth-century prophet and buried for fifteen hundred years near his village. This book, *The Book of Mormon*, recounted the history of Israelite tribes that had come to the American continent long before the Indians, and it revealed that Christ had come to America after his death and resurrection in Jerusalem. Once the book was published, Smith preached the new scriptures, converted his family and neighbors, and founded a church later called the Church of Jesus Christ of Latter-day Saints. In the next decade he and his disciples, including the stalwart Brigham Young, traveled far and wide, making converts not only in New York State but in England, in New England, and as far west as Missouri and Illinois. The Saints made their first removal west immediately after the church was founded, and, though they were much persecuted, their band continued to grow. Smith was murdered in 1844, but when Young embarked on the great trek from Illinois to the salt lake beyond the Rockies, twelve thousand people followed him.

In 1831, a year after the founding of the Mormon church, William Miller, a farmer and a lay Baptist, who had fought as a militia lieutenant in the War of 1812, announced that his own independent study of the Bible showed that Christ would come again to earth in 1844. Licensed as a Baptist preacher, he delivered hundreds of lectures and sermons on the coming Advent across northern New York, and by

1839 a movement had formed about him composed of numerous Baptist preachers and other evangelists as well as lay people. The Adventists, as they were called, published a journal and held camp-meeting
revivals from New England to western New York; as word of the
imminent millennium spread, the crowds at these meetings grew
larger and larger and the excitement more and more intense. By 1843
it was estimated that some fifty thousand people were convinced the
Day was coming, while perhaps a million people across the country
from New England to the frontier waited with skeptical attention. As
the day Miller had appointed approached, hundreds of people gave
up their worldly occupations to preach the good news; some sold
their property and in the end went up to the tops of hills to watch for
Christ's coming. When the day passed without event, they came
down again, much disappointed. Mobs assailed the Adventist meeting places, William Miller was excommunicated, and many left the
movement—some for other enthusiasms. A scattering of Adventists
groups, however, survived—some maintaining that Miller had simply made an error of reckoning, others that Christ had come on the
appointed day but not materially, in the flesh. Eventually a woman
prophet gathered some of these groups into the Seventh-Day Adventist Church.

In 1848 John Humphrey Noyes founded what must still rank as the
most extraordinary social experiment in American history. A Yankee
patrician (his father was a U.S. congressman, his mother a cousin of
Benjamin Harrison), Noyes had attended the theological seminaries
at Andover and at Yale and been ordained as a Presbyterian minister.
Gradually, however, he reached the logical conclusion of the perfectionist doctrines preached farther west and declared that he, personally, was without sin. Forbidden to preach by his colleagues, he
retreated to the family farm in Putney, Vermont, where he persuaded
a number of his neighbors and most of his family—though not his
father—to join him in forming a community of absolute Christian
fellowship where property would be shared and free love practiced.
Noyes explained that the exclusive attachment of a man and a woman
in marriage was incompatible with the absolute fellowship that should
obtain between all regenerate beings. Vermonters, however, would
not put up with this, and they arrested Noyes on charges of adultery.
Noyes, though, had devotees in western New York, and in 1846 he,
with a group of thirty-one adults and fourteen children, moved to a
farm in Oneida County. There the community flourished. The group
doubled in size the first year and doubled again the next year and the
next; in fact there were so many people eager to join that Noyes finally
had to limit the membership to three hundred people—plus a waiting

list. The Oneida Community, as it was called, made an excellent living from farming but also from the manufacture of iron traps and, eventually, silver plate. All three hundred people lived under one roof, sharing the labor, alternating tasks, and working always as a group. The management of the community was democratic—except that Noyes always had the last word. Harmony was maintained by Noyes but also by a system of mutual criticism in which the personal relations and the failings of members were discussed openly by the whole group. Commune members practiced free love, but by a set of formal and mannerly arrangements that ensured the consent of both parties. As Noyes was a believer in eugenics, he insisted on a system of birth control through male continence: there were no children born in the community for many years, and thereafter children were born only to couples designated by him and his senior disciples; the children were cared for by the community. The commune was extremely pious—there were religious services and Bible reading every day; it was also quite cultivated—its members singing Bach chorales and putting on Shakespeare plays. What was extraordinary—particularly in the context of the period—the community enjoyed an almost untroubled relationship with the outside world: tourists would come every Sunday in coaches to tour the commune and take lunch. The commune survived, indeed it prospered, for almost forty years, dispersing only in the 1880s after the death of John Humphrey Noyes.

The Oneida Community was in fact only the largest and most successful of the idealistic communes founded in upstate New York in the years of the Second Great Awakening. The first to appear were Shaker communites. The Shaker prophet, Mother Ann Lee, established the first of them when she came to the new territories from England in the late eighteenth century, and thereafter others grew up. Their intense spirituality, egalitarianism, and communal solidarity impressed the religious radicals of the Burned-over District, and they seem to have influenced Noyes, among others. By the 1840s there was a scattering of religious communes across the district including a breakaway Quaker group, a millenarian group called the Pilgrims, and a number of small groups practicing spiritual adultery. In addition there were a number of secular communes, most of them modeled on the ideas of the European Utopian socialists, Robert Owen and Charles Fourier. Around Rochester, a Fourierist movement had several hundred enthusiasts in the early 1840s, but the secular communes were generally very short-lived.

In 1848, Margaret and Katie Fox, ages fifteen and twelve, the daughters of a farming family established near Newark, New York, heard weird rappings in their house one night and interpreted them

as communications from the spirit world. Going to work on a translation, they finally revealed that the rappings came from the spirit of a
man who had died in the house: a spirit that was omniscient and
infallible and would answer any questions they asked of it. The girls
were introduced into Rochester society by their parents; they gave a
number of public séances and quite quickly gathered quite a large
following. A committee of investigators eventually discovered that the
girls produced the weird rappings with their toe joints, but this did
not seem to discredit them with everyone. Their popularity faded
after a few years, but only because too many competitors appeared
around them. By 1859 there were seventy-one spiritualist mediums in
New York State, and, according to the historian of the Burned-over
District, Whitney Cross, "rappings, table moving, speaking in
tongues, and involuntary operation of musical instruments became
almost commonplace experiences."

The phenomenon of the Fox sisters was only a sign of the times.
During the 1830s and 1840s New Yorkers imported a great variety of
new pseudosciences and psychological techniques from Europe. Uni-
versalist preachers, the most freethinking of the Protestant clergy,
inspired great enthusiams for spiritualism but also for mesmerism,
and phrenology. Swedenborgianism, the philosophy that linked
these techniques with Christianity, had a great vogue for a while in
the district. The people involved with these new disciplines were not,
by and large, credulous country people but rather urbanites, and
religious liberals, and Bostonians as well as New Yorkers. William
James, for one, practiced mesmerism and learned much from it.

In addition to all of these new religions and communal experiments
from the Millerites to the Oneida Community to the spiritualists, the
Burned-over District gave rise to every major reform movement of the
nineteenth century. The temperance movement developed its first
mass following in the district; so, too, did the missionary and Bible
societies that would carry the Protestant gospel across the country
and all the way to China by the end of the century. Then, too, the
district produced a movement for the establishment of the Sabbath
and an educational reform movement devoted to propagating liter-
acy, establishing free schools, and giving a more specifically Protestant content to school curricula. In the twentieth century these
movements would be read a conservative—or mere "status politics."
But in the minds of their creators they were a part of a radical effort
to perfect the society and hasten the reign of Christ on earth. Abolo-
tionism was a part of this perfectionist effort, and, in context, merely
a part of it. The great abolitionist leaders William Lloyd Garrison and
Theodore Weld were protégés of Charles Finney, the central figure in

the perfectionist enterprise. Garrison's American Anti-Slavery Society worked out of Finney's New York City church, and Weld, a convert of Finney's, organized an abolitionist crusade in revival style through upstate New York in the mid-1830s, giving the cause of antislavery its first mass base and making those counties for a time the center of the movement. In upstate New York clergymen from groups as diverse as the Baptists and the Universalists were enthusiastic abolitionists.

Then, too, of course, the feminist movement began in the Burned-over District in the 1840s. Susan B. Anthony and Elizabeth Cady Stanton were upstate New Yorkers, as were Amelia Bloomer, Antoinette Brown Blackwell, and the Grimké sisters. Anthony and Stanton had been organizers in the antislavery movement; they became feminists after journeying to an antislavery convention in London and finding that, as women, they were not allowed in the convention hall. The first feminist convention was held in Seneca Falls, New York, in 1848 —or the same year John Humphrey Noyes established his commune not a hundred miles away. To upstate New Yorkers the feminists may have seemed no less quixotic than Noyes. Indeed, they may have seemed more so, for at the very same time in the district the structure of the family was changing and most middle-class women were retreating into domesticity and the privacy of the home. That is, at a certain class level, the family was becoming "Victorian"; it was taking on the shape that Jerry Falwell in the seventies called "the traditional American family."

What happened in those few counties of upstate New York has always been a matter of considerable interest to historians of religion in this country—and particularly, of course, to historians of the religions that began there. Other historians, however, have given the district only glancing attention until just recently—the one exception being Whitney Cross, whose book, *The Burned-Over District*, published in 1950, remains the one history of the district as a whole. But in the last few years there has been a sudden surge of interest in the district among social historians of the new school—feminists, family historians, and people interested in the lives of working-class people rather than in the political and intellectual leadership. Thus far two of them have shed a great deal of light on the fundamental social changes taking place in the region during the period of the revivals: Paul E. Johnson in *A Shopkeeper's Millennium: Society and Revivals in Rochester, New York, 1815–1837* (published in 1978) and Mary P. Ryan in *Cradle of the Middle Class: The Family in Oneida County, New York, 1790–1865* (published in 1981). Neither Ryan nor Johnson deal with the more sensational results of the revivals; rather, using the new tools of historical ethnography, they look below to the shifting tectonic plates within the society as a whole. To summarize the two accounts briefly and sketchily, what they tell us is this:

In the 1820s upstate New York was settled farming country, the frontier having moved on past it in the 1790s. The westward movement was now well under way, and the nation expanding at an enormous rate, the frontier now pushing out through Ohio, Kansas, and Missouri. But upstate New York was a great and fertile plain compared to New England, and as the Erie Canal had just opened, joining it to the coastal cities, it was fast becoming one of the greatest grain-growing and grain-exporting regions in the world. Its population, largely Yankee, was also growing prodigiously with an influx of New Englanders, whose small farms could not compete with its productivity. Small market towns founded at the turn of the century were burgeoning into cities almost overnight. Rochester, for example, a mere village in 1820, before the arrival of the Erie Canal, was the fastest growing city in the nation by 1827 and the country's first inland boomtown. It was the center of commerce between the coast and the Genesee Valley, but it was also, and increasingly, a manufacturing town: its ten flour mills processed the Genesee wheat, and its hundred workshops and small manufacturing establishments produced everything from guns to furniture—and even jewelry. Economically speaking, upstate New York was an analogue to southern California in the 1960s.

According to Mary Ryan, the settlers of the first generation coming from New England had re-created seventeenth-century Puritan family and community structures in order to deal with the exigencies of the frontier. Before the canal opened, little could be imported, so farm households had not only to grow all the food they consumed, but they had to produce most of the necessities of life: clothes, farm implements, and so on. These households included not only family members but bonded servants and other laborers. The father of the family had authority over all of them, treating the laborers much as children but also treating the children much as laborers in a corporate enterprise. Like its Puritan forebears, the frontier family was strictly hierarchical, and not much affection was exchanged between its members, as affection was thought to undermine obedience and destroy authority. In the towns artisans and shopkeepers ran family businesses much as the farmers did, assimilating extra laborers into the household. When the first factories were built—flour mills, sawmills, and tanneries—the townspeople sent their children and other dependents out to work in them full- or part-time and took their wages (often paid in kind) to support the family unit.

As time went on, however, the factories grew larger and the technology of manufacturing more specialized and technically complex. The owners of large concerns could no longer board all of their immigrant laborers, and families could no longer use or hire out their children and other dependents interchangeably. Inevitably, children and laborers were expelled from the established households, and in cities like Rochester a new phenomenon appeared: a mass of single young men who worked in the factories and paid for their lodgings in the houses of merchants or shopkeepers, whose children had in turn left them. Many of these young men were transients—people coming from the East to make their fortunes or, failing that, to move on out to the frontier. Some stayed, of course, and became skilled workers, but even they were transients in the sense that they had no families, no land, and no social context. As for the young women, those who were born in this frontier settlement had been brought up to run or to serve a productive family unit—and now that unit had disappeared.

Rochester—so Paul Johnson tells us—became an anarchic city where crowds of young, single laborers spent their leisure hours drinking and fighting and terrorizing the new residential neighborhoods—to which the factory owners had retired with their wives and children. Work discipline was lax—men drank on their jobs—for work hours were not yet set off against life in general, but there were no fathers and mothers to set the standards. The churches were of no help, as the churches had always worked through families, assuming the family the guarantor of its members' salvation and social morality. The city goverment, for its part, was paralyzed. Cities like Rochester had been run since their foundation like New England towns, where only men of property came to town meetings, and where issues were decided by voice vote. But universal male suffrage had become the rule in New York—as it had in most northern states in the 1820s—and with the sudden huge increase of population, the system fell apart. Gentry families were now fighting with each other for power in the cities and the state. In the late twenties those out of power stumbled upon an almost magical lever to move popular sentiment against their rivals: anti-Masonry. The Masonic lodges then included a great many of the prominent businessmen, judges, and politicians in the state (as in the country-at-large). But because they were secret societies, conspiracy theories grew up about them, and people fantasized that they were centers of a vast and complicated plot to take over the government—and the banks as well. Finding that these conspiracy theories resonated among workingmen innocent of class politics, prominent businessmen who did not belong to the Masons set about fanning the flames of suspicion. Their efforts were mightily

advanced when the foremost conspiracy theorist of the day—an unemployed stonemason—was abducted after official harassment and
disappeared without a trace. Anti-Masonry was in some sense the
McCarthyism of the day: at any rate, the results were much the same.
In Rochester and cities like it, the political elite became passionately
divided over an issue that was largely trumped up, and that in any
case had nothing to do with the real problems of the day. Whether
the Masons or the anti-Masons won the elections now mattered little,
for neither had a mandate to deal with the real issues, and one group
would automatically oppose the solutions of the other, no matter how
reasonable they were. Then, too, the conflict generated others along
parallel lines: the anti-Masons generally believed that local governments should impose temperance by law, whereas the Masons
thought it should be voluntary. Here again, the churches could not
help, for their congregations were bitterly divided on the Masonry
and temperance issues: the struggles took place inside church congregations and church attendance dropped off. Finally in 1830 one of the
prominent citizens of Rochester called upon Charles Grandison Finney to lead a revival in the city.

Finney spent six months in Rochester that year, leading prayer and
revival meetings every single day. The meetings were held in various
churches around the city, but also on secular or neutral ground, in
people's houses, under tents, and in public halls. They were carefully
organized, with church members, and then converts, going from
door-to-door distributing tracts, holding informal prayer meetings,
and urging people to come to the revivals. People from different denominations came to the meetings—as did the unchurched; and, as
was not the case in the churches, the meetings included people of
different social backgrounds. At the meetings worship was public and
participatory: people prayed aloud, and those leaning toward conversion would sit apart from the rest of the congregation on an "anxious
bench" and would make their moment of conversion into a public
spectacle. Finney, a man of great personal force, would speak directly
to the "sinners" in the congregation, addressing them by name and
describing the choice they faced between heaven and hell.

These tactics, according to Johnson, were extraordinarily successful. Not only did church membership rise precipitously in six months,
but Finney created a small army of militant evangelicals—people who
thereafter gave all their efforts to leading others to conversion. The
militants brought other evangelists to Rochester year after year, including Theodore Weld, who in the early 1830s lectured on temperance reform. The converts from the first revival came, Johnson tells
us, disproportionately from the upper ranks of the society—from

among businessmen, professionals, and master craftsmen. But in the succeeding revivals the proportions changed, and the converts included greater numbers of clerks, small shopkeepers, skilled and semiskilled workingmen. Socially and politically, the results were spectacular: the struggle over Masonry subsided; the political elite united behind a voluntary temperance movement; workingmen joined the movement and the churches—perhaps in part because the businessmen made membership in both conditions of employment and advancement; work discipline improved and civic peace was restored.

For Johnson the revival movement was quite simply a successful attempt on the part of the gentry to impose social controls on an unruly mob of workingmen—a mob which might otherwise have become a working class with its own class culture and class consciousness. For Ryan, however (as for most other historians of the revivals), the movement was far more significant and the transformation it wrought far more profound. According to her, it was not just the local elites that took enthusiastic part in the revivals—it was, from the very beginning, farmers, artisans, and small merchants as well. What was more, women played key roles in all of the revival movements. It was usually women who went from door-to-door distributing tracts, and it was usually the wife in each family who brought her children and her husband to the meetings. This was only as might be expected, for when the social order fell apart, life became far more difficult for those living on the margins than for those who had resources. According to Ryan, it was particularly difficult for young men and women from farm, artisanal, or shopkeeping families; suddenly ejected from their corporate households, they had to struggle mightily to find a place for themselves in the new order of things. It was these young people, Ryan believes, who created much of the religious frenzy of the Burned-over District.

According to Ryan, the revival movement in Oneida County resulted in nothing less than the formation of a new society. A new kind of family emerged from the ruins of the extended, corporate family: a family whose values and domestic practices were to define the new "middle class" taking shape in the cities and towns. The end result, Ryan says, was a new division between "public" and "private" spheres: the home (no longer the center of production) became a private space—a sanctuary for intimate personal relations. Families now required this retreat, for with the growth of manufacturing enterprises and the growth of cities and city governments, the larger society became more and more anonymous. As the two spheres grew distinct, so did gender roles, and the family itself became a specialized unit. Men (often also unmarried women) went out to work in the public sphere, while their wives took charge of the household and the maintenance of family relations. It was now women who brought up children—viewing them now no longer as depraved adults but as innocents in need of love and proper training in the Christian virtues. For young men the virtues now stressed were those of thrift, industry, and self-reliance—but mainly the last, for to work in the outside world, young men had to develop individual initiative and had to be able to compete with the anonymous mass of their peers. The age of the self-made man had just begun.

As it was more specialized, so this new middle-class society was far less authoritarian and hierarchical than Puritan society. The bridge between the two—so Ryan demonstrates—was made by the reform associations. Benevolent societies had existed in the United States long before the nineteenth century, but in the wake of the revivals, a host of new ones sprang up in Oneida County: not just temperance associations but a Maternal Association, a Female Missionary Society, a Young Men's Association, and so on. These societies, she maintains, transcended age, class, and occupational divisions: they mediated class differences, created new social bonds, and acted as training grounds for the new society. They also for a time—that is, until they died out at midcentury—gave women a role in the new public sphere. While they seemed to have pointed most women toward a future of participation in charitable enterprises and good works, they clearly offered an experience that women such as Susan B. Anthony and Elizabeth Cady Stanton never forgot and refused to give up.

Ryan and Johnson do not tell us much about Finney and the other evangelists of the Burned-over District, nor do they really describe what happened within the revival meetings to produce such extraordinary results. All the same, both accounts suggest that the district was going through a cultural transformation of the sort the anthropologist Anthony F. C. Wallace called a "revitalization movement." From a comparison of movements variously known as "reform movements," "cargo cults," "religious revivals," "Utopian communities," and so on, Wallace came to the conclusion that "phenomena of major culture-system innovation" were characterized by a uniform process he called "revitalization." The process began with the disruption or disintegration of a more or less stable cultural system. Initially a few individuals in this system—but then people in increasing numbers—began to experience severe stress as a result of the system breakdown. The next stage was that of "cultural distortion." Now, not just individuals but the majority experienced a disintegration of the mental image they had of the society and its culture. In this period some individuals adapted by making piecemeal changes in their lives; others, however, adopted "regressive" behaviors, such as alcoholism, extreme passivity, violence, disregard of kinship and sexual mores, or states of depression and self-reproach. The third stage was the "revitalization" period in which "elements or subsystems which may already be in currency were combined into a new and internally consistent structure." According to Wallace, religious revitalization movements are usually conceived by a single person—a prophet who experiences a dramatic moment of insight or hallucinatory visions. Generally the prophet gives evidence of a radical change of personality after the vision—perhaps a rather sudden version of the sort of personality change that occurs during maturation or in the rites of passage. The dreamer-prophet then communicates his vision and makes converts. Some of these converts experience an ecstatic vision such as their master had, while others are convinced by rational arguments and still others by questions of expediency. The converts organize and then, almost inevitably, encounter some form of opposition. If the movement is to succeed, it has to deal with this opposition, adapt to the external world, and solve a great variety of practical problems; it must also put forth a program of social and political reform. If the majority of the population (however large or small the society) accepts the new religion, then a cultural transformation occurs, and the group program becomes the established way of doing things: it becomes the system, and the society enters a new period of cultural stability.

Wallace's model may be overly rigid (as many anthropologists now contend) but it is nonetheless suggestive. To add the religious to the social history of the Burned-over District is to see that it works quite well in this case—particularly when Finney enters the picture. Though Finney was far from the only evangelist to work in the district, he was certainly the most influential, and his career seems paradigmatic. Finney had grown up in upstate New York; he had been a schoolteacher briefly, then a lawyer. He had spent four years in a law office when, at the age of twenty-nine, he had an experience of a "mighty Baptism of the Holy Ghost." The next morning he quit his job and gave himself over to religious studies; three years later he was ordained as a minister in the Presbyterian Church. At that time—it was the early 1820s—the Calvinist-Arminian struggles were raging through the seminaries. Finney planted himself firmly in the camp of the New Light preachers, refusing to go to the conservative theological school at Princeton. But then he went a good bit further than the New England evangelists, such as Lyman Beecher, thought it proper to go. To people like Beecher he was something of a contradiction—a man of intellectual tastes, indeed a learned man, and yet a man of the people who would preach in their language and with emotion. He would preach what came to seem the quintessential bourgeois virtues —temperance, thrift, and so on; but he also preached abolition, political reform, and reform in the way merchants and manufacturers conducted their businesses. The revivals he led were not particularly emotional by the standards of the Burned-over District, and yet many of his converts did experience ecstatic visions or states of religious enthusiasm. What he promised "sinners" was immediate and complete absolution. For Calvinists carrying around crippling burdens of guilt for their inability to fulfill the old injunctions to be a "father" to their employees, or to be obedient "children" when there were no more "fathers"—the release from this guilt might in itself feel like an ecstatic experience. (It might feel like "coming out" or being "born again.") But Finney did not stop there. He insisted that his converts had an obligation to perfect themselves and to realize the vision of Christ on earth. Temperance, as he described it, was not a form of repression or social control but rather a form of purification—another kind of release, different but nonetheless analogous to the abolition of slavery. As the individual could be redeemed, so by individual efforts the whole society might purify itself and become regenerate. This state of regeneration or "perfection" would be the society of Christ's disciples at the beginning of Christian history, and it would put an end to history (and all its tragic dilemmas) with the return of Christ to earth. Finney was nothing if not an optimist, and in the middle of one of his successful revival cycles he predicted that, as a result of man's efforts at reform, the millennial Kingdom would come very soon—perhaps in five years.

To look once again at the Wallace model is to see that many of the other millenarian or Utopian movements of the Burned-over District were also "revitalization movements"; it was just that they were more limited in their appeal or in their duration than Finney's. The Mormon leaders, for example, passed successfully through all kinds of trials and adversities, but by comparison to Finney and his colleagues they attracted a relatively small group of people at the time. And because they left the district, they had relatively little impact on its particular cultural transformation. The Millerites, by contrast, had a built-in self-destruct mechanism in the literalness of their prophecy: the movement would have ended whether or not the End came on the date Miller predicted. As for the Oneida Community, it for all intents and purposes died with John Humphrey Noyes, having failed to institutionalize itself sufficiently—or, as Weber would have it, to "routinize the charisma" of its founder-leader. Abolition and temperance were, of course, parts of Finney's whole "revitalization" program, though they had their own leaders and their own constituencies. Feminism, however, was not; as a social movement it resembled abolitionism but it was a secondary explosion from the fires of revival and it created its own independent program.

How such an extraordinary variety of movements could rise up in the same few counties in the same short space of time is, of course, the great puzzle of the Burned-over District. For twenty years the society was a veritable fireworks display of extraordinary ideas and extraordinary enthusiasms: projects taking off skyward, creating bursts of brilliance and then—for the most part—fading out. This is also, of course, the puzzle of the 1960s and 1970s. And here the work of the anthropologist Victor Turner is of some help. In his *Dramas, Fields, and Metaphors,* Turner talks about groups of people in the process of major social change; his focus, unlike Wallace's, is on those in a state of transition, or in what he calls "liminal," or threshold, states. In stable societies thresholds, or "limina," may be rites of passage: initiations into manhood or the priesthood. Or they may be simply "in-between" periods, such as adolescence or "midlife crisis." In highly ritualized societies (Hindu society, certain tribal groups) these periods of transition, and the people going through them, are often hedged about by taboos, for people in transition are neither this nor that, but anomalies who have no "identity" and no structural position within the society. And having no identity, they are in some sense dangerous, for they are people who might think anything. In ritualized societies these people in transition have a well-known propensity to bond very tightly among themselves: they look upon each other as equals; their relationships are direct, immediate, face-to-face, and not constrained by any of the normal social rules or roles; and thus they become very quickly a brother- or sisterhood. In certain societies those going through these "liminal" periods, these rites of passage, have an obligation to contemplate the mysteries of life, their own personal problems, and the functioning of their society. They are free, so they must take the opportunity—of which there are few in life—to think about things. The danger is, of course, that they will actually *see* the social structure and want to change it: thus the taboos.

As it is with individuals in rites of passage, so it is, Turner says, with whole societies in the midst of drastic social change. In times of change groups, or whole societies, may bond together for a while in what Turner calls *communitas*—or the kind of community where people relate as total persons, free, equal, and completely open to each other—and to suggestion from the outside world. The biological analogy is perhaps to molting—and specifically, perhaps, to the molting of eider ducks. Losing all their feathers at the same time, these sea ducks as individuals lose all their capacity to avoid predators both from above and below; so, when they are molting, they join together in huge naked bands or "rafts" to paddle and skim the surface of the ocean pretending (for the benefit of larger predatory fish and fowl) that they are one large thing. For humans, as for birds, this period of molting is dangerous, but for humans it is also a period of great creativity. The image of molting appears in the *I Ching*, the ancient Chinese Book of Changes, and it signifies both revolution and the coming of spring.

Revolution is, of course, a directed change, but when the change is —for a time at least—undirected, people in transitional states are open and vulnerable to all kinds of ideas. "The world over," Turner says, "millenarian and revivalistic movements originate in periods when societies are in liminal transition between major orderings of the social structure." And not only revivals but crusades, or collective journeys to new or unknown destinations; hegiras such as the early Muslims took, or such as the Mormons took across the United States. In stable societies these voyages are not hegiras but pilgrimages to known sacred places along more or less well-defined routes. Pilgrims on their way to Mecca or to Lourdes have the opportunity to experience a sense of community with people whose like they have never met before—a sense of brotherhood which transcends class, race, and nationality: they have the opportunity to become Muslims or Catholics in the broadest sense—beyond their own local definitions. This is a well-known phenomenon, but, according to Turner, it is also true of people on hegiras. The destination may be unimportant: it is the journey that changes them, for it reveals the possibility of *communitas,* and the community itself is sacralized along the way.

All societies, Turner says, contain elements of "structure" and elements of "anti-structure." By "structure" what he means is not just social structure or laws and customs but everything that holds people apart and defines their differences. "Anti-structure" is all that which brings people together (*communitas*) and resolves oppositions and contradictions. It is the art or the mysticism of a society as opposed to its mathematics; it is its intuitive, as opposed to its discursive, reasoning. Both are necessary, for a society that is too rigidly structured is stifling and a society with too little structure is the same—as a result of its need to suppress individual differences and repress all tendencies to independence. But in periods of major social change, when the structure of a society seems unworkable, groups often try to maximize *communitas*—for the alternative seems to be a state of total disjunction and anomie. Religious groups, but others as well, have traditionally used certain well-defined strategies to this end. They try to eliminate the outward signs of rank—often by taking up the dress and behavior of the poor, because it seems to them the most "natural," or in any case, the simplest. Second, they give up their property—or share it among themselves and hold it in common. Third, they attack the institution of marriage and repudiate sexual exclusivity, preferring celibacy or nonexclusive sexuality for the sake of group bonding. And fourth (though the list is surely not exhaustive), they attempt to minimize or conceal gender differences. For Turner all of this is still liminal behavior, and not the end of a social change process. As all societies require some structure, so these groups cannot last unless they eventually acquire it—or unless they become content to take a very small place within the interstices of a larger, more structured society.

Turner's conception of *liminality* explains, it seems to me, a great deal of what happened in the Burned-over District. To begin with, it illuminates the prophetic and mystical state that so many people—and particularly the young—seemed to experience at the time. And it goes a long way to explaining why people living almost next door to each other might have had such an extraordinary variety of responses to the same situation. Also why certain ideas that now seem bizarre or eccentric might have had equal weight with ideas that now seem to be truly prophetic or mainstream. The search for *communitas* explains, for example, why such properly brought-up people as John Humphrey Noyes and his relatives should suddenly pool their property and take up group marriage—and why Presbyterian clergymen, equally well brought up, should engage in antinomian behavior of an even more scandalous sort. It illuminates the early Mormon practice of polygamy and the decision of the Shakers to remain celibate. Then, too, it points to the function of the voluntary associations as described by Mary Ryan. The notion of *liminality* gives a clue to the great vogue for spiritualism in the Burned-over District, for spirits of the dead who communicate with the living are, precisely, liminal figures, somewhere between man and God, life and death. The mesmeric trance is equally liminal, for the subject under hypnosis reveals what is normally concealed or unknown. Those who practiced mesmerism or spiritualism were clearly looking for an oracle, or a guide to the future —their usual guides having proved useless or wrong. In periods of cultural transition people do not feel that their ideas or projects must be constrained by current intellectual assumptions or current social realities; they conceive of all kinds of idealistic solutions—and carry some of them out. Most societies, however, are small or centralized enough that at a certain point one system or solution prevails, and the rest are overwhelmed by majority opinion. But in a society at the edge of a vast and expanding frontier, many different solutions or experiments could coexist for a long period. Thus the Mormons could survive, and thus feminism could survive—if not flourish—even while most women were turning inward to Victorian domesticity.

The history of the Burned-over District, as illuminated by Wallace and Turner, suggests some new ways of looking at the "cultural politics" of the sixties and the seventies and some of its cultural creations —among them, the Rajneeshee, the Castro, Sun City, and Falwell's church. Certainly there are obvious parallels between the religious revival movements of the two periods. (One thinks of Falwell, halfway between the world of Appalachia and the world of engineering school, on his knees in an unused administration room of the Baptist Bible College crying out to God for help.) As for the new and imported "youth religions" and occult practices, they seem quite clearly successors to some of the more apparently eccentric religious movements and practices in the Burned-over District. (The Rajneeshee themselves referred to the Oneida Community and, rather more hopefully, to the Mormons as historical precedents.) But religious revival did not play so central a role in the sixties and the seventies as it did during the Second Great Awakening—and nor did charismatic leadership. (The most important exception to this rule was surely the role played by Dr. Martin Luther King, Jr., in the civil rights movement in the South. The march on Selma was a kind of hegira that brought blacks and whites from a great variety of backgrounds together for the first time.) Most of the sixties' youth rebellions and youth movements were secular in nature. Yet, to consider what Turner and Wallace say about revivals or revitalization movements, there clearly was such a movement at work in that large and amorphous phenomenon, the counterculture.

What happened, after all, was that sometime in the mid-sixties large numbers of white, middle-class young people suddenly and quite spontaneously took off their middle-class clothes and put on the dress of workingmen—blue jeans—and took up the erotic music of the black working class. The men grew their hair long and the women took to wearing pants (blue jeans, perhaps, with denim jackets). And together they turned on their elders and went on the road. They traveled endlessly, their journeys having no destination most of the time and no purpose except that which lay in the journey itself. They went looking for their peers, and whether they found them at antiwar demonstrations, at Woodstock, or in India along the ashram routes, the discovery was the same: they were a brother- and sisterhood, and they shared a secret understanding—one not vouchsafed to Eleanor Rigby or Mr. Jones. The secret was that they alone were real and authentic. Their parents and elders were living lies—they were stuck in their role-playing and in their absurd social conformity. For the young the supreme virtues were those of openness and risk-taking: all institutions of society were empty and had to go. The sexual revolution was on one hand an attack on just another empty institution and on the other hand an acting-out of the emotions flowing so freely around this community of equals. The counterculture—as Turner's work would suggest—was not an alternate culture so much as an anticulture where all structures and conventions were dissolved. For the young it was quite precisely a melting pot. It was a melting pot in the original sense where "all the races of Europe were melting and reforming." But it was also a melting pot for the remnants of Victorian bourgeois culture that had survived into the sixties. It was not—as many at the time supposed—an end in itself; rather, it was a beginning. It was the creative ooze from which new life-forms would emerge.

And of course a great deal did come out of it: a host of new and imported religions, all the political and social movements of the late sixties and early seventies, literally hundreds of communes and other experiments in communal living, a new psychotherapy and enthusiasm for a wild variety of pseudosciences and occult practices; also, of course, the drug culture, the new popular music, a new visual aesthetic, and so on. The counterculture was prodigiously fertile and hugely profligate. Thus it was not surprising that some of its creations proved short-lived.

The Rajneeshee were merely one of the new religious movements, but not a wholly unrepresentative one in the spectrum that ran from Scientology to TM and the Maharishi Mahesh Yogi to the Tibetan Buddhist community of Trungpa Rimpoche. Oregonians called them a "cult," but then in the 1840s they would have had to put the Oneida Community and Joseph Smith's following under the same rubric. In Wallace's terms they were a revitalization movement—except that they failed to adapt and to institutionalize themselves. In Turner's vocabulary they suffered from a surfeit of *communitas*. The flowing, liquid, egalitarian community had to erect high walls around itself lest its members took to loving others and simply flowing away. Also, of course, their ideology left no room for individual differences, and they in the end could not tolerate dissent, independence of mind, idiosyncrasy—or even bad temper. In their attempt to suppress their differences they developed a kind of totalitarianism. The Oneida

Community might well have ended the same way, and the fact that it did not says a great deal for the character of John Humphrey Noyes.

In the development of the gay community in the Castro there was something of the same thing at work. Its origins were also in the counterculture, and for a time it had the same liquid tribal quality and the same surfeit of *communitas*. Throughout history, plagues have established themselves in new environmental niches—such as the new cities in medieval Europe. Not just the gay community but the sexual revolution and the drug culture in general created such a niche. AIDS—with its destruction of the body's immune system—was perhaps the quintessential disease of *communitas*. But the Castro, unlike the Rajneeshee, developed a good deal of structure—a political structure, in the first place, that allowed it to adapt and survive. Beyond that, of course, the gay movement, like the feminist movement, proved a major force in the reshaping of the whole culture.

Sun City did not come out of the counterculture, but it was an adaptation to social transformation going on throughout the country. In particular it was a response to the enormous increase in longevity and the change in relationship between parents and their adult children. Sun Citians thought of themselves as occupying a transitional stage in life; a number of them understood how new and undefined this stage was and actively sought solutions and a new kind of community. The future of retirement communities such as Sun City depends a great deal on the economy, but it also depends on the manner in which "the American family" is eventually recast. Possibly the retirement communities bear some relationship to the voluntary associations of the 1840s: that is, they may be transitional forms. But then it is altogether possible that in the future there will be not one American middle-class family, but several, a variety. In that case age-segregated communities may remain as an alternative—as a choice for some people. Possibly also all the various Sun Cities may be the first rough drafts for institutions in which many Americans of future generations will choose to live.

Falwell's church—along with all the other evangelical churches—makes the historical connection between the Second Great Awakening and the present day. Those people who poured into the evangelical churches during the late seventies were, after all, walking much the same path that Finney and the other preachers of the New Light had blazed. Falwell himself could claim direct descent from Finney through the line of the great mass revivalists: Dwight L. Moody, Billy Sunday, and Billy Graham. Finney, of course, was a visionary, an innovator, and a political, social, and theological progressive. His successors, by clinging close to his Victorian vision of family life and middle-class society, were conservatives or reactionaries in terms of the society of the day. But then their constituency seemed to be the same generation after generation: the people flocking to the mass revival meetings (as opposed to those who grew up and remained in evangelical churches) always seemed to be people moving from the country to the city, from a small and relatively simple world to a large and relatively complicated one. They were people who felt a great need for structure. Like Falwell, Moody, Sunday, and Graham were premillennialists—their theology reflecting the fury of the rootless, of those who did not know what was to be done. (Finney's perfectionism was carried on historically by those who thought they knew what was to be done.) Graham, of course, moved into the mainstream and became more of a liberal, politically and theologically, over the years, leaving his fundamentalist constituency behind him. Falwell, however, moved slowly toward the center, trying at once to change "the world" and bring his fundamentalist constituency into it. While to liberals he seemed dogmatic and unbending, he was in fact experimental and pragmatic. Doctrinal issues did not interest him very much. And practically speaking, his achievement was enormous. Leading fundamentalists away from separation and premillennial resignation and despair, he enfranchised and empowered what was perhaps the last unenfranchised and unempowered sector of the white population in the United States. He changed fundamentalist culture and in the process changed the tone and temper of the radical Right (whether permanently or not remains to be seen). To the extent that fundamentalists had influence in Washington and the competence to deal with "Ivy Leaguers" and "bureaucrats," the paranoid style faded out. It was a historic achievement—though in other quarters the price of it seemed unacceptably high.

The history of the Burned-over District suggests the impulse and the dynamic of change within all four groups, but it is instructive in other ways as well. To begin with, the Rajneeshee, but also the fundamentalists, had strong intellectual affinities with the movements of the 1840s. The antecedents of the Rajneeshee were the Universalists and Swedenborgians who practiced mesmerism, spiritualism, and phrenology. These were, after all, well-educated urbanites, who conceived of a mystical monism, who used imported "mind sciences" to create transcendent states of consciousness and who secretly espoused millenarianism. Ranging the various religious movements in the Burned-over District by the degree of their optimism about the perfectibility of human nature, Whitney Cross put these people on the extreme left of the spectrum along with "ultraist" perfectionists such as John Humphrey Noyes. On the extreme right he put the Millerites, who despaired of human nature and of the future, without divine intervention (a position Falwell once held). To look at the class base of the movements was, however, to see that the "left" was made up of relatively rich and well-educated people, whereas the "right" was composed of relatively poor and ill-educated people—some of them small farmers suffering from a recent fall in grain prices. In class terms, then, the "left" and the "right" should be reversed (and similarly with their heirs, the Rajneeshee and the fundamentalists). Still, it is understandable why the rich and the educated should be more optimistic about human nature and the future in *saecula saeculorum* than the uneducated and the dispossessed. What is notable, too, is that the Swedenborgians and the "ultraists" did not believe in social reform or have any interest in changing the society-at-large. Like the Rajneeshee, they worked on making an elite breakthrough into a realm of higher consciousness, leaving everyone else to follow or not as they could. (The esoteric millenarianism of these groups consisted in the view that they would make the breakthrough and be the only ones to survive.) Like the twentieth-century premillennialists, the Millerites for their part did not believe that social reform was possible. Thus there was complete social and political passivity on the extreme "right" and the extreme "left." Only the centrist religious groups planned action in the world.

As there were strong elements of continuity between the religious movements of the two periods, there were notable differences as well. In the 1840s a number of the religious movements—the Mormons, the Oneida Community—were separatists in the tradition of the Puritans, or more precisely and more to the point, the tradition of Roger Williams. That is, they cut their ties with the society and went about building their own world in isolation, allowing others to do as they would. In the twentieth century there were others like them—the Hutterites, the Mennonites, the last remaining separatist Baptists—but they were all groups founded in the nineteenth century or before. The new movements were not "separatist" in this sense—or they did not remain separatist for very long. Either they were social change movements, or they were world-rejecting movements which, while they had no intention of changing the society, ended up by trying to conquer it. Gay liberation, for example, was by its nature a social change movement. The gay community in the Castro, however, began by seeing itself as a separatist group—the Castro was a "ghetto" or a bastion against the world—but then grew to imagine it would take over all of San Francisco. The Rajneeshee, for their part, had no interest in social change whatsoever, and yet it was they who in the end went to the extremity of trying to conquer Oregon. As for Falwell, he, moving in the other direction from the Rajneeshee, transformed his constituency from a separatist to a social change movement; in the intermediate stages, however, his "disciplined charging army" had conquest on its mind.

Just why it was that the new world-rejecting (or apparently world-rejecting) groups could no longer seem to live and let live was an interesting question, for, as the cases of Rajneeshpuram and of Falwell's church showed, it had nothing to do with the closing of the frontier or the lack of wide-open spaces. (The Rajneeshee had plenty of room, and Falwell's church remained in the same place before and after.) Falwell said that his own change of heart was caused by the change in government and in society. Yet separatist Baptists had always considered both of these lost causes. While direct governmental interference with the autonomy of religious schools and other fundamentalist institutions increased somewhat in the sixties and seventies, it was not enough to convince ministers like Bob Jones, Jr., to go into politics. Fundamentalists, after all, did not have to practice abortion because of the existence of *Roe* v. *Wade*. What had changed, however, was the volume of information flowing about the country. In the case of Falwell's constituency, the critical instrument was television. Television not only brought what Falwell and others considered pornography into Baptist living rooms, but it brought "secular humanists" as well. It brought the government and other parts of the society into focus—close up for the first time. Television penetrated the "walls of separation" and made large numbers of fundamentalists see the possibilities of this larger world and at the same time see that they had to legitimate their own beliefs and way of life in the context of the nation-at-large. Falwell's first answer, sensibly enough, was to put himself on television; his next answer—after the civil rights movement had freed him—was to go into politics and try to gain national support for his views. As for the gay activists and the Rajneeshee, they had been brought up in the world of the mass media, and even when there were no television sets or newspapers around, they could not (or so it seemed) withdraw from the web of information.

During the sixties and seventies a great many people in this country —and not just the fundamentalists—felt a real sense of threat from watching the antiwar demonstrators, the radical feminists, the gay liberationists, the hippies, and so on. They felt that everything they stood for, believed in, everything they were, was challenged, violated, discredited: that they were becoming a powerless minority. Similarly in the eighties many liberals felt the same sense of threat from the fundamentalist crusaders and the radical Right in Washington. To both sides it seemed quite possible that the country would be riven down the middle by moral and religious issues which could not be compromised—and which could not be dealt with by the two-party system.

There was, of course, a precedent for this. In the 1840s the trouble-makers were the New Light revivalists and reformers of Charles Finney's ilk, for they changed the culture of the North, and as the South (rural and agrarian as well as slave-owning) did not change in the same way, they divided the country right through the middle. Then, with the fires of religious revival in them, the abolitionists made slavery an issue which could not be compromised, and the result was civil war. In the twentieth century, however, there was little geographical division between the two cultures (and between the two economic and social systems). States were divided, but so also were towns and even school districts. In certain ways the lack of geographic separation made the division more acutely felt and more dangerous. When, for example, school board members banned a book from a school library, they might—as in the Supreme Court case of *Pico* v. *Island Trees*—act in the name of the whole community but represent only a majority of its voters. The minority would then have the choice of giving in or turning its problems over to the state or the federal government. Local disputes thus quickly became national ones. In addition, of course, the mass media tended to erase whatever geographical differences there were, bringing, for example, the gay demonstrations in San Francisco into the homes of fundamentalists in Virginia and Florida. Then, too, as journalists give more attention to the exceptional than to the run of the mill, they tended to give more space, or airtime, to the radicals than to the moderates. The radicals on both sides thus seemed more powerful than they actually were.

In other ways, however, the very lack of distance between the contending groups helped to prevent a national breakdown. The partisans of radical movements tended to meet their opponents early on. They found them, as it were, in the house next door, but also in the national press, for reactions built swiftly. Movements could thus not develop their internal logic or their evangelistic fervor as well as they might have in isolation; nor could they so completely transform their opponents into monsters. (To read Henry Adams's *Education* is to have some feeling for the degree of repulsion Northerners felt for Southerners before the Civil War.) They could try, and they did, but there was always the rub of their neighbors and of the press. While journalists would give them space or airtime, they would, by a convention quite unique to the American press, give their opponents equal time and then represent a position somewhere between the two. Movements were thus often blunted before they gathered force. Then, too, there was always the possibility of corruption or co-optation. The purists in such movements charged corruption quite generally—and sometimes they were right, for the leaders of successful movements encountered not just opposition but the enticements of power early in the game. And then, like Jerry Falwell, many of them faced the choice between leading a charge with their own small armies and risking destruction or gaining a larger, though vaguer, influence in the country.

By 1985 the conflict had in fact abated somewhat. The argument, however, continued, for there was still no consensus on important matters of personal conduct and the social good. There was still no basic agreement on the nature of the culture, such as obtained in England and France. Yet Americans managed to put up with a great deal of disagreement, even when it came electronically into their living rooms. This was a measure of their tolerance and liberality—or it was a measure of their philosophic acceptance of the particular nature of their country. The country was, after all, too large and too various for any detailed cultural agreement, and the society was always in motion with economic change, new immigrant groups, new money, and new ideas. The constant was merely this condition of turbulence: nothing much else lasted for very long. Small wonder, then, that the evangelical tradition proved so durable, and so influential beyond its own domain, for with its promise of rebirth—or liberation and transformation—it was antitraditional and thus acceptable, or even a necessity, to Americans. Because of it the country sometimes presented bizarre and even comic spectacles to the world. As an American historian, Robert Wiebe, remarked, "In times of discontent Americans traditionally resisted the elementary proposition that every social system carries a composite price. They would not relinquish the hope of finding somewhere in the world an ideal remedy—European high culture, South Seas happiness, mystical Asian peace—to cure their nagging pains." This continuing comedy was at least reassuring, for it was equality, de Toqueville maintained, that suggested the very idea of human perfectibility. "Aristocratic nations," he wrote in the 1830s after a visit to the United States, "are naturally too liable to narrow the scope of human perfectibility; democratic nations, to expand it beyond reason." The very appearance of the Castro, Sun City, Jerry Falwell's church, and Rajneeshpuram showed that the United States had not changed too drastically in a century and a half.